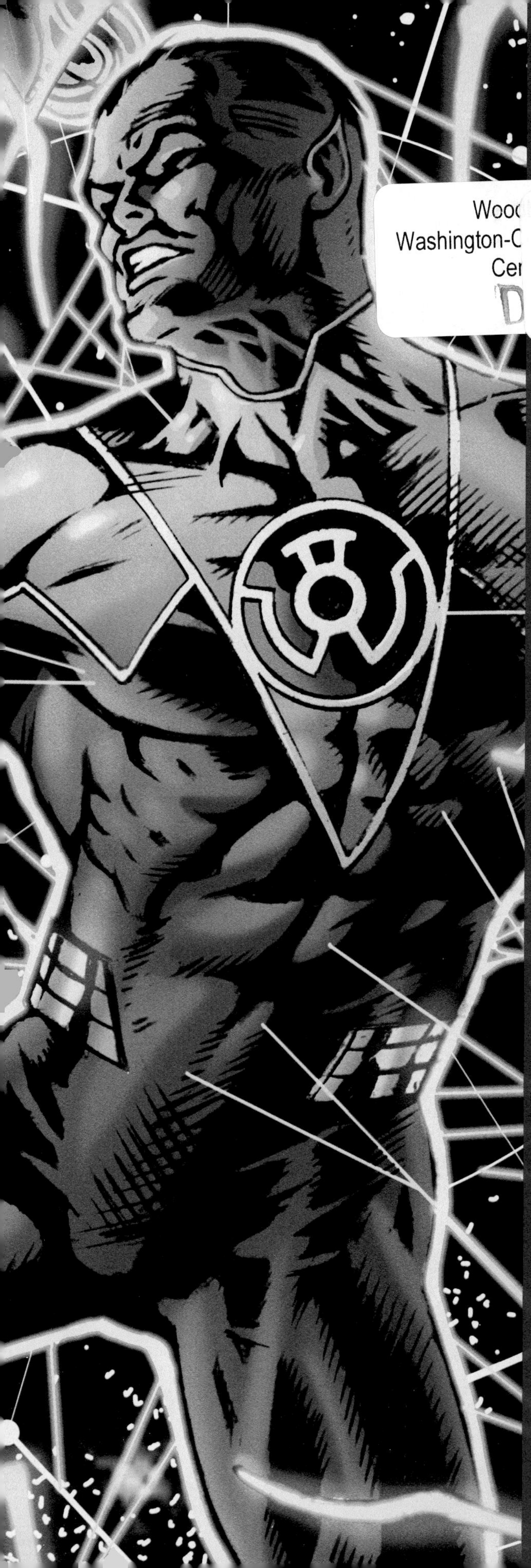

SINESTRO

VOLUME 2
SACRIFICE

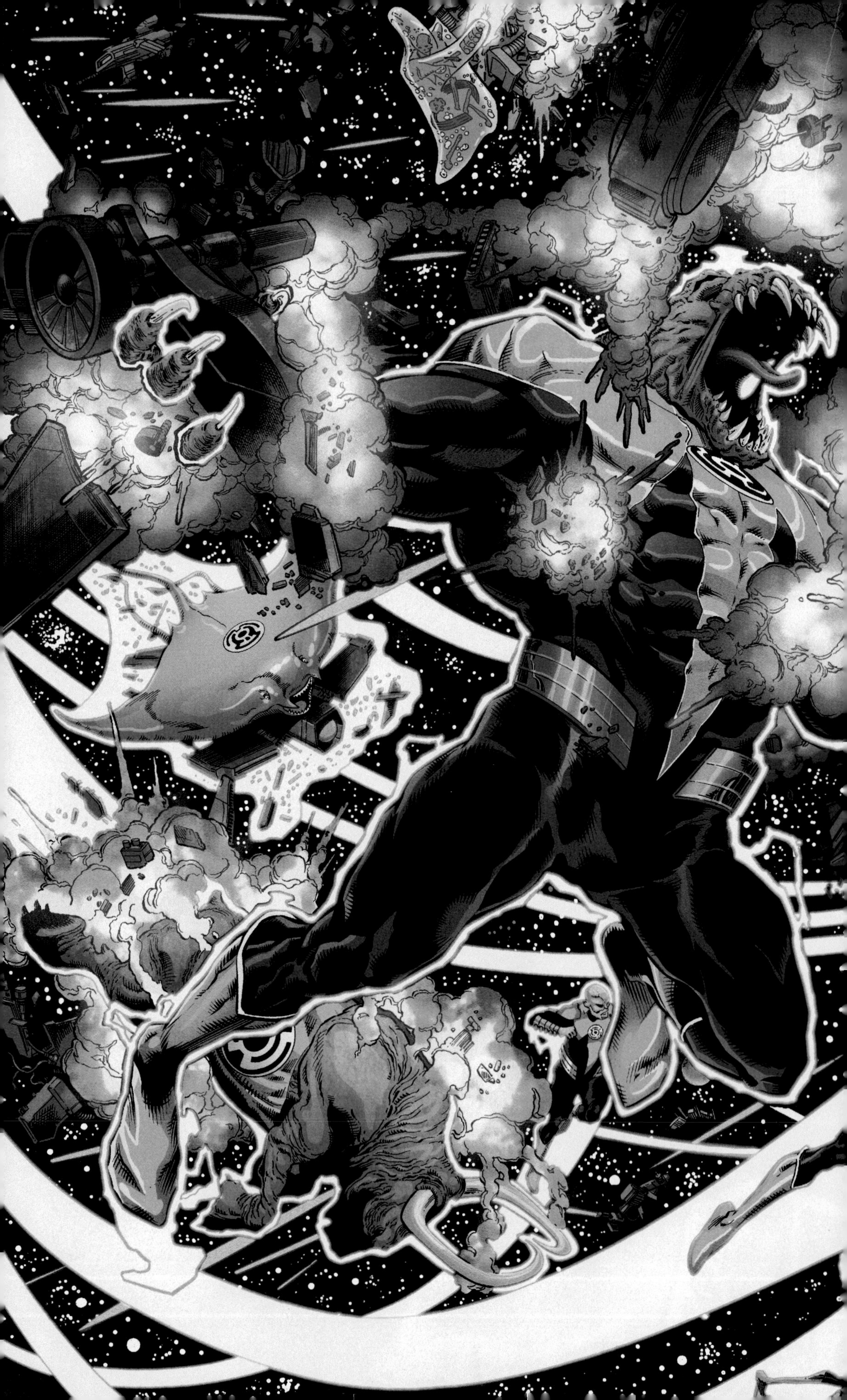

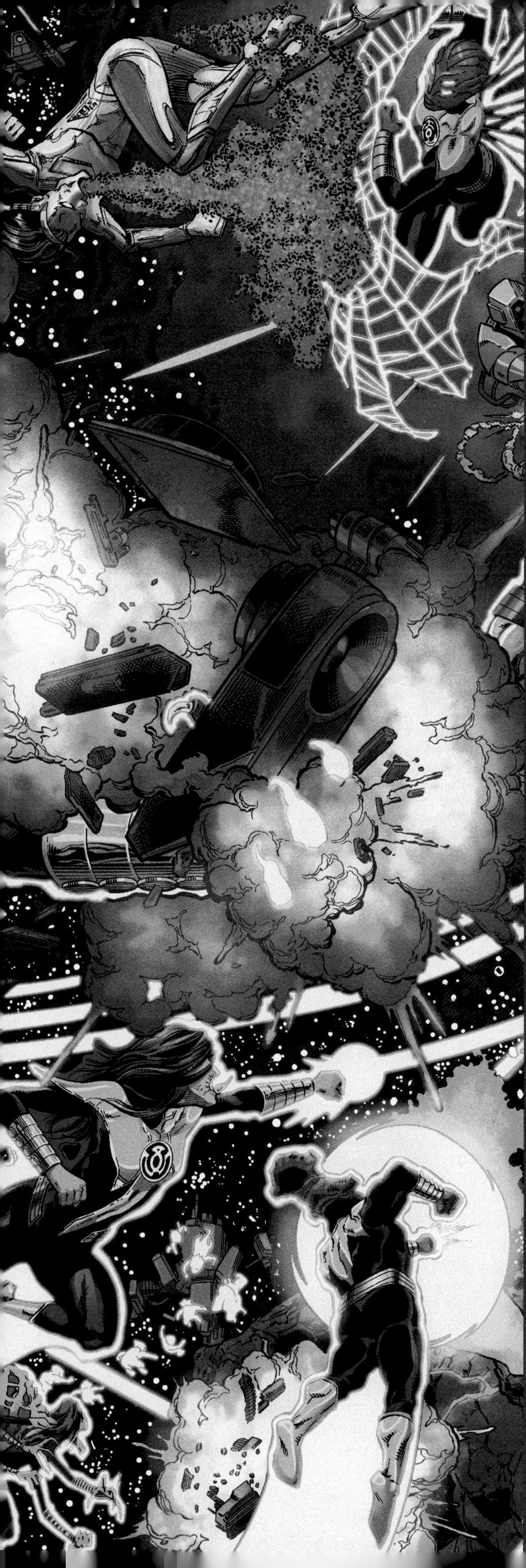

SINESTRO

VOLUME 2
SINESTRO

WRITTEN BY
CULLEN BUNN

ART BY
BRAD WALKER
ANDREW HENNESSY
DALE EAGLESHAM
MARTIN COCCOLO
SCOTT HANNA
ETHAN VAN SCIVER
GERALDO BORGES
IGOR LIMA
JOSÉ MARZÁN JR.
OCLAIR ALBERT
VICTOR IBANEZ
DANIEL WARREN JOHNSON
MIRKO COLAK
ANDY KUHN
RONAN CLIQUET

COLOR BY
JASON WRIGHT
TONY AVIÑA

LETTERS BY
TAYLOR ESPOSITO
DAVE SHARPE

COLLECTION COVER ARTISTS
GUILLEM MARCH AND
TOMEU MOREY

MATT IDELSON Editor – Original Series
DARREN SHAN Associate Editor– Original Series
PAUL SANTOS Editor
ROBBIN BROSTERMAN Design Director – Books
DAMIAN RYLAND Publication Design

BOB HARRAS Senior VP – Editor-in-Chief, DC Comics

DIANE NELSON President
DAN DIDIO and JIM LEE Co-Publishers
GEOFF JOHNS Chief Creative Officer
AMIT DESAI Senior VP – Marketing & Franchise Management
AMY GENKINS Senior VP – Business & Legal Affairs
NAIRI GARDINER Senior VP – Finance
JEFF BOISON VP – Publishing Planning
MARK CHIARELLO VP – Art Direction & Design
JOHN CUNNINGHAM VP – Marketing
TERRI CUNNINGHAM VP – Editorial Administration
ALISON GILL Senior VP – Manufacturing & Operations
HANK KANALZ Senior VP – Vertigo & Integrated Publishing
JAY KOGAN VP – Business & Legal Affairs, Publishing
JACK MAHAN VP – Business Affairs, Talent
NICK NAPOLITANO VP – Manufacturing Administration
SUE POHJA VP – Book Sales
COURTNEY SIMMONS Senior VP – Publicity
BOB WAYNE Senior VP – Sales

SINESTRO VOLUME 2: SACRIFICE

Published by DC Comics. Compilation Copyright © 2015 DC Comics. All Rights Reserved.

Originally published in single magazine form in SINESTRO 6-11, SINESTRO ANNUAL 1 © 2014, 2015 DC Comics. All Rights Reserved. All characters, their distinctive likenesses and related elements featured in this publication are trademarks of DC Comics. The stories, characters and incidents featured in this publication are entirely fictional. DC Comics does not read or accept unsolicited ideas, stories or artwork.

DC Comics, 4000 Warner Blvd. | Burbank, CA 91522
A Warner Bros. Entertainment Company.
Printed by RR Donnelley, Owensville, MO, USA. 6/05/15 First Printing.
ISBN: 978-1-4012-5486-5

Library of Congress Cataloging-in-Publication Data

Bunn, Cullen, author.
Sinestro. Volume 2, Sacrifice / Cullen Bunn, writer ; Dale Eaglesham, artist.
pages cm
ISBN 978-1-4012-5486-5 (pbk.)
1. Graphic novels. I. Eaglesham, Dale, illustrator. II. Title. III. Title: Sacrifice.

PN6728.S496B86 2015
741.5'973—dc23

2014034200

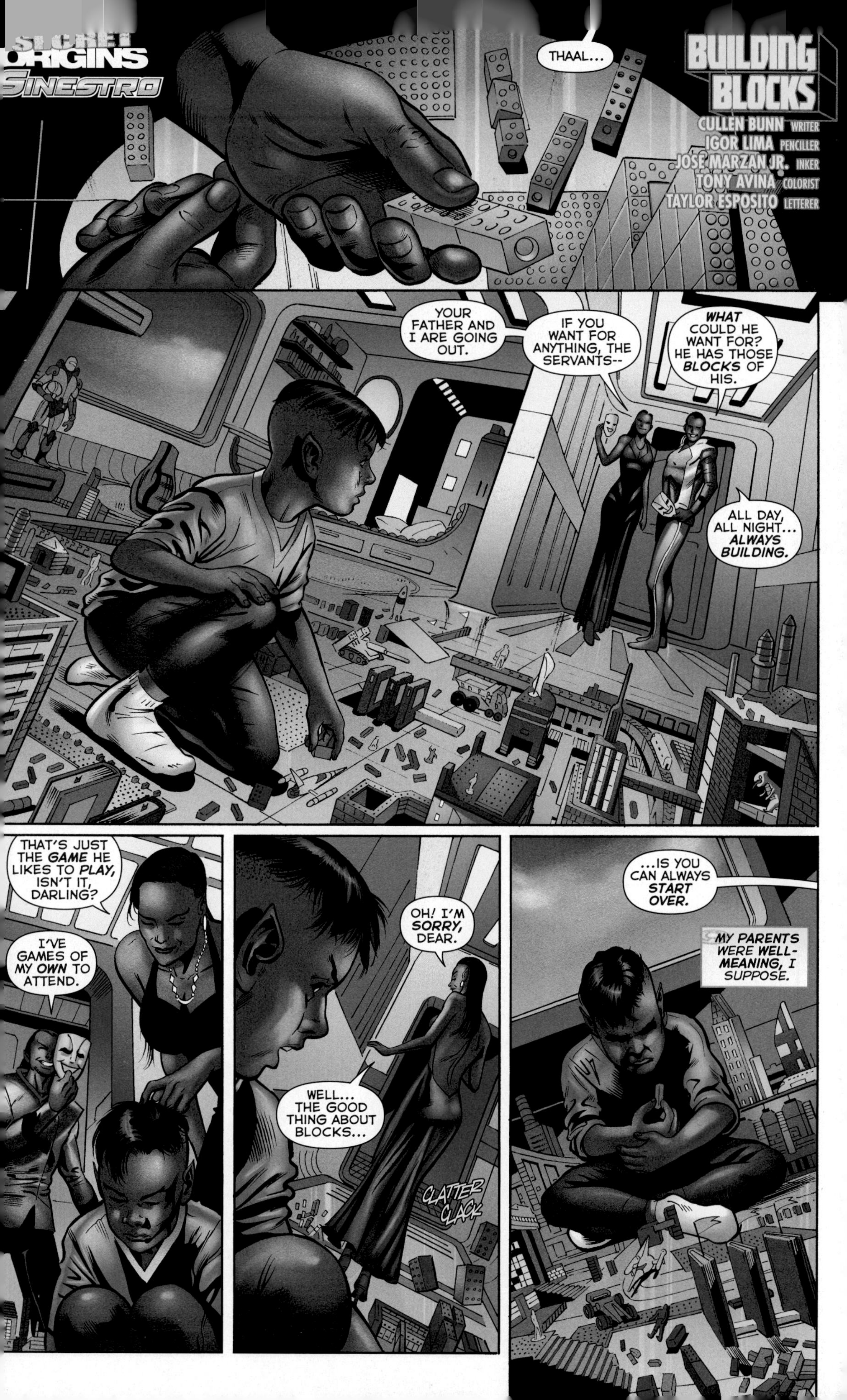
SECRET ORIGINS
SINESTRO
THAAL...
BUILDING BLOCKS
CULLEN BUNN WRITER
IGOR LIMA PENCILLER
JOSÉ MARZAN JR. INKER
TONY AVINA COLORIST
TAYLOR ESPOSITO LETTERER
YOUR FATHER AND I ARE GOING OUT.
IF YOU WANT FOR ANYTHING, THE SERVANTS--
WHAT COULD HE WANT FOR? HE HAS THOSE BLOCKS OF HIS.
ALL DAY, ALL NIGHT... ALWAYS BUILDING.
THAT'S JUST THE GAME HE LIKES TO PLAY, ISN'T IT, DARLING?
I'VE GAMES OF MY OWN TO ATTEND.
OH! I'M SORRY, DEAR.
WELL... THE GOOD THING ABOUT BLOCKS...
CLATTER CLACK
...IS YOU CAN ALWAYS START OVER.
MY PARENTS WERE WELL-MEANING, I SUPPOSE.

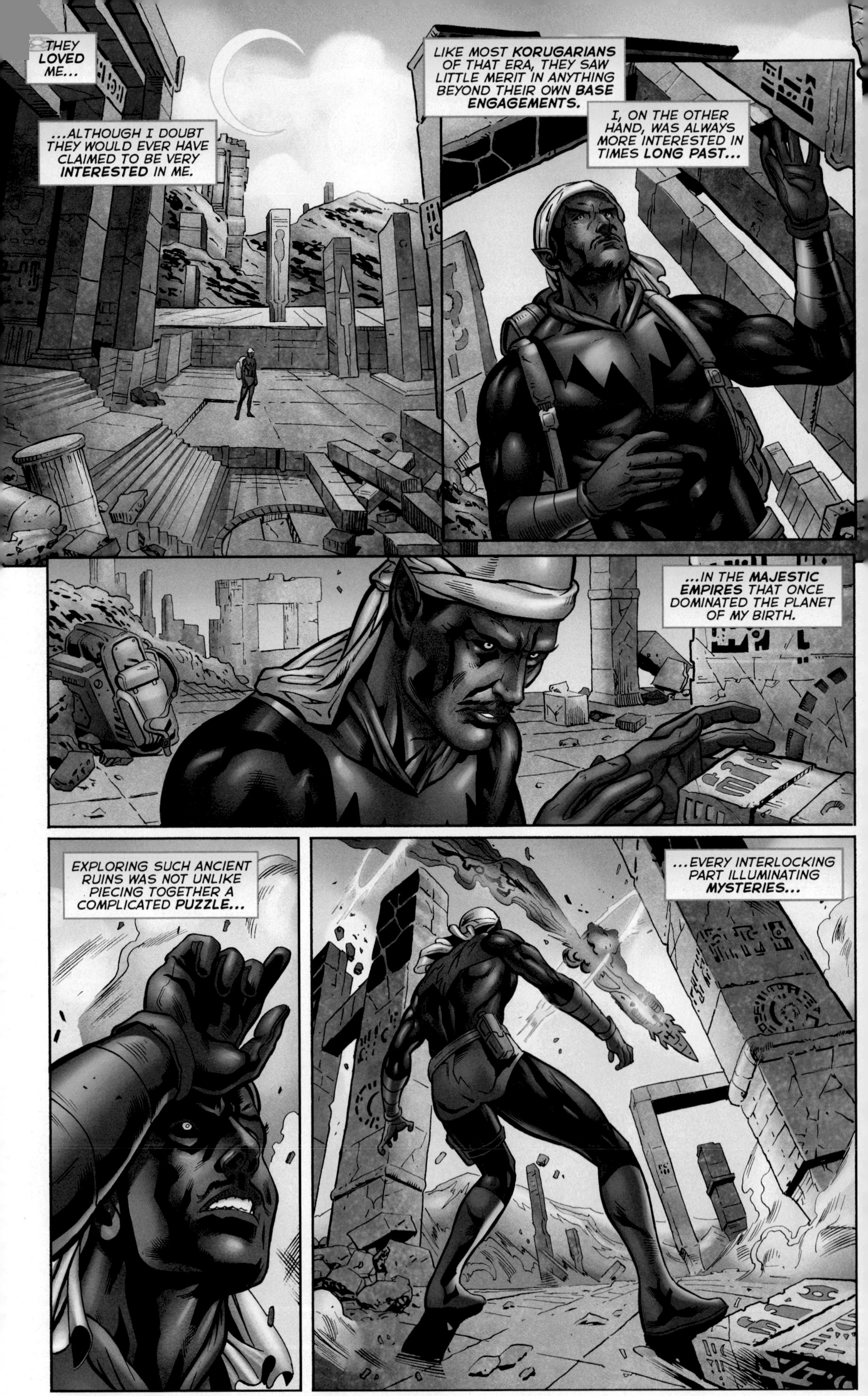
THEY LOVED ME...
...ALTHOUGH I DOUBT THEY WOULD EVER HAVE CLAIMED TO BE VERY INTERESTED IN ME.
LIKE MOST KORUGARIANS OF THAT ERA, THEY SAW LITTLE MERIT IN ANYTHING BEYOND THEIR OWN BASE ENGAGEMENTS.
I, ON THE OTHER HAND, WAS ALWAYS MORE INTERESTED IN TIMES LONG PAST...
...IN THE MAJESTIC EMPIRES THAT ONCE DOMINATED THE PLANET OF MY BIRTH.
EXPLORING SUCH ANCIENT RUINS WAS NOT UNLIKE PIECING TOGETHER A COMPLICATED PUZZLE...
...EVERY INTERLOCKING PART ILLUMINATING MYSTERIES...

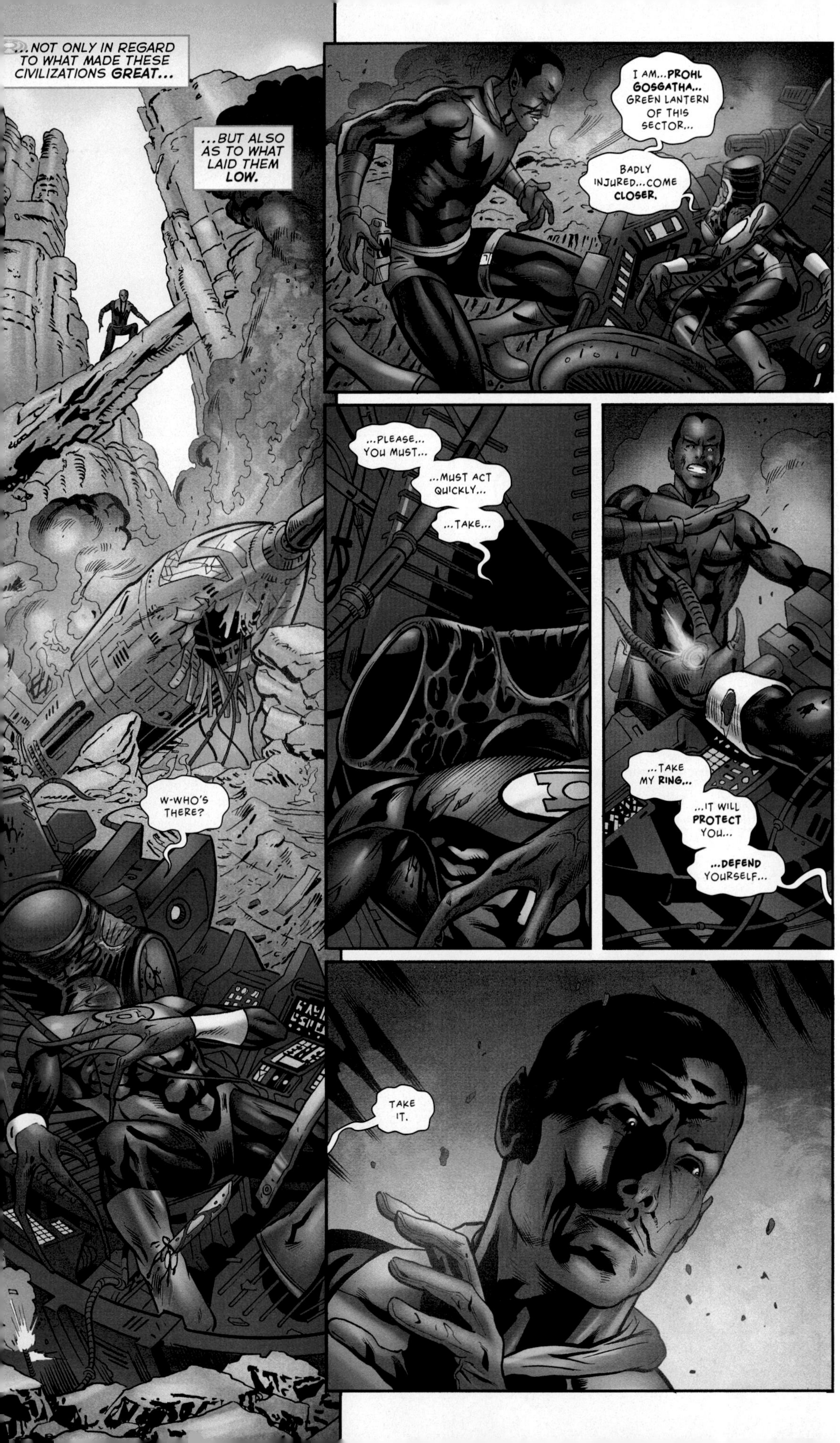
...NOT ONLY IN REGARD TO WHAT MADE THESE CIVILIZATIONS GREAT...
...BUT ALSO AS TO WHAT LAID THEM LOW.
W-WHO'S THERE?
I AM...PROHL GOSGATHA... GREEN LANTERN OF THIS SECTOR...
BADLY INJURED...COME CLOSER.
...PLEASE... YOU MUST...
...MUST ACT QUICKLY...
...TAKE...
...TAKE MY RING...
...IT WILL PROTECT YOU...
...DEFEND YOURSELF...
TAKE IT.

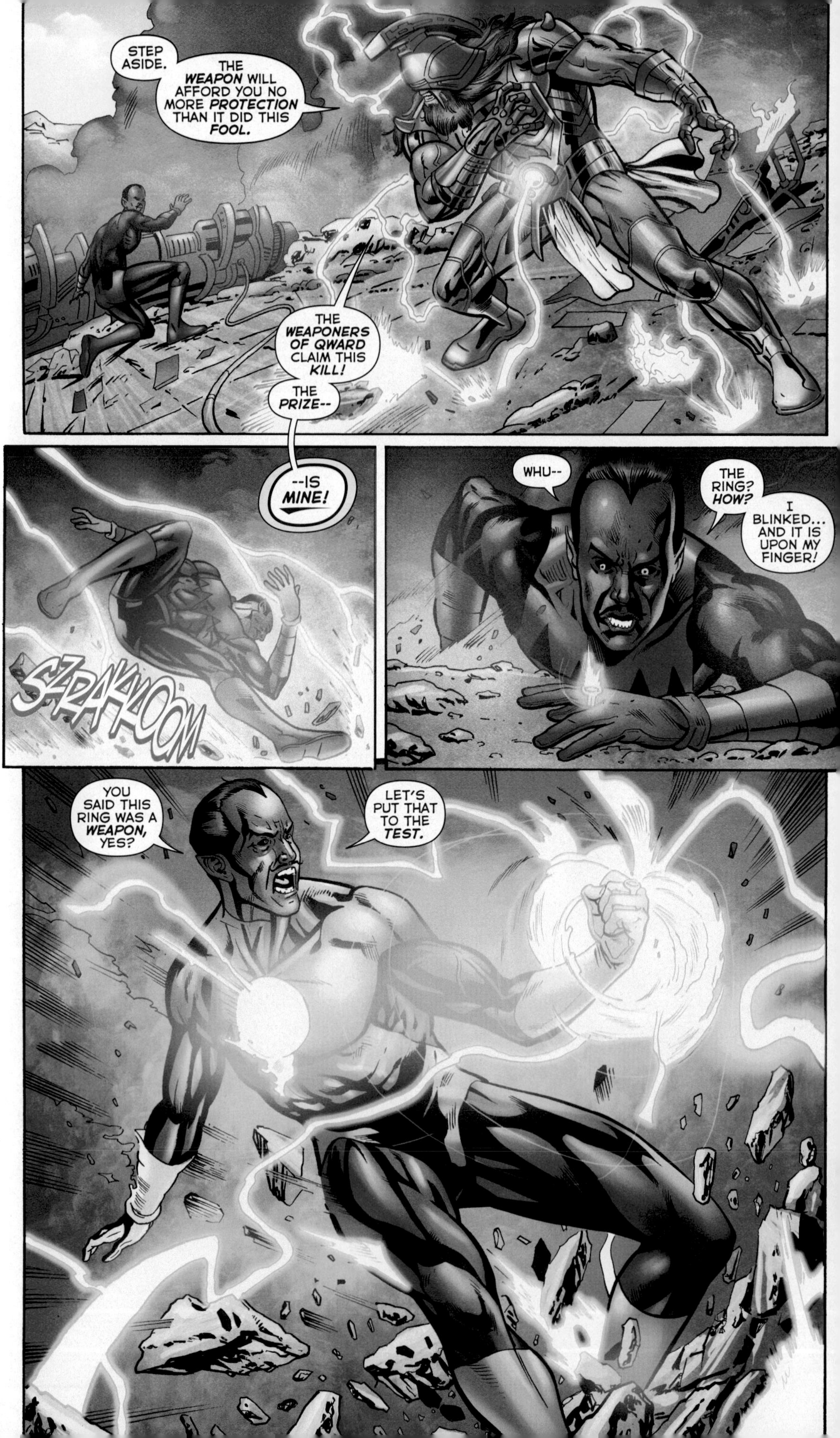
STEP ASIDE.
THE WEAPON WILL AFFORD YOU NO MORE PROTECTION THAN IT DID THIS FOOL.
THE WEAPONERS OF QWARD CLAIM THIS KILL!
THE PRIZE--
--IS MINE!
SZZRAKAKAKOOM
WHU--
THE RING? HOW?
I BLINKED... AND IT IS UPON MY FINGER!
YOU SAID THIS RING WAS A WEAPON, YES?
LET'S PUT THAT TO THE TEST.

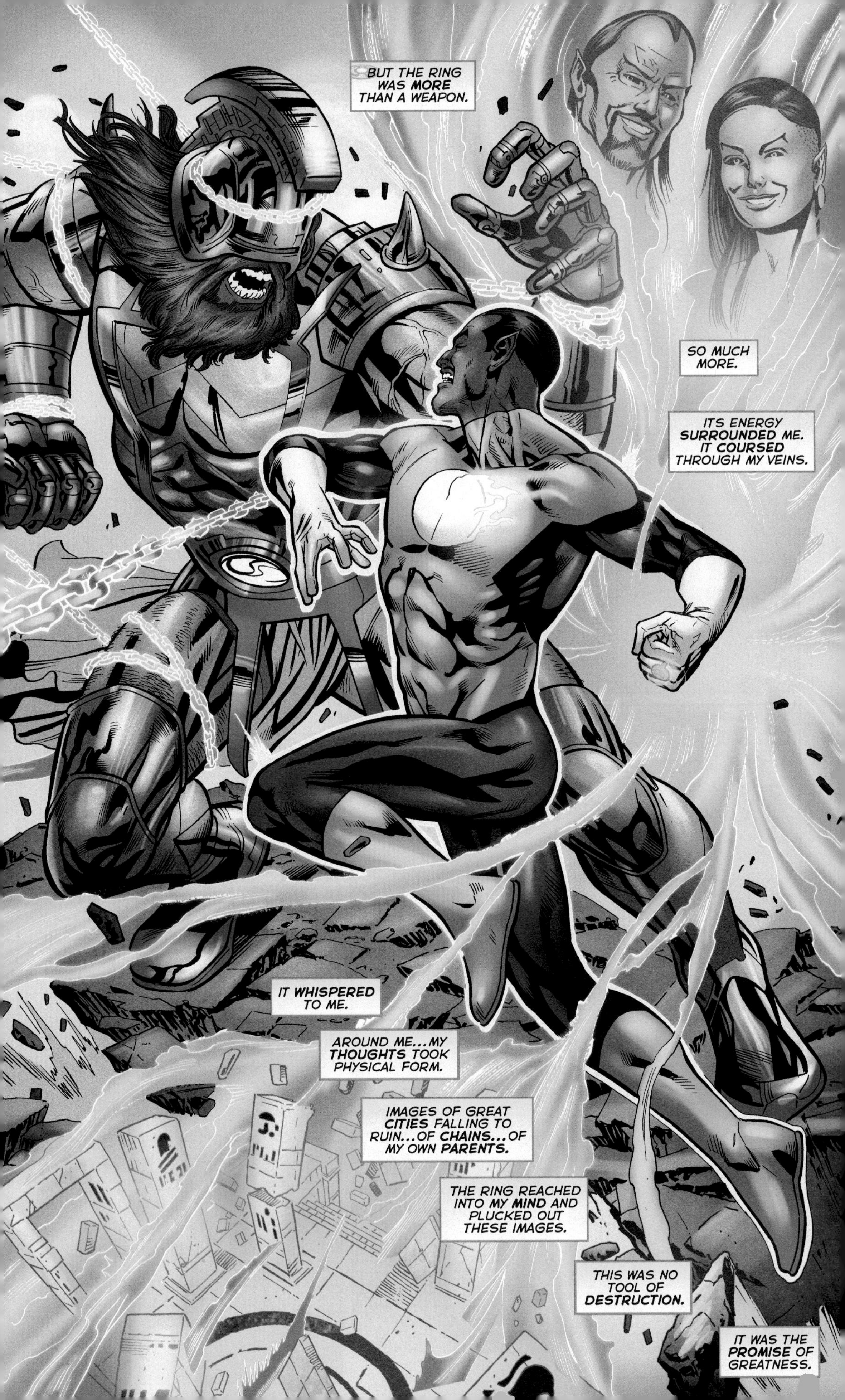
BUT THE RING WAS MORE THAN A WEAPON.
SO MUCH MORE.
ITS ENERGY SURROUNDED ME. IT COURSED THROUGH MY VEINS.
IT WHISPERED TO ME.
AROUND ME...MY THOUGHTS TOOK PHYSICAL FORM.
IMAGES OF GREAT CITIES FALLING TO RUIN...OF CHAINS...OF MY OWN PARENTS.
THE RING REACHED INTO MY MIND AND PLUCKED OUT THESE IMAGES.
THIS WAS NO TOOL OF DESTRUCTION.
IT WAS THE PROMISE OF GREATNESS.

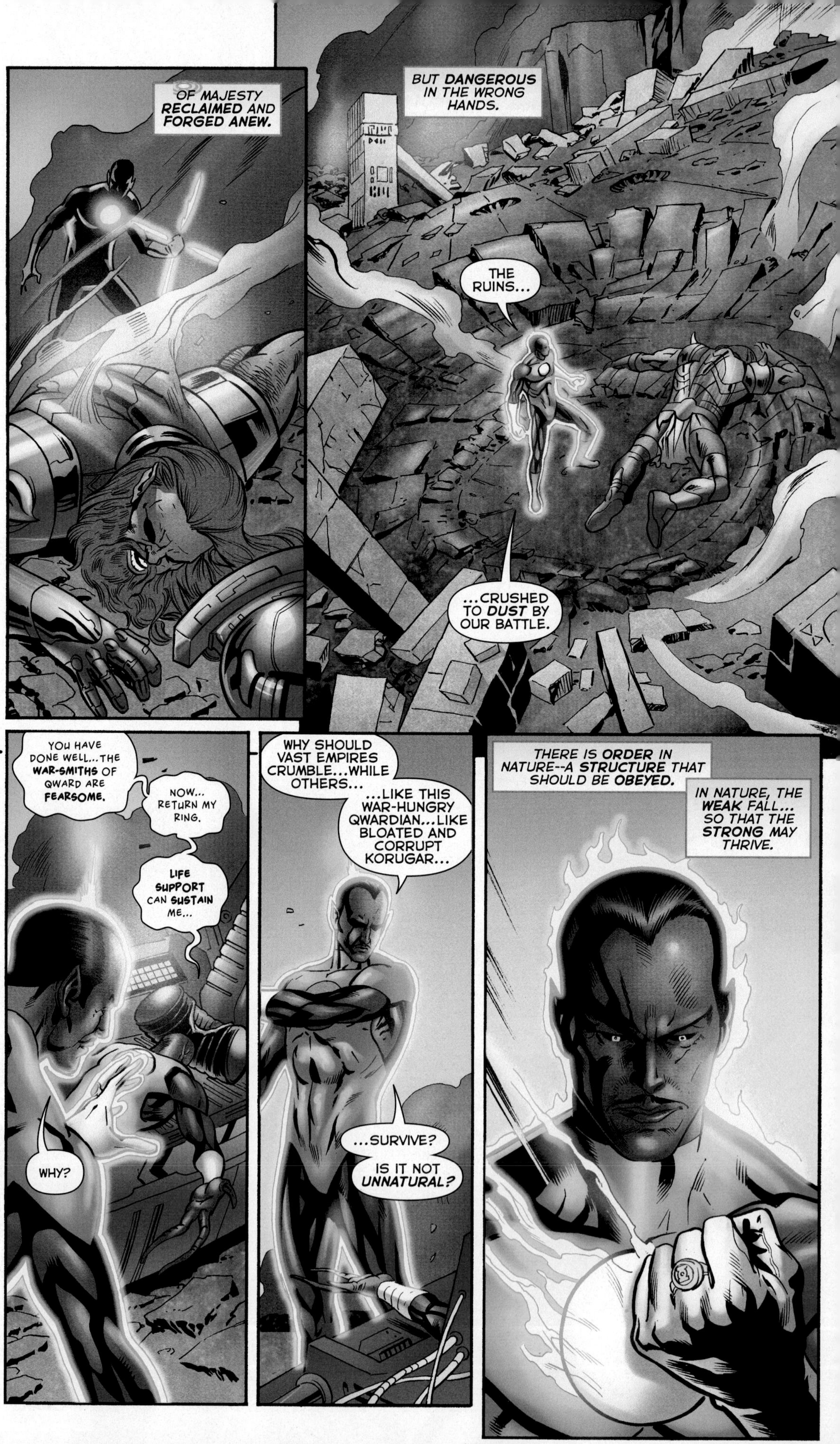
OF MAJESTY RECLAIMED AND FORGED ANEW.
BUT DANGEROUS IN THE WRONG HANDS.
THE RUINS...
...CRUSHED TO DUST BY OUR BATTLE.
YOU HAVE DONE WELL...THE WAR-SMITHS OF QWARD ARE FEARSOME.
NOW... RETURN MY RING.
LIFE SUPPORT CAN SUSTAIN ME...
WHY?
WHY SHOULD VAST EMPIRES CRUMBLE...WHILE OTHERS...
...LIKE THIS WAR-HUNGRY QWARDIAN...LIKE BLOATED AND CORRUPT KORUGAR...
...SURVIVE?
IS IT NOT UNNATURAL?
THERE IS ORDER IN NATURE--A STRUCTURE THAT SHOULD BE OBEYED.
IN NATURE, THE WEAK FALL... SO THAT THE STRONG MAY THRIVE.

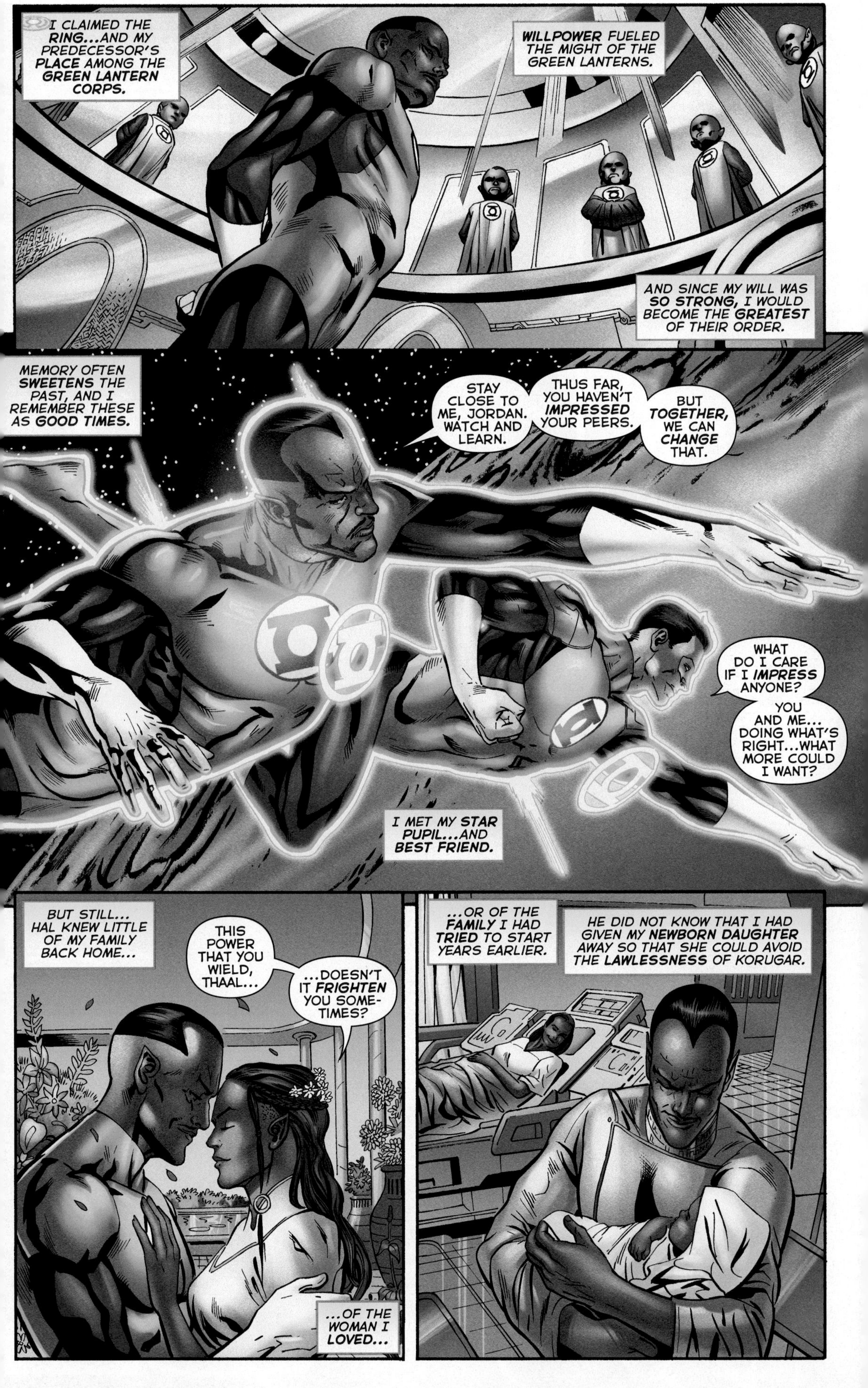
I CLAIMED THE RING...AND MY PREDECESSOR'S PLACE AMONG THE GREEN LANTERN CORPS.
WILLPOWER FUELED THE MIGHT OF THE GREEN LANTERNS.
AND SINCE MY WILL WAS SO STRONG, I WOULD BECOME THE GREATEST OF THEIR ORDER.
MEMORY OFTEN SWEETENS THE PAST, AND I REMEMBER THESE AS GOOD TIMES.
STAY CLOSE TO ME, JORDAN. WATCH AND LEARN.
THUS FAR, YOU HAVEN'T IMPRESSED YOUR PEERS.
BUT TOGETHER, WE CAN CHANGE THAT.
WHAT DO I CARE IF I IMPRESS ANYONE?
YOU AND ME... DOING WHAT'S RIGHT...WHAT MORE COULD I WANT?
I MET MY STAR PUPIL...AND BEST FRIEND.
BUT STILL... HAL KNEW LITTLE OF MY FAMILY BACK HOME...
THIS POWER THAT YOU WIELD, THAAL...
...DOESN'T IT FRIGHTEN YOU SOME-TIMES?
...OF THE WOMAN I LOVED...
...OR OF THE FAMILY I HAD TRIED TO START YEARS EARLIER.
HE DID NOT KNOW THAT I HAD GIVEN MY NEWBORN DAUGHTER AWAY SO THAT SHE COULD AVOID THE LAWLESSNESS OF KORUGAR.

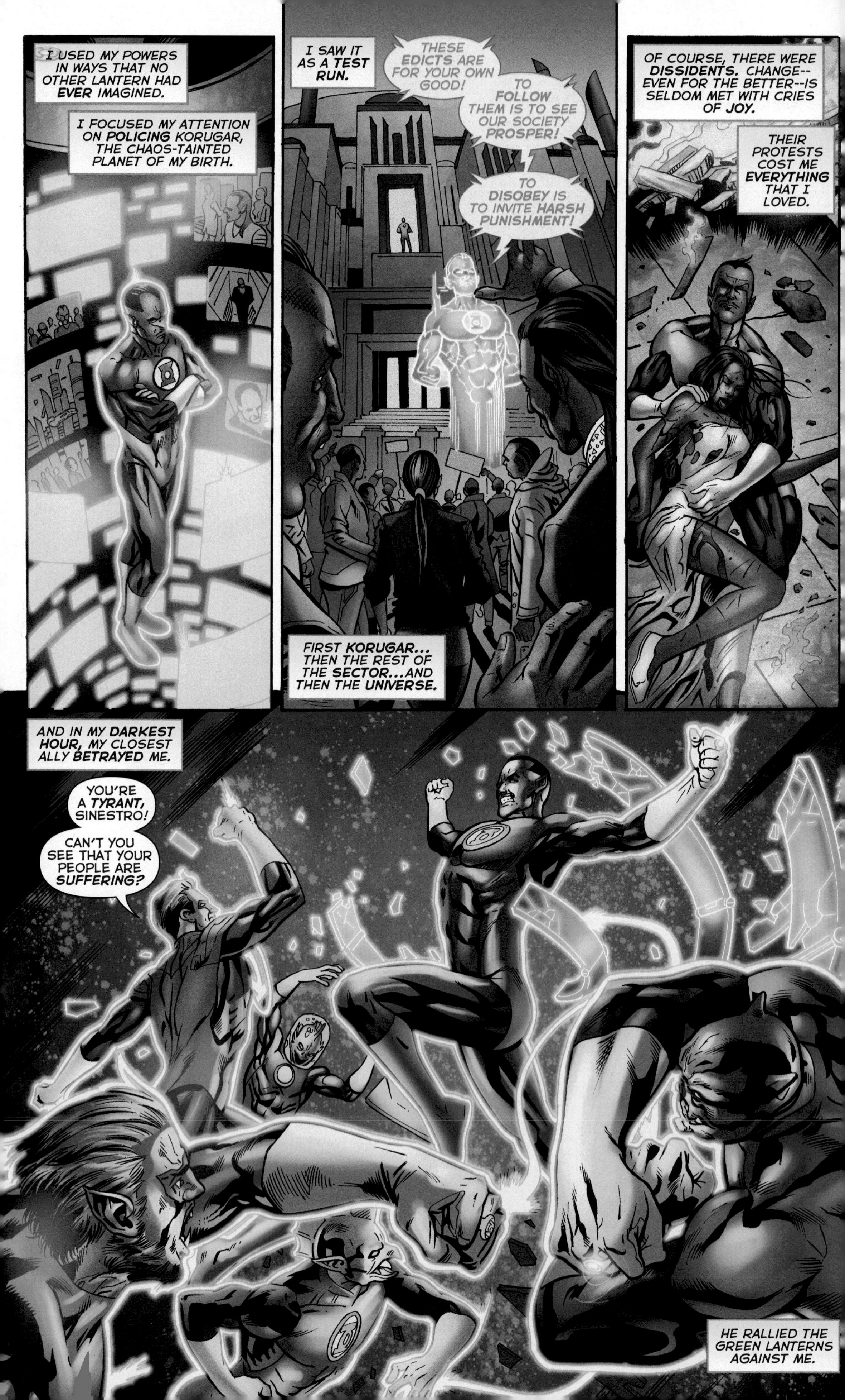
I USED MY POWERS IN WAYS THAT NO OTHER LANTERN HAD EVER IMAGINED.
I FOCUSED MY ATTENTION ON POLICING KORUGAR, THE CHAOS-TAINTED PLANET OF MY BIRTH.
I SAW IT AS A TEST RUN.
THESE EDICTS ARE FOR YOUR OWN GOOD!
TO FOLLOW THEM IS TO SEE OUR SOCIETY PROSPER!
TO DISOBEY IS TO INVITE HARSH PUNISHMENT!
FIRST KORUGAR... THEN THE REST OF THE SECTOR...AND THEN THE UNIVERSE.
OF COURSE, THERE WERE DISSIDENTS. CHANGE-- EVEN FOR THE BETTER--IS SELDOM MET WITH CRIES OF JOY.
THEIR PROTESTS COST ME EVERYTHING THAT I LOVED.
AND IN MY DARKEST HOUR, MY CLOSEST ALLY BETRAYED ME.
YOU'RE A TYRANT, SINESTRO!
CAN'T YOU SEE THAT YOUR PEOPLE ARE SUFFERING?
HE RALLIED THE GREEN LANTERNS AGAINST ME.

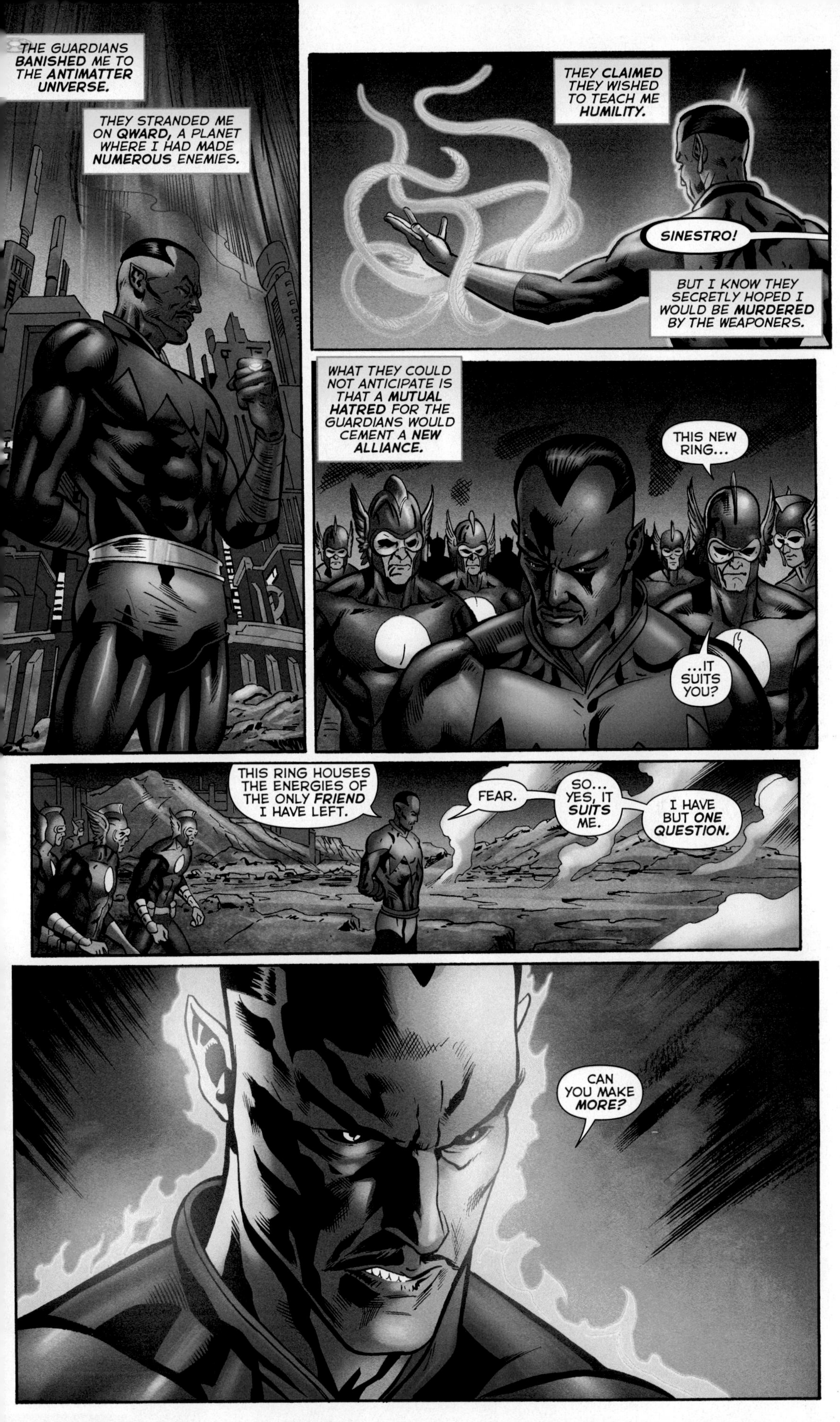
THE GUARDIANS BANISHED ME TO THE ANTIMATTER UNIVERSE.
THEY STRANDED ME ON QWARD, A PLANET WHERE I HAD MADE NUMEROUS ENEMIES.
THEY CLAIMED THEY WISHED TO TEACH ME HUMILITY.
SINESTRO!
BUT I KNOW THEY SECRETLY HOPED I WOULD BE MURDERED BY THE WEAPONERS.
WHAT THEY COULD NOT ANTICIPATE IS THAT A MUTUAL HATRED FOR THE GUARDIANS WOULD CEMENT A NEW ALLIANCE.
THIS NEW RING...
...IT SUITS YOU?
THIS RING HOUSES THE ENERGIES OF THE ONLY FRIEND I HAVE LEFT.
FEAR.
SO... YES, IT SUITS ME.
I HAVE BUT ONE QUESTION.
CAN YOU MAKE MORE?

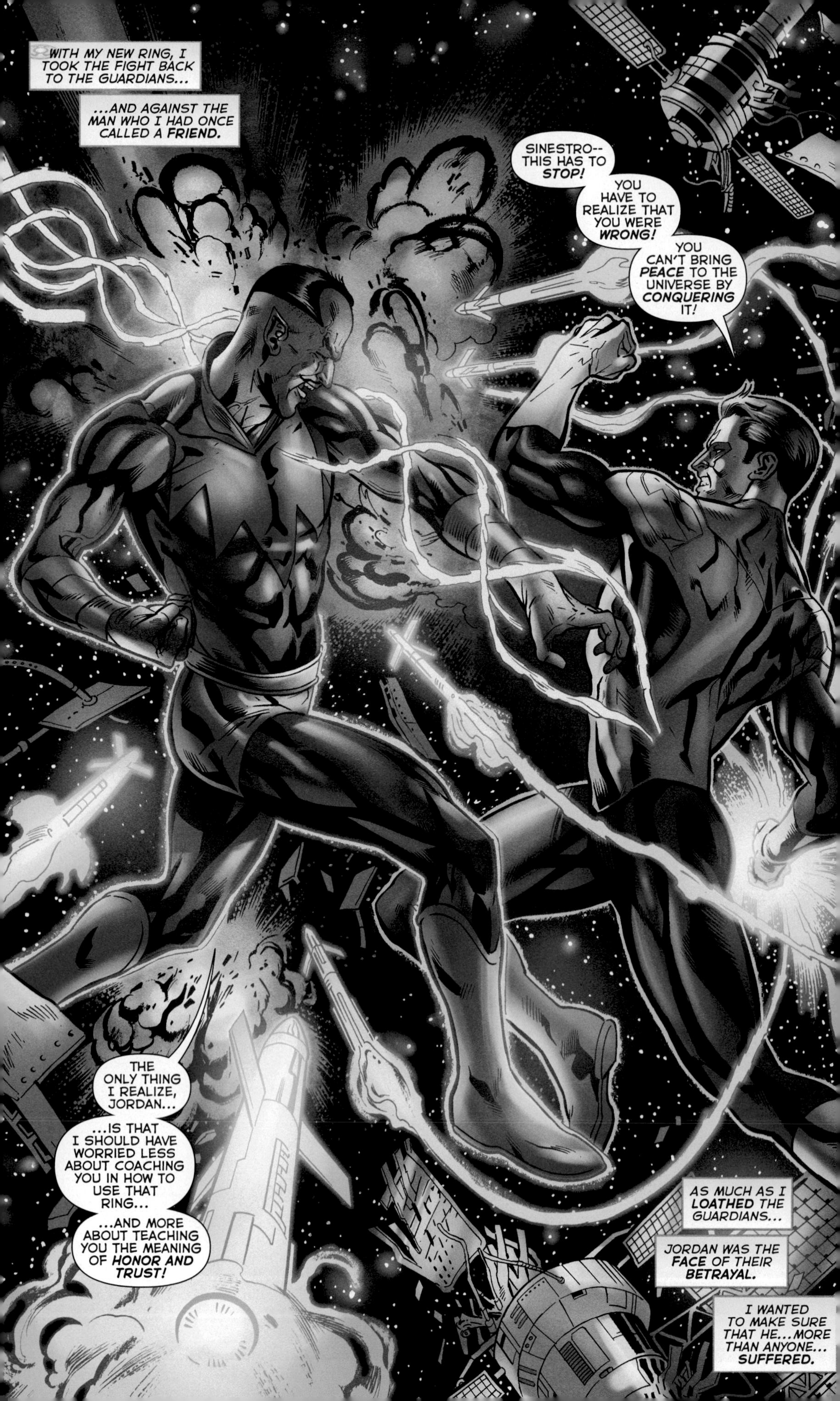

WITH MY NEW RING, I TOOK THE FIGHT BACK TO THE GUARDIANS...
...AND AGAINST THE MAN WHO I HAD ONCE CALLED A FRIEND.
SINESTRO-- THIS HAS TO STOP!
YOU HAVE TO REALIZE THAT YOU WERE WRONG!
YOU CAN'T BRING PEACE TO THE UNIVERSE BY CONQUERING IT!
THE ONLY THING I REALIZE, JORDAN...
...IS THAT I SHOULD HAVE WORRIED LESS ABOUT COACHING YOU IN HOW TO USE THAT RING...
...AND MORE ABOUT TEACHING YOU THE MEANING OF HONOR AND TRUST!
AS MUCH AS I LOATHED THE GUARDIANS...
JORDAN WAS THE FACE OF THEIR BETRAYAL.
I WANTED TO MAKE SURE THAT HE...MORE THAN ANYONE... SUFFERED.

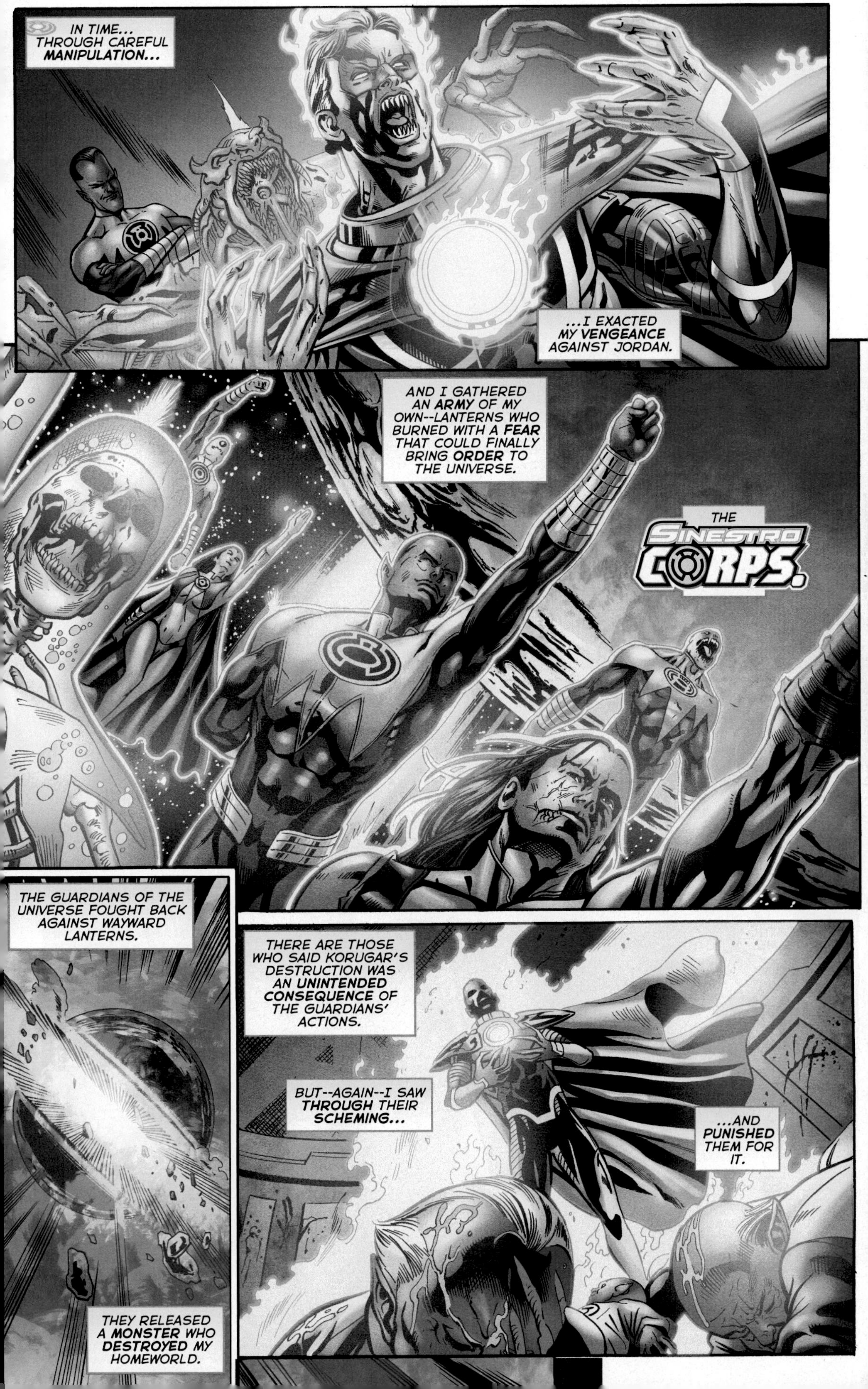
IN TIME... THROUGH CAREFUL MANIPULATION...
...I EXACTED MY VENGEANCE AGAINST JORDAN.
AND I GATHERED AN ARMY OF MY OWN--LANTERNS WHO BURNED WITH A FEAR THAT COULD FINALLY BRING ORDER TO THE UNIVERSE.
THE SINESTRO CORPS.
THE GUARDIANS OF THE UNIVERSE FOUGHT BACK AGAINST WAYWARD LANTERNS.
THEY RELEASED A MONSTER WHO DESTROYED MY HOMEWORLD.
THERE ARE THOSE WHO SAID KORUGAR'S DESTRUCTION WAS AN UNINTENDED CONSEQUENCE OF THE GUARDIANS' ACTIONS.
BUT--AGAIN--I SAW THROUGH THEIR SCHEMING...
...AND PUNISHED THEM FOR IT.

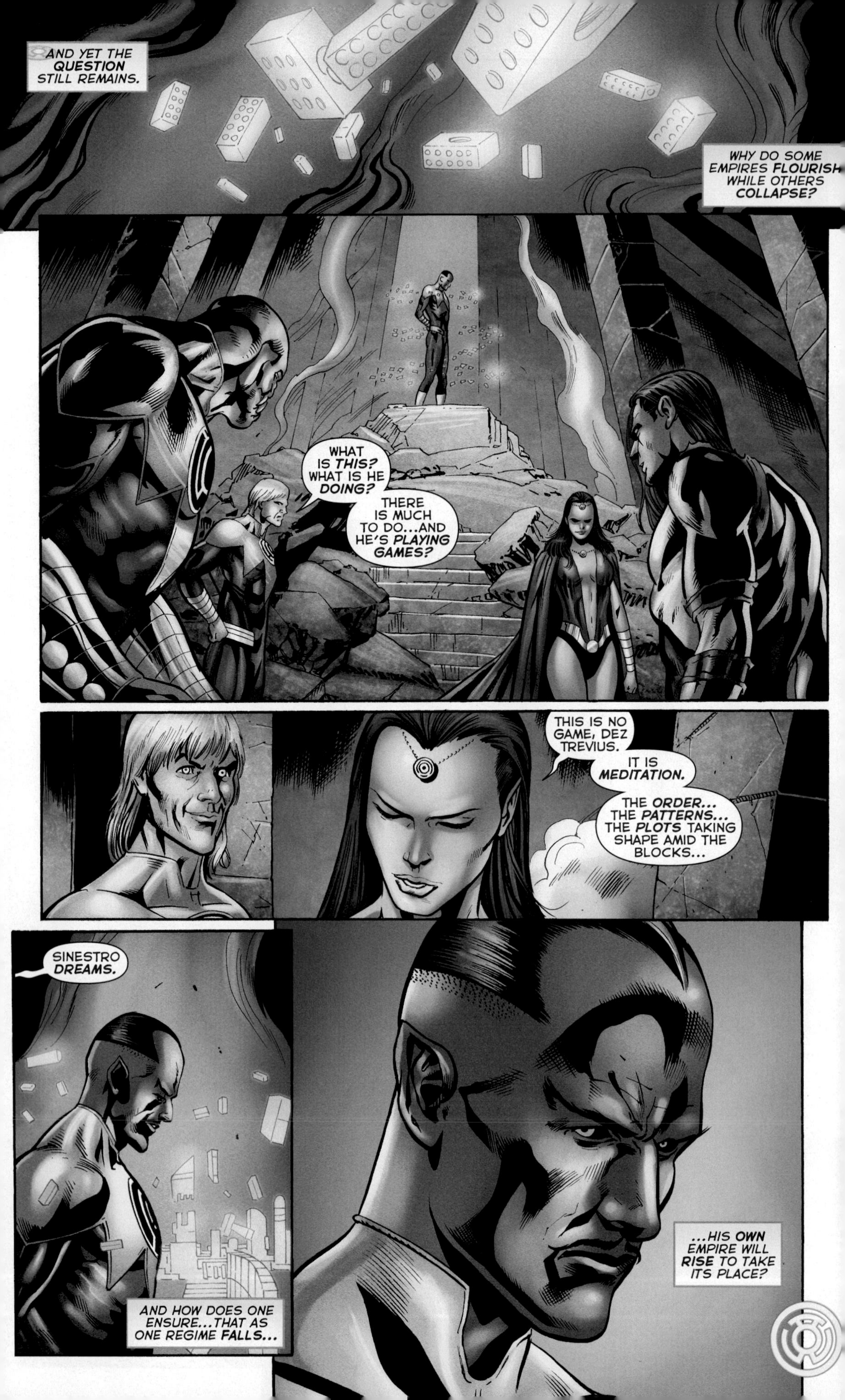
AND YET THE QUESTION STILL REMAINS.
WHY DO SOME EMPIRES FLOURISH WHILE OTHERS COLLAPSE?
WHAT IS THIS? WHAT IS HE DOING?
THERE IS MUCH TO DO...AND HE'S PLAYING GAMES?
THIS IS NO GAME, DEZ TREVIUS.
IT IS MEDITATION.
THE ORDER... THE PATTERNS... THE PLOTS TAKING SHAPE AMID THE BLOCKS...
SINESTRO DREAMS.
AND HOW DOES ONE ENSURE...THAT AS ONE REGIME FALLS...
...HIS OWN EMPIRE WILL RISE TO TAKE ITS PLACE?

WHAT
USE IS
FEAR
AGAINST
THE FURY
OF A
GOD?

GODHEAD ACT I, PART VI: SACRIFICE

CULLEN BUNN writer **DALE EAGLESHAM MARTIN COCCOLO** pencillers **DALE EAGLESHAM SCOTT HANNA** inkers **JASON WRIGHT** colorist **DAVE SHARPE** letterer
cover art by **GUILLEM MARCH & TOMEU MOREY**

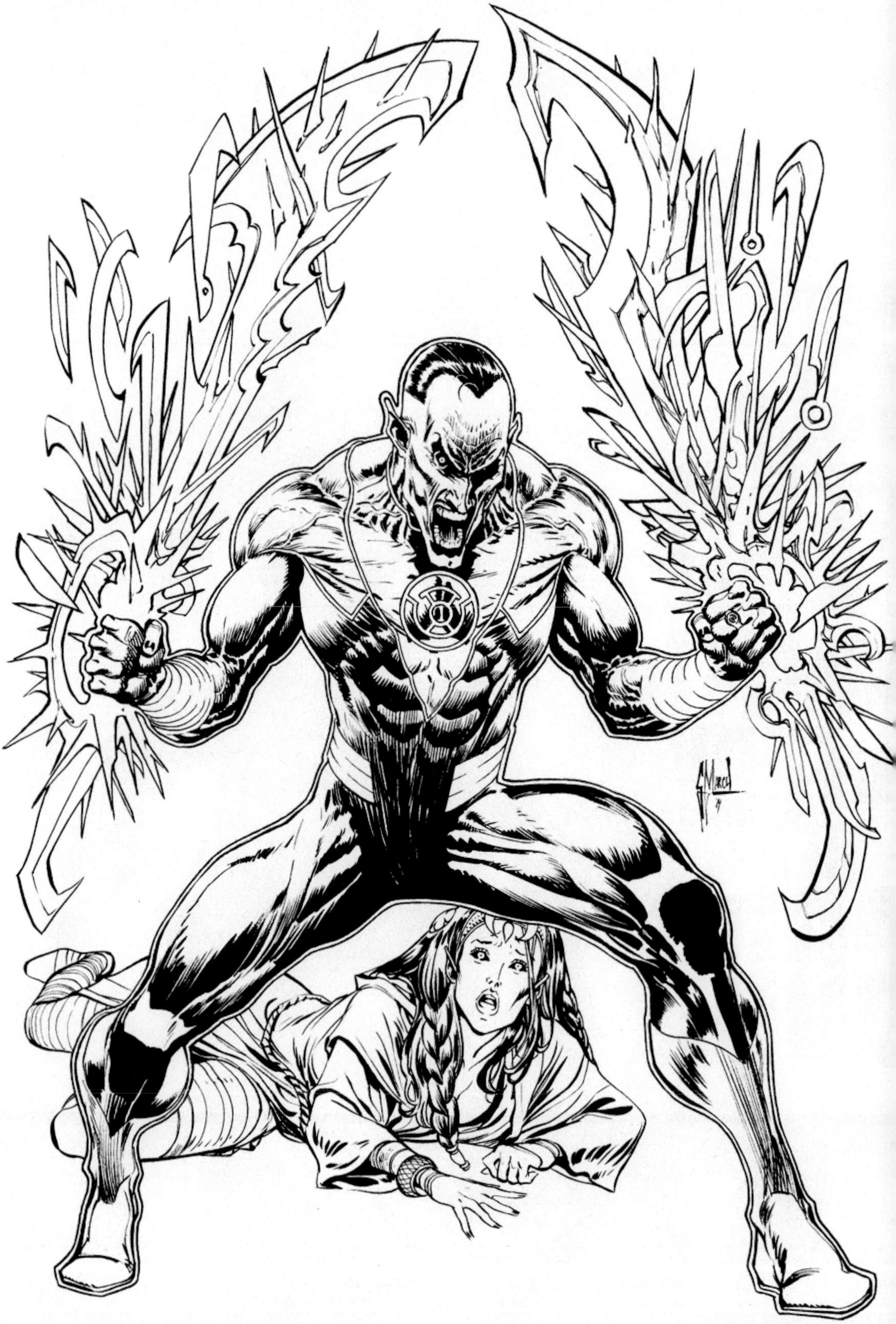

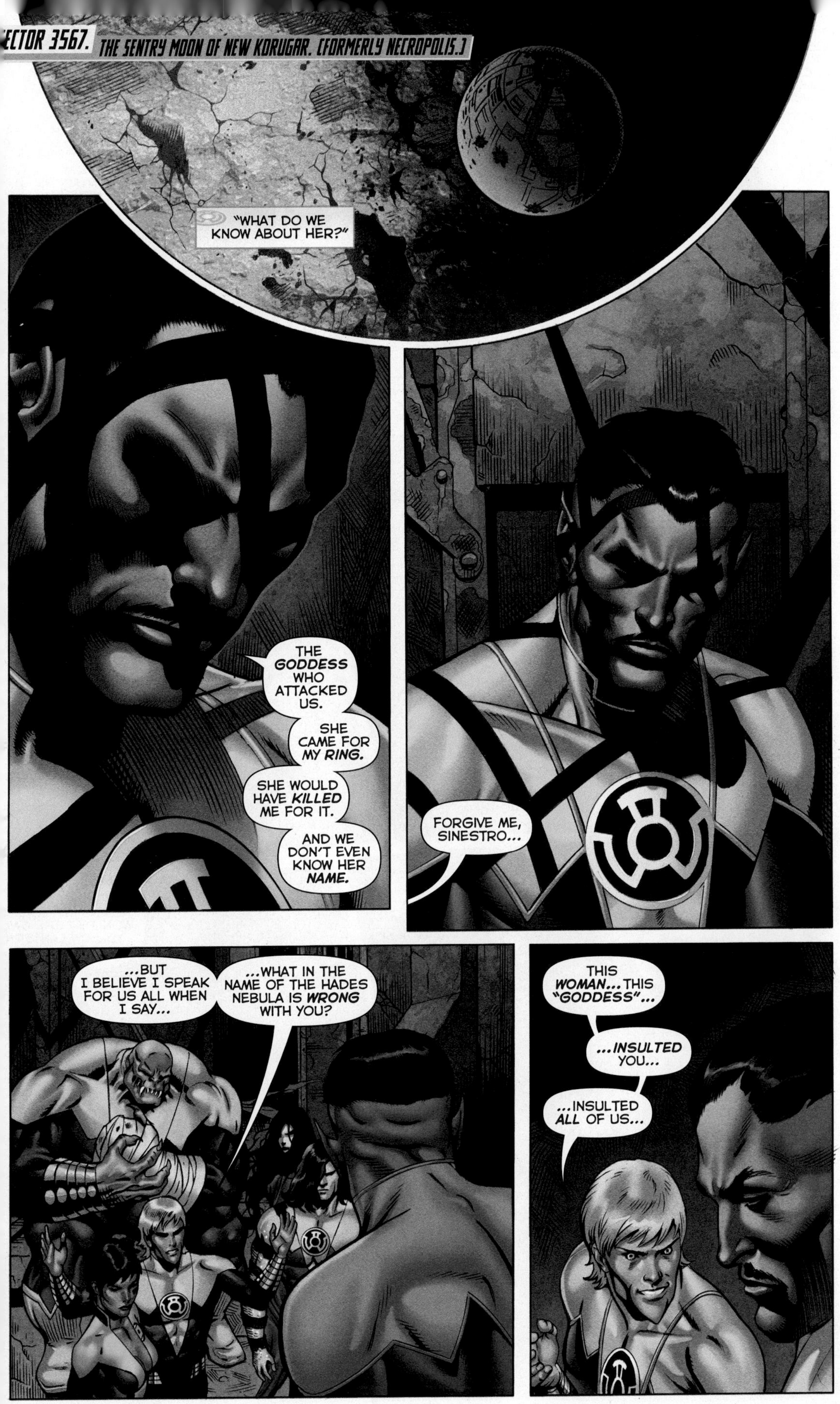

ECTOR 3567. THE SENTRY MOON OF NEW KORUGAR. [FORMERLY NECROPOLIS.]
"WHAT DO WE KNOW ABOUT HER?"
THE GODDESS WHO ATTACKED US.
SHE CAME FOR MY RING.
SHE WOULD HAVE KILLED ME FOR IT.
AND WE DON'T EVEN KNOW HER NAME.
FORGIVE ME, SINESTRO...
...BUT I BELIEVE I SPEAK FOR US ALL WHEN I SAY...
...WHAT IN THE NAME OF THE HADES NEBULA IS WRONG WITH YOU?
THIS WOMAN... THIS "GODDESS"...
...INSULTED YOU...
...INSULTED ALL OF US...

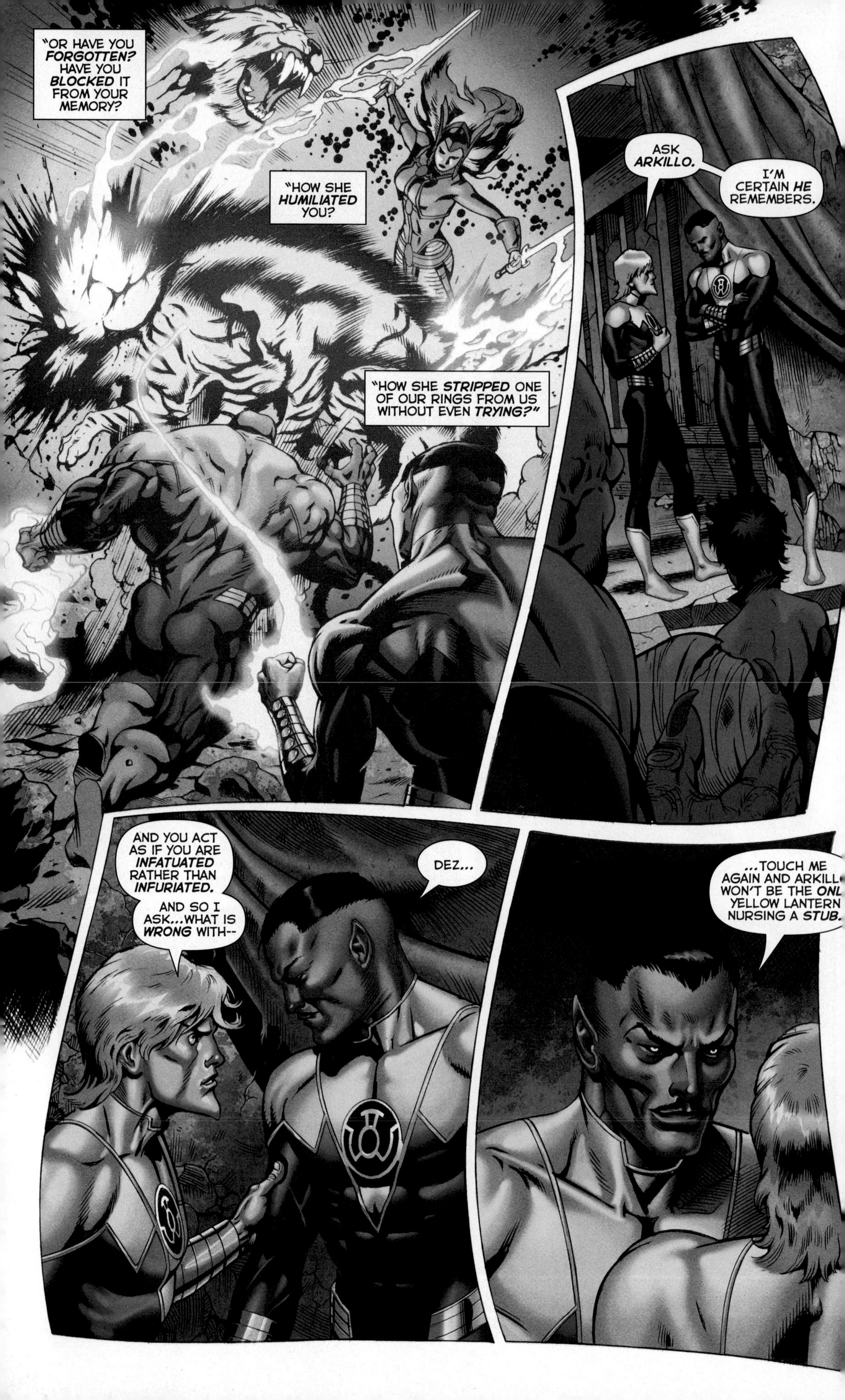
"OR HAVE YOU FORGOTTEN? HAVE YOU BLOCKED IT FROM YOUR MEMORY?
"HOW SHE HUMILIATED YOU?
"HOW SHE STRIPPED ONE OF OUR RINGS FROM US WITHOUT EVEN TRYING?"
ASK ARKILLO.
I'M CERTAIN HE REMEMBERS.
AND YOU ACT AS IF YOU ARE INFATUATED RATHER THAN INFURIATED.
AND SO I ASK...WHAT IS WRONG WITH--
DEZ...
...TOUCH ME AGAIN AND ARKILL WON'T BE THE ONL YELLOW LANTERN NURSING A STUB.

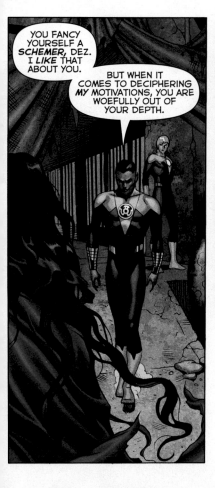

YOU FANCY YOURSELF A *SCHEMER*, DEZ. I *LIKE* THAT ABOUT YOU.

BUT WHEN IT COMES TO DECIPHERING *MY* MOTIVATIONS, YOU ARE WOEFULLY OUT OF YOUR DEPTH.

NOT THAT I LIKE AGREEING WITH TREVIUS, BUT HE *DOES* HAVE A POINT.

THIS WOMAN ATTACKED YOU ON *NEW KORUGAR.*

SHE COULD HAVE *KILLED* EVERY *KORUGARIAN* REFUGEE WE'VE SAVED.

EVER SINCE THAT ENCOUNTER, THOUGH, YOU SEEM MORE INTERESTED IN *COURTING* HER THAN *FIGHTING* HER.

LYSSA, CAN YOU *SENSE* HER? CAN YOU TELL ME WHERE TO FIND THIS WOMAN?

I'D VERY MUCH LIKE TO HAVE A *WORD* WITH HER.

IT COULD BE *DANGEROUS* TO TRACK HER.

I SAW YOUR *DEMISE* AT HER HANDS.

AND YET HERE I AM.

WHAT DO YOUR *VISIONS* TELL YOU NOW?

I SEE...

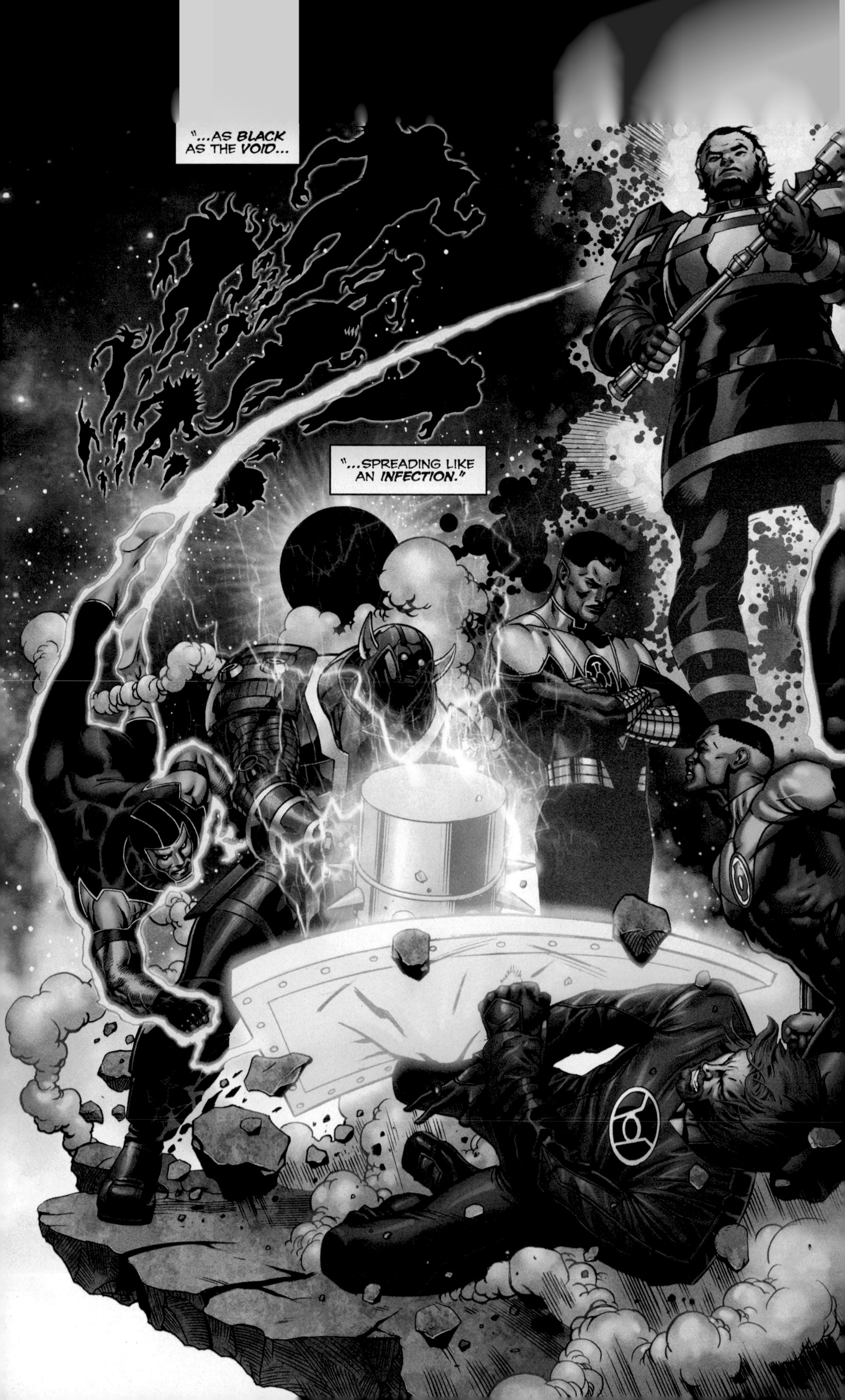
"...AS BLACK AS THE VOID...
"...SPREADING LIKE AN INFECTION."

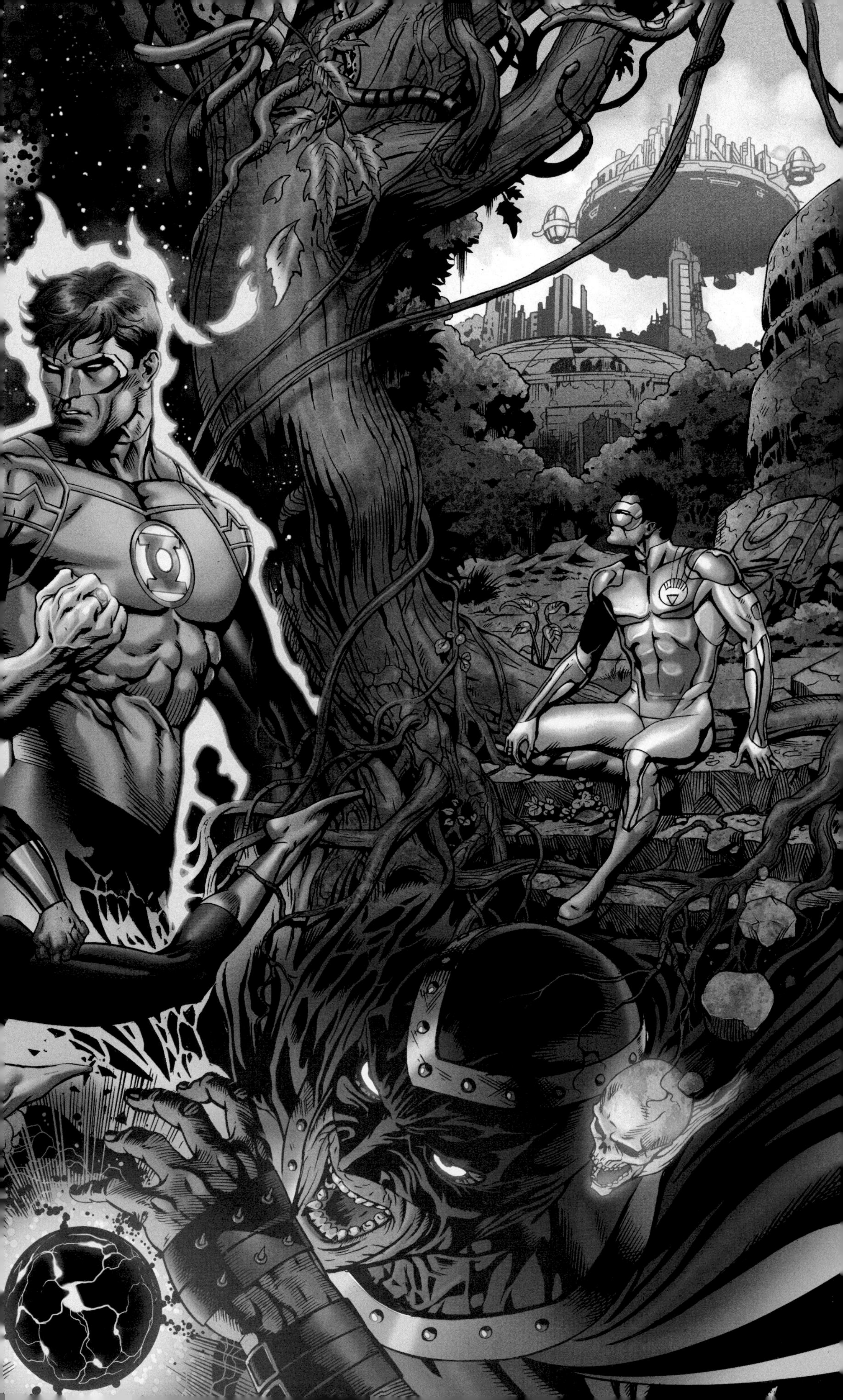

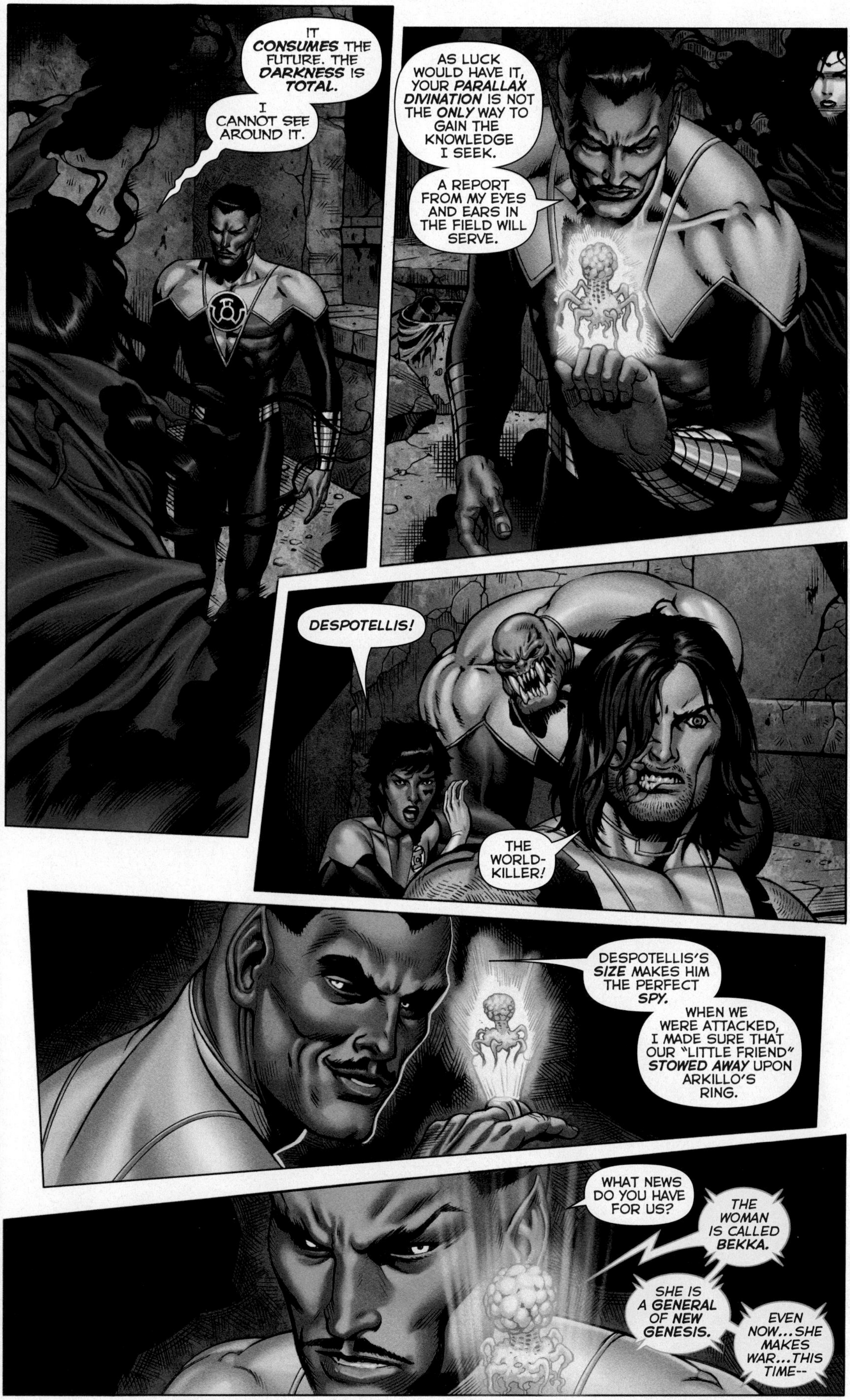
IT CONSUMES THE FUTURE. THE DARKNESS IS TOTAL.
I CANNOT SEE AROUND IT.
AS LUCK WOULD HAVE IT, YOUR PARALLAX DIVINATION IS NOT THE ONLY WAY TO GAIN THE KNOWLEDGE I SEEK.
A REPORT FROM MY EYES AND EARS IN THE FIELD WILL SERVE.
DESPOTELLIS!
THE WORLD-KILLER!
DESPOTELLIS'S SIZE MAKES HIM THE PERFECT SPY.
WHEN WE WERE ATTACKED, I MADE SURE THAT OUR "LITTLE FRIEND" STOWED AWAY UPON ARKILLO'S RING.
WHAT NEWS DO YOU HAVE FOR US?
THE WOMAN IS CALLED BEKKA.
SHE IS A GENERAL OF NEW GENESIS.
EVEN NOW...SHE MAKES WAR...THIS TIME--

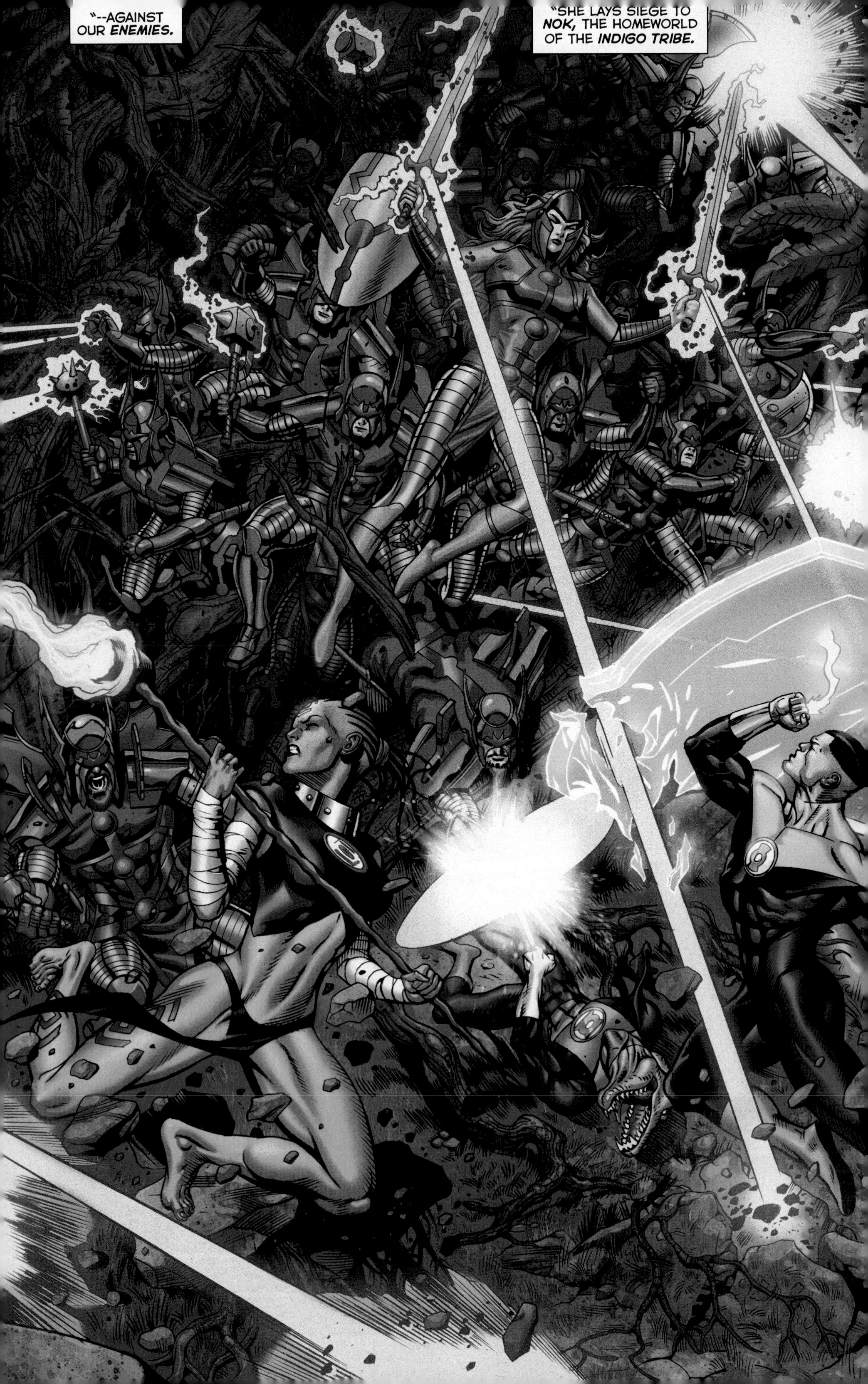
"--AGAINST OUR *ENEMIES.*
"SHE LAYS SIEGE TO *NOK,* THE HOMEWORLD OF THE *INDIGO TRIBE.*

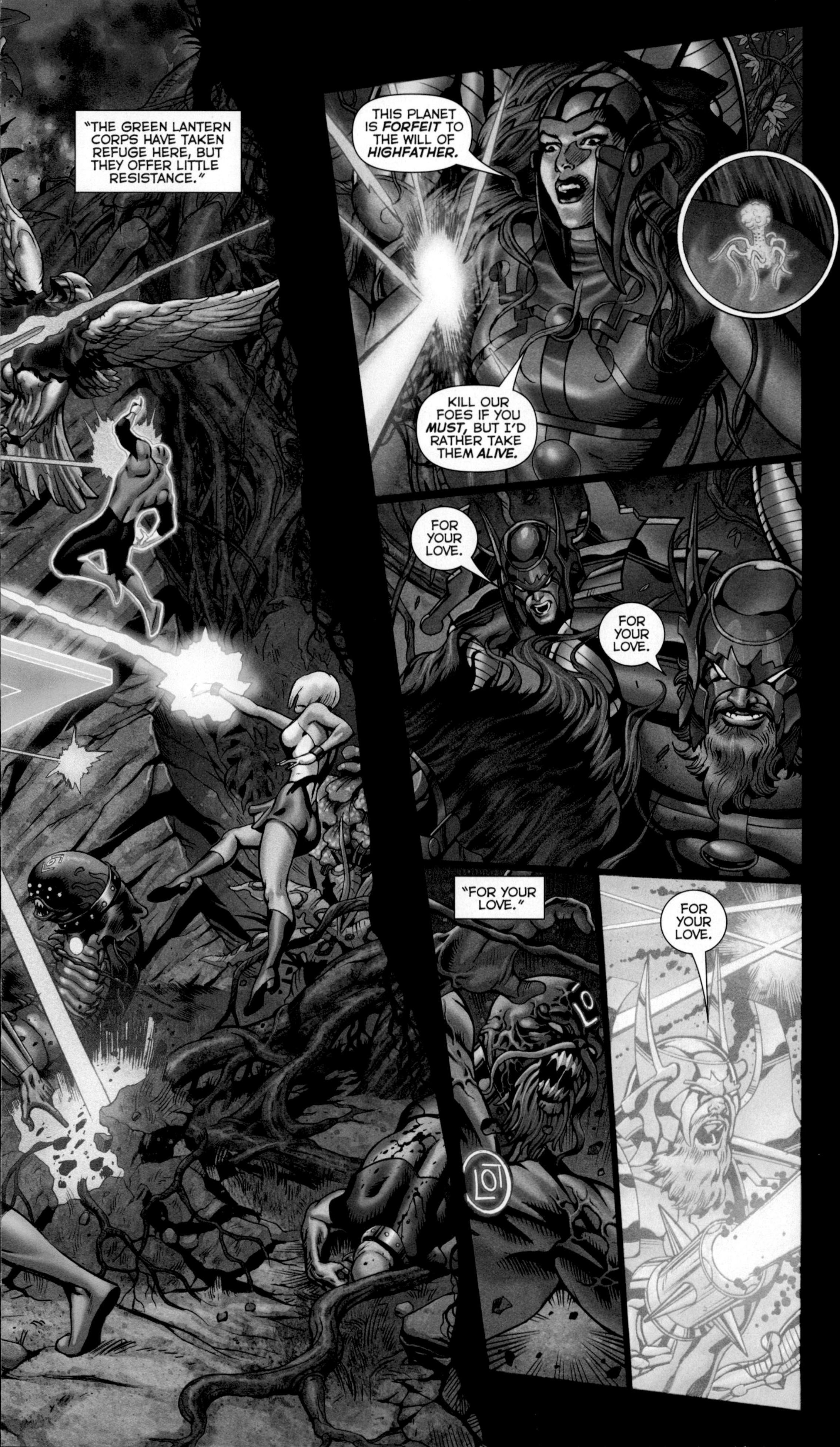
"THE GREEN LANTERN CORPS HAVE TAKEN REFUGE HERE, BUT THEY OFFER LITTLE RESISTANCE."
THIS PLANET IS ***FORFEIT*** TO THE WILL OF ***HIGHFATHER.***
KILL OUR FOES IF YOU ***MUST,*** BUT I'D RATHER TAKE THEM ***ALIVE.***
FOR YOUR LOVE.
FOR YOUR LOVE.
"FOR YOUR LOVE."
FOR YOUR LOVE.

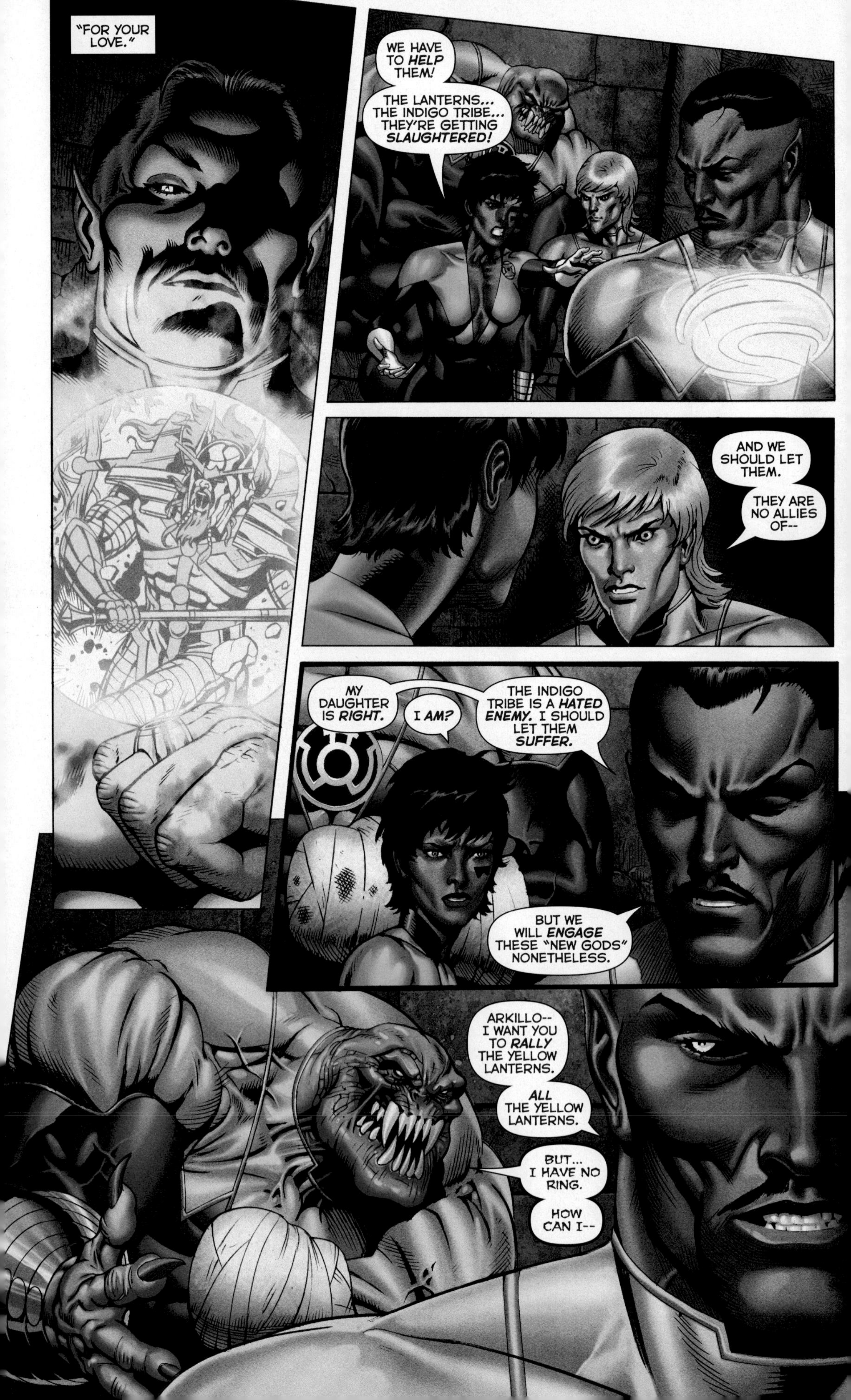
"FOR YOUR LOVE."
WE HAVE TO HELP THEM!
THE LANTERNS... THE INDIGO TRIBE... THEY'RE GETTING SLAUGHTERED!
AND WE SHOULD LET THEM.
THEY ARE NO ALLIES OF--
MY DAUGHTER IS RIGHT.
I AM?
THE INDIGO TRIBE IS A HATED ENEMY. I SHOULD LET THEM SUFFER.
BUT WE WILL ENGAGE THESE "NEW GODS" NONETHELESS.
ARKILLO-- I WANT YOU TO RALLY THE YELLOW LANTERNS.
ALL THE YELLOW LANTERNS.
BUT... I HAVE NO RING.
HOW CAN I--

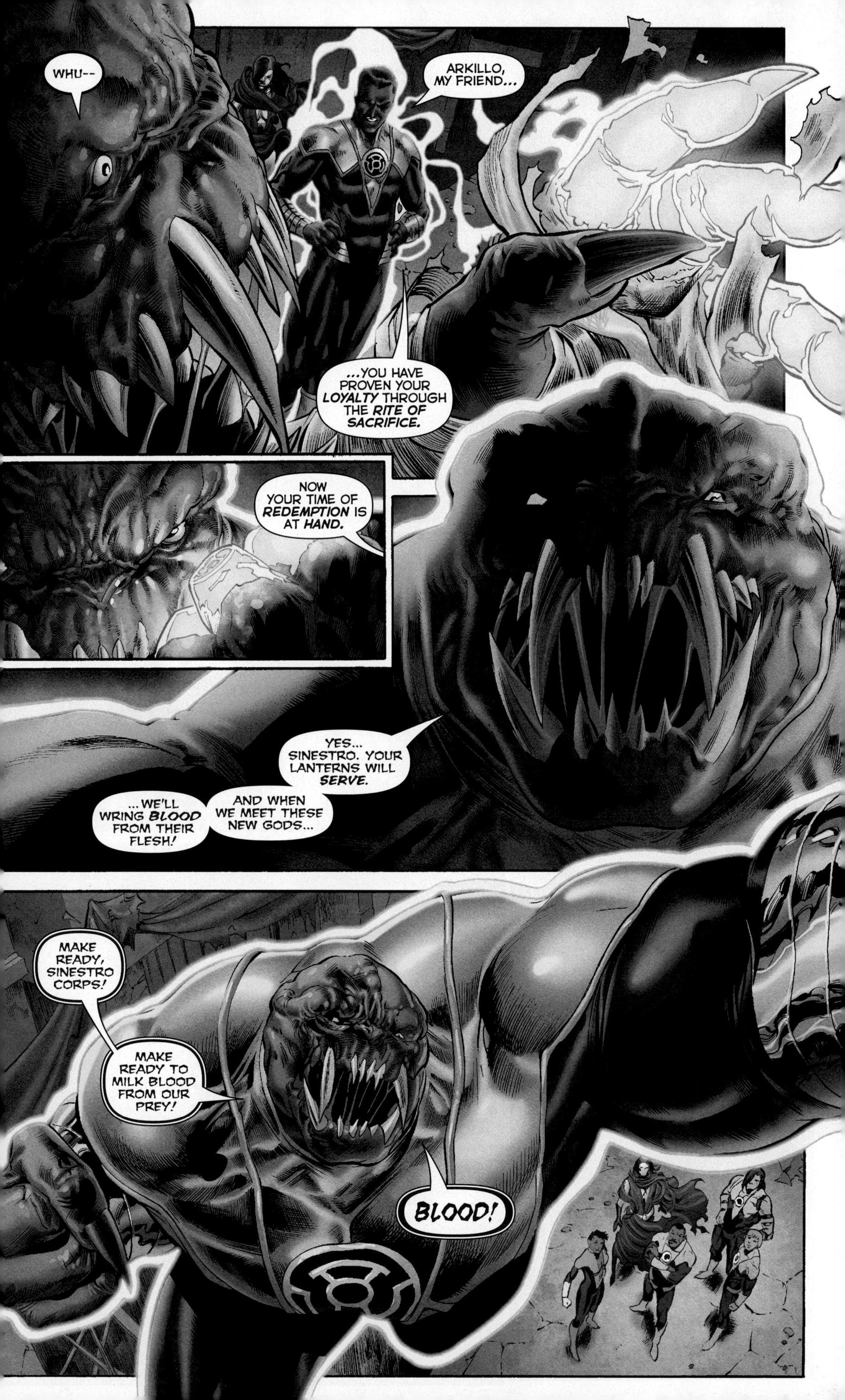
WHU--
ARKILLO, MY FRIEND...
...YOU HAVE PROVEN YOUR LOYALTY THROUGH THE RITE OF SACRIFICE.
NOW YOUR TIME OF REDEMPTION IS AT HAND.
YES... SINESTRO. YOUR LANTERNS WILL SERVE.
AND WHEN WE MEET THESE NEW GODS...
...WE'LL WRING BLOOD FROM THEIR FLESH!
MAKE READY, SINESTRO CORPS!
MAKE READY TO MILK BLOOD FROM OUR PREY!
BLOOD!

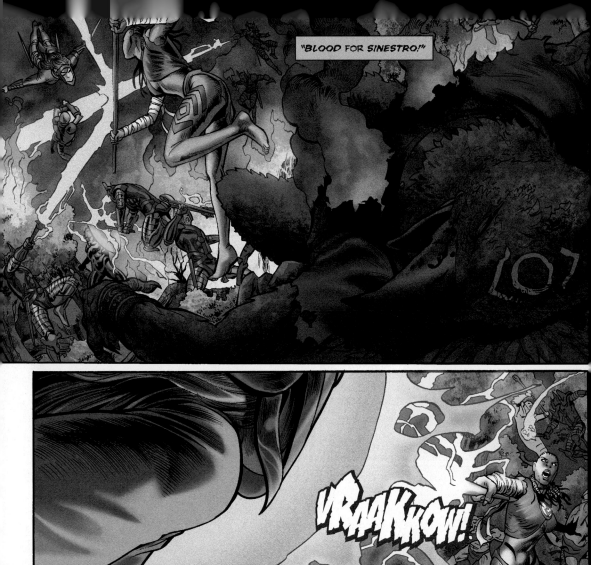

"BLOOD FOR SINESTRO!"

VRAAKKOW!

N-NOK.

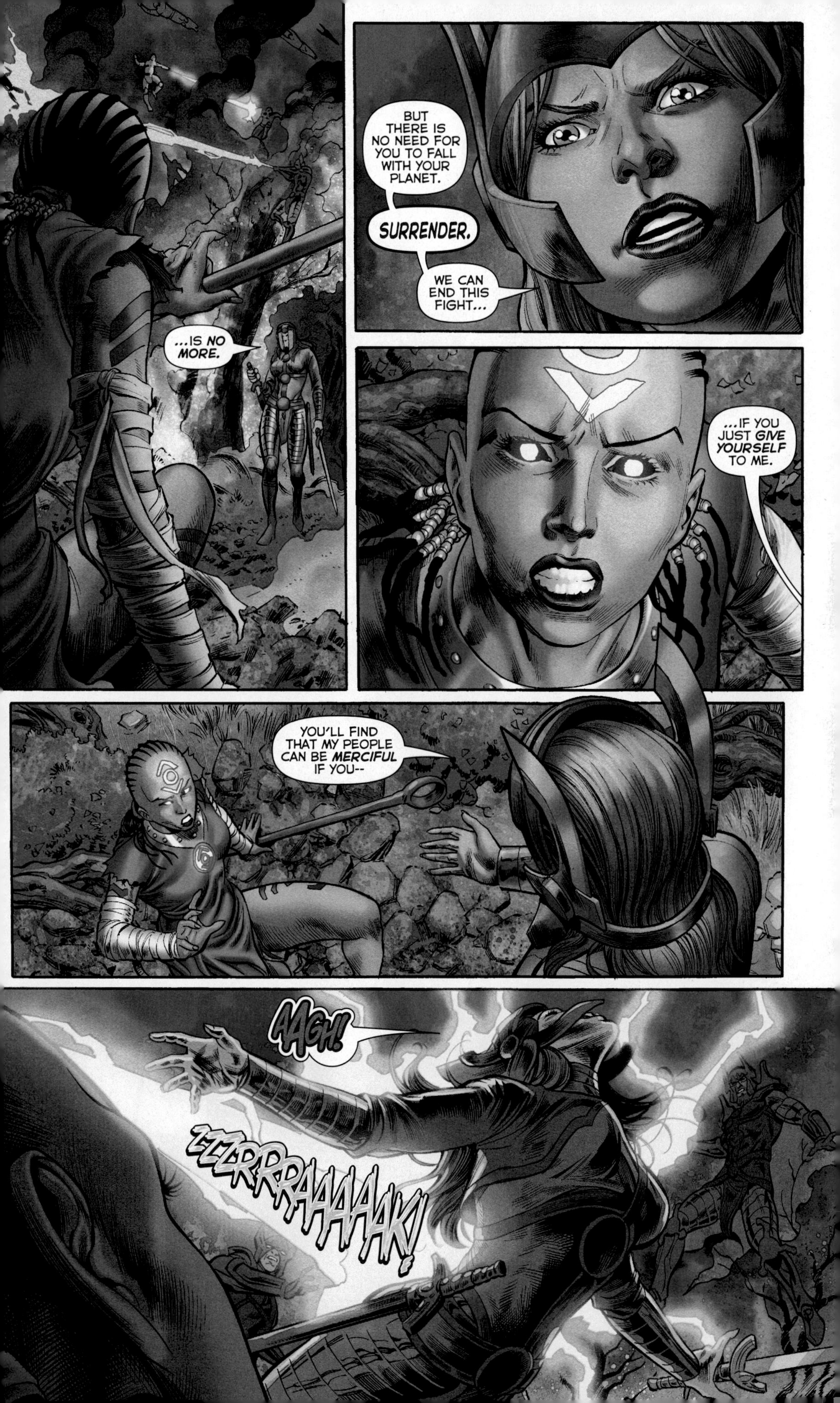
...IS NO MORE.
BUT THERE IS NO NEED FOR YOU TO FALL WITH YOUR PLANET.
SURRENDER.
WE CAN END THIS FIGHT...
...IF YOU JUST GIVE YOURSELF TO ME.
YOU'LL FIND THAT MY PEOPLE CAN BE MERCIFUL IF YOU--
AAGH!
ZZZRRRRAAAAAAK!

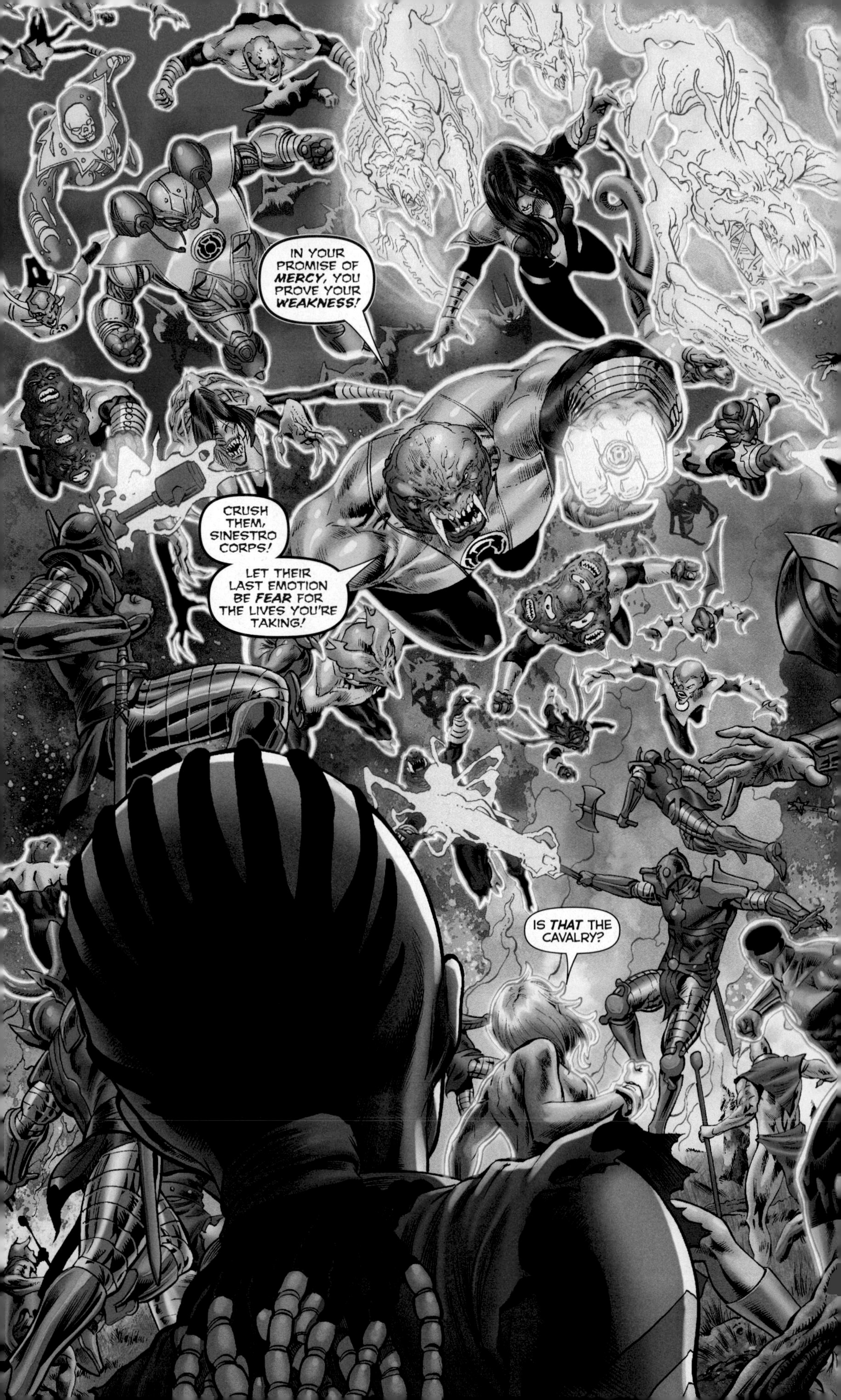

IN YOUR PROMISE OF MERCY, YOU PROVE YOUR WEAKNESS!
CRUSH THEM, SINESTRO CORPS!
LET THEIR LAST EMOTION BE FEAR FOR THE LIVES YOU'RE TAKING!
IS THAT THE CAVALRY?

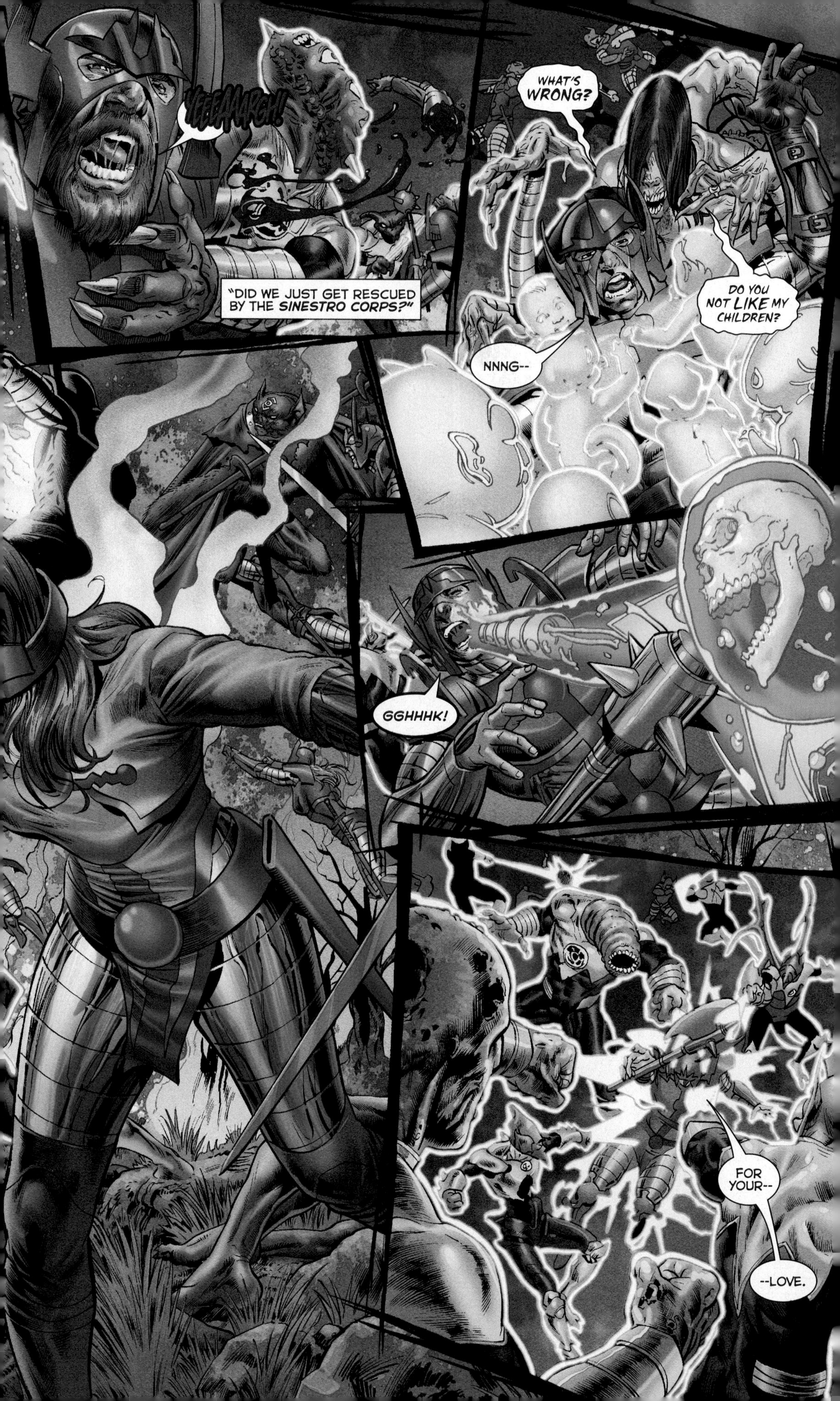
YEEEAAARGH!!
"DID WE JUST GET RESCUED BY THE SINESTRO CORPS?"
WHAT'S WRONG?
DO YOU NOT LIKE MY CHILDREN?
NNNG--
GGHHHK!
FOR YOUR--
--LOVE.

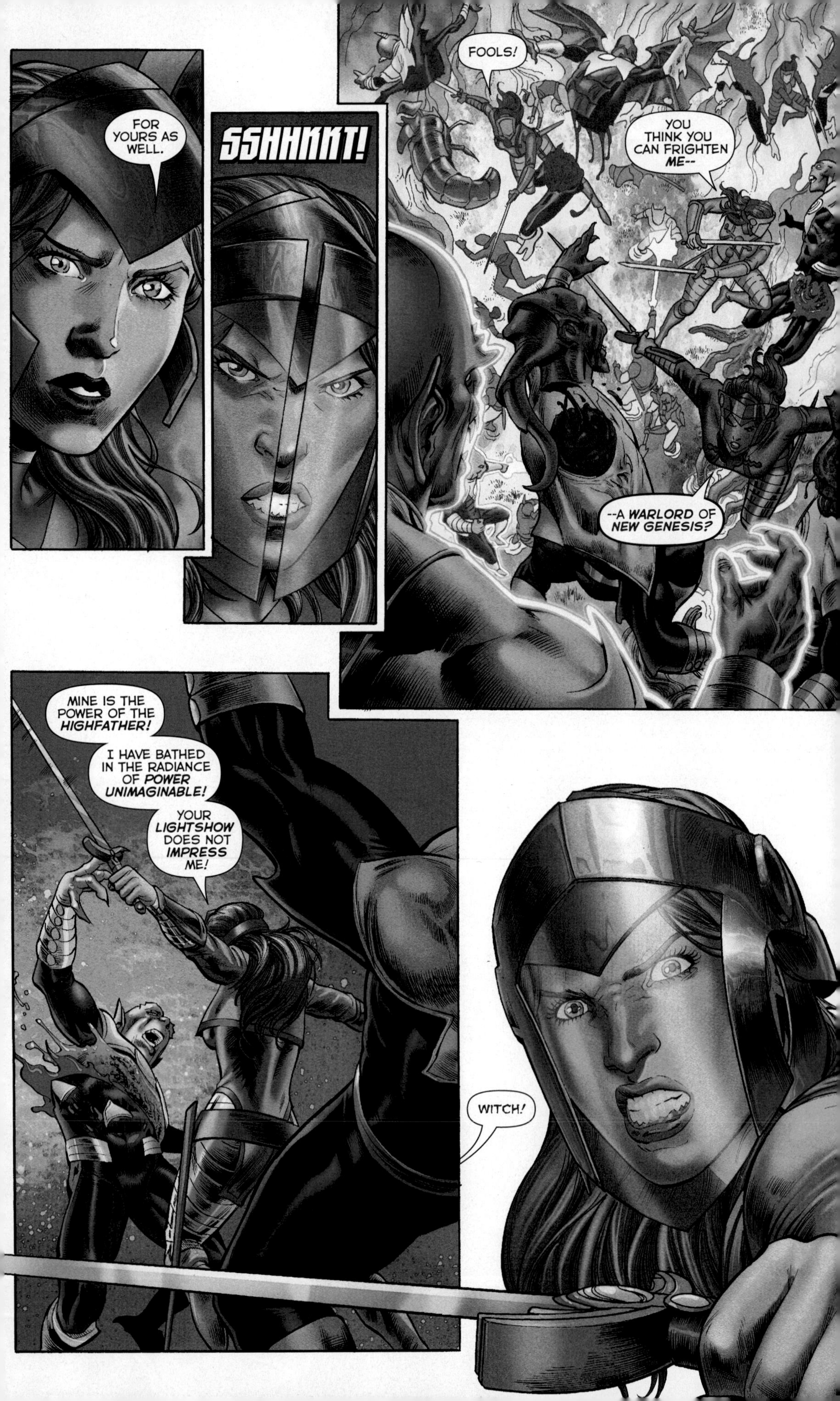

FOR YOURS AS WELL.
SSHHKKT!
FOOLS!
YOU THINK YOU CAN FRIGHTEN ME--
--A WARLORD OF NEW GENESIS?
MINE IS THE POWER OF THE HIGHFATHER!
I HAVE BATHED IN THE RADIANCE OF POWER UNIMAGINABLE!
YOUR LIGHTSHOW DOES NOT IMPRESS ME!
WITCH!

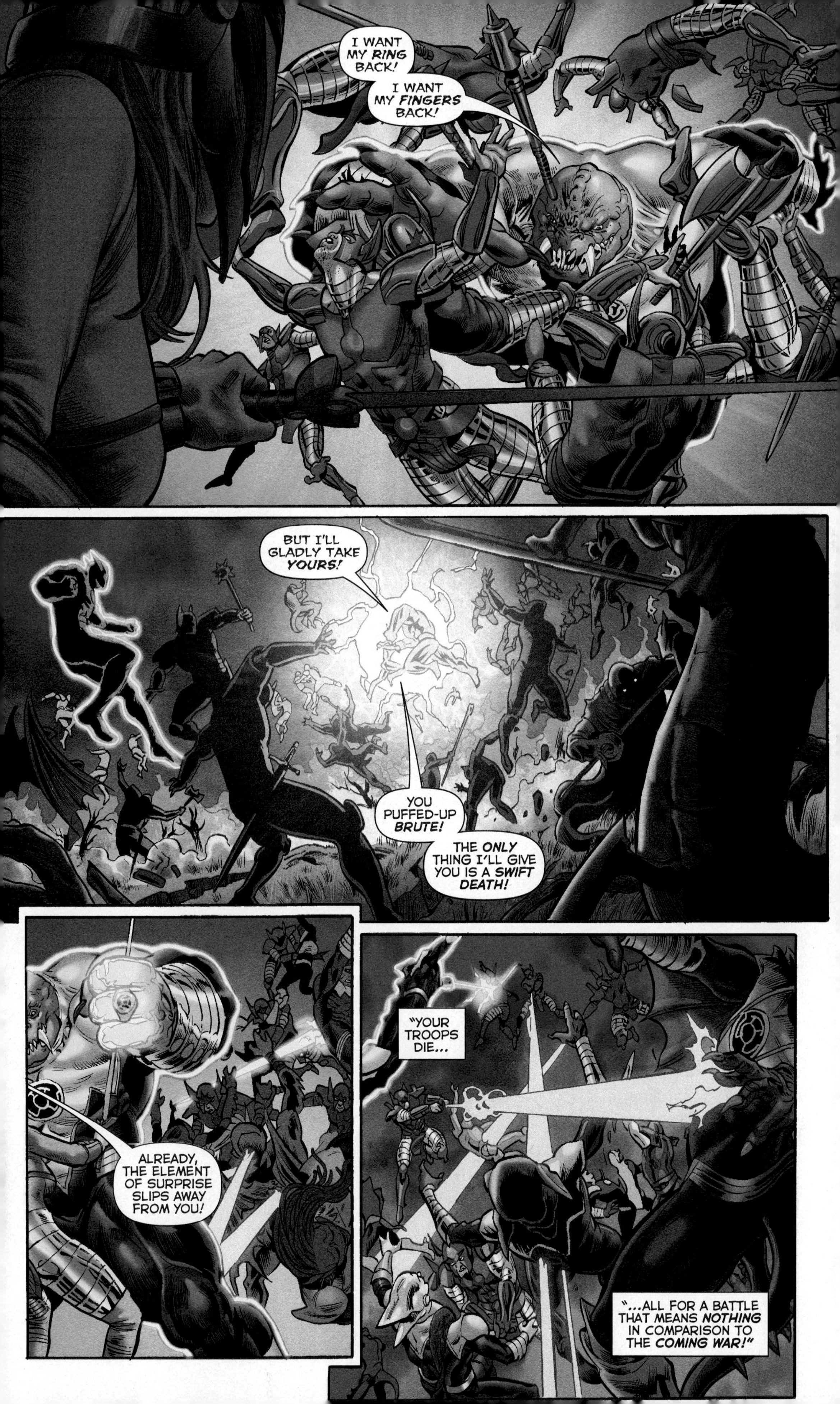
I WANT MY RING BACK!
I WANT MY FINGERS BACK!
BUT I'LL GLADLY TAKE YOURS!
YOU PUFFED-UP BRUTE!
THE ONLY THING I'LL GIVE YOU IS A SWIFT DEATH!
ALREADY, THE ELEMENT OF SURPRISE SLIPS AWAY FROM YOU!
"YOUR TROOPS DIE...
"...ALL FOR A BATTLE THAT MEANS NOTHING IN COMPARISON TO THE COMING WAR!"

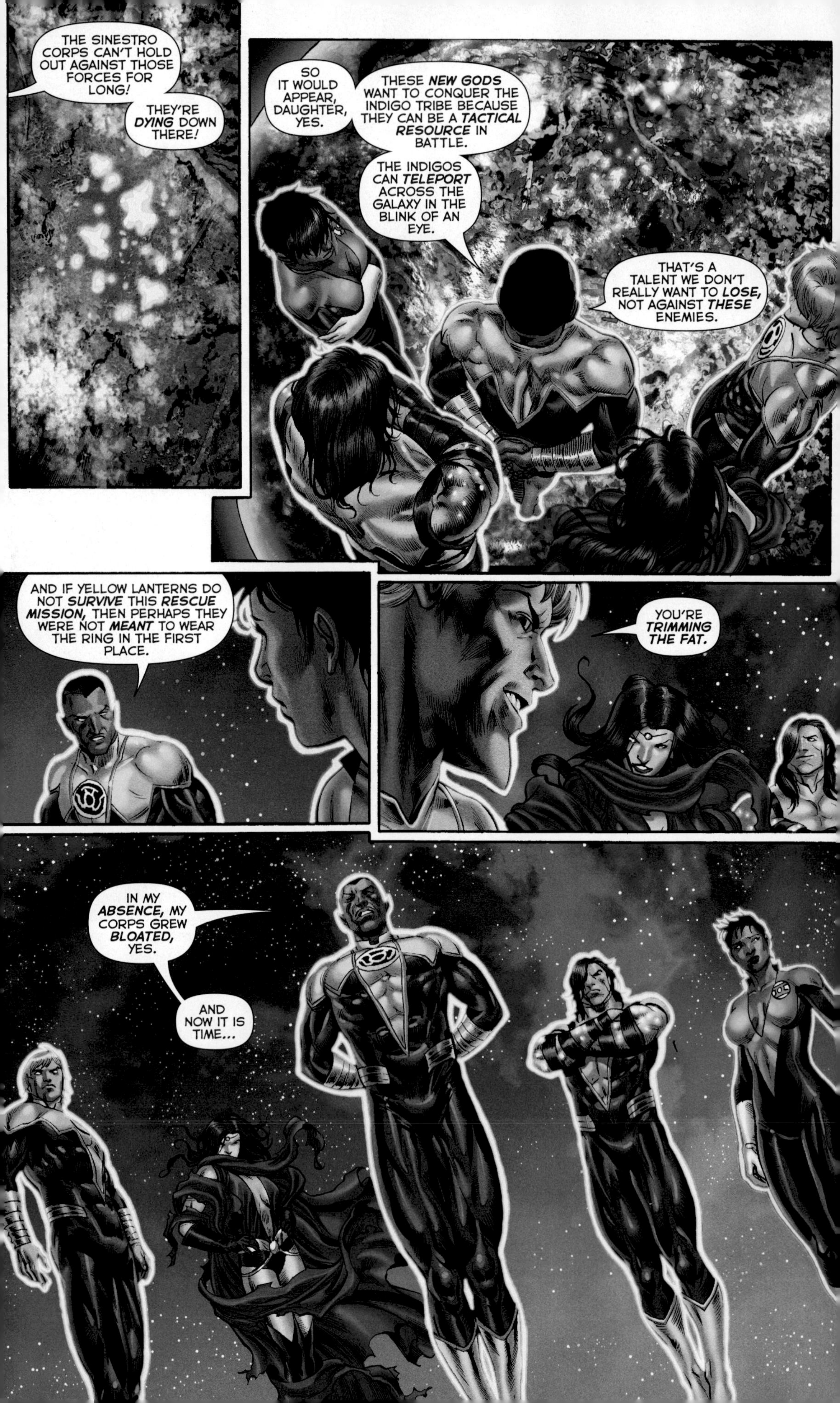
THE SINESTRO CORPS CAN'T HOLD OUT AGAINST THOSE FORCES FOR LONG!
THEY'RE DYING DOWN THERE!
SO IT WOULD APPEAR, DAUGHTER, YES.
THESE NEW GODS WANT TO CONQUER THE INDIGO TRIBE BECAUSE THEY CAN BE A TACTICAL RESOURCE IN BATTLE.
THE INDIGOS CAN TELEPORT ACROSS THE GALAXY IN THE BLINK OF AN EYE.
THAT'S A TALENT WE DON'T REALLY WANT TO LOSE, NOT AGAINST THESE ENEMIES.
AND IF YELLOW LANTERNS DO NOT SURVIVE THIS RESCUE MISSION, THEN PERHAPS THEY WERE NOT MEANT TO WEAR THE RING IN THE FIRST PLACE.
YOU'RE TRIMMING THE FAT.
IN MY ABSENCE, MY CORPS GREW BLOATED, YES.
AND NOW IT IS TIME...

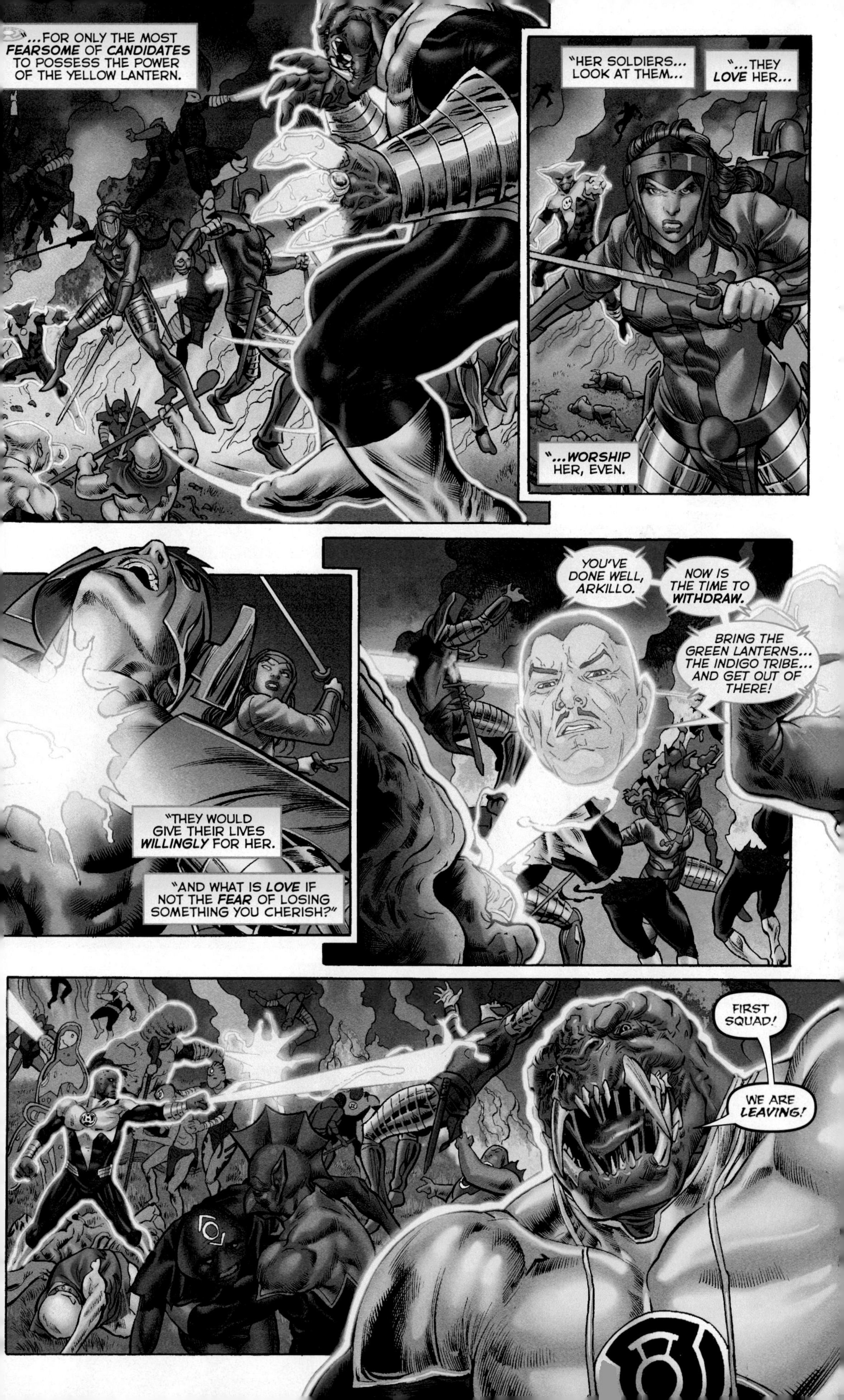
"...FOR ONLY THE MOST FEARSOME OF CANDIDATES TO POSSESS THE POWER OF THE YELLOW LANTERN.
"HER SOLDIERS... LOOK AT THEM...
"...THEY LOVE HER...
"...WORSHIP HER, EVEN.
"THEY WOULD GIVE THEIR LIVES WILLINGLY FOR HER.
"AND WHAT IS LOVE IF NOT THE FEAR OF LOSING SOMETHING YOU CHERISH?"
YOU'VE DONE WELL, ARKILLO.
NOW IS THE TIME TO WITHDRAW.
BRING THE GREEN LANTERNS... THE INDIGO TRIBE... AND GET OUT OF THERE!
FIRST SQUAD!
WE ARE LEAVING!

THIS PLANET IS *DONE!* THIS BATTLE IS *FINISHED!*

SINESTRO CORPS! *COVER US!*

"HOLD THE LINE!"

IS HE SERIOUS? THE LINE IS ALREADY BROKEN!

WE STAY HERE ANY LONGER AND WE'RE--

HNH?

SELF-DESTRUCT PROTOCOL INITIATED.

SINESTRO?

YOU BAS--

SELF-DESTRUCT PROTOCOL INITIATED.

SELF-DESTRUCT PROTOCOL INITIATED.

SELF-DESTRUCT PROTOCOL INITIATED.

SELF-DESTRUCT PROTOCOL INITIATED.

SELF-DESTRUCT PROTOCOL INITIATED.

SELF-DESTRUCT PROTOCOL INITIATED.

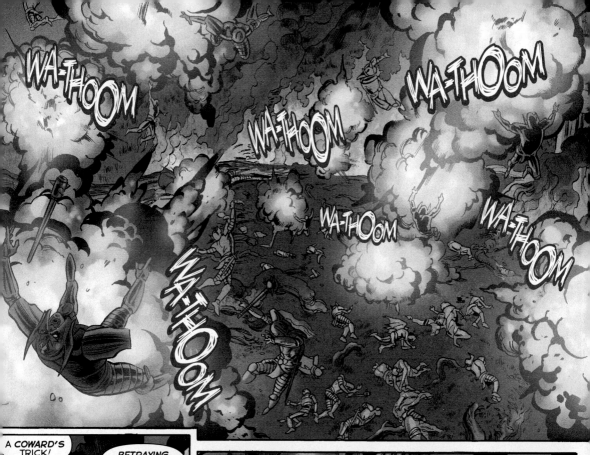

WA-THOOM

WA-THOOM

WA-THOOM

WA-THOOM

WA-THOOM

WA-THOOM

WA-THOOM

A COWARD'S TRICK!

SACRIFICING UNWITTING PAWNS TO COVER YOUR ESCAPE!

BETRAYING THE LOYALTY OF YOUR SUBJECTS LIKE SOME--

FOR YOUR L-LOVE.

LOVE.

LOVE FOR YOU, MY SOLDIERS.

BUT FOR YOU, SINESTRO...FOR WHAT WE HAVE BOTH DONE HERE TODAY...

...ONLY DAMNATION AWAITS.

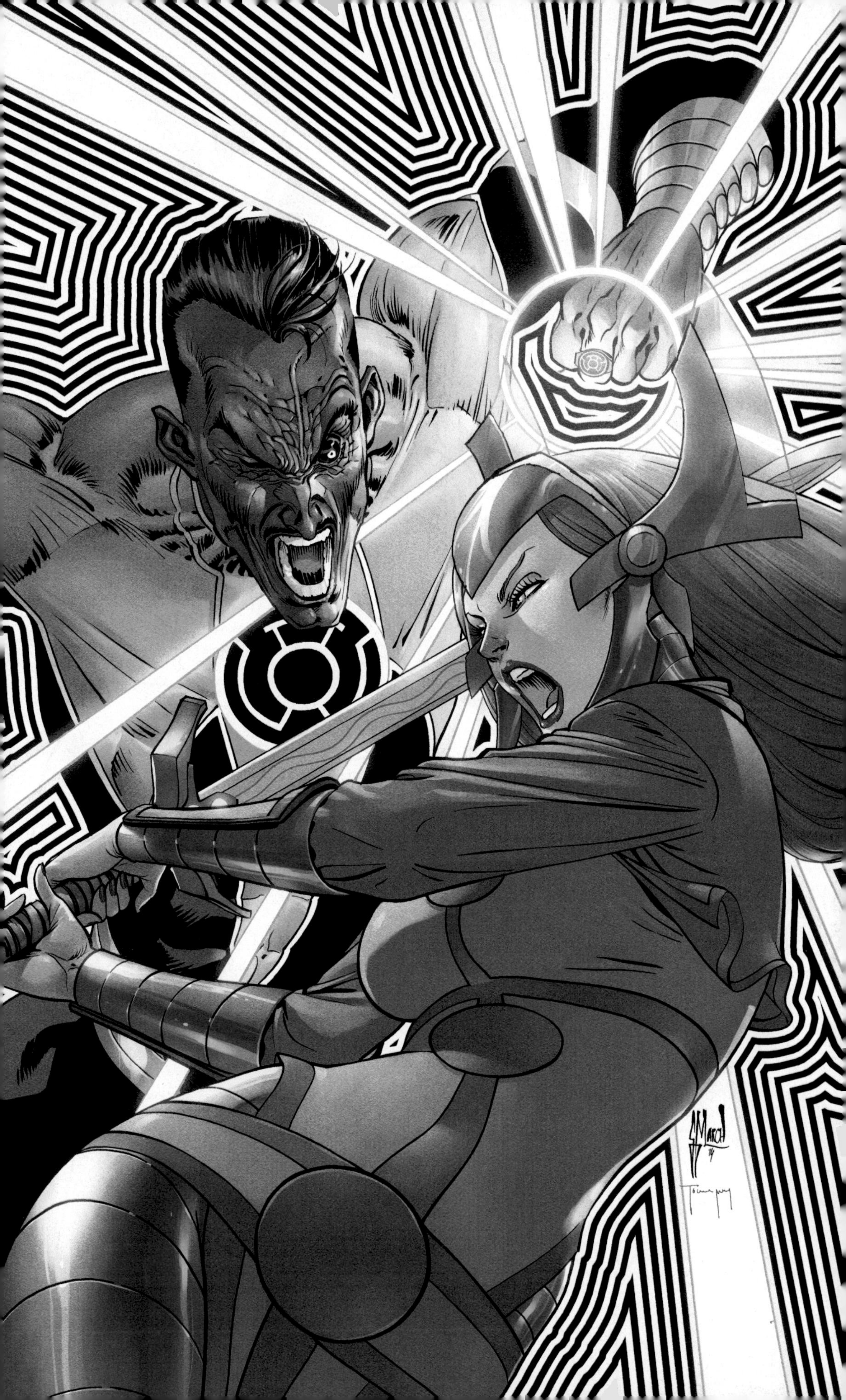

GODHEAD ACT II, PART V: BATTLEPLANS

CULLEN BUNN writer **ETHAN VAN SCIVER** penciller **GERALDO BORGES** inker **JASON WRIGHT** colorist **DAVE SHARPE** letterer cover art by **GUILLEM MARCH & TOMEU MOREY**

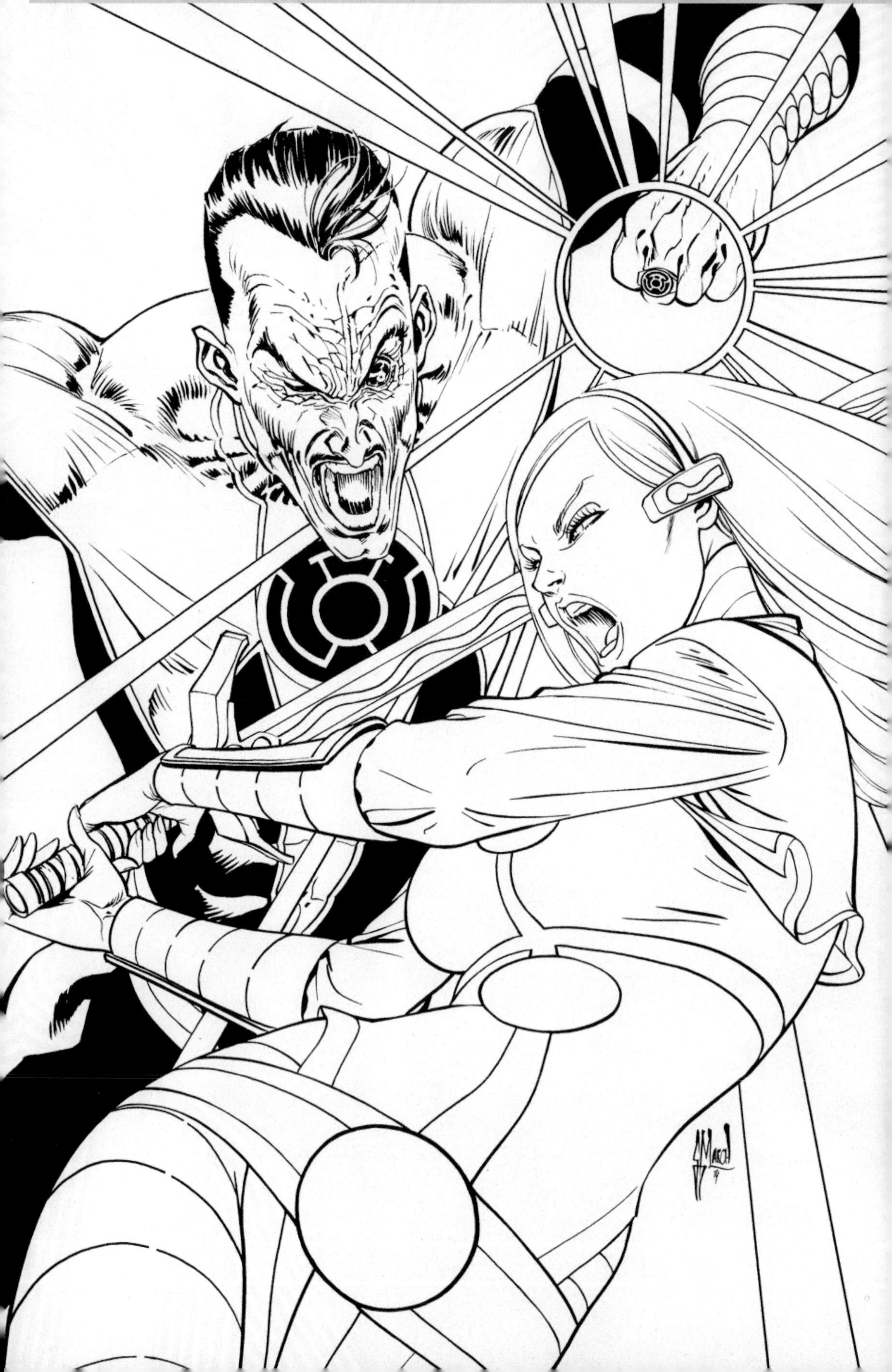

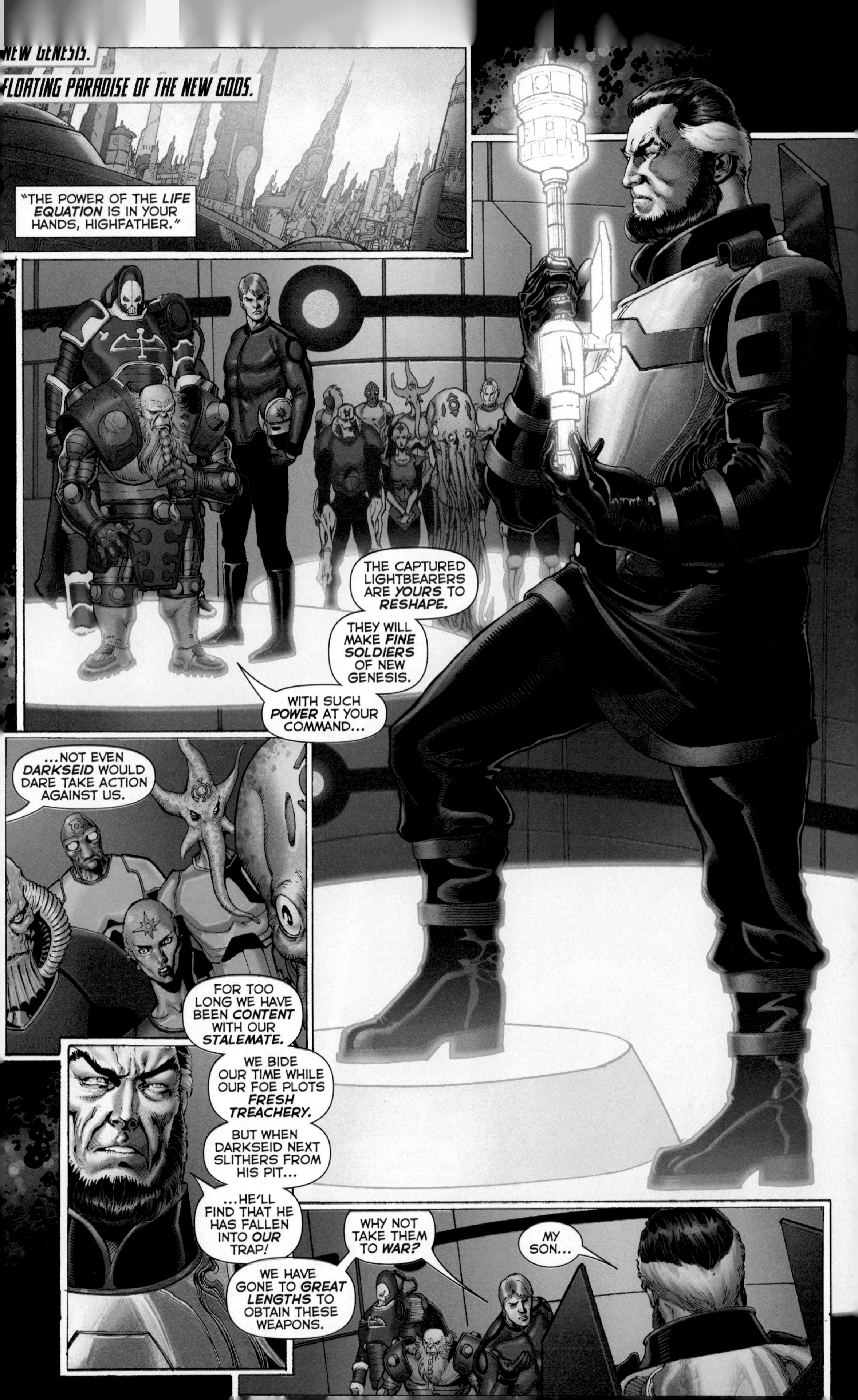

NEW GENESIS.
FLOATING PARADISE OF THE NEW GODS.
"THE POWER OF THE LIFE EQUATION IS IN YOUR HANDS, HIGHFATHER."
THE CAPTURED LIGHTBEARERS ARE YOURS TO RESHAPE.
THEY WILL MAKE FINE SOLDIERS OF NEW GENESIS.
WITH SUCH POWER AT YOUR COMMAND...
...NOT EVEN DARKSEID WOULD DARE TAKE ACTION AGAINST US.
FOR TOO LONG WE HAVE BEEN CONTENT WITH OUR STALEMATE.
WE BIDE OUR TIME WHILE OUR FOE PLOTS FRESH TREACHERY.
BUT WHEN DARKSEID NEXT SLITHERS FROM HIS PIT...
...HE'LL FIND THAT HE HAS FALLEN INTO OUR TRAP!
WHY NOT TAKE THEM TO WAR?
WE HAVE GONE TO GREAT LENGTHS TO OBTAIN THESE WEAPONS.
MY SON...

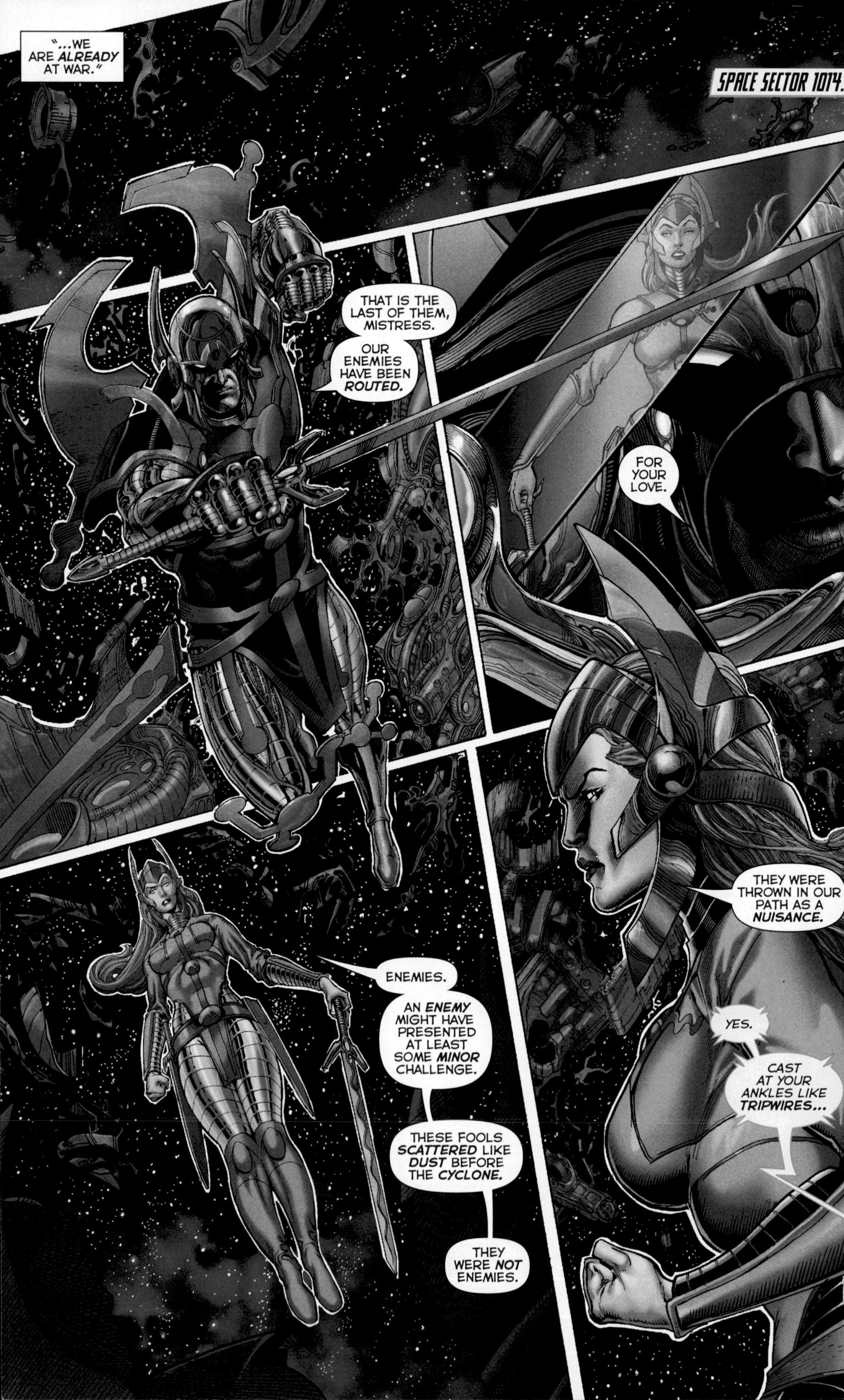
"...WE ARE *ALREADY* AT WAR."
SPACE SECTOR 1014.
THAT IS THE LAST OF THEM, MISTRESS.
OUR ENEMIES HAVE BEEN *ROUTED.*
FOR YOUR LOVE.
ENEMIES.
AN *ENEMY* MIGHT HAVE PRESENTED AT LEAST SOME *MINOR* CHALLENGE.
THESE FOOLS *SCATTERED* LIKE *DUST* BEFORE THE *CYCLONE.*
THEY WERE *NOT* ENEMIES.
THEY WERE THROWN IN OUR PATH AS A *NUISANCE.*
YES.
CAST AT YOUR ANKLES LIKE *TRIPWIRES...*

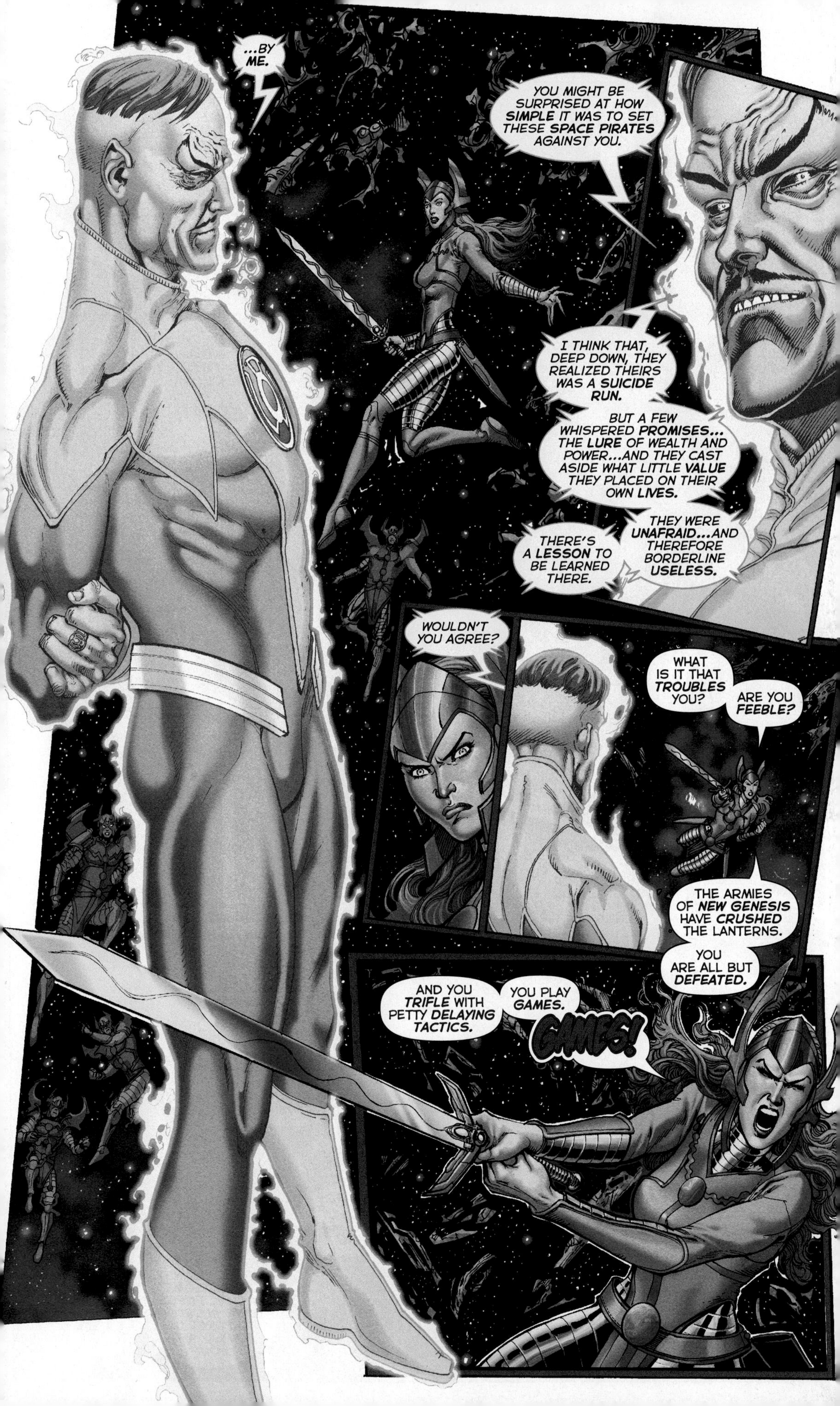
...BY ME.
YOU MIGHT BE SURPRISED AT HOW SIMPLE IT WAS TO SET THESE SPACE PIRATES AGAINST YOU.
I THINK THAT, DEEP DOWN, THEY REALIZED THEIRS WAS A SUICIDE RUN.
BUT A FEW WHISPERED PROMISES... THE LURE OF WEALTH AND POWER...AND THEY CAST ASIDE WHAT LITTLE VALUE THEY PLACED ON THEIR OWN LIVES.
THEY WERE UNAFRAID...AND THEREFORE BORDERLINE USELESS.
THERE'S A LESSON TO BE LEARNED THERE.
WOULDN'T YOU AGREE?
WHAT IS IT THAT TROUBLES YOU?
ARE YOU FEEBLE?
THE ARMIES OF NEW GENESIS HAVE CRUSHED THE LANTERNS.
YOU ARE ALL BUT DEFEATED.
YOU PLAY GAMES.
GAMES!
AND YOU TRIFLE WITH PETTY DELAYING TACTICS.

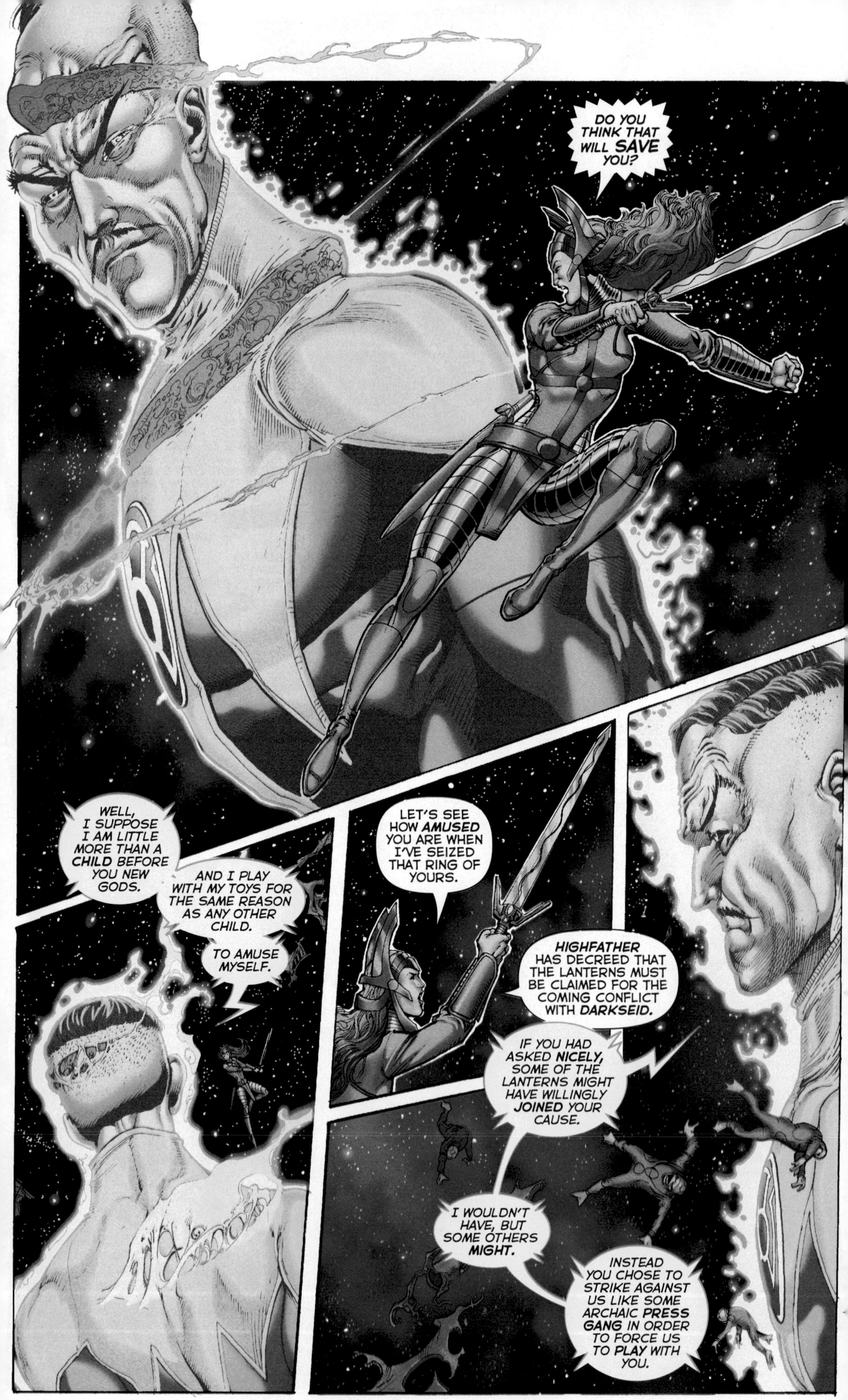

DO YOU THINK THAT WILL SAVE YOU?
WELL, I SUPPOSE I AM LITTLE MORE THAN A CHILD BEFORE YOU NEW GODS.
AND I PLAY WITH MY TOYS FOR THE SAME REASON AS ANY OTHER CHILD.
TO AMUSE MYSELF.
LET'S SEE HOW AMUSED YOU ARE WHEN I'VE SEIZED THAT RING OF YOURS.
HIGHFATHER HAS DECREED THAT THE LANTERNS MUST BE CLAIMED FOR THE COMING CONFLICT WITH DARKSEID.
IF YOU HAD ASKED NICELY, SOME OF THE LANTERNS MIGHT HAVE WILLINGLY JOINED YOUR CAUSE.
I WOULDN'T HAVE, BUT SOME OTHERS MIGHT.
INSTEAD YOU CHOSE TO STRIKE AGAINST US LIKE SOME ARCHAIC PRESS GANG IN ORDER TO FORCE US TO PLAY WITH YOU.

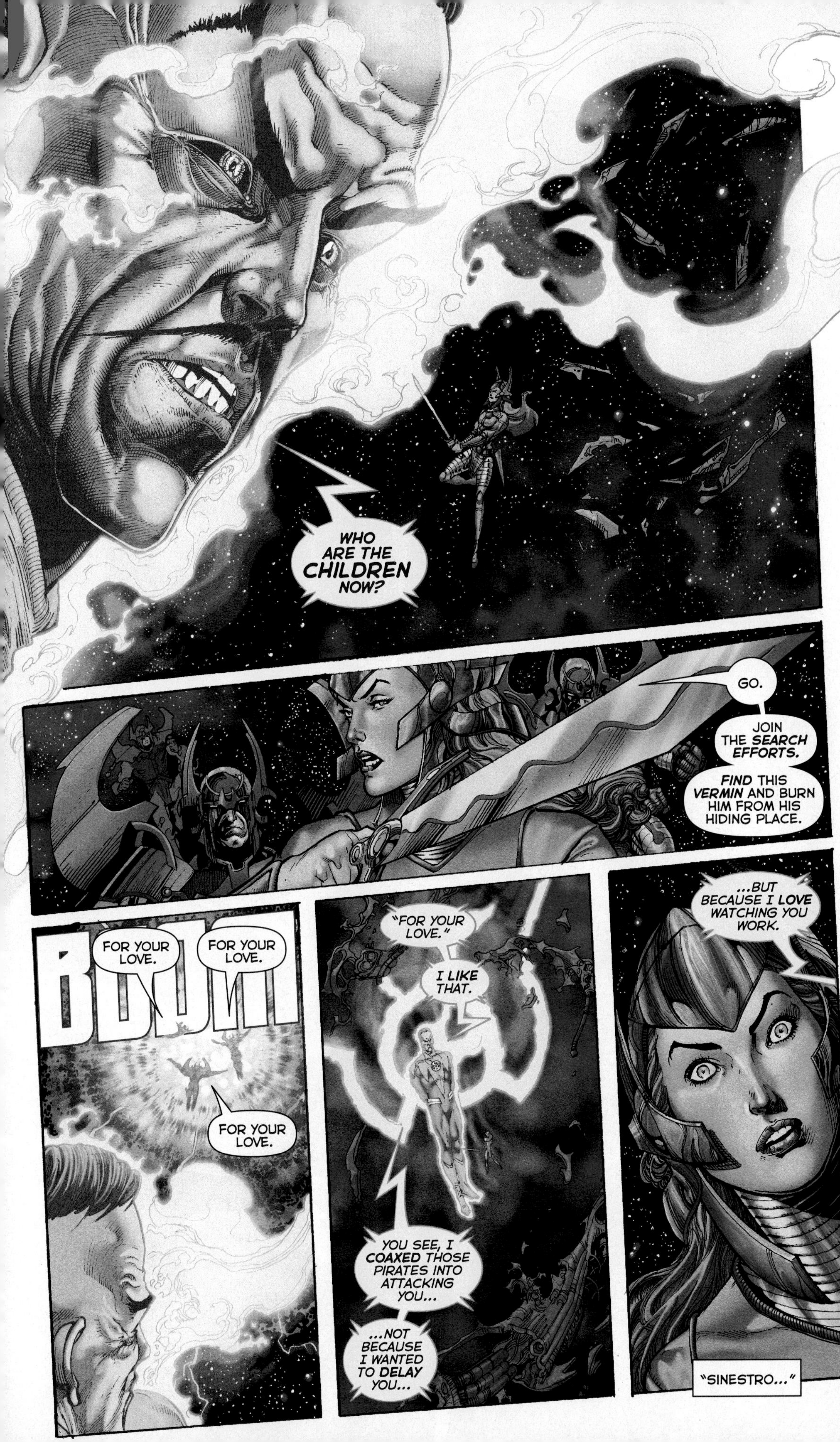
WHO ARE THE CHILDREN NOW?
GO.
JOIN THE SEARCH EFFORTS.
FIND THIS VERMIN AND BURN HIM FROM HIS HIDING PLACE.
BOOM
FOR YOUR LOVE.
FOR YOUR LOVE.
FOR YOUR LOVE.
"FOR YOUR LOVE."
I LIKE THAT.
YOU SEE, I COAXED THOSE PIRATES INTO ATTACKING YOU...
...NOT BECAUSE I WANTED TO DELAY YOU...
...BUT BECAUSE I LOVE WATCHING YOU WORK.
"SINESTRO..."

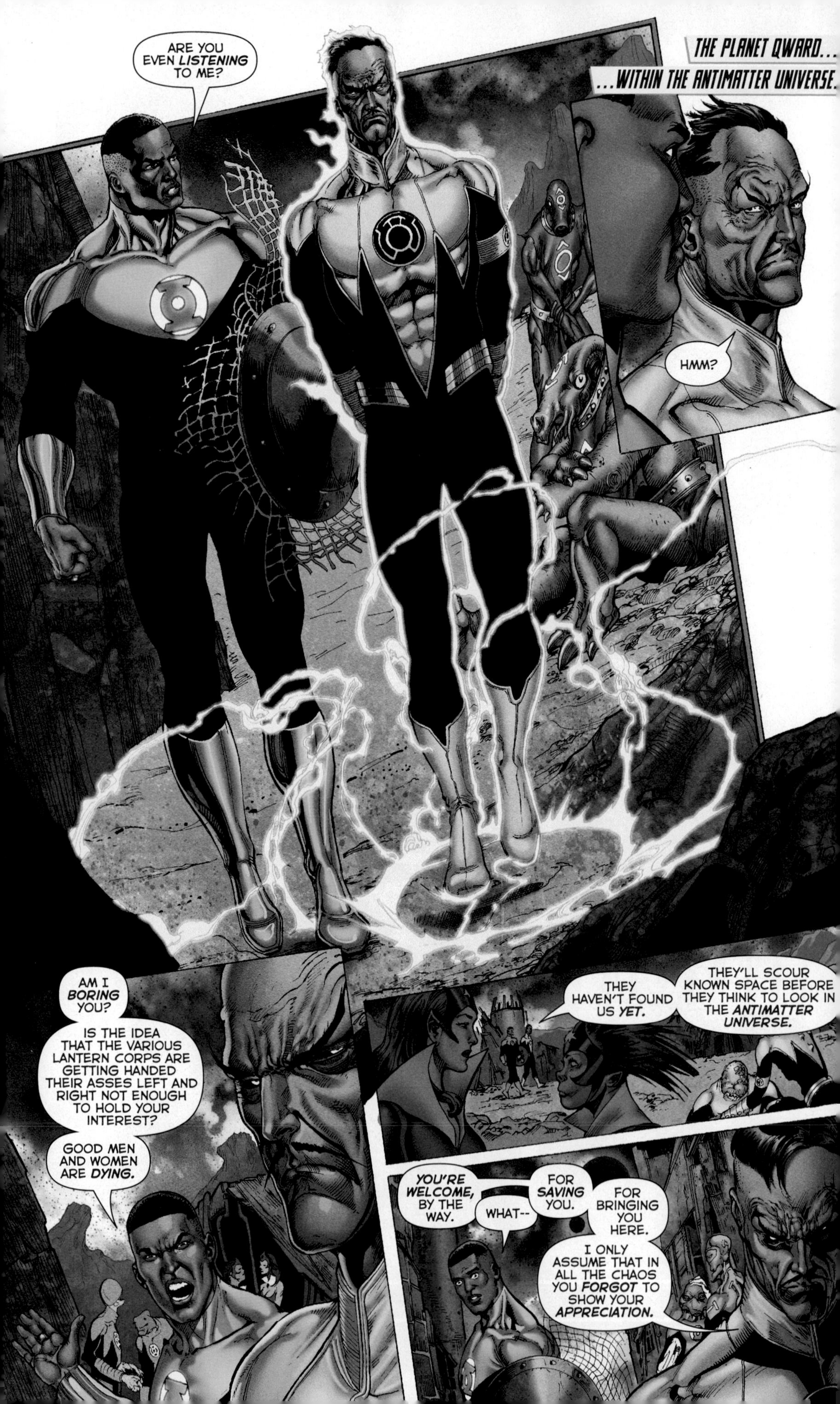
THE PLANET QWARD...
...WITHIN THE ANTIMATTER UNIVERSE.
ARE YOU EVEN LISTENING TO ME?
HMM?
AM I BORING YOU?
IS THE IDEA THAT THE VARIOUS LANTERN CORPS ARE GETTING HANDED THEIR ASSES LEFT AND RIGHT NOT ENOUGH TO HOLD YOUR INTEREST?
GOOD MEN AND WOMEN ARE DYING.
THEY HAVEN'T FOUND US YET.
THEY'LL SCOUR KNOWN SPACE BEFORE THEY THINK TO LOOK IN THE ANTIMATTER UNIVERSE.
YOU'RE WELCOME, BY THE WAY.
WHAT--
FOR SAVING YOU.
FOR BRINGING YOU HERE.
I ONLY ASSUME THAT IN ALL THE CHAOS YOU FORGOT TO SHOW YOUR APPRECIATION.

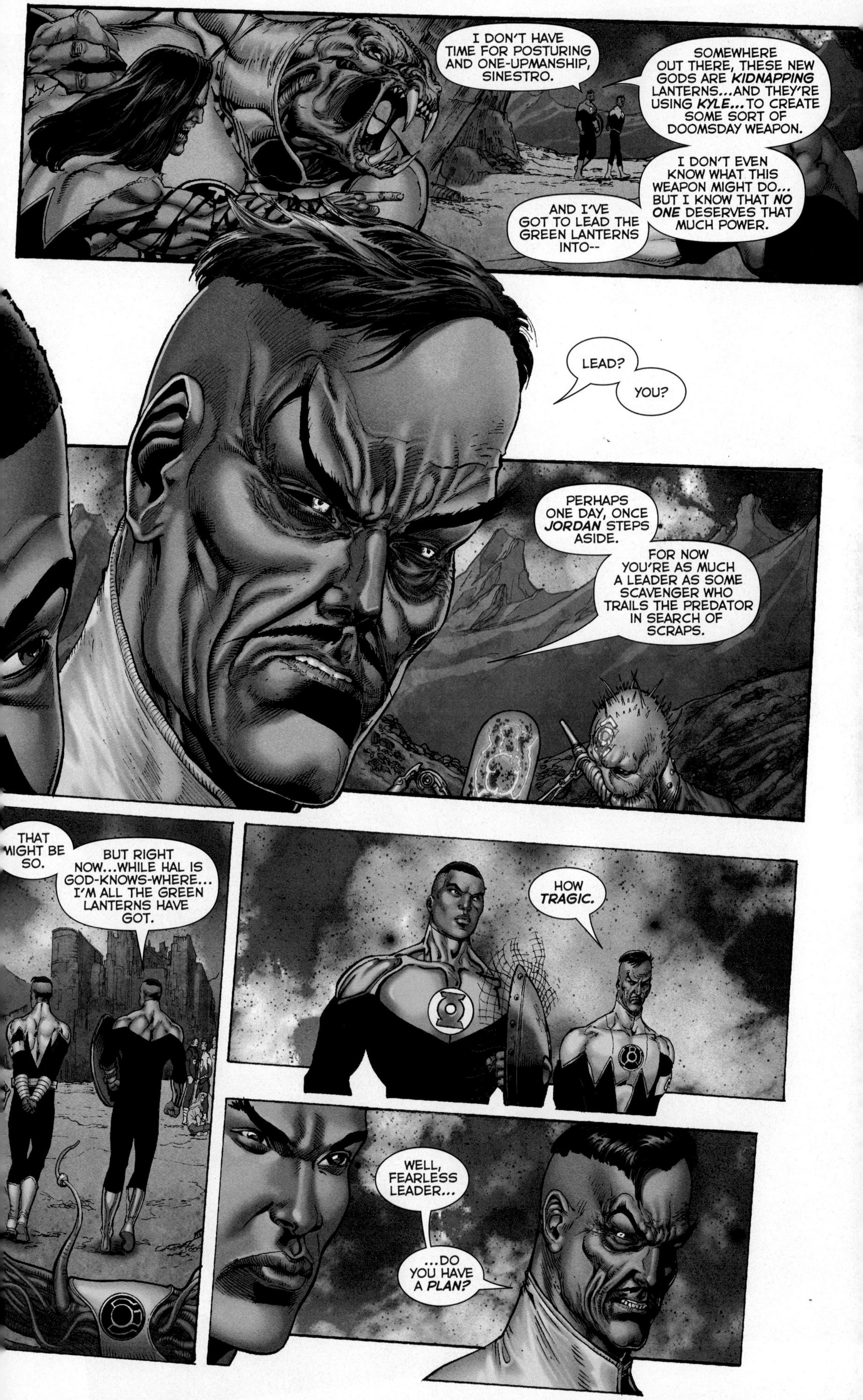

I DON'T HAVE TIME FOR POSTURING AND ONE-UPMANSHIP, SINESTRO.
SOMEWHERE OUT THERE, THESE NEW GODS ARE KIDNAPPING LANTERNS...AND THEY'RE USING KYLE...TO CREATE SOME SORT OF DOOMSDAY WEAPON.
I DON'T EVEN KNOW WHAT THIS WEAPON MIGHT DO... BUT I KNOW THAT NO ONE DESERVES THAT MUCH POWER.
AND I'VE GOT TO LEAD THE GREEN LANTERNS INTO--
LEAD?
YOU?
PERHAPS ONE DAY, ONCE JORDAN STEPS ASIDE.
FOR NOW YOU'RE AS MUCH A LEADER AS SOME SCAVENGER WHO TRAILS THE PREDATOR IN SEARCH OF SCRAPS.
THAT MIGHT BE SO.
BUT RIGHT NOW...WHILE HAL IS GOD-KNOWS-WHERE... I'M ALL THE GREEN LANTERNS HAVE GOT.
HOW TRAGIC.
WELL, FEARLESS LEADER...
...DO YOU HAVE A PLAN?

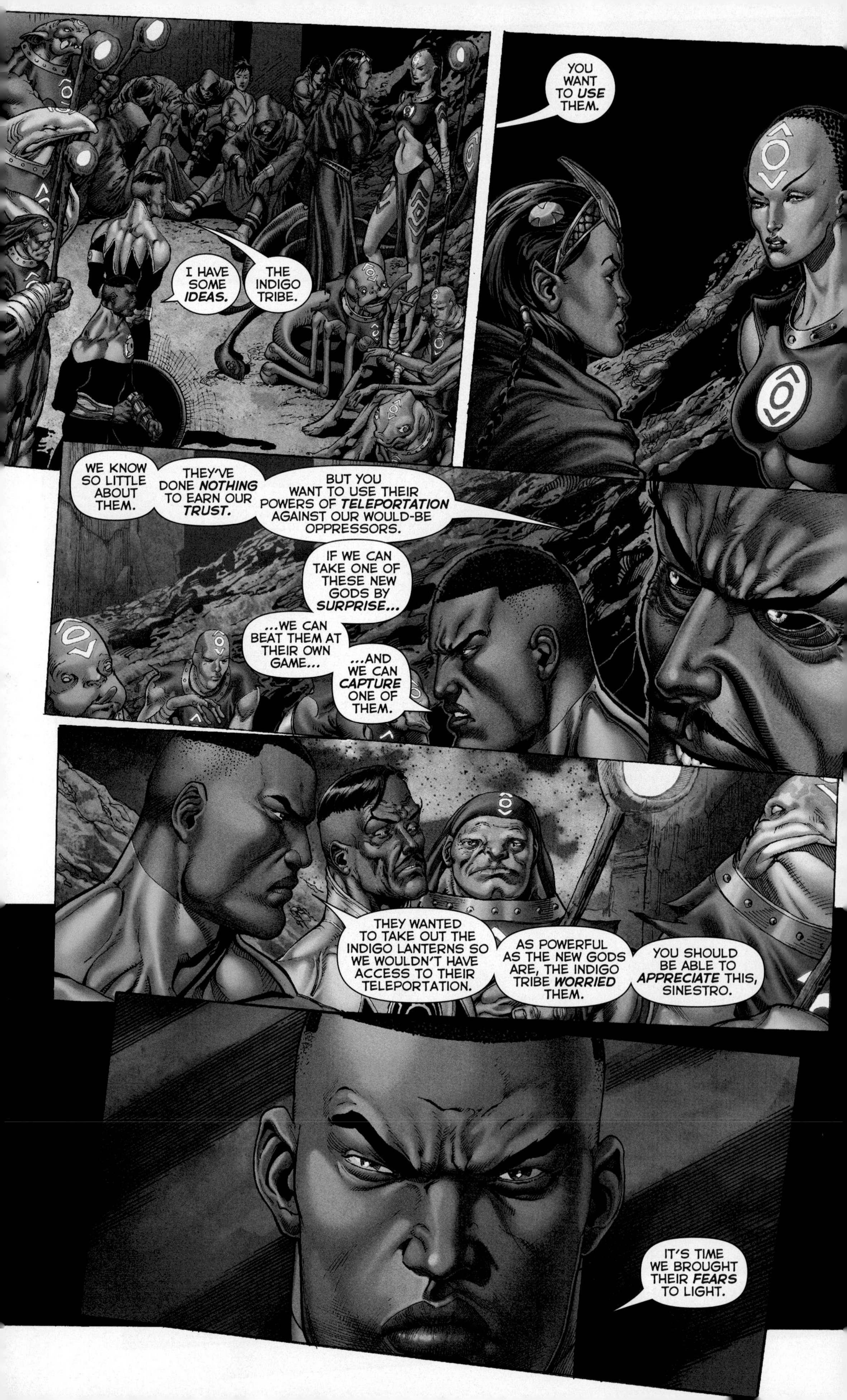
THE INDIGO TRIBE.
I HAVE SOME IDEAS.
YOU WANT TO USE THEM.
WE KNOW SO LITTLE ABOUT THEM.
THEY'VE DONE NOTHING TO EARN OUR TRUST.
BUT YOU WANT TO USE THEIR POWERS OF TELEPORTATION AGAINST OUR WOULD-BE OPPRESSORS.
IF WE CAN TAKE ONE OF THESE NEW GODS BY SURPRISE...
...WE CAN BEAT THEM AT THEIR OWN GAME...
...AND WE CAN CAPTURE ONE OF THEM.
THEY WANTED TO TAKE OUT THE INDIGO LANTERNS SO WE WOULDN'T HAVE ACCESS TO THEIR TELEPORTATION.
AS POWERFUL AS THE NEW GODS ARE, THE INDIGO TRIBE WORRIED THEM.
YOU SHOULD BE ABLE TO APPRECIATE THIS, SINESTRO.
IT'S TIME WE BROUGHT THEIR FEARS TO LIGHT.

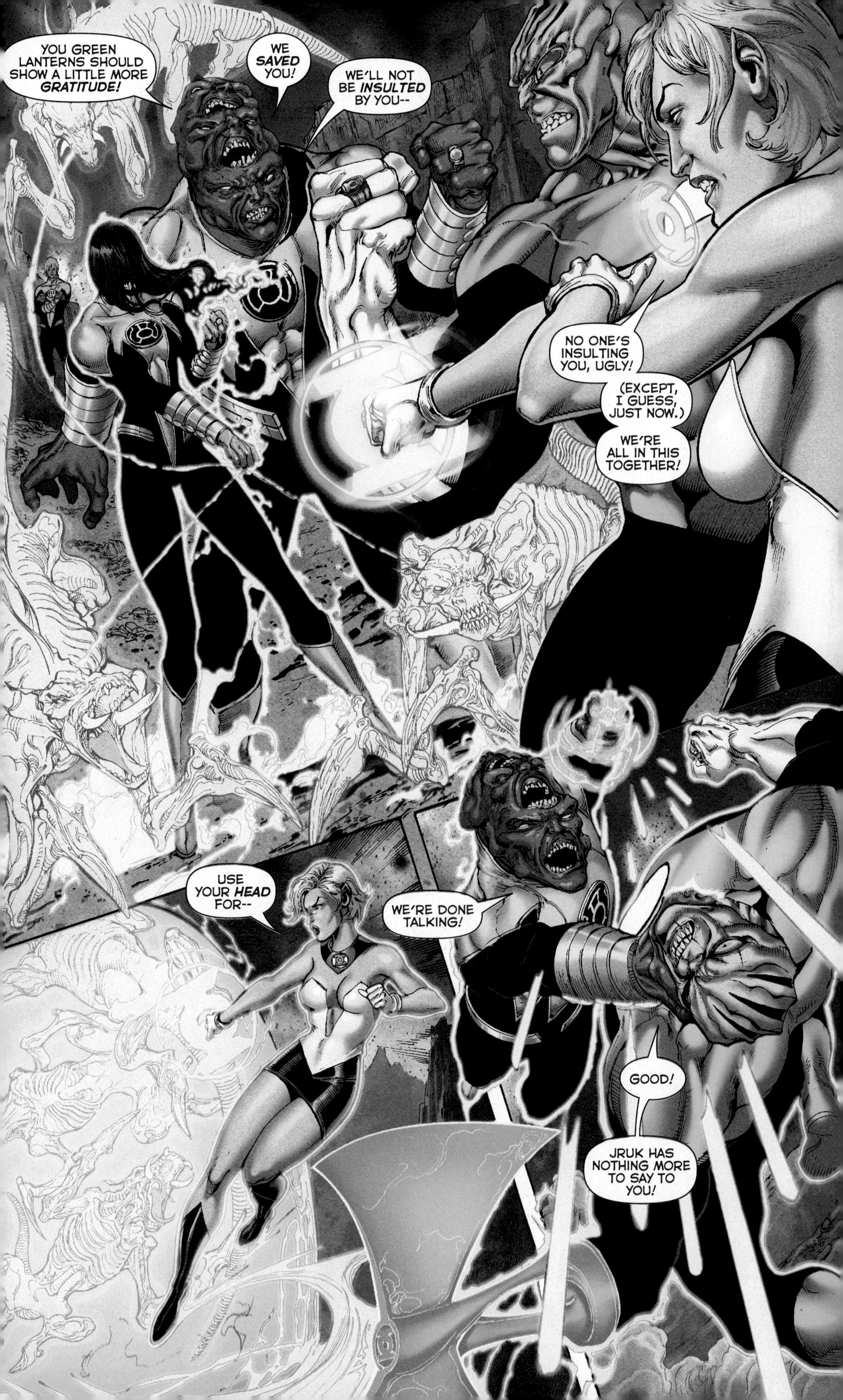
YOU GREEN LANTERNS SHOULD SHOW A LITTLE MORE GRATITUDE!
WE SAVED YOU!
WE'LL NOT BE INSULTED BY YOU--
NO ONE'S INSULTING YOU, UGLY!
(EXCEPT, I GUESS, JUST NOW.)
WE'RE ALL IN THIS TOGETHER!
USE YOUR HEAD FOR--
WE'RE DONE TALKING!
GOOD!
JRUK HAS NOTHING MORE TO SAY TO YOU!

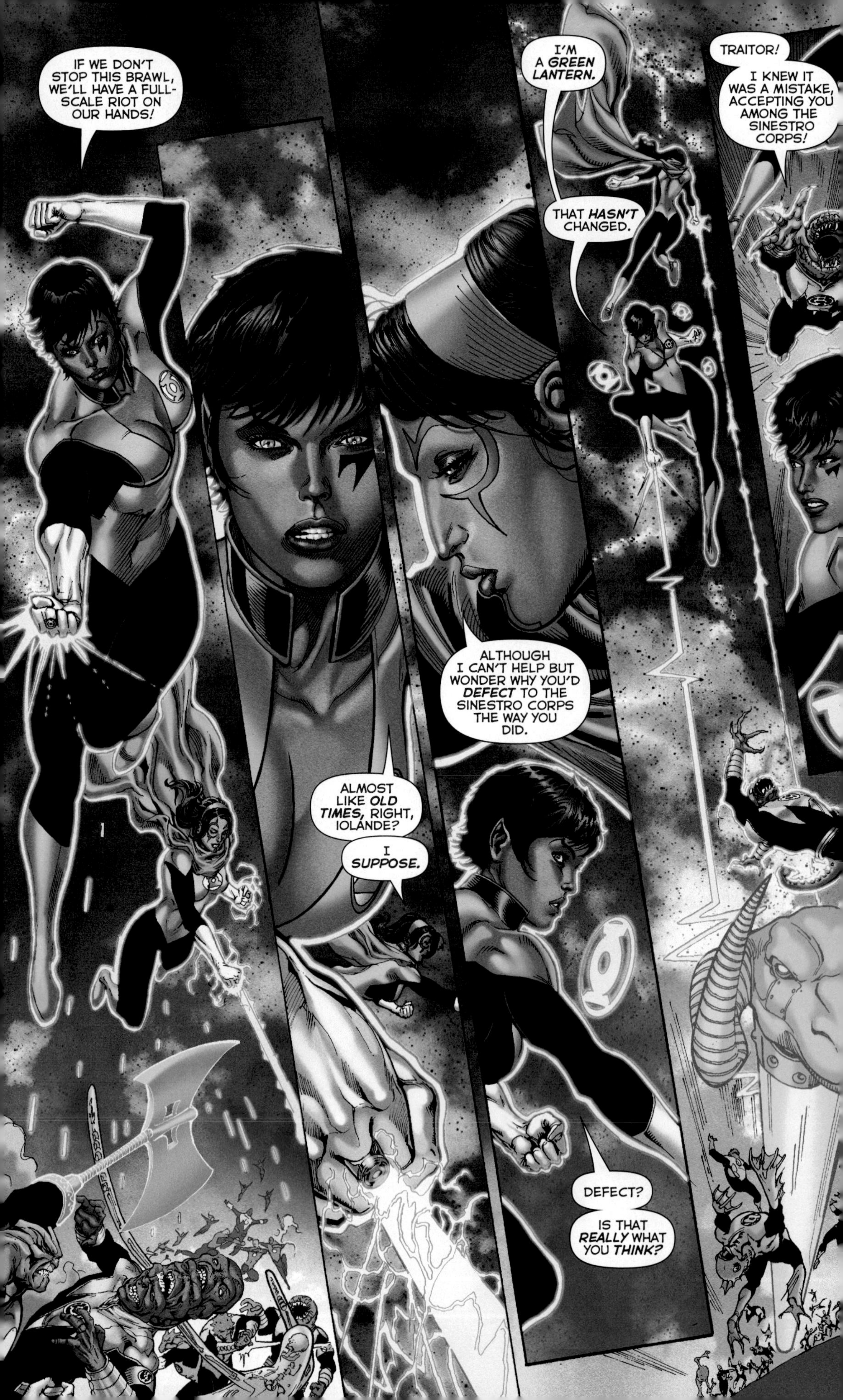

IF WE DON'T STOP THIS BRAWL, WE'LL HAVE A FULL-SCALE RIOT ON OUR HANDS!
ALMOST LIKE OLD TIMES, RIGHT, IOLANDE?
I SUPPOSE.
ALTHOUGH I CAN'T HELP BUT WONDER WHY YOU'D DEFECT TO THE SINESTRO CORPS THE WAY YOU DID.
DEFECT?
IS THAT REALLY WHAT YOU THINK?
I'M A GREEN LANTERN.
THAT HASN'T CHANGED.
TRAITOR!
I KNEW IT WAS A MISTAKE, ACCEPTING YOU AMONG THE SINESTRO CORPS!

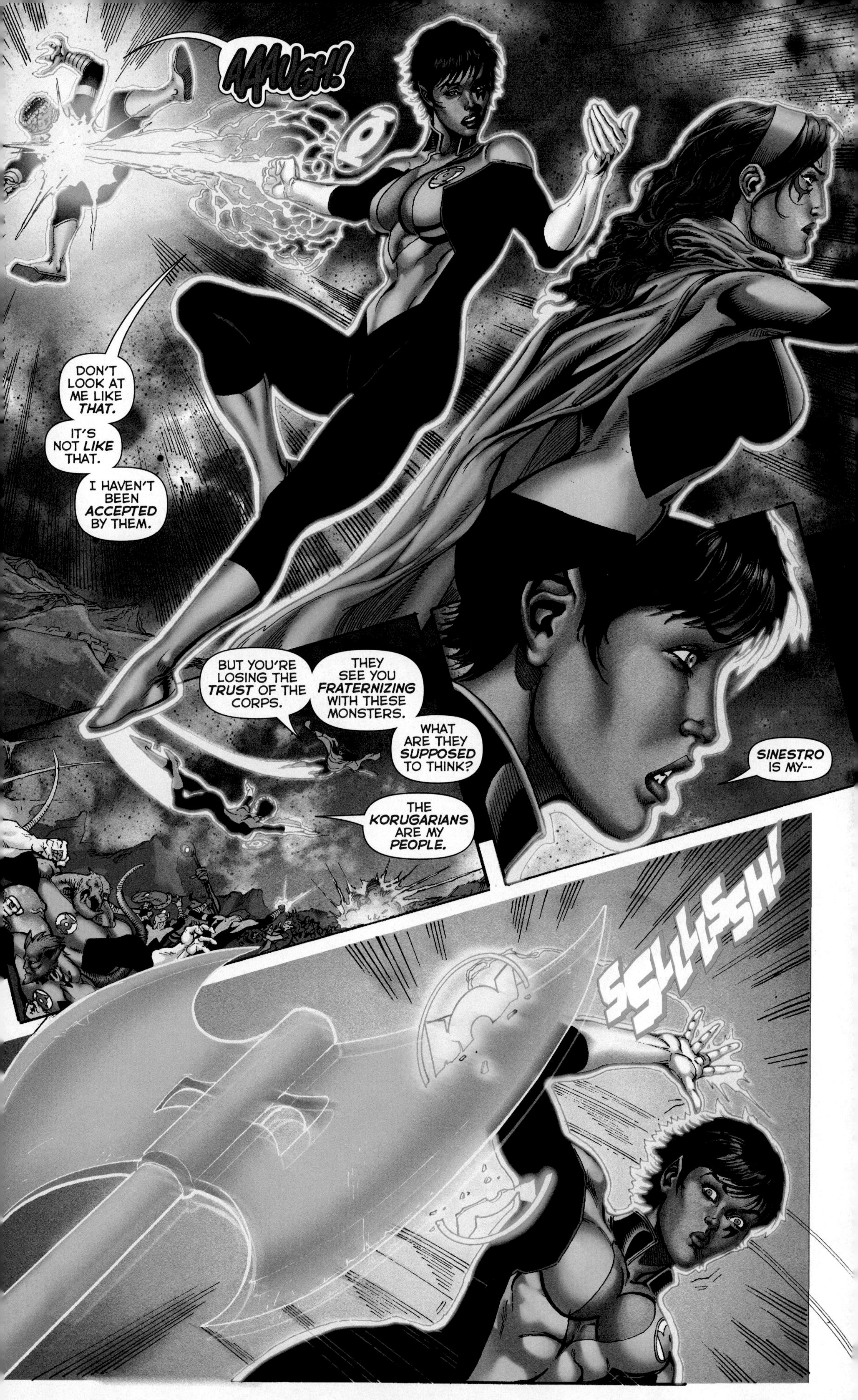
AAAUGH!
DON'T LOOK AT ME LIKE THAT.
IT'S NOT LIKE THAT.
I HAVEN'T BEEN ACCEPTED BY THEM.
BUT YOU'RE LOSING THE TRUST OF THE CORPS.
THEY SEE YOU FRATERNIZING WITH THESE MONSTERS.
WHAT ARE THEY SUPPOSED TO THINK?
THE KORUGARIANS ARE MY PEOPLE.
SINESTRO IS MY--
SSLLLSSH!

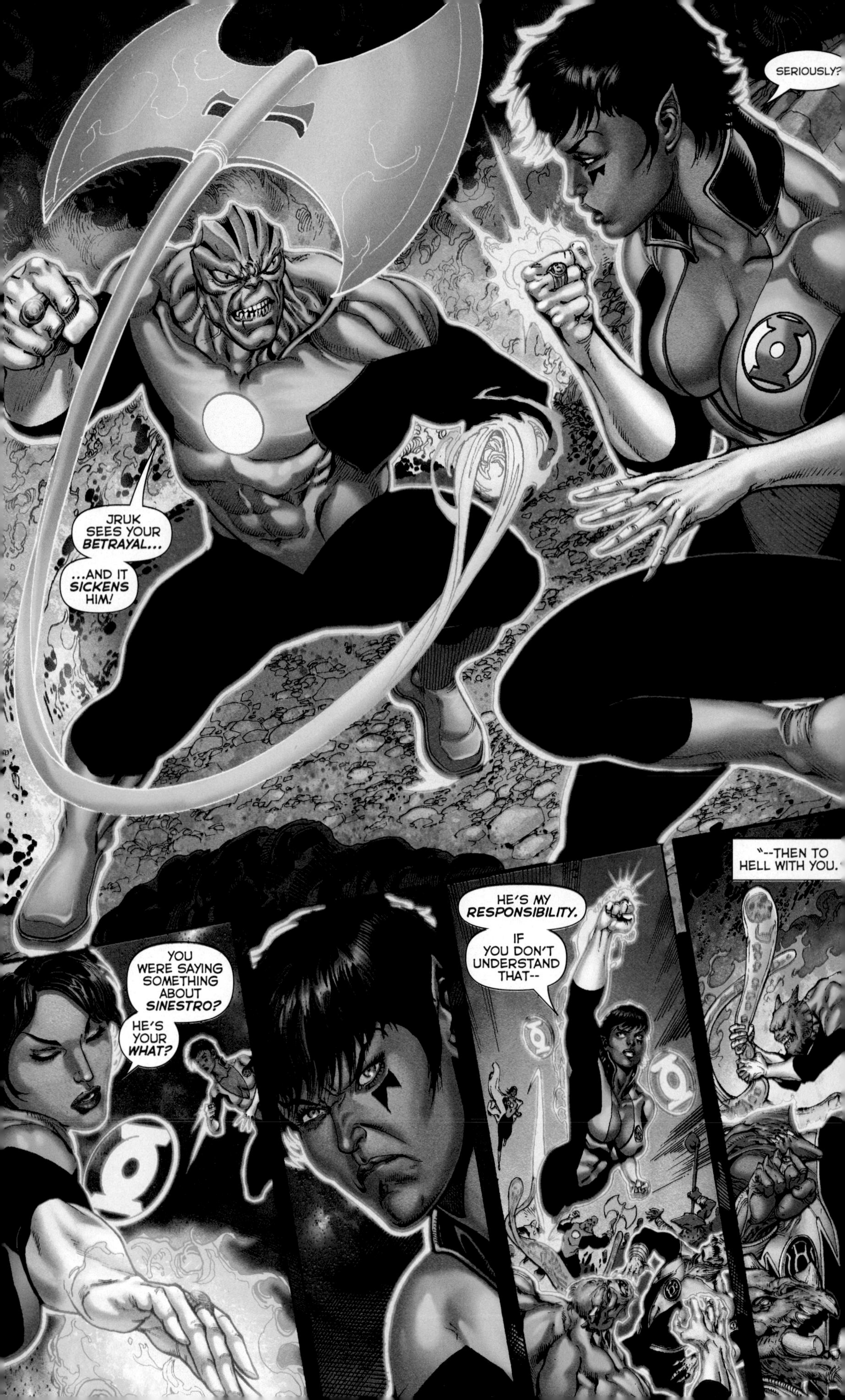
SERIOUSLY?
JRUK SEES YOUR BETRAYAL...
...AND IT SICKENS HIM!
YOU WERE SAYING SOMETHING ABOUT SINESTRO?
HE'S YOUR WHAT?
HE'S MY RESPONSIBILITY.
IF YOU DON'T UNDERSTAND THAT--
"--THEN TO HELL WITH YOU."

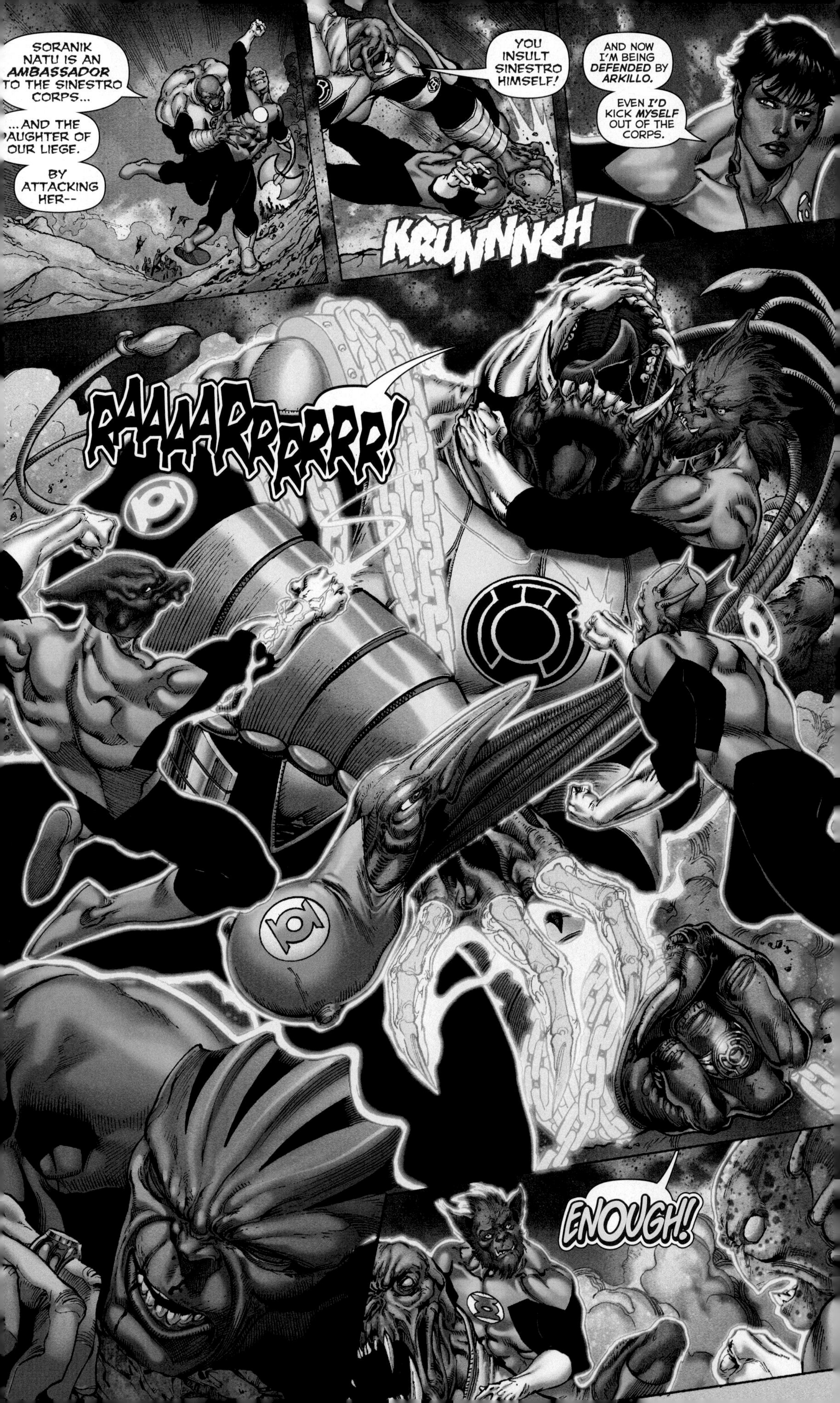

SORANIK NATU IS AN AMBASSADOR TO THE SINESTRO CORPS...
...AND THE DAUGHTER OF OUR LIEGE.
BY ATTACKING HER--
YOU INSULT SINESTRO HIMSELF!
AND NOW I'M BEING DEFENDED BY ARKILLO.
EVEN I'D KICK MYSELF OUT OF THE CORPS.
KRUNNNCH
RAAAARRRRRR!
ENOUGH!

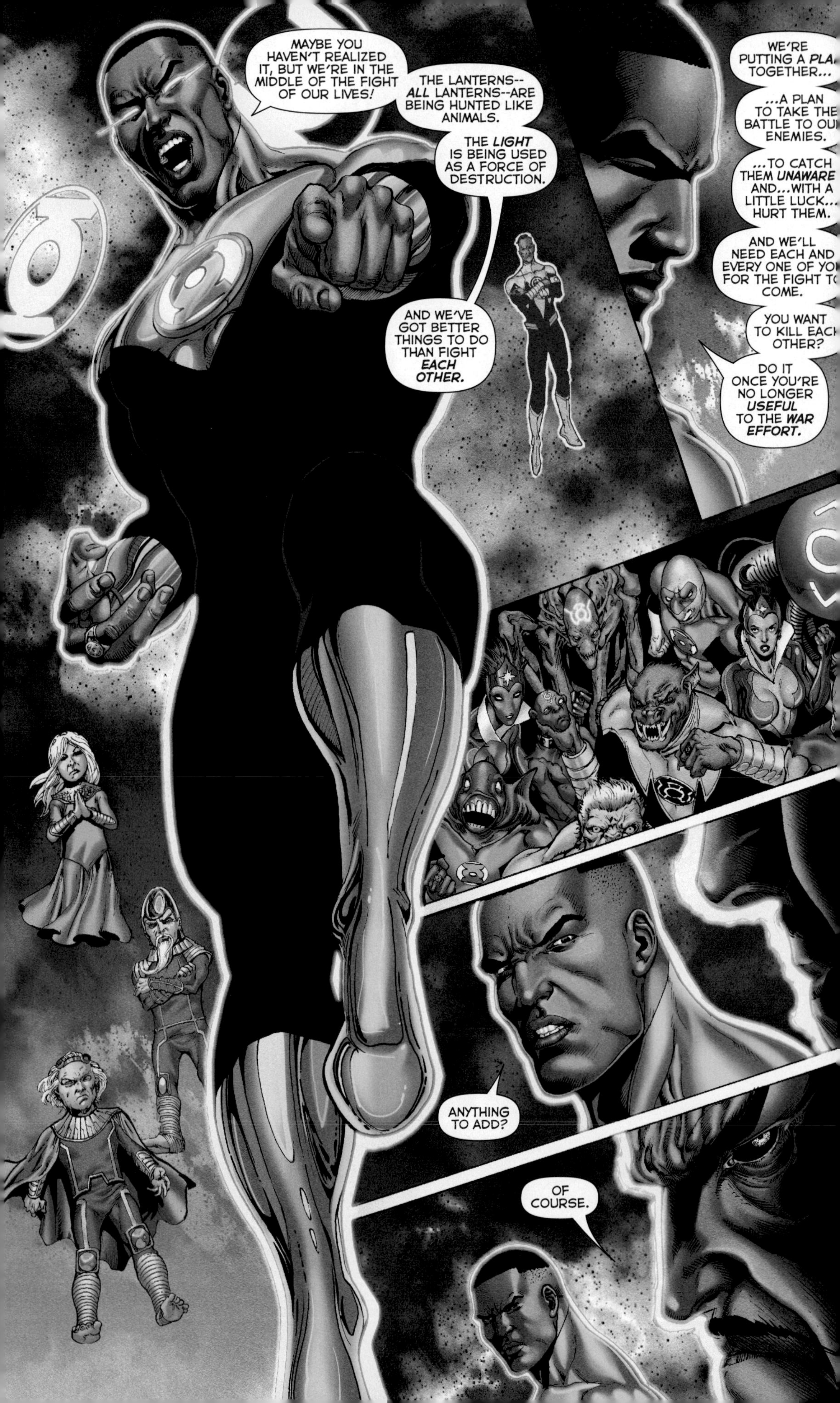

MAYBE YOU HAVEN'T REALIZED IT, BUT WE'RE IN THE MIDDLE OF THE FIGHT OF OUR LIVES!
THE LANTERNS-- ALL LANTERNS--ARE BEING HUNTED LIKE ANIMALS.
THE LIGHT IS BEING USED AS A FORCE OF DESTRUCTION.
AND WE'VE GOT BETTER THINGS TO DO THAN FIGHT EACH OTHER.
WE'RE PUTTING A PLA TOGETHER...
...A PLAN TO TAKE THE BATTLE TO OU ENEMIES.
...TO CATCH THEM UNAWARE AND...WITH A LITTLE LUCK... HURT THEM.
AND WE'LL NEED EACH AND EVERY ONE OF YO FOR THE FIGHT T COME.
YOU WANT TO KILL EAC OTHER?
DO IT ONCE YOU'RE NO LONGER USEFUL TO THE WAR EFFORT.
ANYTHING TO ADD?
OF COURSE.

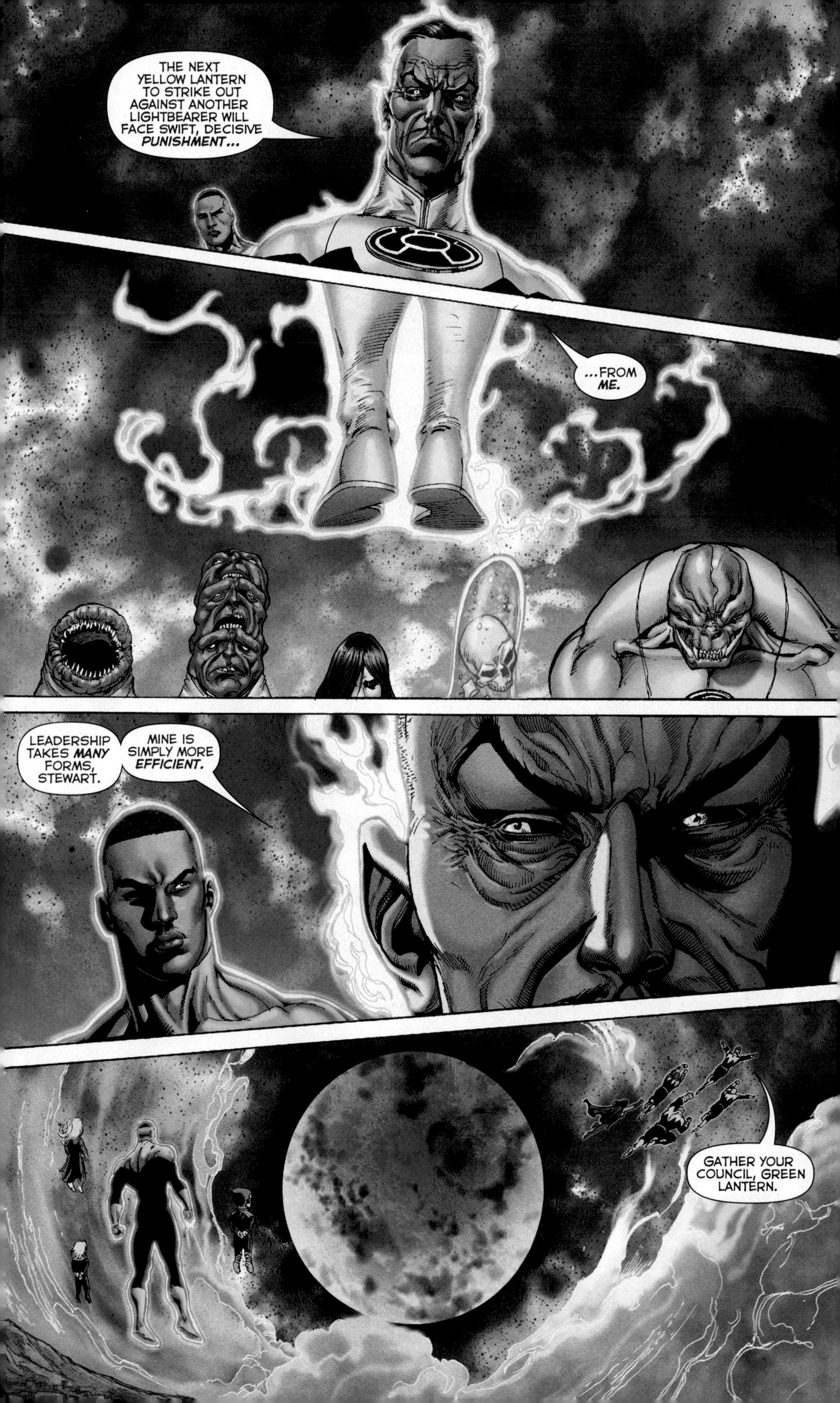
THE NEXT YELLOW LANTERN TO STRIKE OUT AGAINST ANOTHER LIGHTBEARER WILL FACE SWIFT, DECISIVE *PUNISHMENT...*
...FROM *ME.*
LEADERSHIP TAKES *MANY* FORMS, STEWART.
MINE IS SIMPLY MORE *EFFICIENT.*
GATHER YOUR COUNCIL, GREEN LANTERN.

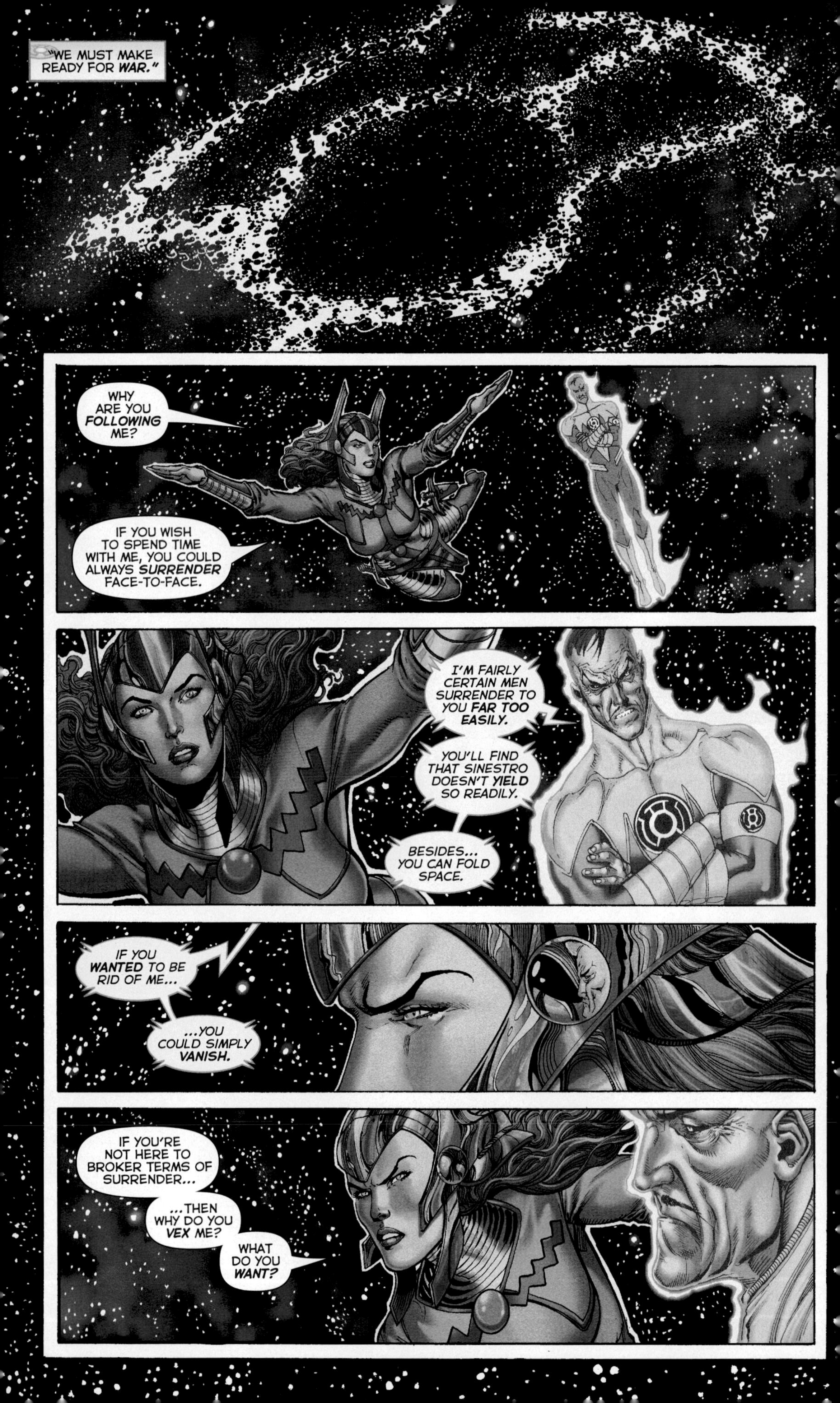

"WE MUST MAKE READY FOR WAR."
WHY ARE YOU FOLLOWING ME?
IF YOU WISH TO SPEND TIME WITH ME, YOU COULD ALWAYS SURRENDER FACE-TO-FACE.
I'M FAIRLY CERTAIN MEN SURRENDER TO YOU FAR TOO EASILY.
YOU'LL FIND THAT SINESTRO DOESN'T YIELD SO READILY.
BESIDES... YOU CAN FOLD SPACE.
IF YOU WANTED TO BE RID OF ME...
...YOU COULD SIMPLY VANISH.
IF YOU'RE NOT HERE TO BROKER TERMS OF SURRENDER...
...THEN WHY DO YOU VEX ME?
WHAT DO YOU WANT?

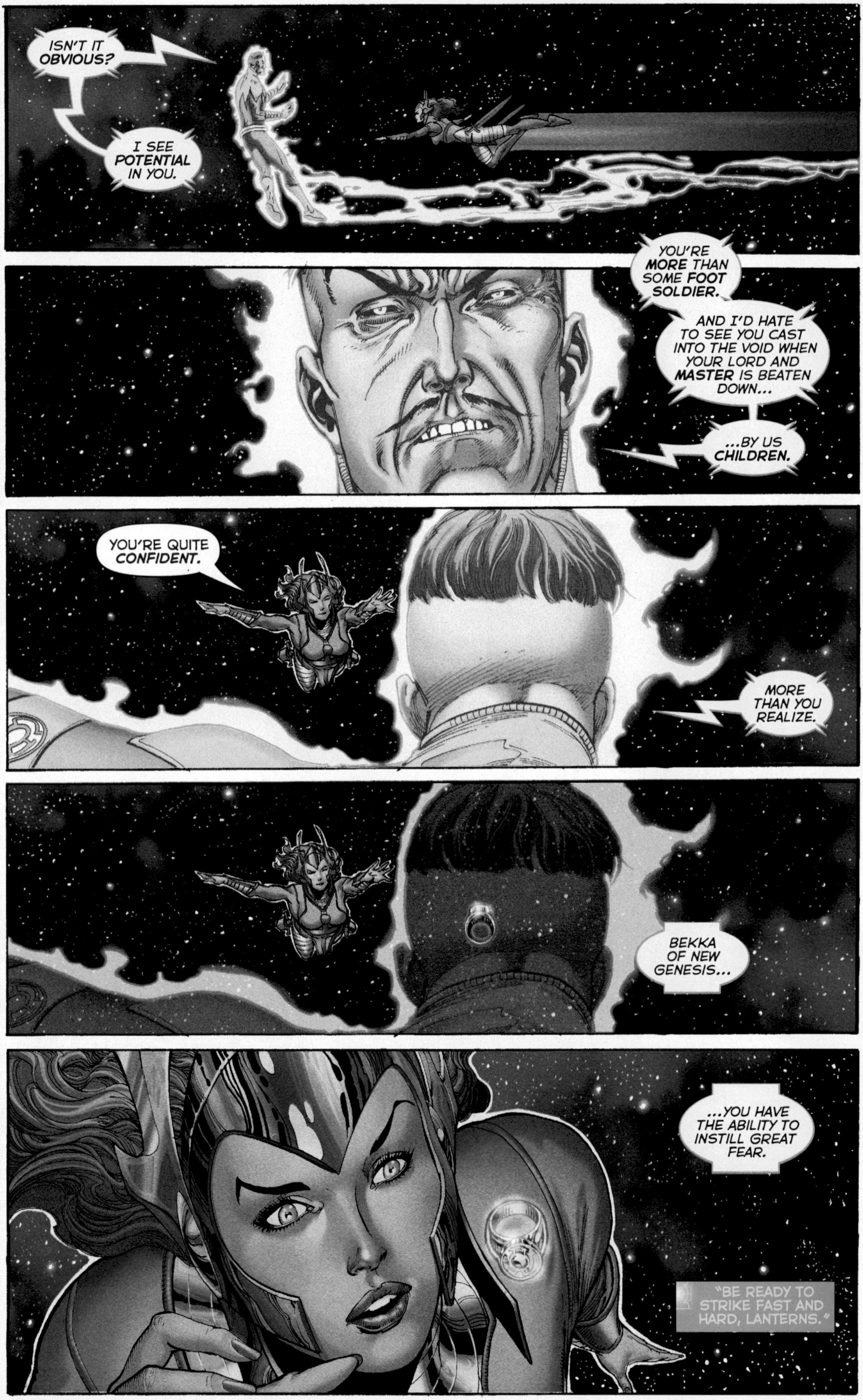

ISN'T IT OBVIOUS?
I SEE POTENTIAL IN YOU.
YOU'RE MORE THAN SOME FOOT SOLDIER.
AND I'D HATE TO SEE YOU CAST INTO THE VOID WHEN YOUR LORD AND MASTER IS BEATEN DOWN...
...BY US CHILDREN.
YOU'RE QUITE CONFIDENT.
MORE THAN YOU REALIZE.
BEKKA OF NEW GENESIS...
...YOU HAVE THE ABILITY TO INSTILL GREAT FEAR.
"BE READY TO STRIKE FAST AND HARD, LANTERNS."

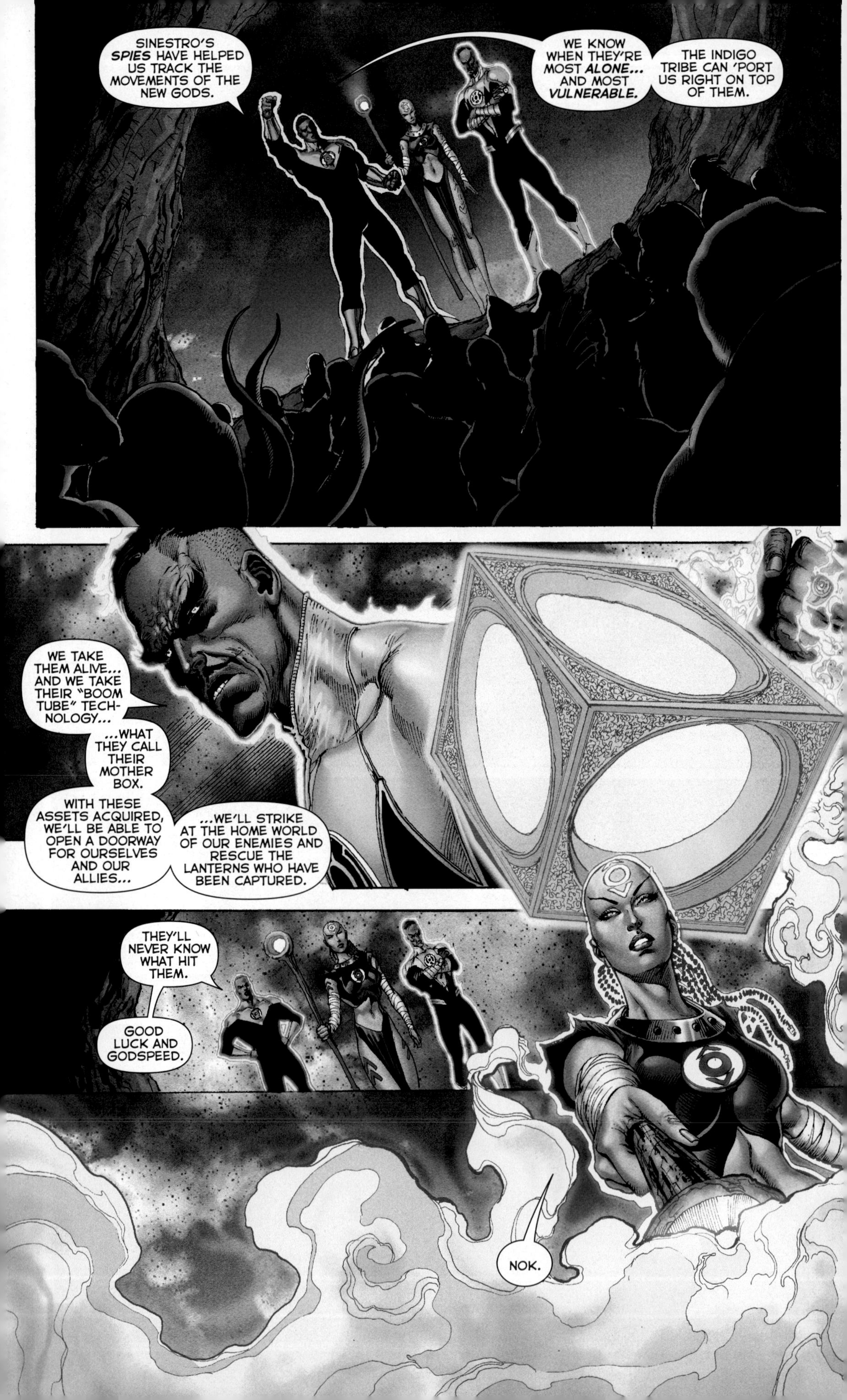
SINESTRO'S SPIES HAVE HELPED US TRACK THE MOVEMENTS OF THE NEW GODS.
WE KNOW WHEN THEY'RE MOST ALONE... AND MOST VULNERABLE.
THE INDIGO TRIBE CAN 'PORT US RIGHT ON TOP OF THEM.
WE TAKE THEM ALIVE... AND WE TAKE THEIR "BOOM TUBE" TECH-NOLOGY...
...WHAT THEY CALL THEIR MOTHER BOX.
WITH THESE ASSETS ACQUIRED, WE'LL BE ABLE TO OPEN A DOORWAY FOR OURSELVES AND OUR ALLIES...
...WE'LL STRIKE AT THE HOME WORLD OF OUR ENEMIES AND RESCUE THE LANTERNS WHO HAVE BEEN CAPTURED.
THEY'LL NEVER KNOW WHAT HIT THEM.
GOOD LUCK AND GODSPEED.
NOK.

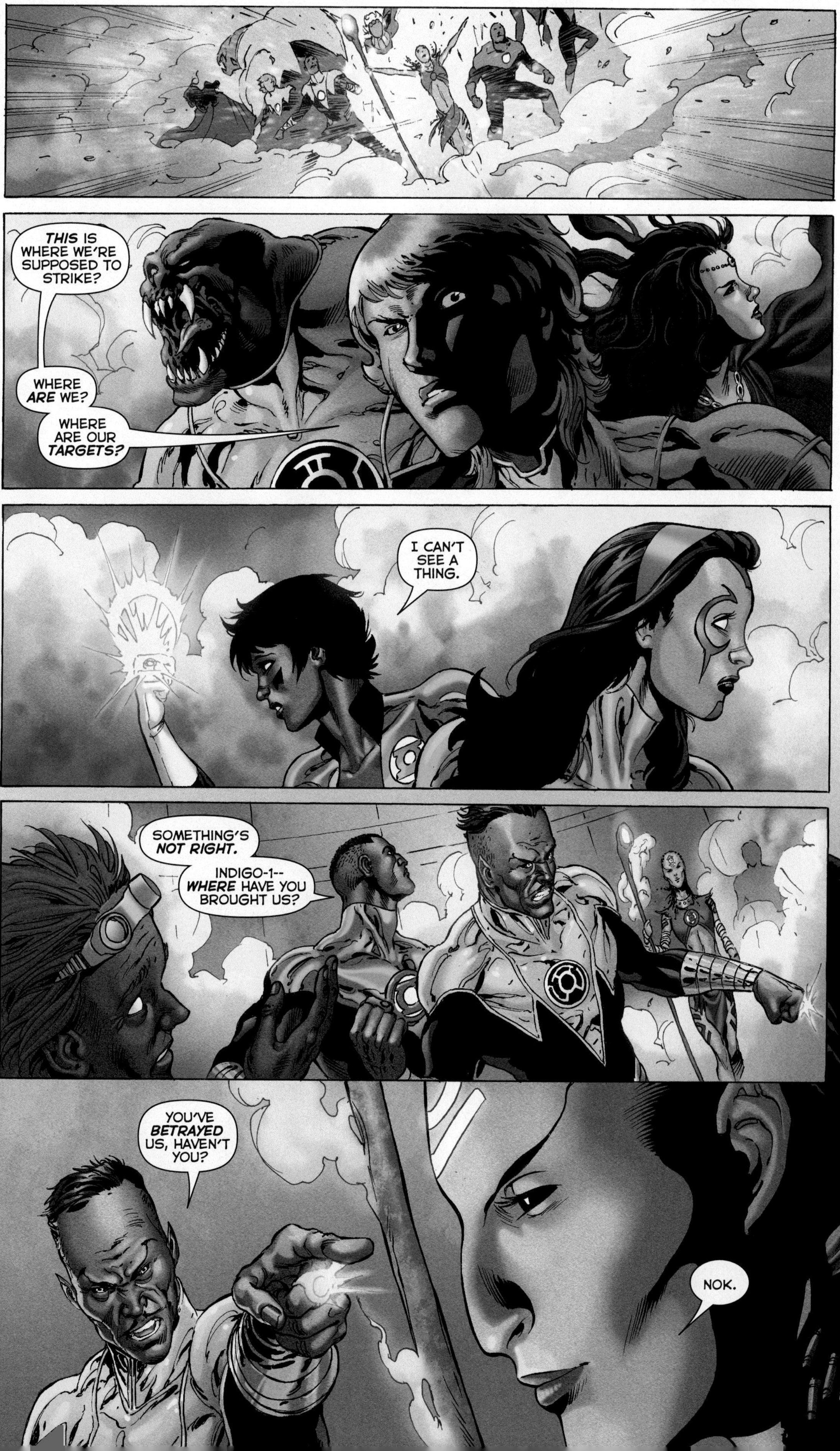
THIS IS WHERE WE'RE SUPPOSED TO STRIKE?
WHERE ARE WE?
WHERE ARE OUR TARGETS?
I CAN'T SEE A THING.
SOMETHING'S NOT RIGHT.
INDIGO-1-- WHERE HAVE YOU BROUGHT US?
YOU'VE BETRAYED US, HAVEN'T YOU?
NOK.

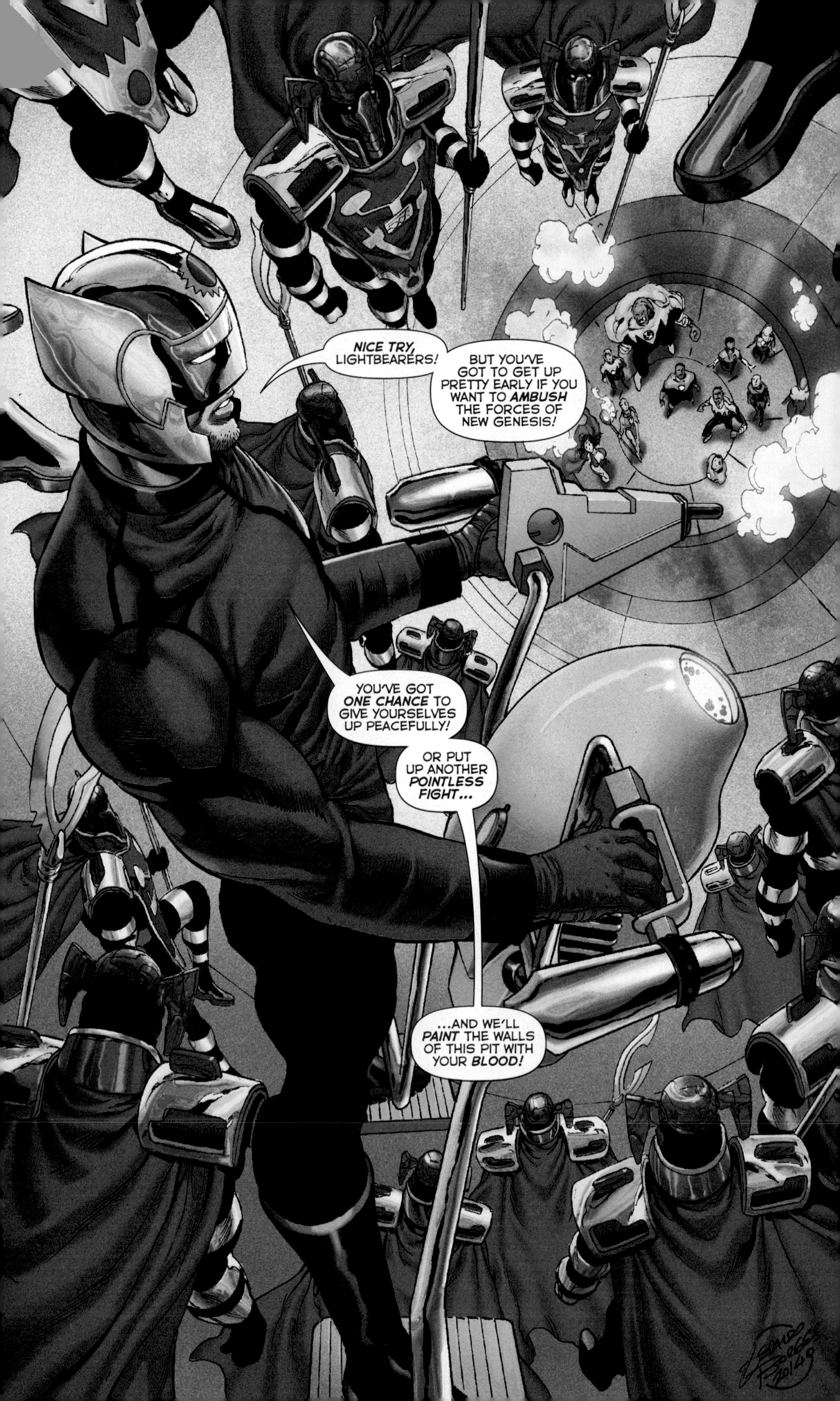
NICE TRY, LIGHTBEARERS!
BUT YOU'VE GOT TO GET UP PRETTY EARLY IF YOU WANT TO AMBUSH THE FORCES OF NEW GENESIS!
YOU'VE GOT ONE CHANCE TO GIVE YOURSELVES UP PEACEFULLY!
OR PUT UP ANOTHER POINTLESS FIGHT...
...AND WE'LL PAINT THE WALLS OF THIS PIT WITH YOUR BLOOD!

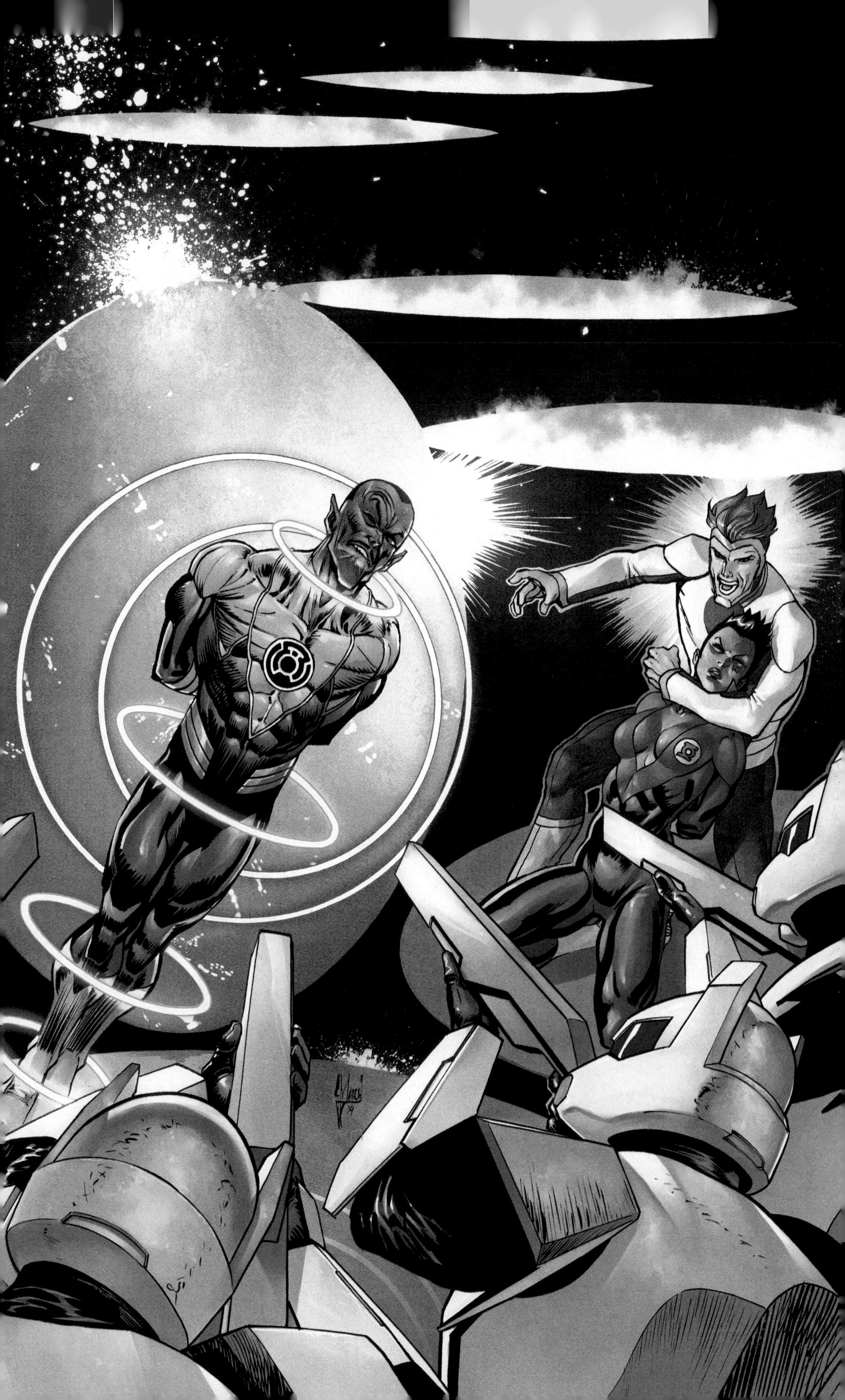

GODHEAD ACT III, PART V: WAR COUNCIL

CULLEN BUNN writer **MARTIN COCCOLO** penciller **SCOTT HANNA** inker **JASON WRIGHT** colorist **TAYLOR ESPOSITO** letterer cover art by **GUILLEM MARCH & TOMEU MOREY**

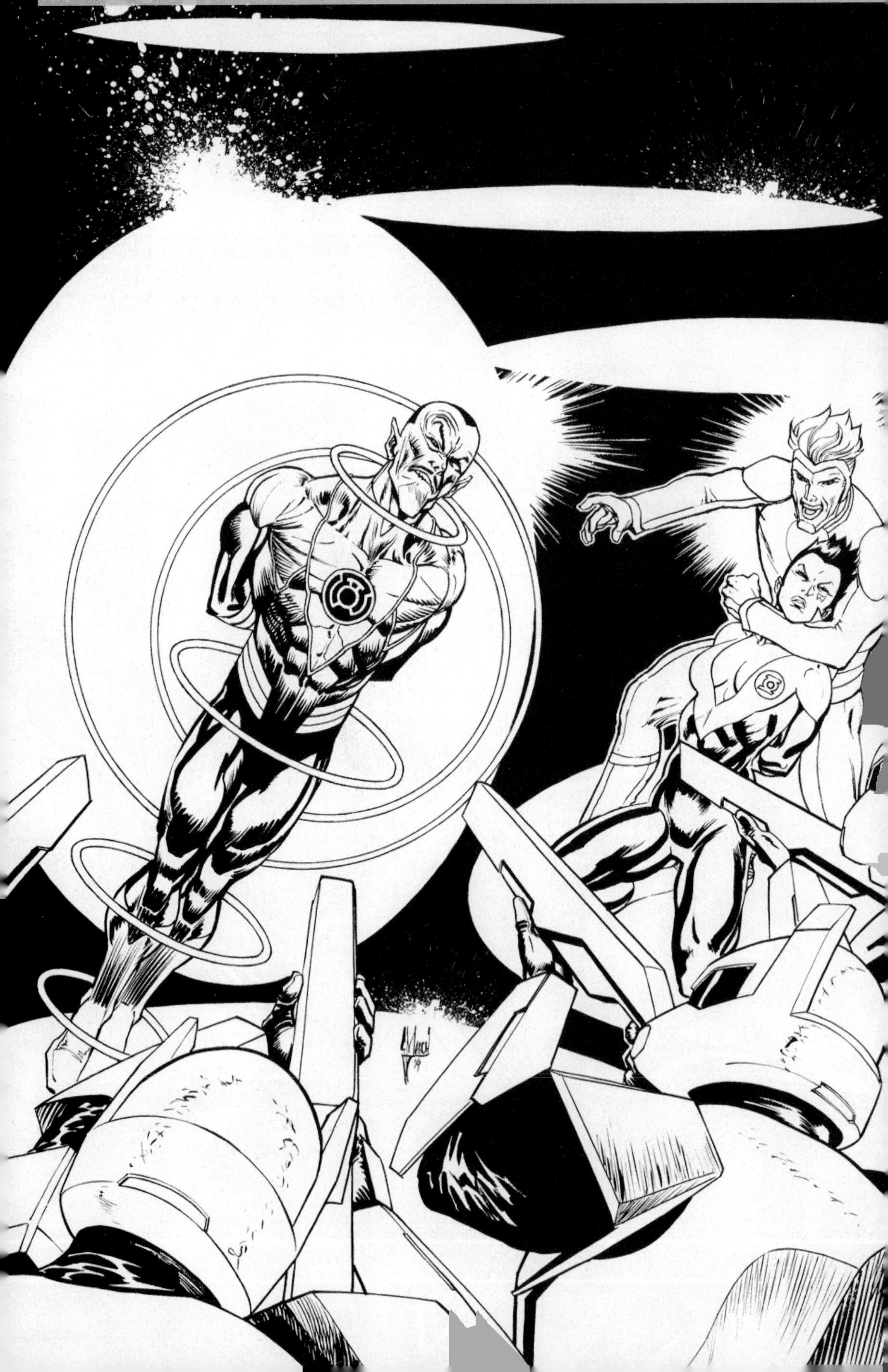

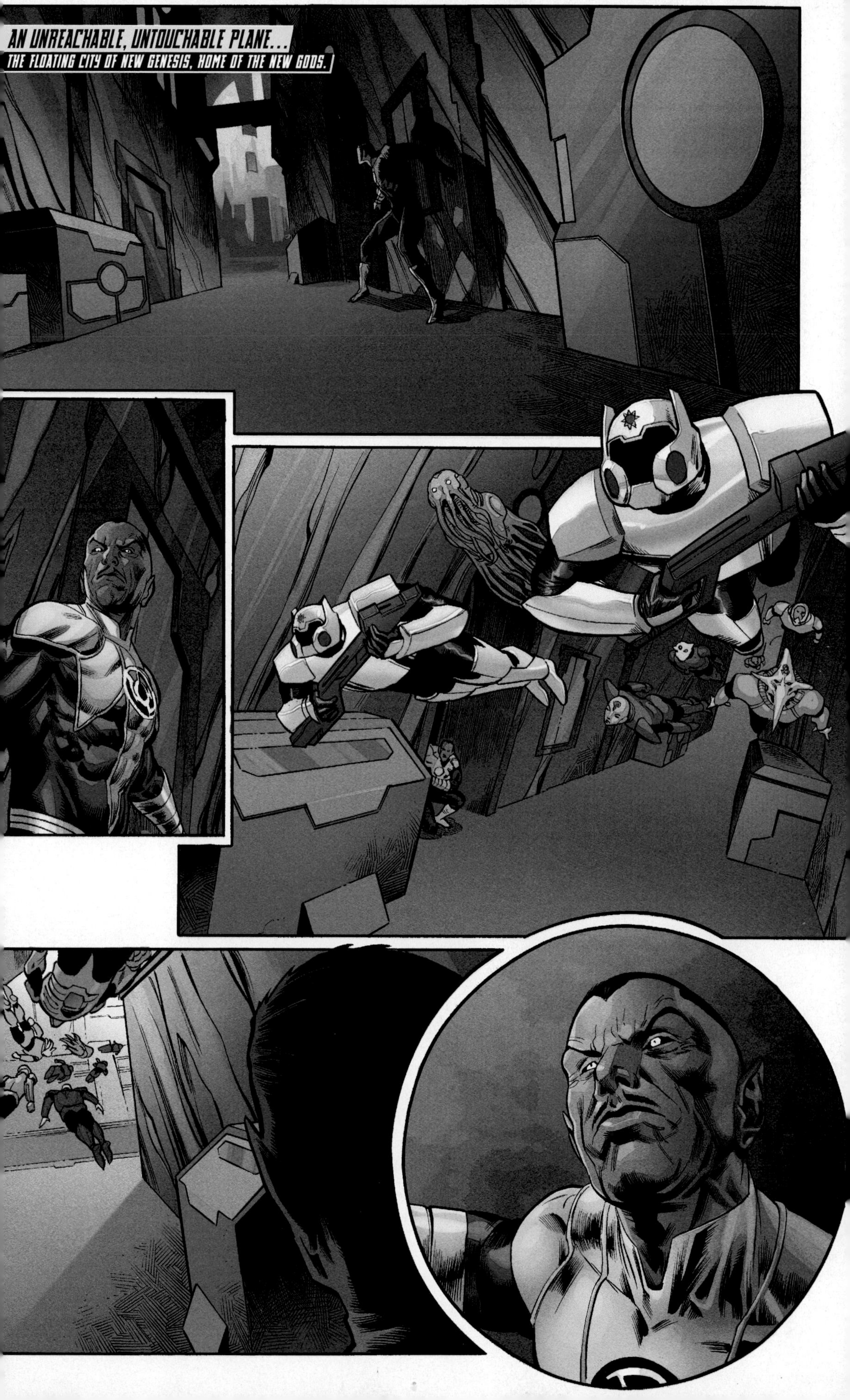
AN UNREACHABLE, UNTOUCHABLE PLANE...
THE FLOATING CITY OF NEW GENESIS, HOME OF THE NEW GODS.

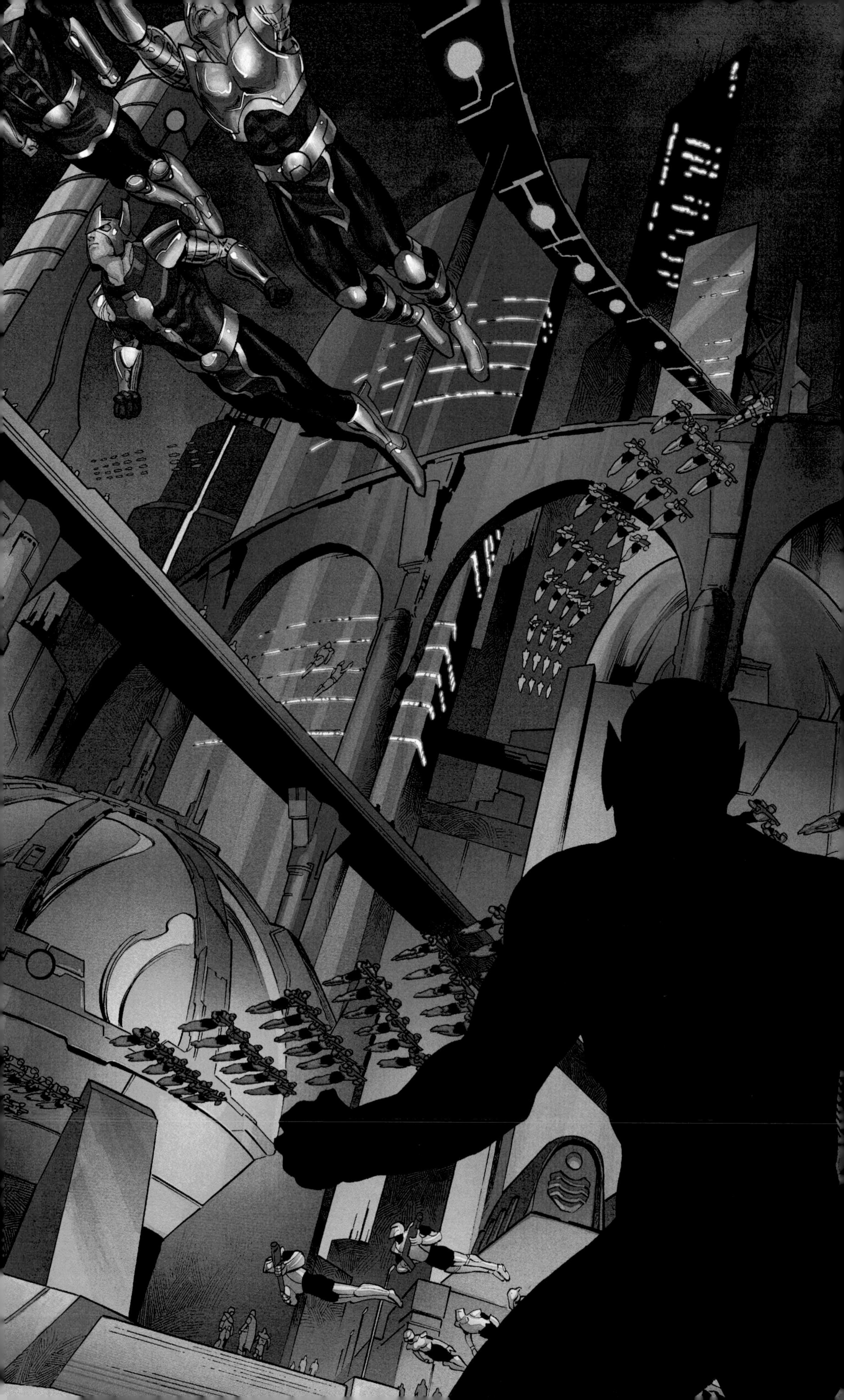

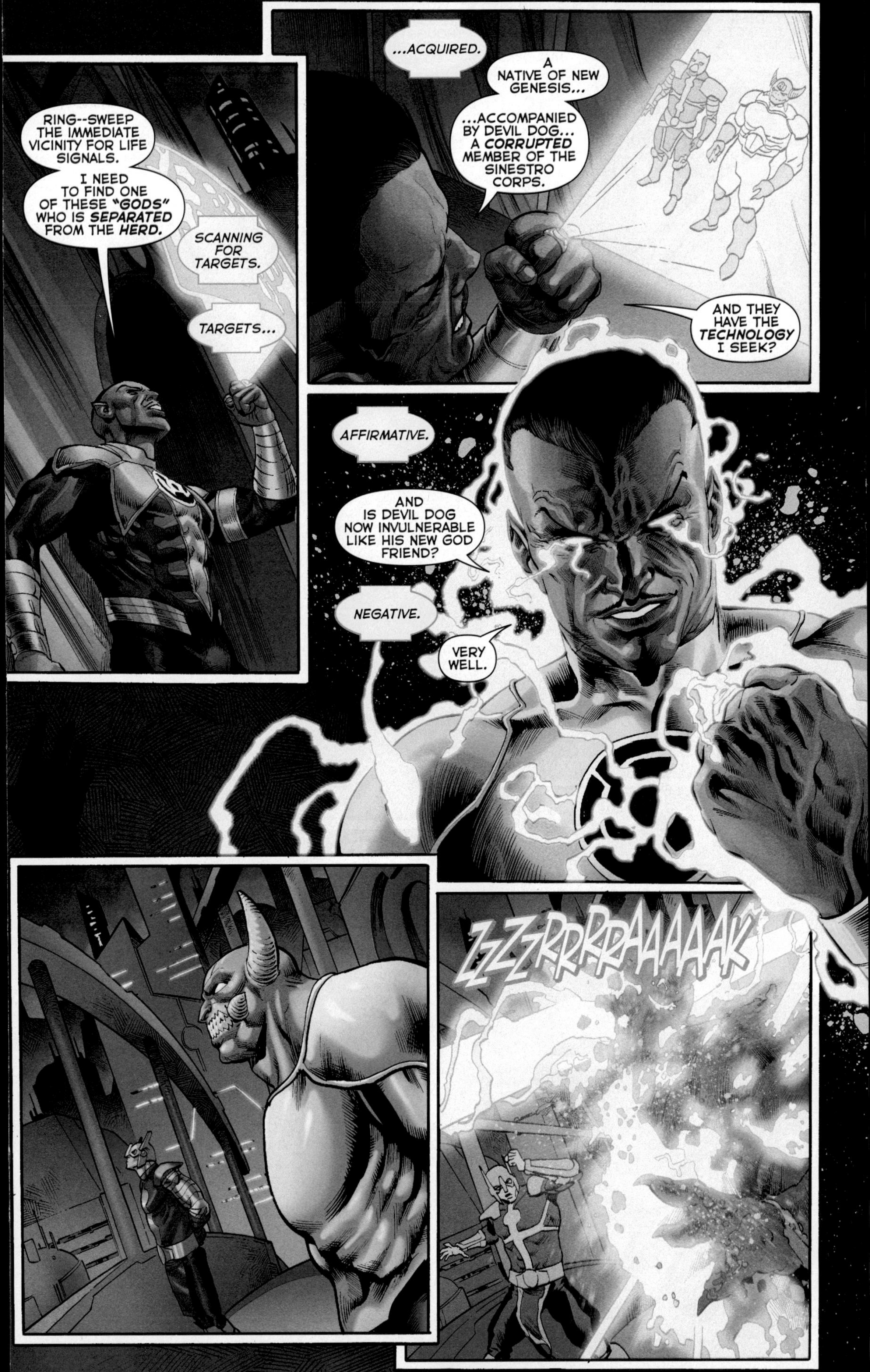
RING--SWEEP THE IMMEDIATE VICINITY FOR LIFE SIGNALS.
I NEED TO FIND ONE OF THESE "GODS" WHO IS SEPARATED FROM THE HERD.
SCANNING FOR TARGETS.
TARGETS...
...ACQUIRED.
A NATIVE OF NEW GENESIS...
...ACCOMPANIED BY DEVIL DOG... A CORRUPTED MEMBER OF THE SINESTRO CORPS.
AND THEY HAVE THE TECHNOLOGY I SEEK?
AFFIRMATIVE.
AND IS DEVIL DOG NOW INVULNERABLE LIKE HIS NEW GOD FRIEND?
NEGATIVE.
VERY WELL.
ZZZZRRRRRAAAAAAK

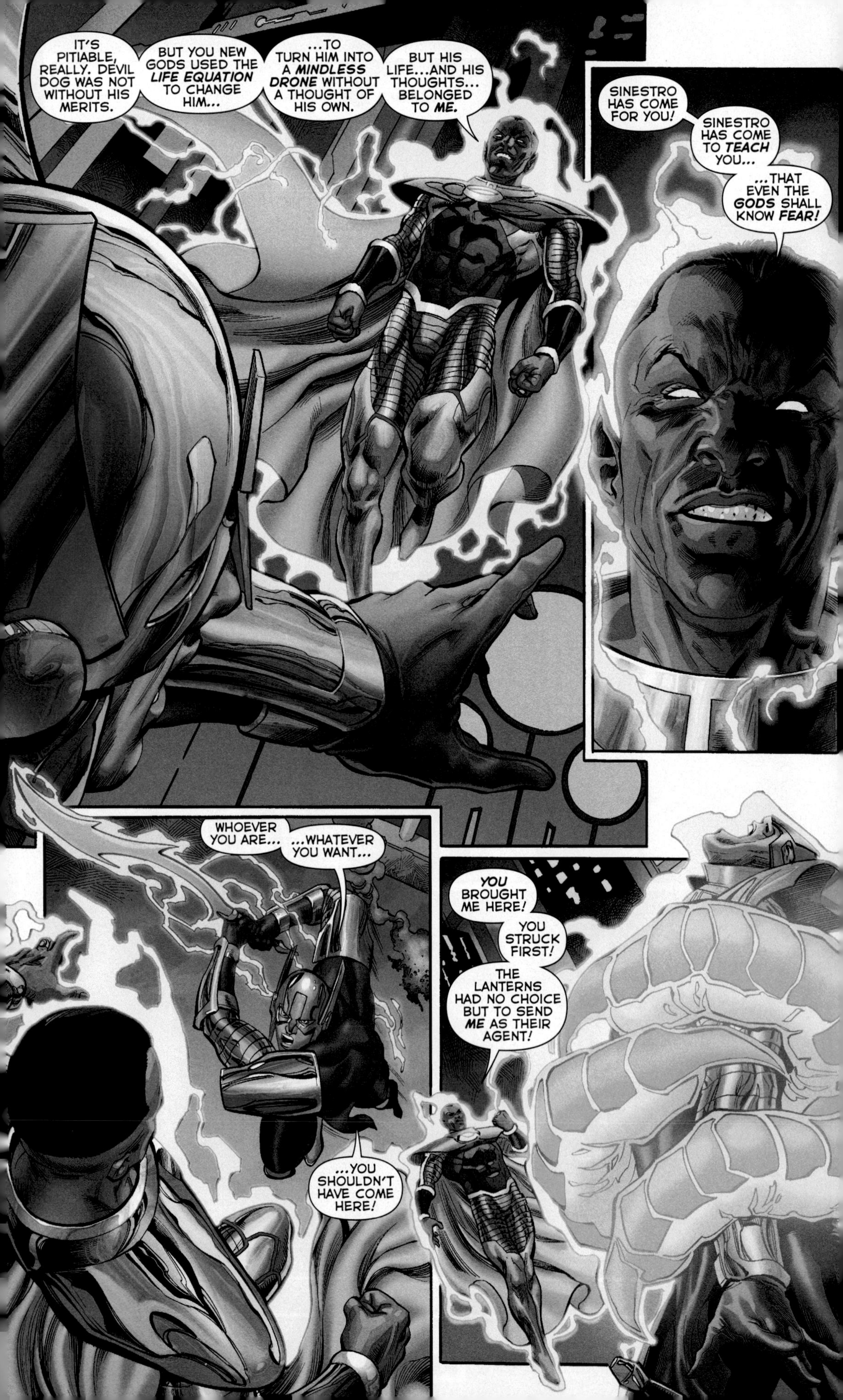
IT'S PITIABLE, REALLY. DEVIL DOG WAS NOT WITHOUT HIS MERITS.
BUT YOU NEW GODS USED THE ***LIFE EQUATION*** TO CHANGE HIM...
...TO TURN HIM INTO A ***MINDLESS DRONE*** WITHOUT A THOUGHT OF HIS OWN.
BUT HIS LIFE...AND HIS THOUGHTS... BELONGED TO ***ME.***
SINESTRO HAS COME FOR YOU!
SINESTRO HAS COME TO ***TEACH*** YOU...
...THAT EVEN THE ***GODS*** SHALL KNOW ***FEAR!***
WHOEVER YOU ARE...
...WHATEVER YOU WANT...
...YOU SHOULDN'T HAVE COME HERE!
YOU BROUGHT ME HERE!
YOU STRUCK FIRST!
THE LANTERNS HAD NO CHOICE BUT TO SEND ***ME*** AS THEIR AGENT!

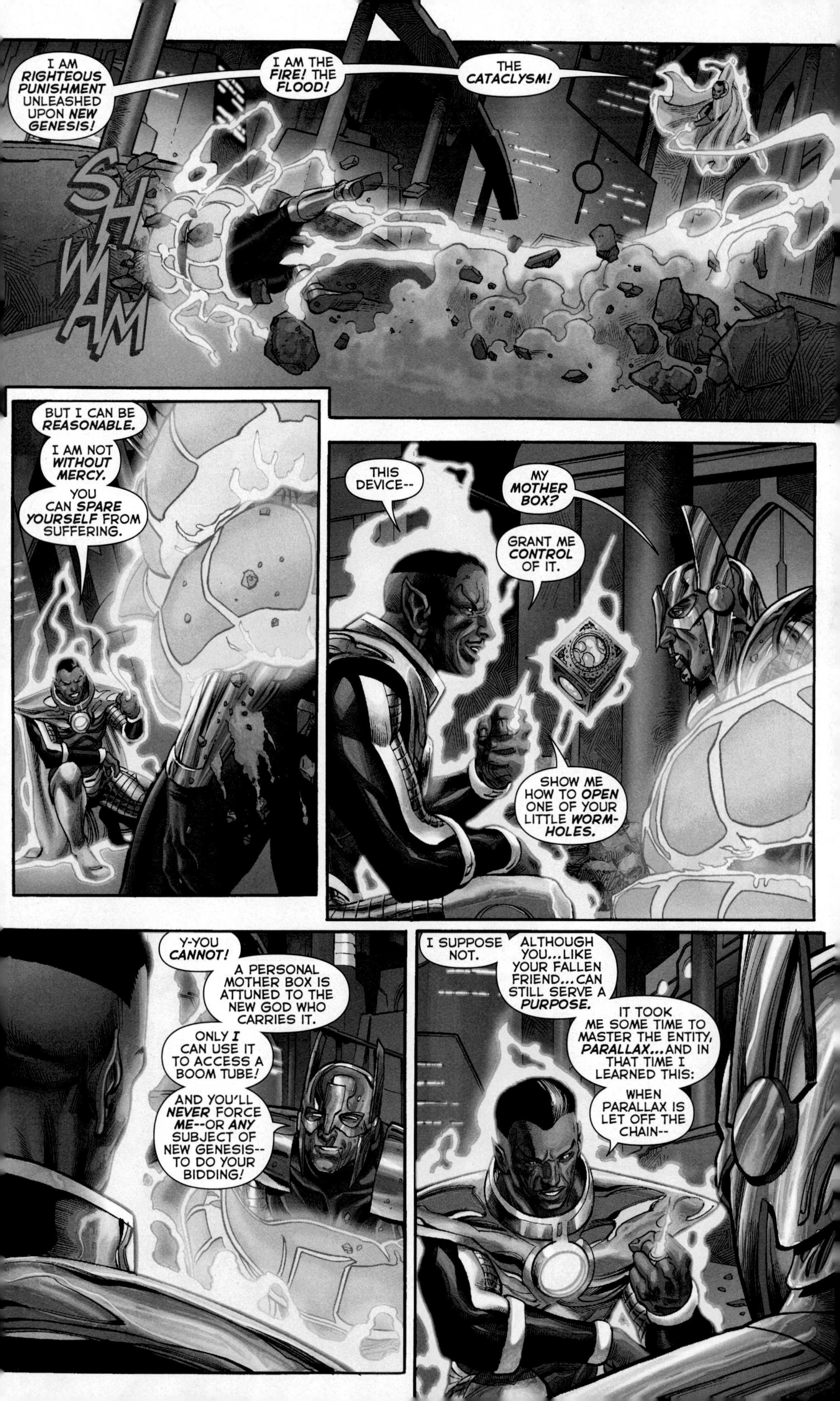
I AM RIGHTEOUS PUNISHMENT UNLEASHED UPON NEW GENESIS!
I AM THE FIRE! THE FLOOD!
THE CATACLYSM!
SHWAM
BUT I CAN BE REASONABLE.
I AM NOT WITHOUT MERCY.
YOU CAN SPARE YOURSELF FROM SUFFERING.
THIS DEVICE--
MY MOTHER BOX?
GRANT ME CONTROL OF IT.
SHOW ME HOW TO OPEN ONE OF YOUR LITTLE WORM-HOLES.
Y-YOU CANNOT!
A PERSONAL MOTHER BOX IS ATTUNED TO THE NEW GOD WHO CARRIES IT.
ONLY I CAN USE IT TO ACCESS A BOOM TUBE!
AND YOU'LL NEVER FORCE ME--OR ANY SUBJECT OF NEW GENESIS--TO DO YOUR BIDDING!
I SUPPOSE NOT.
ALTHOUGH YOU...LIKE YOUR FALLEN FRIEND...CAN STILL SERVE A PURPOSE.
IT TOOK ME SOME TIME TO MASTER THE ENTITY, PARALLAX...AND IN THAT TIME I LEARNED THIS:
WHEN PARALLAX IS LET OFF THE CHAIN--

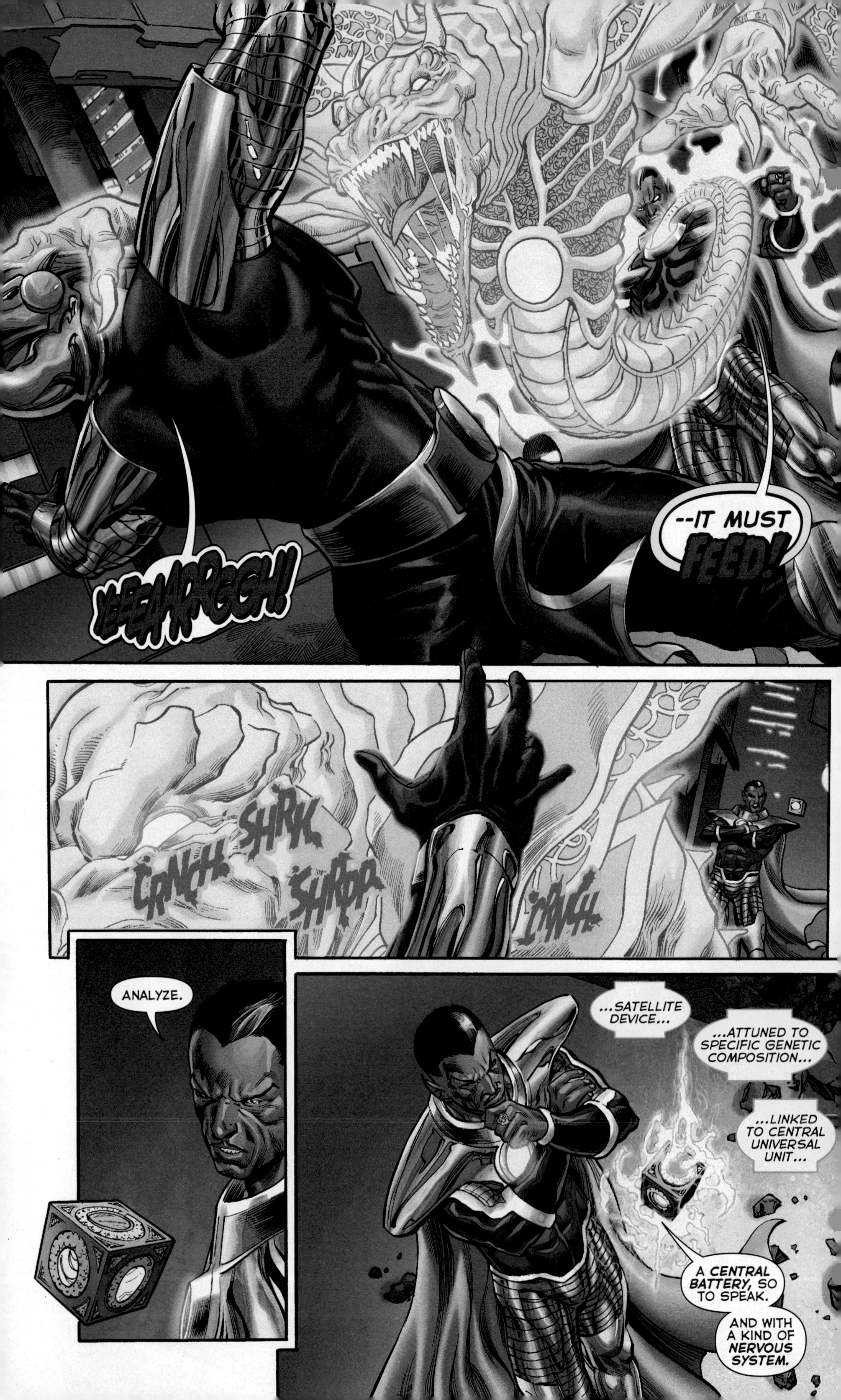
YEEEAARRGGH!
--IT MUST FEED!
CRNCH
SHRK
SHRDR
CRNCH
ANALYZE.
...SATELLITE DEVICE...
...ATTUNED TO SPECIFIC GENETIC COMPOSITION...
...LINKED TO CENTRAL UNIVERSAL UNIT...
A CENTRAL BATTERY, SO TO SPEAK.
AND WITH A KIND OF NERVOUS SYSTEM.

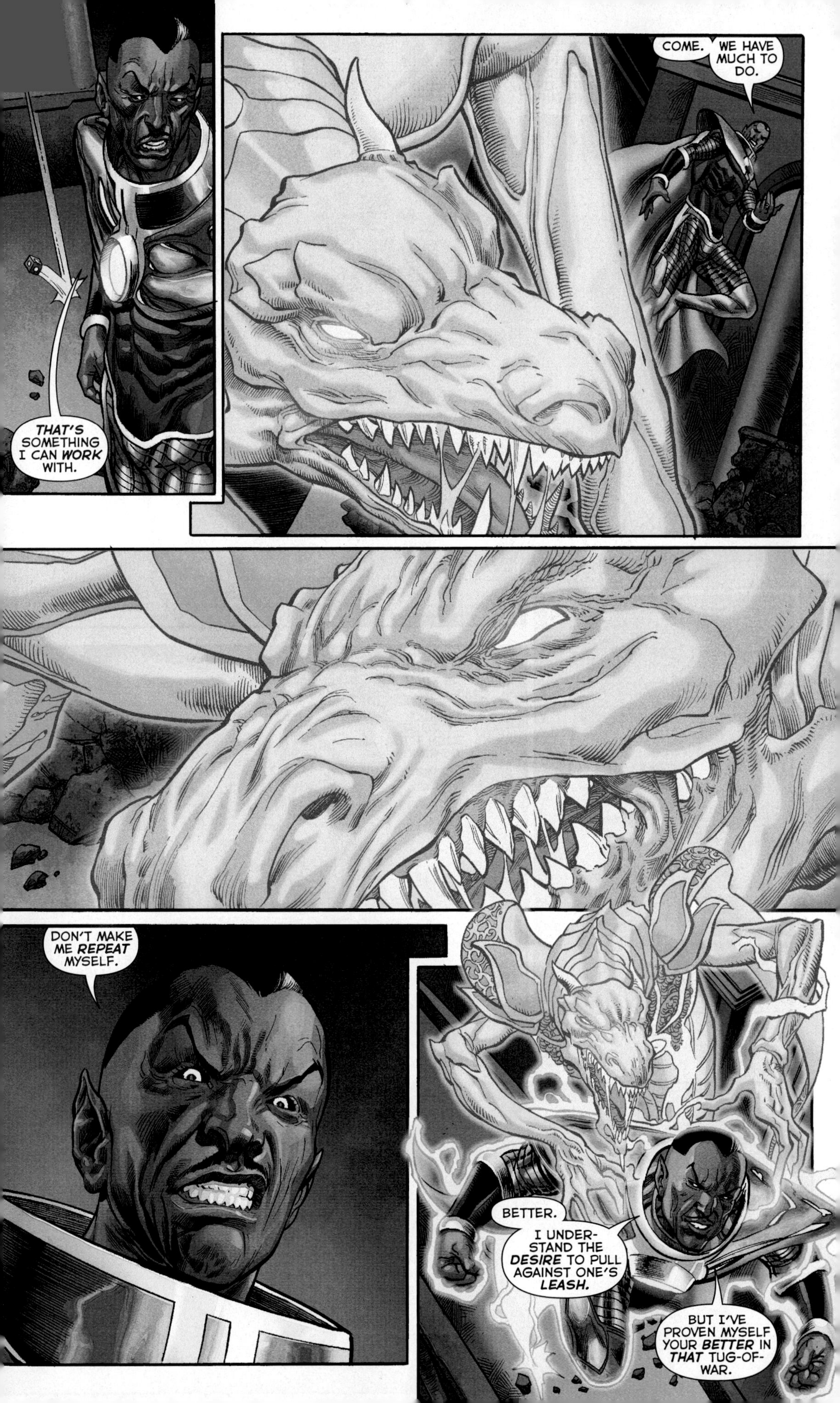
THAT'S SOMETHING I CAN WORK WITH.
COME.
WE HAVE MUCH TO DO.
DON'T MAKE ME REPEAT MYSELF.
BETTER.
I UNDERSTAND THE DESIRE TO PULL AGAINST ONE'S LEASH.
BUT I'VE PROVEN MYSELF YOUR BETTER IN THAT TUG-OF-WAR.

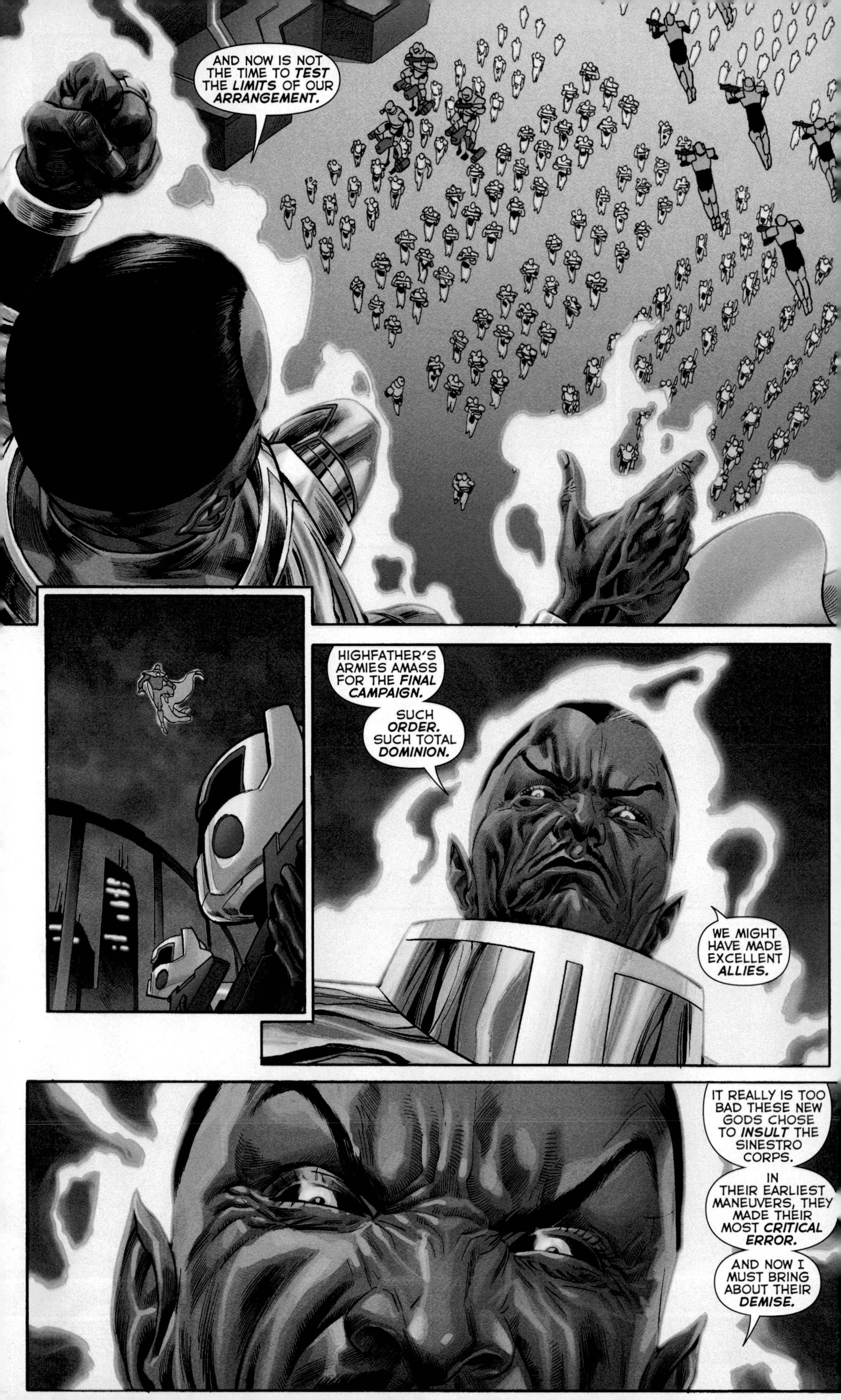
AND NOW IS NOT THE TIME TO TEST THE LIMITS OF OUR ARRANGEMENT.
HIGHFATHER'S ARMIES AMASS FOR THE FINAL CAMPAIGN.
SUCH ORDER. SUCH TOTAL DOMINION.
WE MIGHT HAVE MADE EXCELLENT ALLIES.
IT REALLY IS TOO BAD THESE NEW GODS CHOSE TO INSULT THE SINESTRO CORPS.
IN THEIR EARLIEST MANEUVERS, THEY MADE THEIR MOST CRITICAL ERROR.
AND NOW I MUST BRING ABOUT THEIR DEMISE.

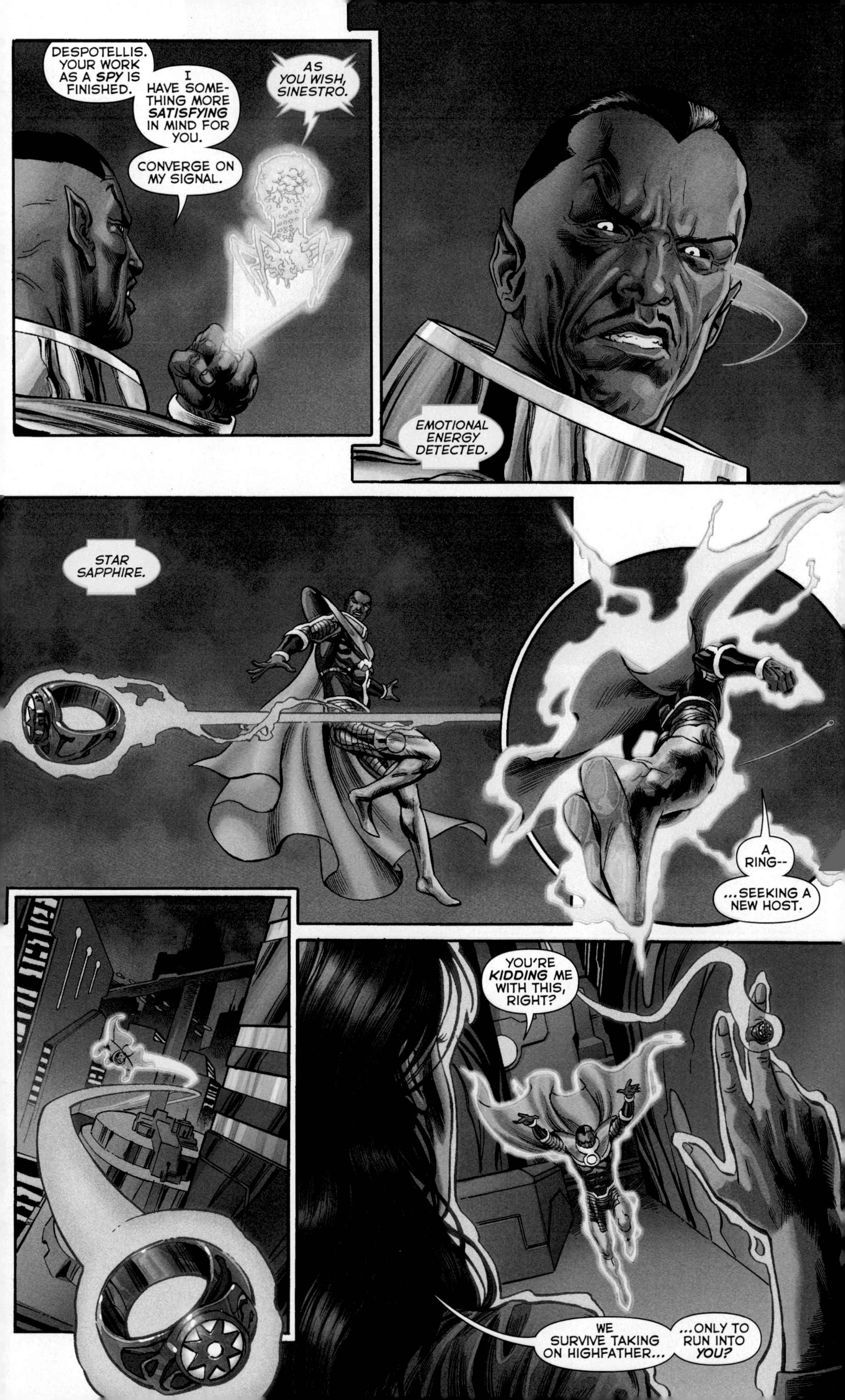
DESPOTELLIS. YOUR WORK AS A SPY IS FINISHED.
I HAVE SOMETHING MORE SATISFYING IN MIND FOR YOU.
CONVERGE ON MY SIGNAL.
AS YOU WISH, SINESTRO.
EMOTIONAL ENERGY DETECTED.
STAR SAPPHIRE.
A RING--
...SEEKING A NEW HOST.
YOU'RE KIDDING ME WITH THIS, RIGHT?
WE SURVIVE TAKING ON HIGHFATHER...
...ONLY TO RUN INTO YOU?

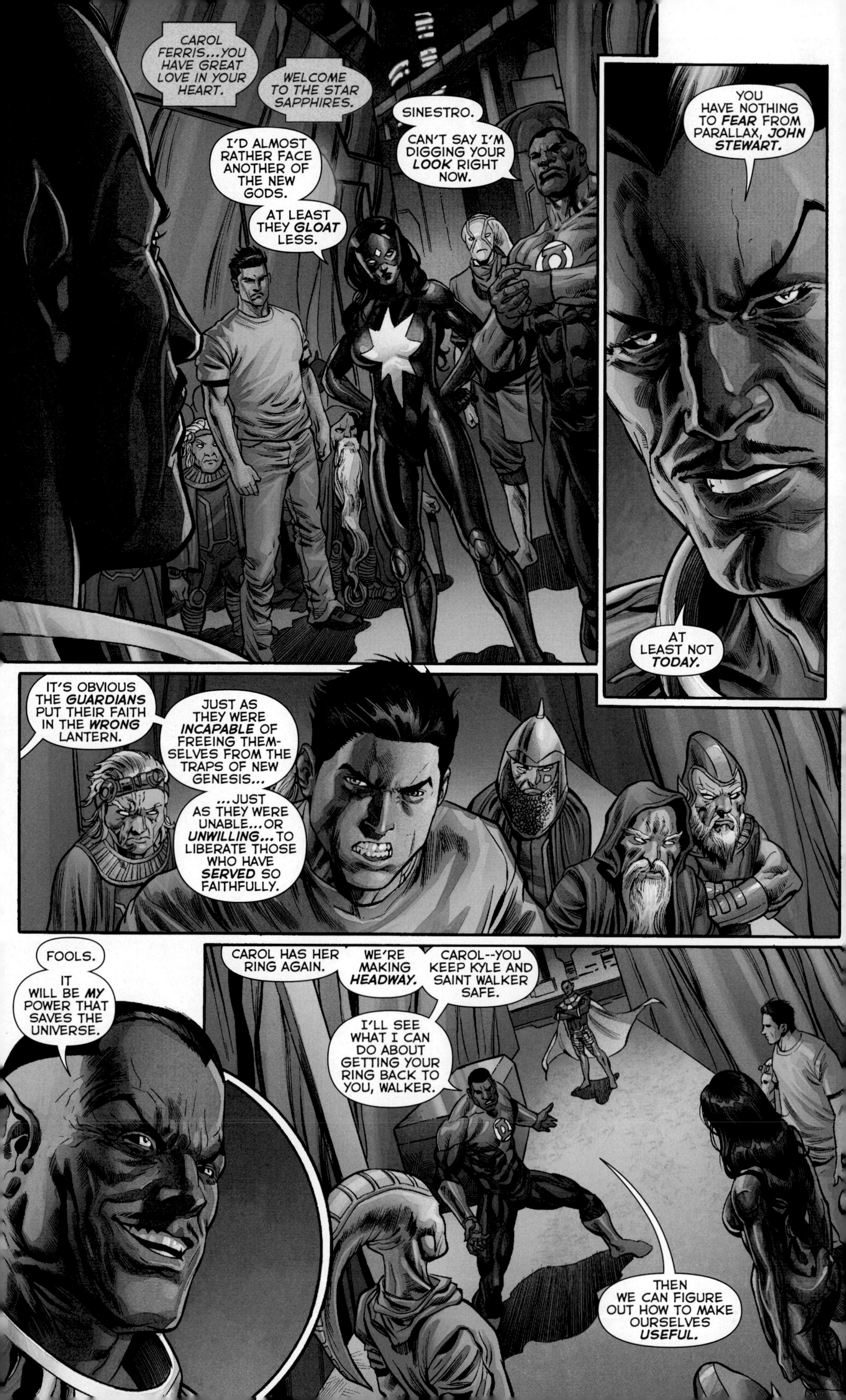
CAROL FERRIS...YOU HAVE GREAT LOVE IN YOUR HEART.
WELCOME TO THE STAR SAPPHIRES.
I'D ALMOST RATHER FACE ANOTHER OF THE NEW GODS.
AT LEAST THEY GLOAT LESS.
SINESTRO.
CAN'T SAY I'M DIGGING YOUR LOOK RIGHT NOW.
YOU HAVE NOTHING TO FEAR FROM PARALLAX, JOHN STEWART.
AT LEAST NOT TODAY.
IT'S OBVIOUS THE GUARDIANS PUT THEIR FAITH IN THE WRONG LANTERN.
JUST AS THEY WERE INCAPABLE OF FREEING THEMSELVES FROM THE TRAPS OF NEW GENESIS...
...JUST AS THEY WERE UNABLE...OR UNWILLING...TO LIBERATE THOSE WHO HAVE SERVED SO FAITHFULLY.
FOOLS.
IT WILL BE MY POWER THAT SAVES THE UNIVERSE.
CAROL HAS HER RING AGAIN.
WE'RE MAKING HEADWAY.
CAROL--YOU KEEP KYLE AND SAINT WALKER SAFE.
I'LL SEE WHAT I CAN DO ABOUT GETTING YOUR RING BACK TO YOU, WALKER.
THEN WE CAN FIGURE OUT HOW TO MAKE OURSELVES USEFUL.

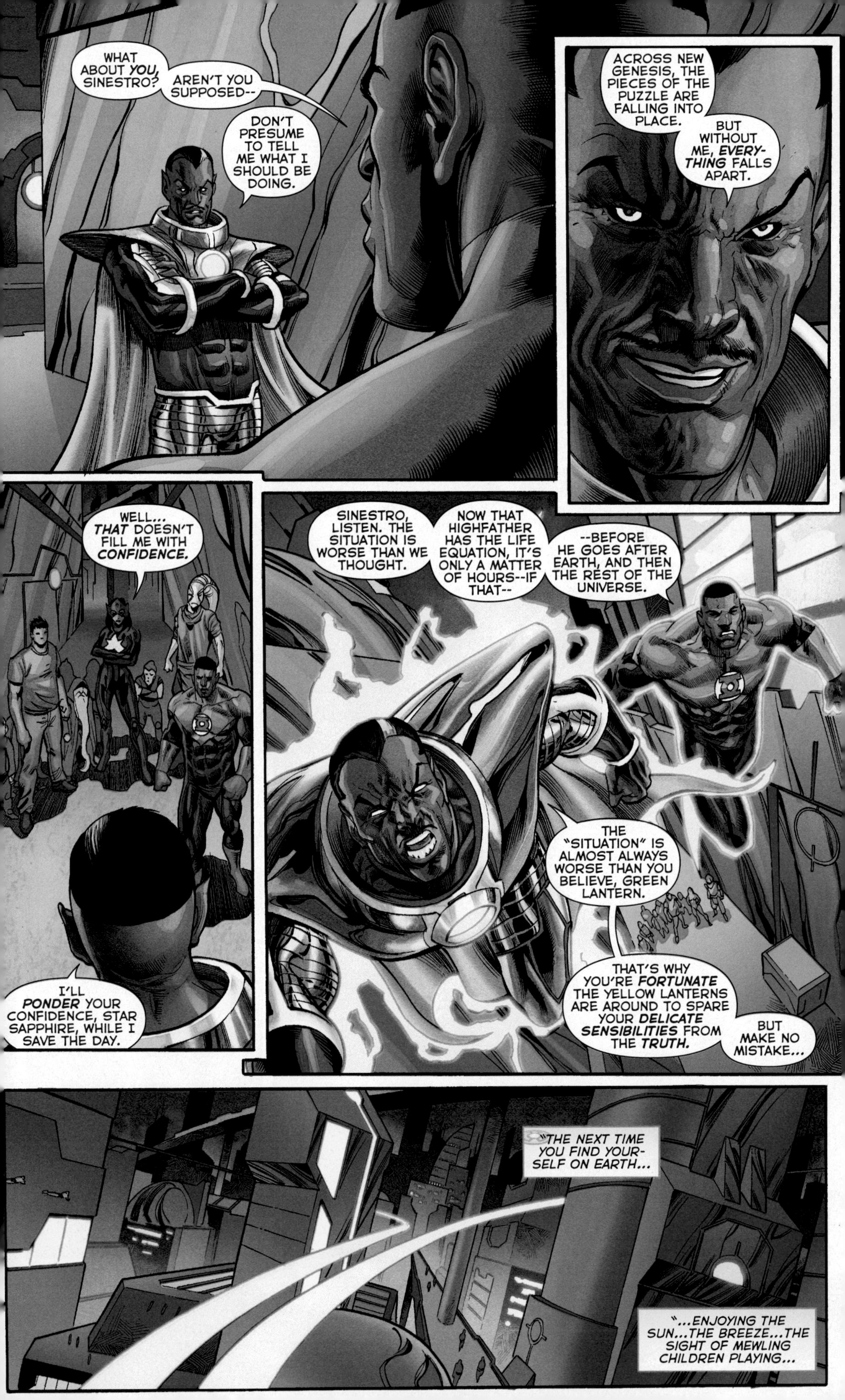
WHAT ABOUT *YOU,* SINESTRO?
AREN'T YOU SUPPOSED--
DON'T PRESUME TO TELL ME WHAT I SHOULD BE DOING.
ACROSS NEW GENESIS, THE PIECES OF THE PUZZLE ARE FALLING INTO PLACE.
BUT WITHOUT ME, *EVERYTHING* FALLS APART.
WELL... *THAT* DOESN'T FILL ME WITH *CONFIDENCE.*
I'LL *PONDER* YOUR CONFIDENCE, STAR SAPPHIRE, WHILE I SAVE THE DAY.
SINESTRO, LISTEN. THE SITUATION IS WORSE THAN WE THOUGHT.
NOW THAT HIGHFATHER HAS THE LIFE EQUATION, IT'S ONLY A MATTER OF HOURS--IF THAT--
--BEFORE HE GOES AFTER EARTH, AND THEN THE REST OF THE UNIVERSE.
THE "SITUATION" IS ALMOST ALWAYS WORSE THAN YOU BELIEVE, GREEN LANTERN.
THAT'S WHY YOU'RE *FORTUNATE* THE YELLOW LANTERNS ARE AROUND TO SPARE YOUR *DELICATE SENSIBILITIES* FROM THE *TRUTH.*
BUT MAKE NO MISTAKE...
"THE NEXT TIME YOU FIND YOURSELF ON EARTH...
"...ENJOYING THE SUN...THE BREEZE...THE SIGHT OF MEWLING CHILDREN PLAYING...

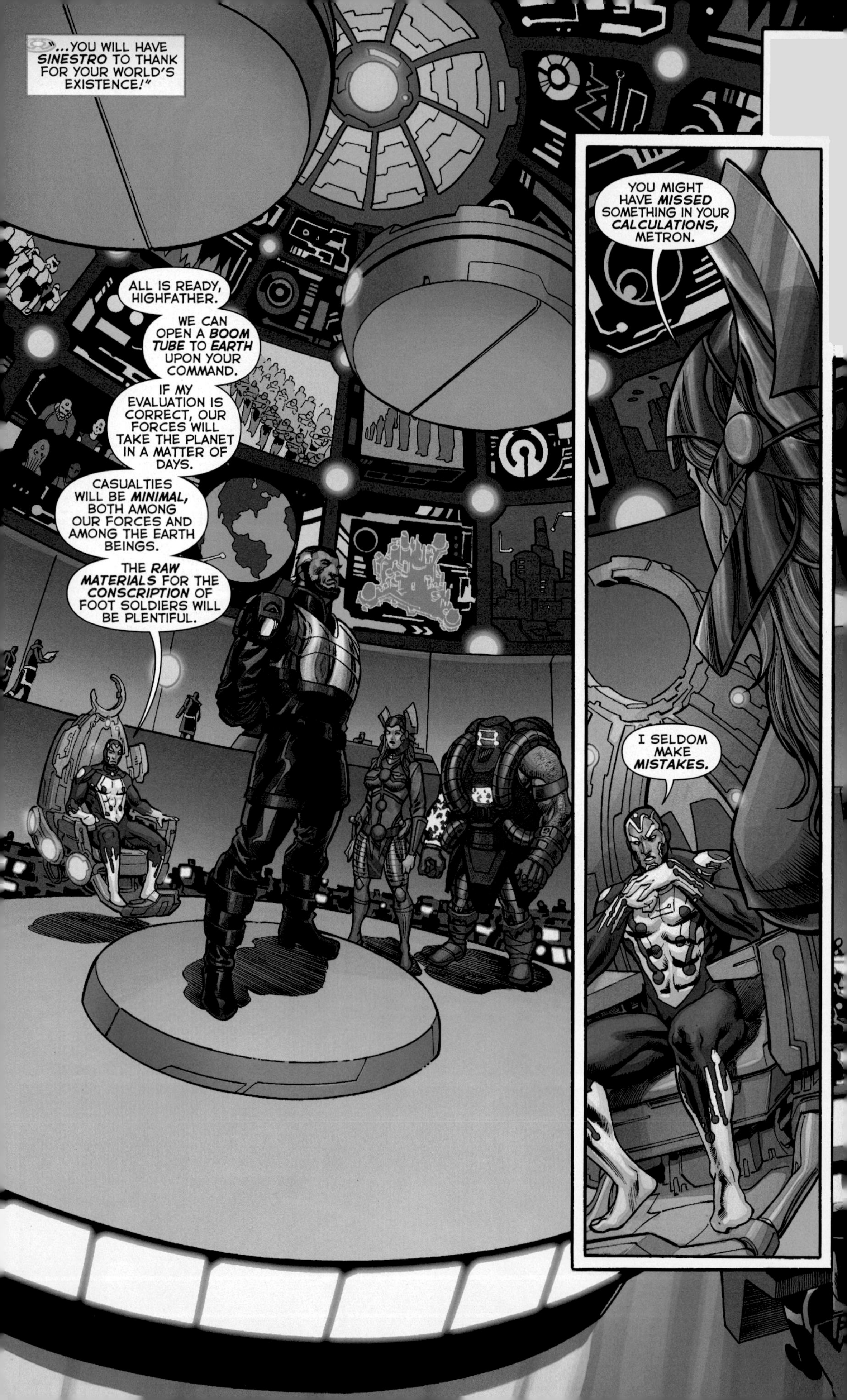

...YOU WILL HAVE SINESTRO TO THANK FOR YOUR WORLD'S EXISTENCE!"
ALL IS READY, HIGHFATHER.
WE CAN OPEN A BOOM TUBE TO EARTH UPON YOUR COMMAND.
IF MY EVALUATION IS CORRECT, OUR FORCES WILL TAKE THE PLANET IN A MATTER OF DAYS.
CASUALTIES WILL BE MINIMAL, BOTH AMONG OUR FORCES AND AMONG THE EARTH BEINGS.
THE RAW MATERIALS FOR THE CONSCRIPTION OF FOOT SOLDIERS WILL BE PLENTIFUL.
YOU MIGHT HAVE MISSED SOMETHING IN YOUR CALCULATIONS, METRON.
I SELDOM MAKE MISTAKES.

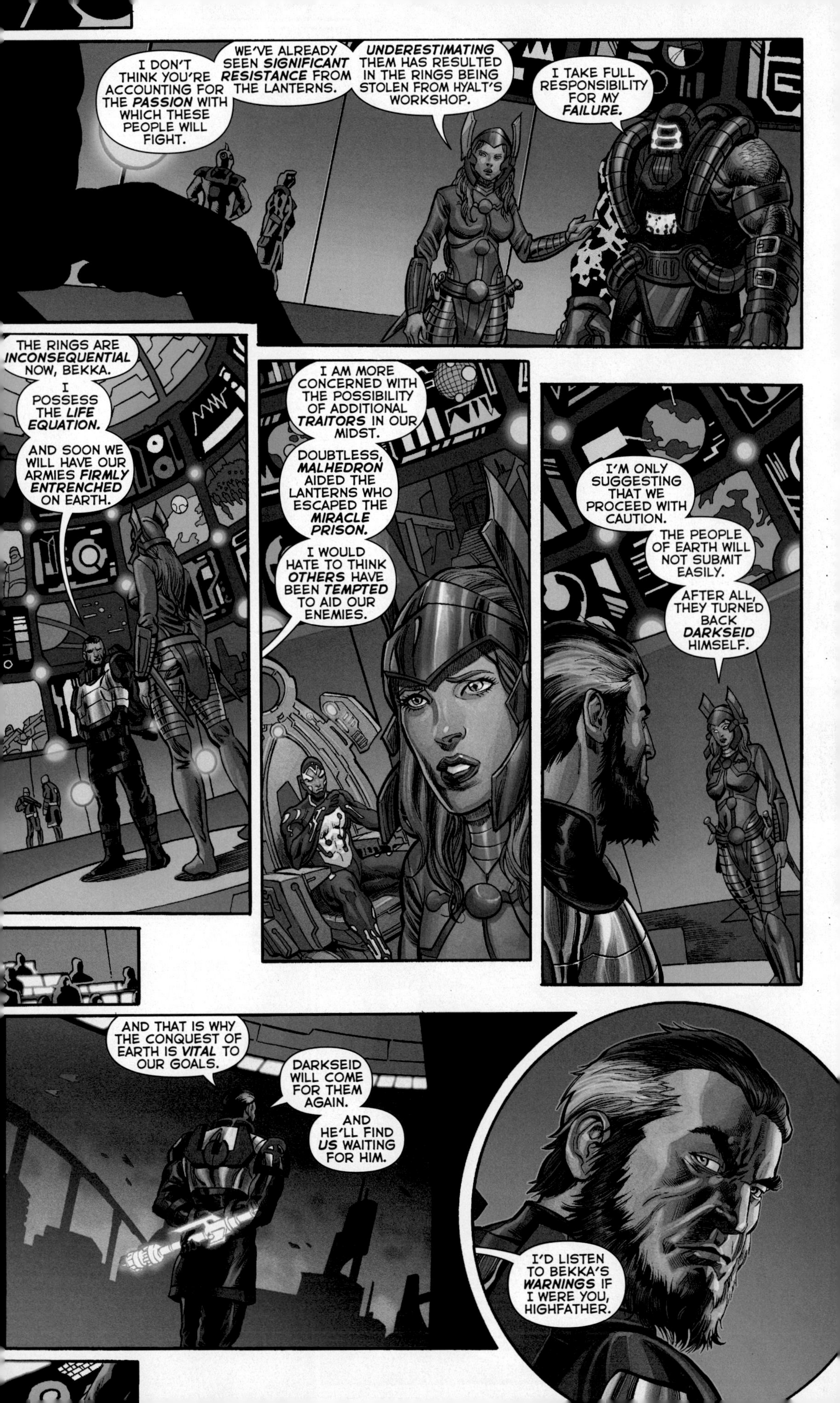
I DON'T THINK YOU'RE ACCOUNTING FOR THE PASSION WITH WHICH THESE PEOPLE WILL FIGHT.
WE'VE ALREADY SEEN SIGNIFICANT RESISTANCE FROM THE LANTERNS.
UNDERESTIMATING THEM HAS RESULTED IN THE RINGS BEING STOLEN FROM HYALT'S WORKSHOP.
I TAKE FULL RESPONSIBILITY FOR MY FAILURE.
THE RINGS ARE INCONSEQUENTIAL NOW, BEKKA.
I POSSESS THE LIFE EQUATION.
AND SOON WE WILL HAVE OUR ARMIES FIRMLY ENTRENCHED ON EARTH.
I AM MORE CONCERNED WITH THE POSSIBILITY OF ADDITIONAL TRAITORS IN OUR MIDST.
DOUBTLESS, MALHEDRON AIDED THE LANTERNS WHO ESCAPED THE MIRACLE PRISON.
I WOULD HATE TO THINK OTHERS HAVE BEEN TEMPTED TO AID OUR ENEMIES.
I'M ONLY SUGGESTING THAT WE PROCEED WITH CAUTION.
THE PEOPLE OF EARTH WILL NOT SUBMIT EASILY.
AFTER ALL, THEY TURNED BACK DARKSEID HIMSELF.
AND THAT IS WHY THE CONQUEST OF EARTH IS VITAL TO OUR GOALS.
DARKSEID WILL COME FOR THEM AGAIN.
AND HE'LL FIND US WAITING FOR HIM.
I'D LISTEN TO BEKKA'S WARNINGS IF I WERE YOU, HIGHFATHER.

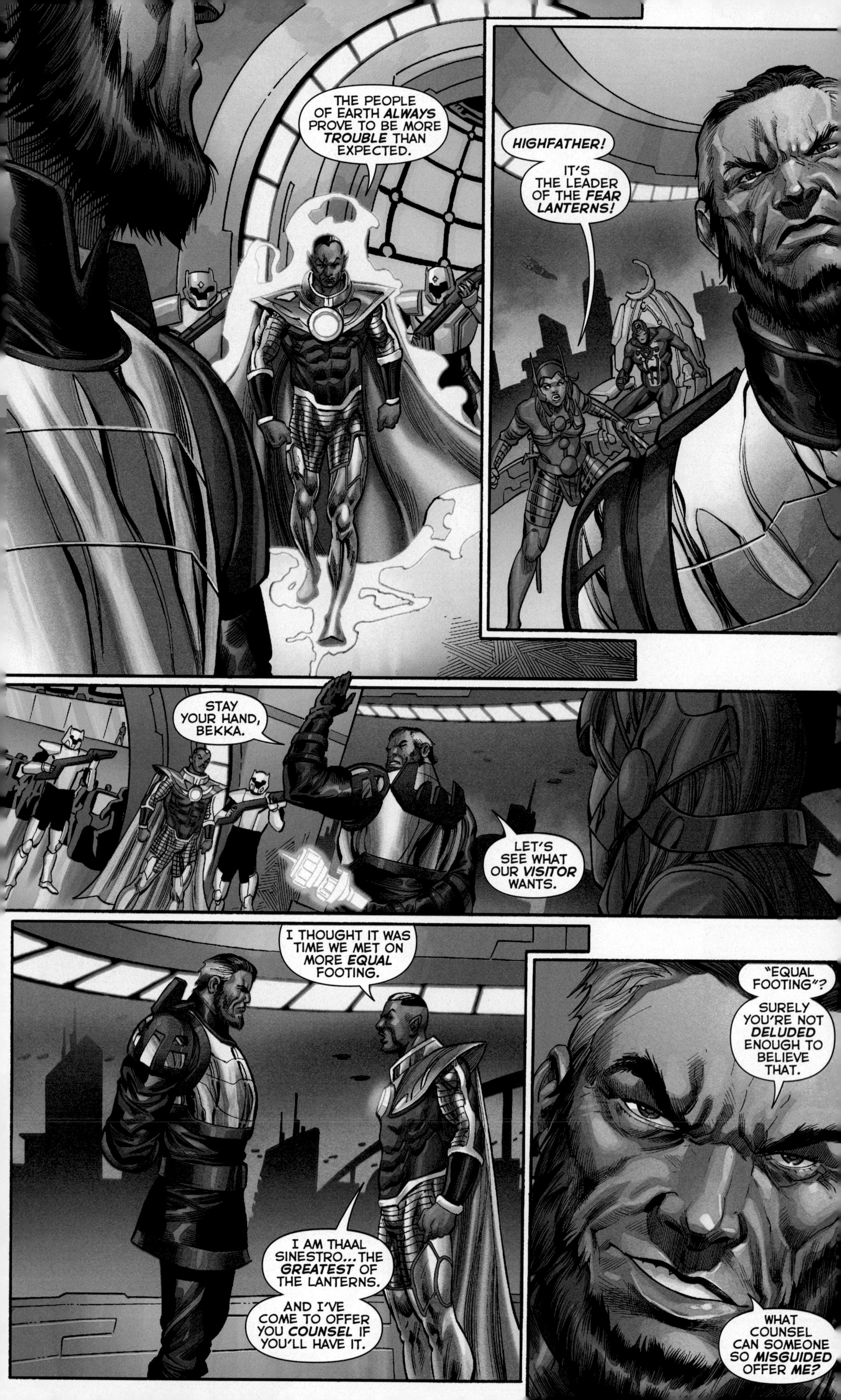
THE PEOPLE OF EARTH ALWAYS PROVE TO BE MORE TROUBLE THAN EXPECTED.
HIGHFATHER!
IT'S THE LEADER OF THE FEAR LANTERNS!
STAY YOUR HAND, BEKKA.
LET'S SEE WHAT OUR VISITOR WANTS.
I THOUGHT IT WAS TIME WE MET ON MORE EQUAL FOOTING.
I AM THAAL SINESTRO...THE GREATEST OF THE LANTERNS.
AND I'VE COME TO OFFER YOU COUNSEL IF YOU'LL HAVE IT.
"EQUAL FOOTING"?
SURELY YOU'RE NOT DELUDED ENOUGH TO BELIEVE THAT.
WHAT COUNSEL CAN SOMEONE SO MISGUIDED OFFER ME?

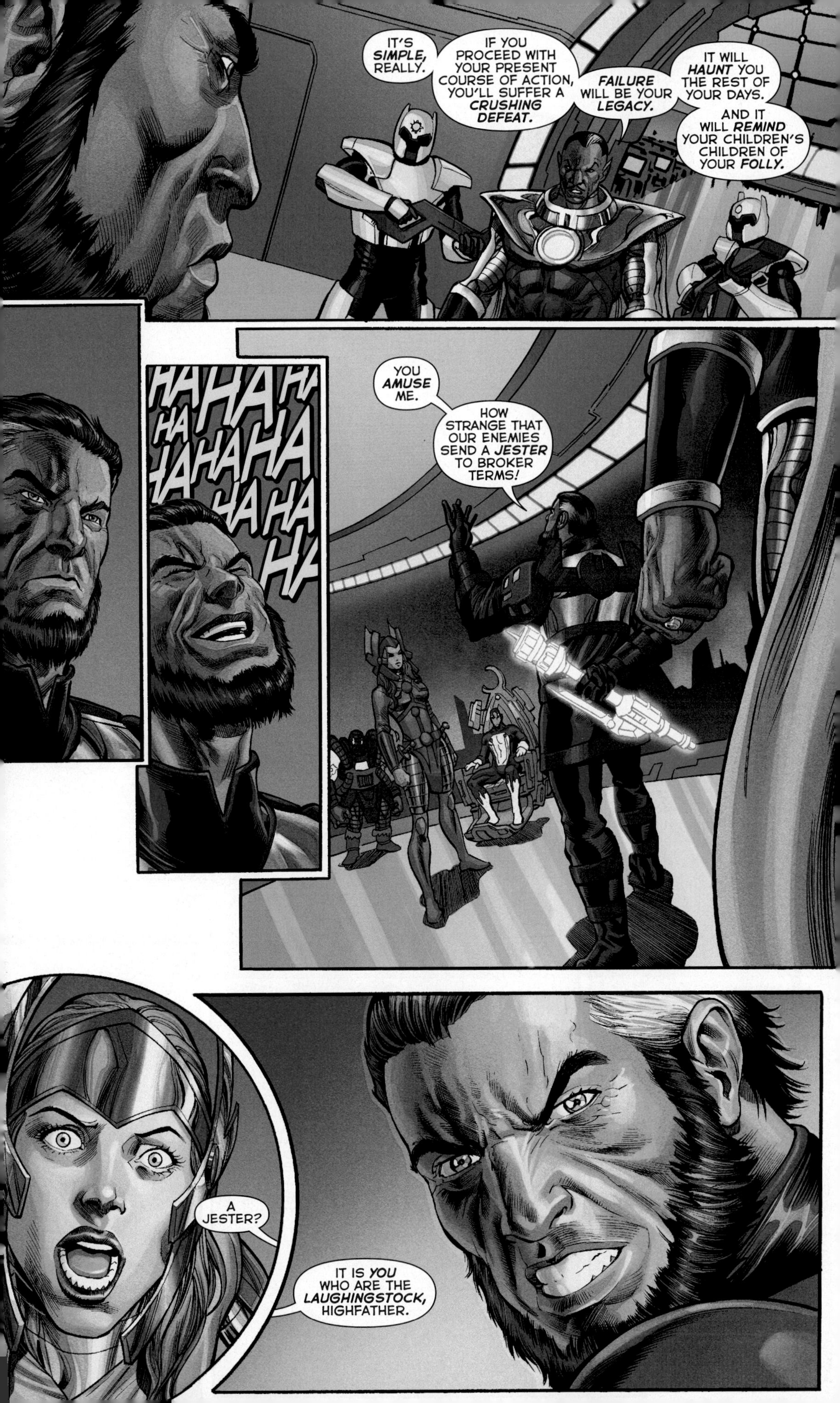
IT'S SIMPLE, REALLY.
IF YOU PROCEED WITH YOUR PRESENT COURSE OF ACTION, YOU'LL SUFFER A CRUSHING DEFEAT.
FAILURE WILL BE YOUR LEGACY.
IT WILL HAUNT YOU THE REST OF YOUR DAYS.
AND IT WILL REMIND YOUR CHILDREN'S CHILDREN OF YOUR FOLLY.
HAHAHA HA HAHAHA HAHA HA
YOU AMUSE ME.
HOW STRANGE THAT OUR ENEMIES SEND A JESTER TO BROKER TERMS!
A JESTER?
IT IS YOU WHO ARE THE LAUGHINGSTOCK, HIGHFATHER.

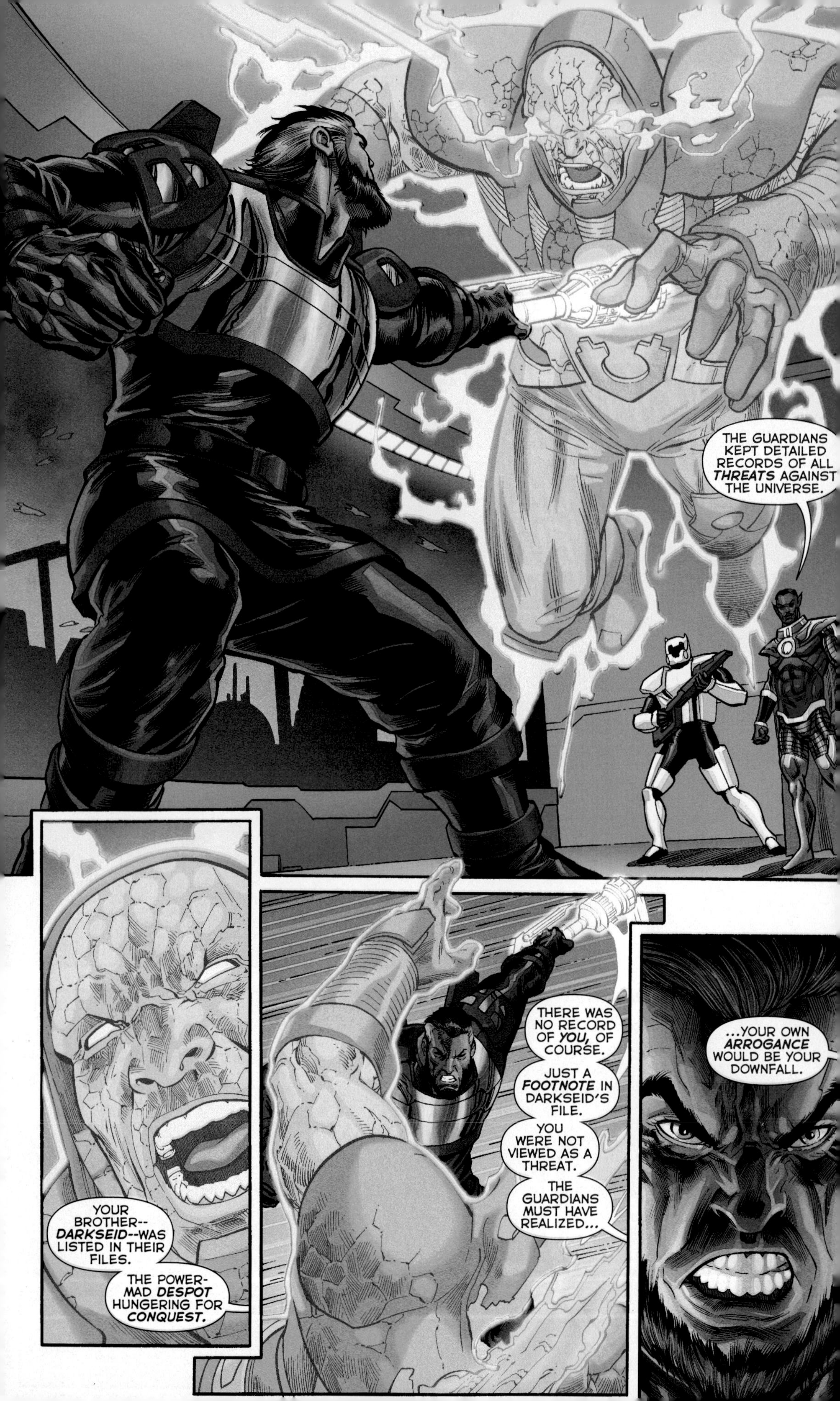
THE GUARDIANS KEPT DETAILED RECORDS OF ALL THREATS AGAINST THE UNIVERSE.
YOUR BROTHER--DARKSEID--WAS LISTED IN THEIR FILES.
THE POWER-MAD DESPOT HUNGERING FOR CONQUEST.
THERE WAS NO RECORD OF YOU, OF COURSE.
JUST A FOOTNOTE IN DARKSEID'S FILE.
YOU WERE NOT VIEWED AS A THREAT.
THE GUARDIANS MUST HAVE REALIZED...
...YOUR OWN ARROGANCE WOULD BE YOUR DOWNFALL.

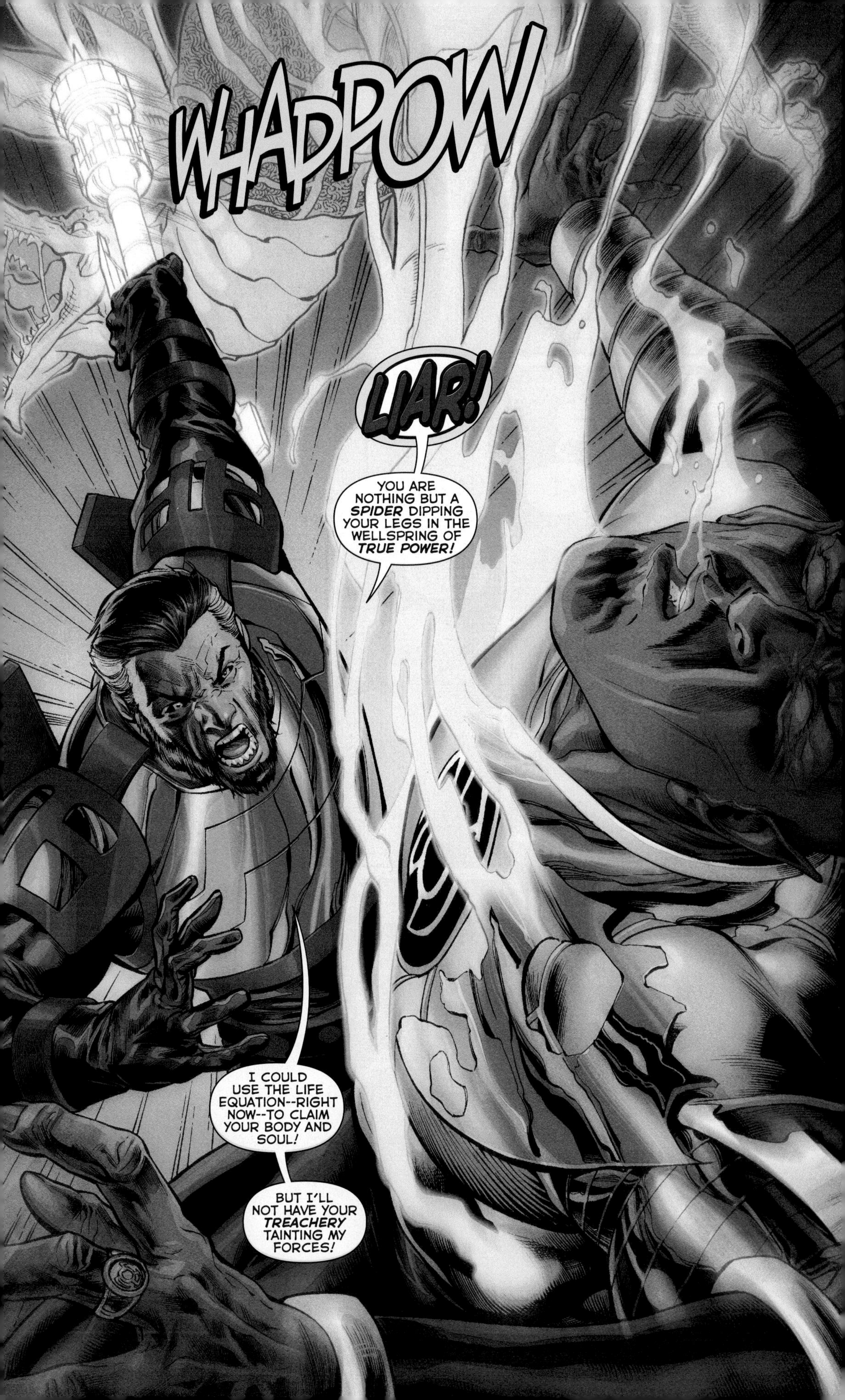
WHADPOW
LIAR!
YOU ARE NOTHING BUT A SPIDER DIPPING YOUR LEGS IN THE WELLSPRING OF TRUE POWER!
I COULD USE THE LIFE EQUATION--RIGHT NOW--TO CLAIM YOUR BODY AND SOUL!
BUT I'LL NOT HAVE YOUR TREACHERY TAINTING MY FORCES!

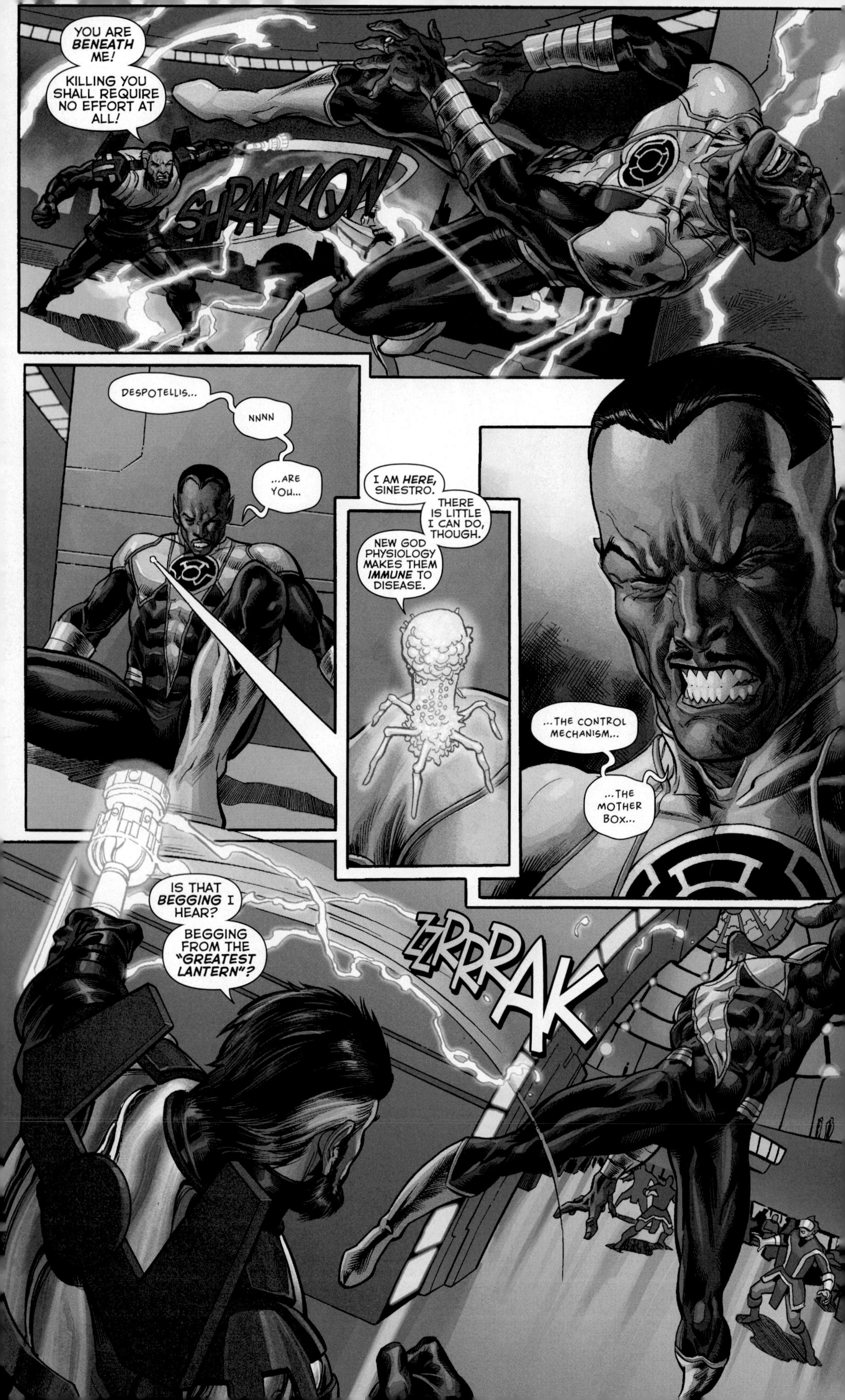
YOU ARE BENEATH ME!
KILLING YOU SHALL REQUIRE NO EFFORT AT ALL!
SHRAKKOW!
DESPOTELLIS...
NNNN
...ARE YOU...
I AM HERE, SINESTRO.
THERE IS LITTLE I CAN DO, THOUGH.
NEW GOD PHYSIOLOGY MAKES THEM IMMUNE TO DISEASE.
...THE CONTROL MECHANISM...
...THE MOTHER BOX...
IS THAT BEGGING I HEAR?
BEGGING FROM THE "GREATEST LANTERN"?
ZZRRRRAK

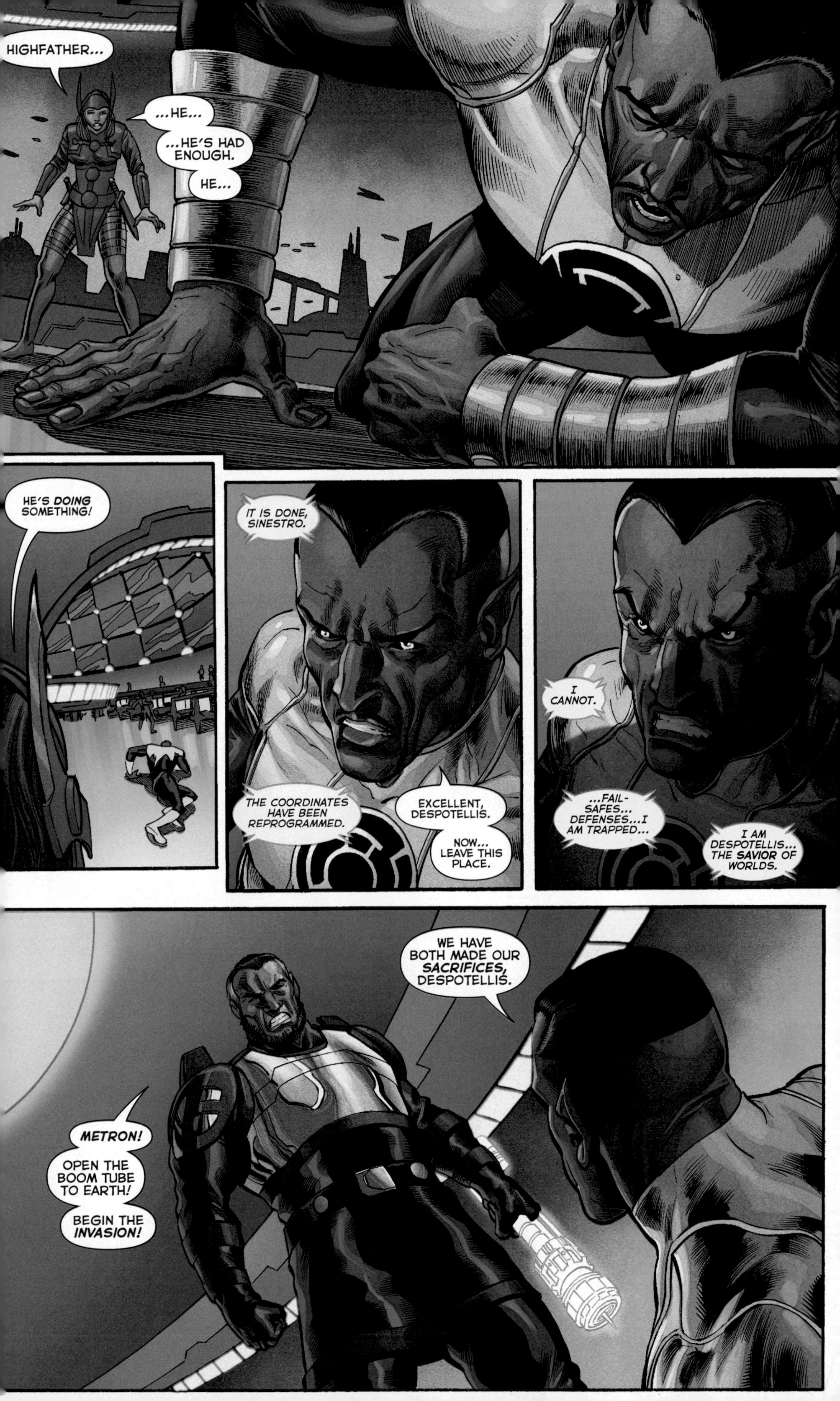

HIGHFATHER...
...HE...
...HE'S HAD ENOUGH.
HE...
HE'S *DOING* SOMETHING!
IT IS DONE, SINESTRO.
THE COORDINATES HAVE BEEN REPROGRAMMED.
EXCELLENT, DESPOTELLIS.
NOW... LEAVE THIS PLACE.
I CANNOT.
...FAIL-SAFES... DEFENSES...I AM TRAPPED...
*I AM DESPOTELLIS... THE **SAVIOR** OF WORLDS.*
WE HAVE BOTH MADE OUR ***SACRIFICES,*** DESPOTELLIS.
METRON!
OPEN THE BOOM TUBE TO EARTH!
BEGIN THE ***INVASION!***

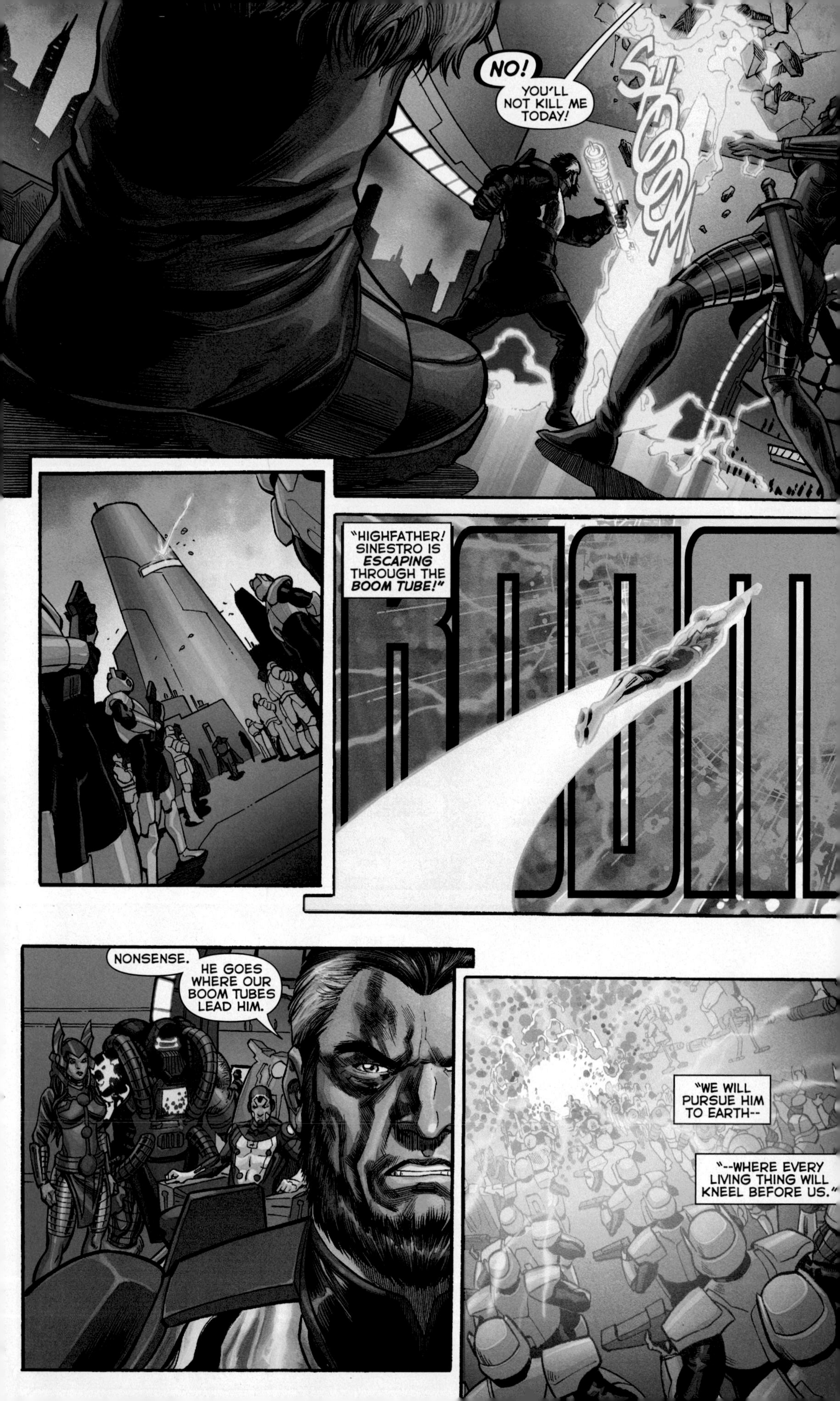
NO!
YOU'LL NOT KILL ME TODAY!
SHOOOM
"HIGHFATHER! SINESTRO IS ESCAPING THROUGH THE BOOM TUBE!"
BOOM
NONSENSE.
HE GOES WHERE OUR BOOM TUBES LEAD HIM.
"WE WILL PURSUE HIM TO EARTH--
"--WHERE EVERY LIVING THING WILL KNEEL BEFORE US."

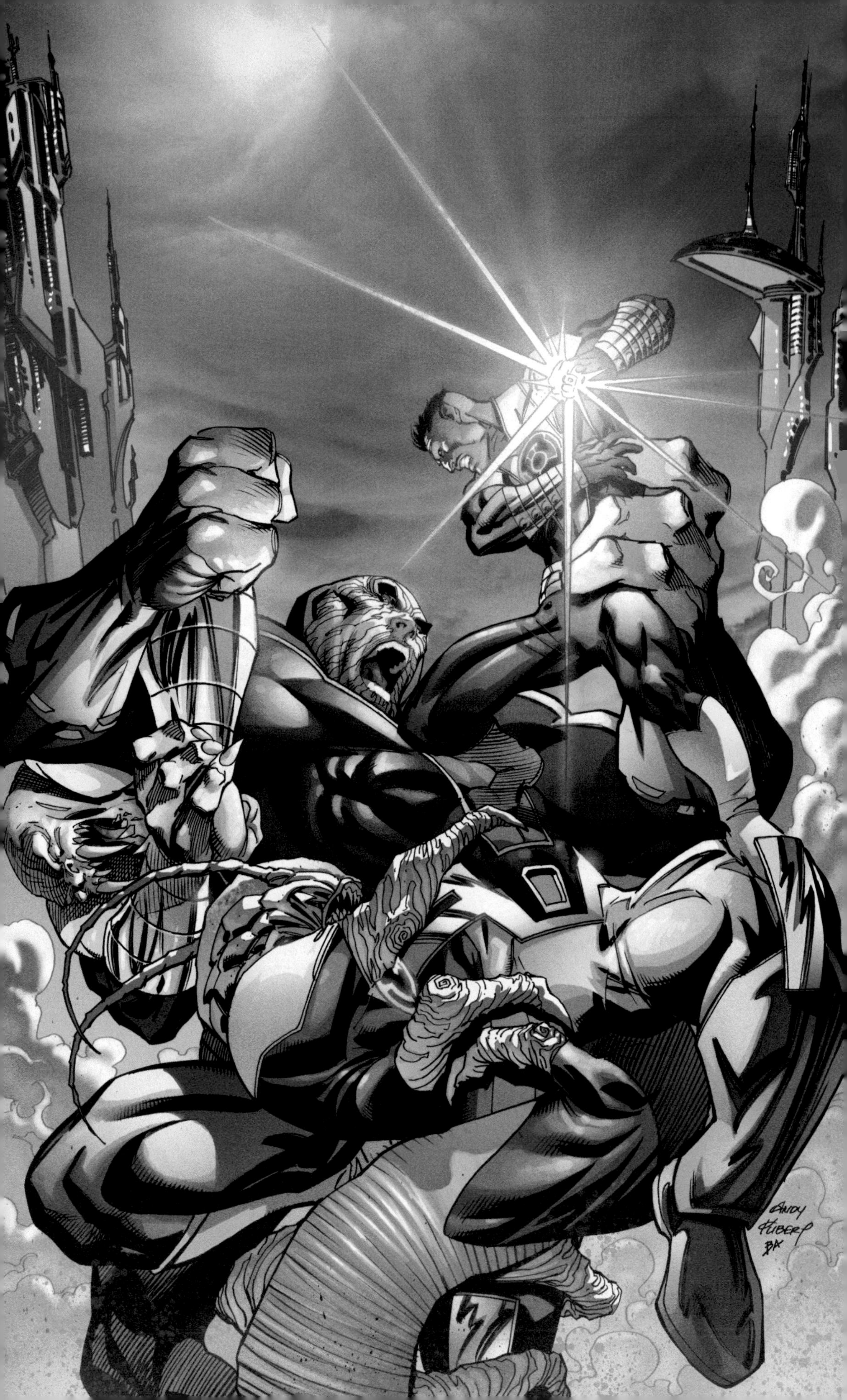
ANDY
KUBERT
BA

LIMITS OF WAR

CULLEN BUNN writer **BRAD WALKER** penciller **ANDREW HENNESSY** inker **DAVE SHARPE** letterer **JASON WRIGHT** colorist cover art by **ANDY KUBERT & BRAD ANDERSON**

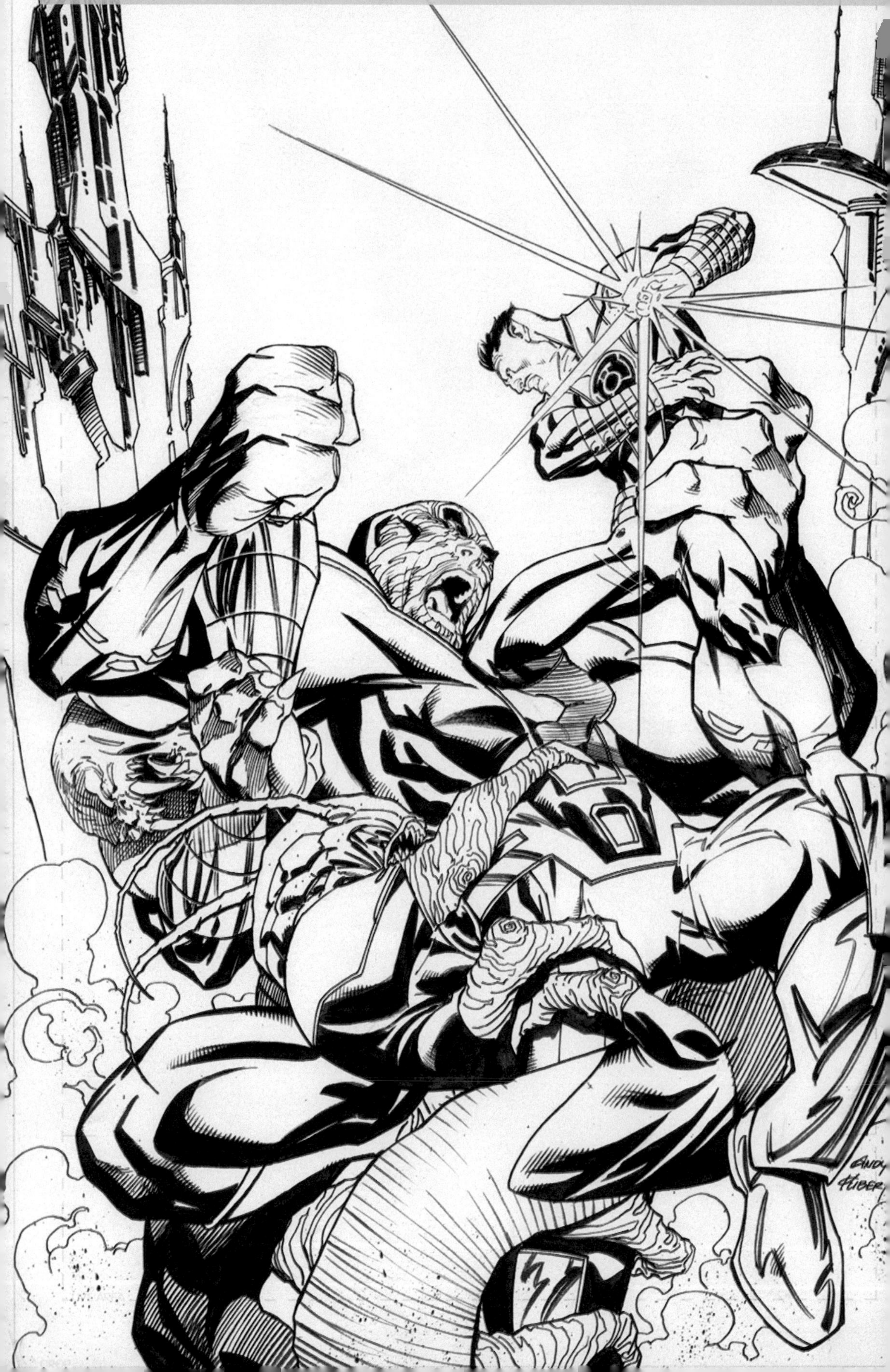

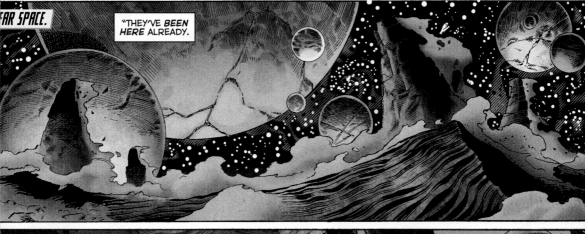

"THEY'VE *BEEN HERE* ALREADY.

"THIS *WORLD*... IT WAS SUPPOSED TO BE A *PARADISE*...

"...RICH JUNGLES... TEEMING WITH WILDLIFE...

"...HOME TO A PRIMITIVE BUT PEACEFUL PEOPLE.

"ONCE EVERY DECADE, ALL THE PEOPLE OF THIS WORLD WOULD JOIN TOGETHER IN A *VAST FESTIVAL.*

"A CELEBRATION OF *BOUNTY* AND *JOY* THAT SPANNED THE ENTIRE WORLD.

"IT WAS THEIR *HAPPINESS* THAT BROUGHT ABOUT THEIR *DESTRUCTION.*

"THE *PALING*.

"THEY WERE DRAWN TO THE *EMOTION*.

"THE PALE VICARS...

"...CAME TO PREACH THEIR GOSPEL OF NOTHINGNESS.

"THEY *HARVESTED* ALL THE *LIFE*...

"...STRIPPED ALL THE *NATURAL RESOURCES* FROM THE PLANET.

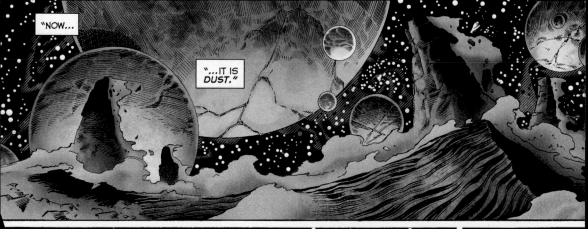

"NOW...

"...IT IS *DUST*."

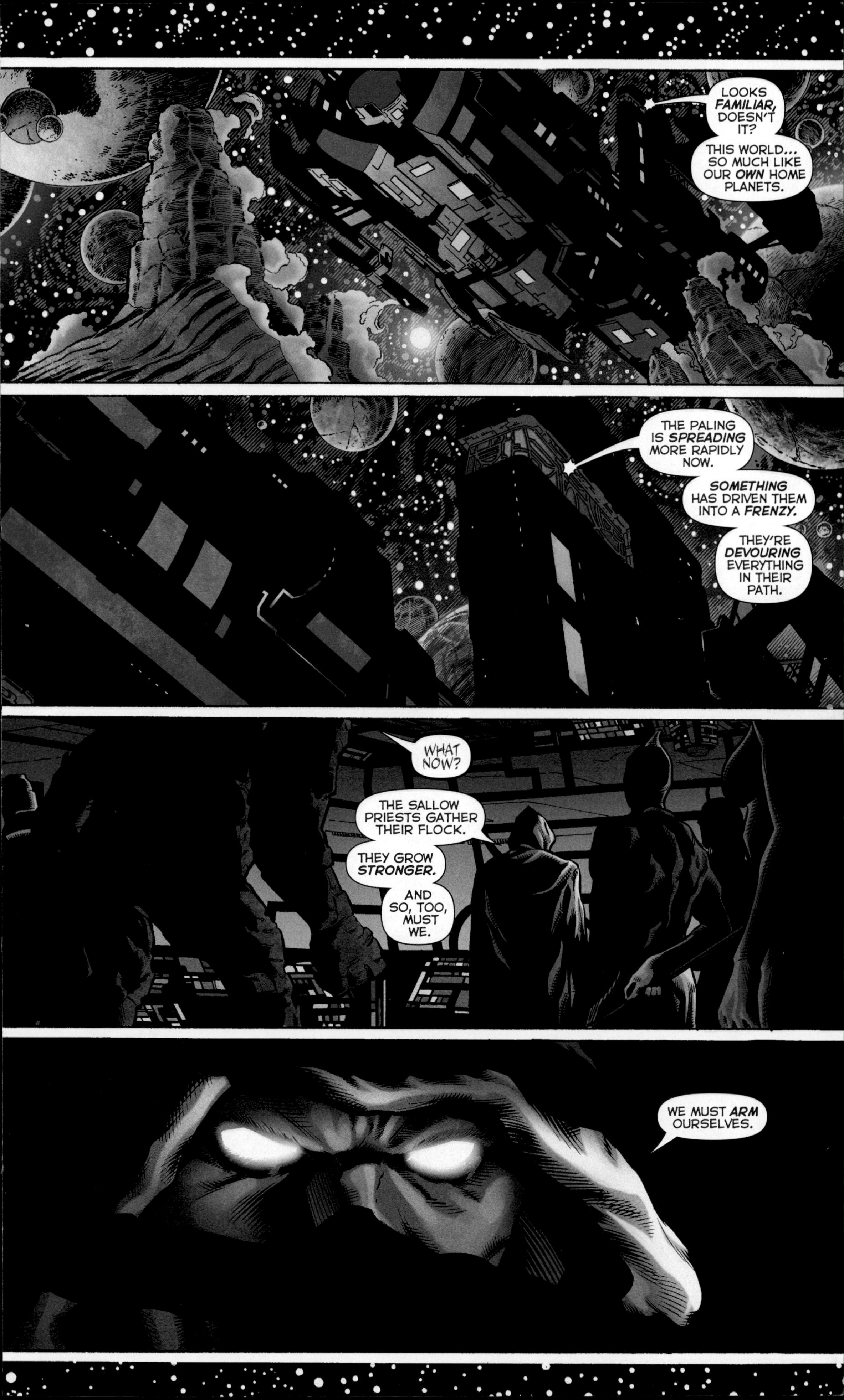
LOOKS FAMILIAR, DOESN'T IT?
THIS WORLD... SO MUCH LIKE OUR OWN HOME PLANETS.
THE PALING IS SPREADING MORE RAPIDLY NOW.
SOMETHING HAS DRIVEN THEM INTO A FRENZY.
THEY'RE DEVOURING EVERYTHING IN THEIR PATH.
WHAT NOW?
THE SALLOW PRIESTS GATHER THEIR FLOCK.
THEY GROW STRONGER.
AND SO, TOO, MUST WE.
WE MUST ARM OURSELVES.

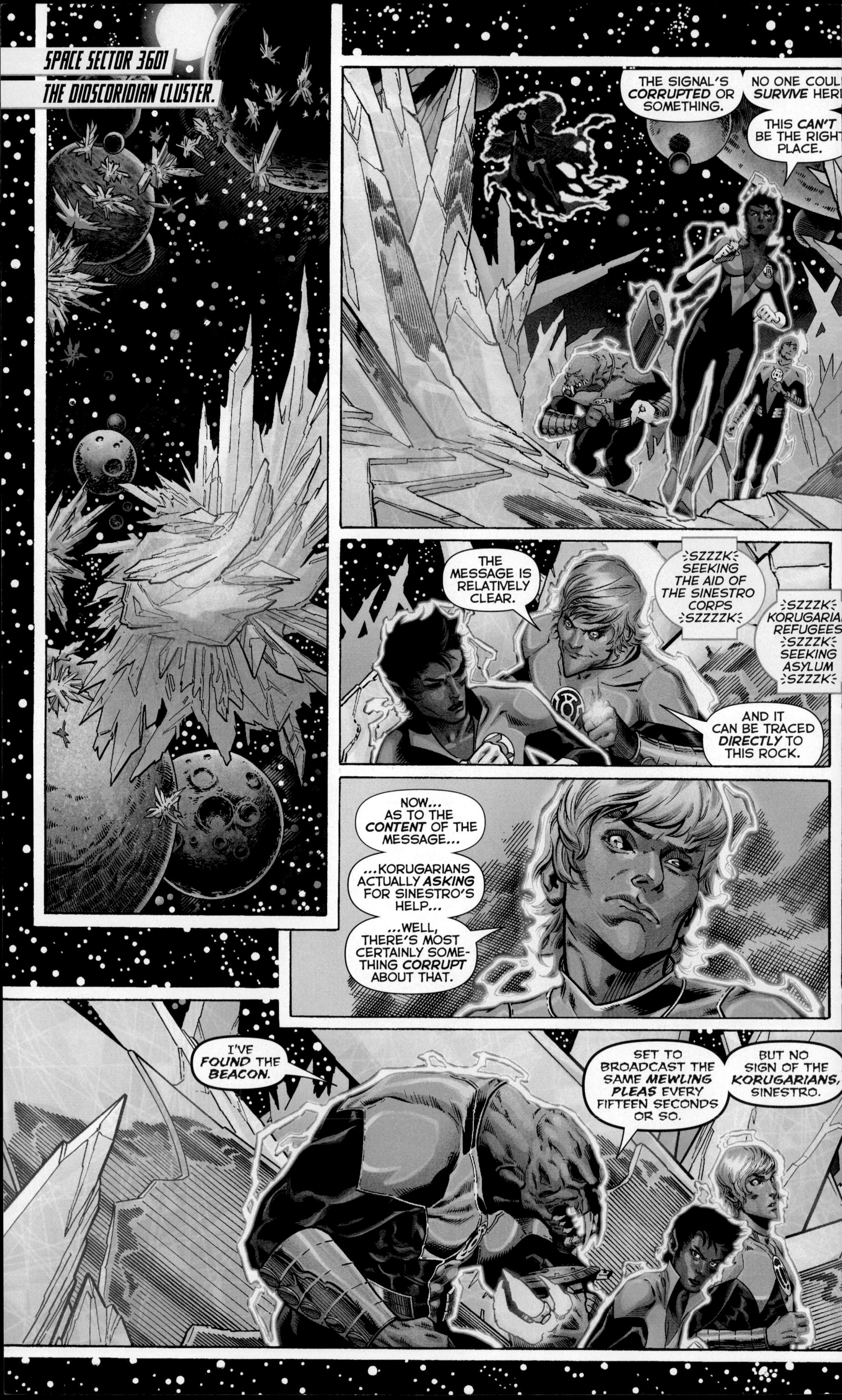
SPACE SECTOR 3601
THE DIOSCORIDIAN CLUSTER.
THE SIGNAL'S CORRUPTED OR SOMETHING.
NO ONE COULD SURVIVE HERE
THIS CAN'T BE THE RIGHT PLACE.
THE MESSAGE IS RELATIVELY CLEAR.
SZZZK SEEKING THE AID OF THE SINESTRO CORPS SZZZZK
SZZZK KORUGARIAN REFUGEES SZZZK SEEKING ASYLUM SZZZK
AND IT CAN BE TRACED DIRECTLY TO THIS ROCK.
NOW... AS TO THE CONTENT OF THE MESSAGE...
...KORUGARIANS ACTUALLY ASKING FOR SINESTRO'S HELP...
...WELL, THERE'S MOST CERTAINLY SOMETHING CORRUPT ABOUT THAT.
I'VE FOUND THE BEACON.
SET TO BROADCAST THE SAME MEWLING PLEAS EVERY FIFTEEN SECONDS OR SO.
BUT NO SIGN OF THE KORUGARIANS, SINESTRO.

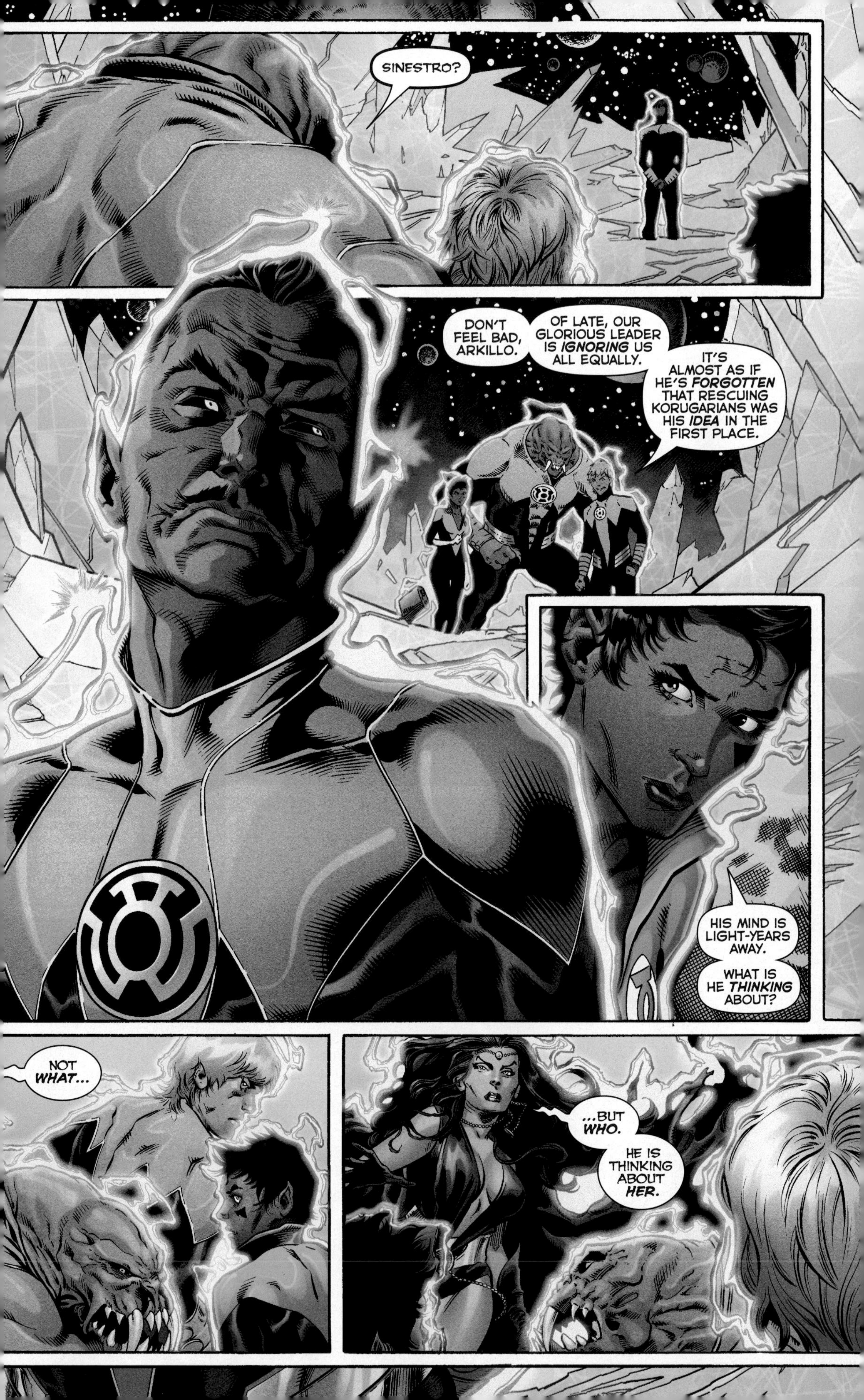

SINESTRO?
DON'T FEEL BAD, ARKILLO.
OF LATE, OUR GLORIOUS LEADER IS *IGNORING* US ALL EQUALLY.
IT'S ALMOST AS IF HE'S *FORGOTTEN* THAT RESCUING KORUGARIANS WAS HIS *IDEA* IN THE FIRST PLACE.
HIS MIND IS LIGHT-YEARS AWAY.
WHAT IS HE *THINKING* ABOUT?
NOT *WHAT*...
...BUT *WHO*.
HE IS THINKING ABOUT *HER*.

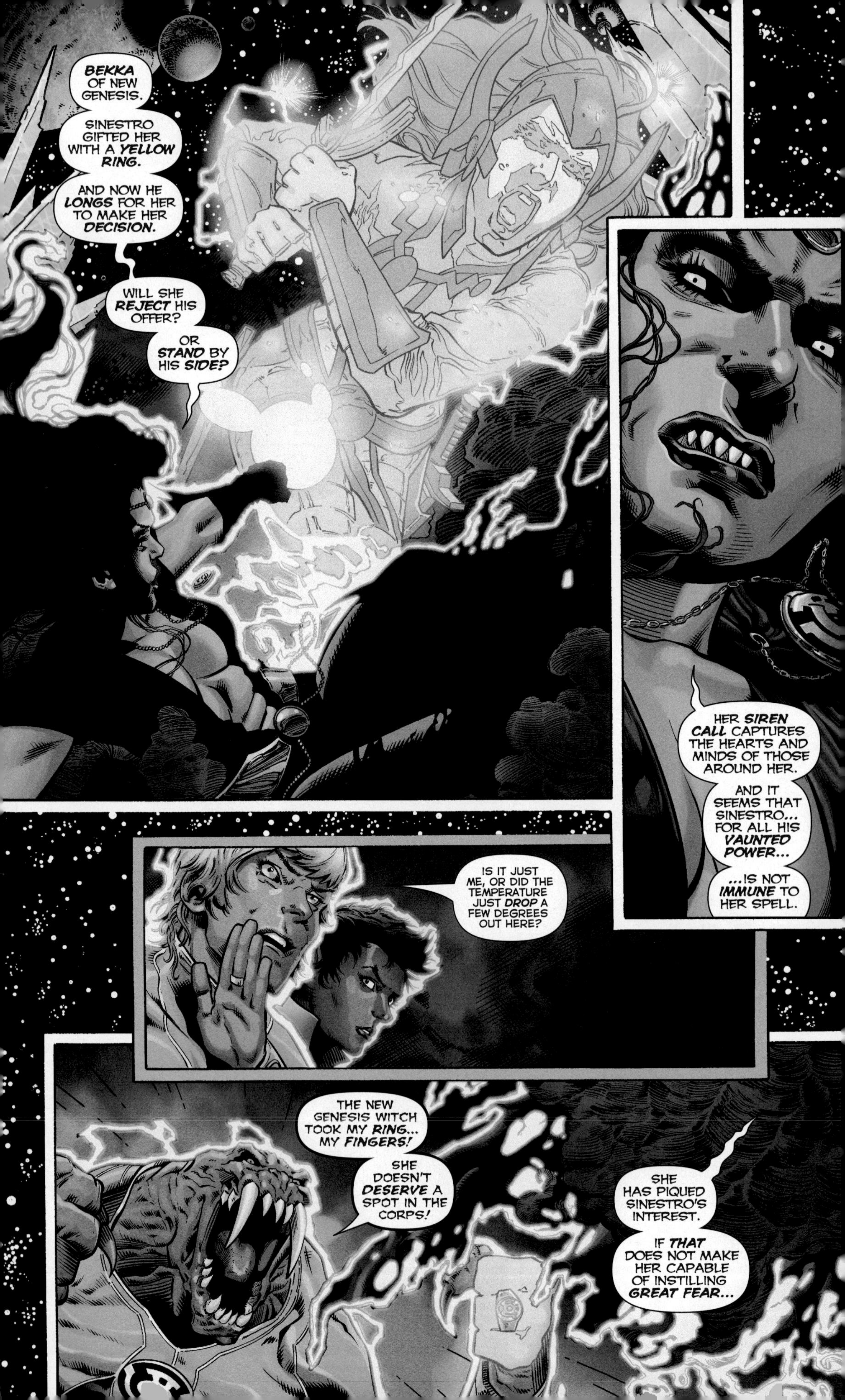
BEKKA OF NEW GENESIS.
SINESTRO GIFTED HER WITH A YELLOW RING.
AND NOW HE LONGS FOR HER TO MAKE HER DECISION.
WILL SHE REJECT HIS OFFER?
OR STAND BY HIS SIDE?
HER SIREN CALL CAPTURES THE HEARTS AND MINDS OF THOSE AROUND HER.
AND IT SEEMS THAT SINESTRO... FOR ALL HIS VAUNTED POWER...
...IS NOT IMMUNE TO HER SPELL.
IS IT JUST ME, OR DID THE TEMPERATURE JUST DROP A FEW DEGREES OUT HERE?
THE NEW GENESIS WITCH TOOK MY RING... MY FINGERS!
SHE DOESN'T DESERVE A SPOT IN THE CORPS!
SHE HAS PIQUED SINESTRO'S INTEREST.
IF THAT DOES NOT MAKE HER CAPABLE OF INSTILLING GREAT FEAR...

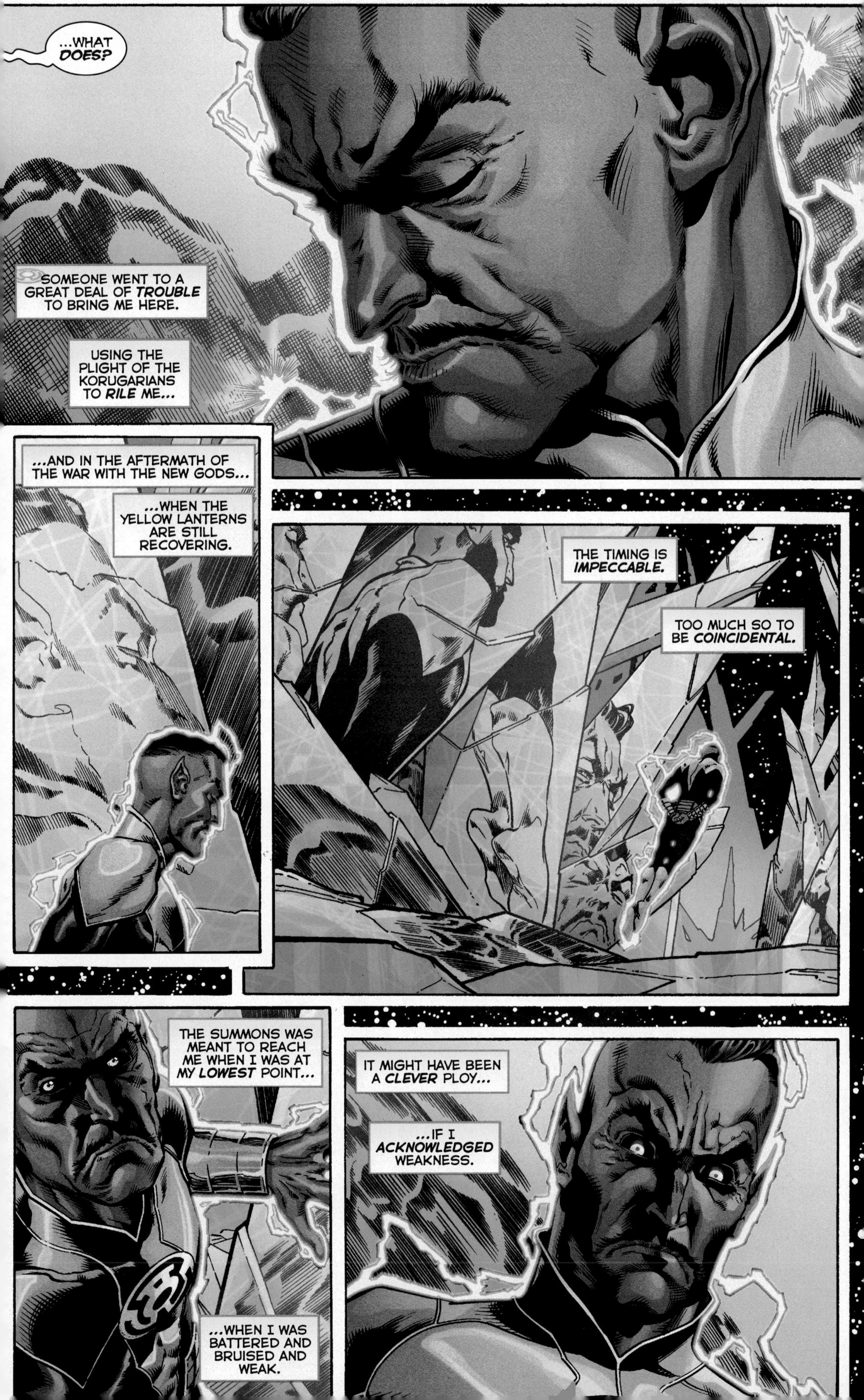
...WHAT DOES?
SOMEONE WENT TO A GREAT DEAL OF TROUBLE TO BRING ME HERE.
USING THE PLIGHT OF THE KORUGARIANS TO RILE ME...
...AND IN THE AFTERMATH OF THE WAR WITH THE NEW GODS...
...WHEN THE YELLOW LANTERNS ARE STILL RECOVERING.
THE TIMING IS IMPECCABLE.
TOO MUCH SO TO BE COINCIDENTAL.
THE SUMMONS WAS MEANT TO REACH ME WHEN I WAS AT MY LOWEST POINT...
...WHEN I WAS BATTERED AND BRUISED AND WEAK.
IT MIGHT HAVE BEEN A CLEVER PLOY...
...IF I ACKNOWLEDGED WEAKNESS.

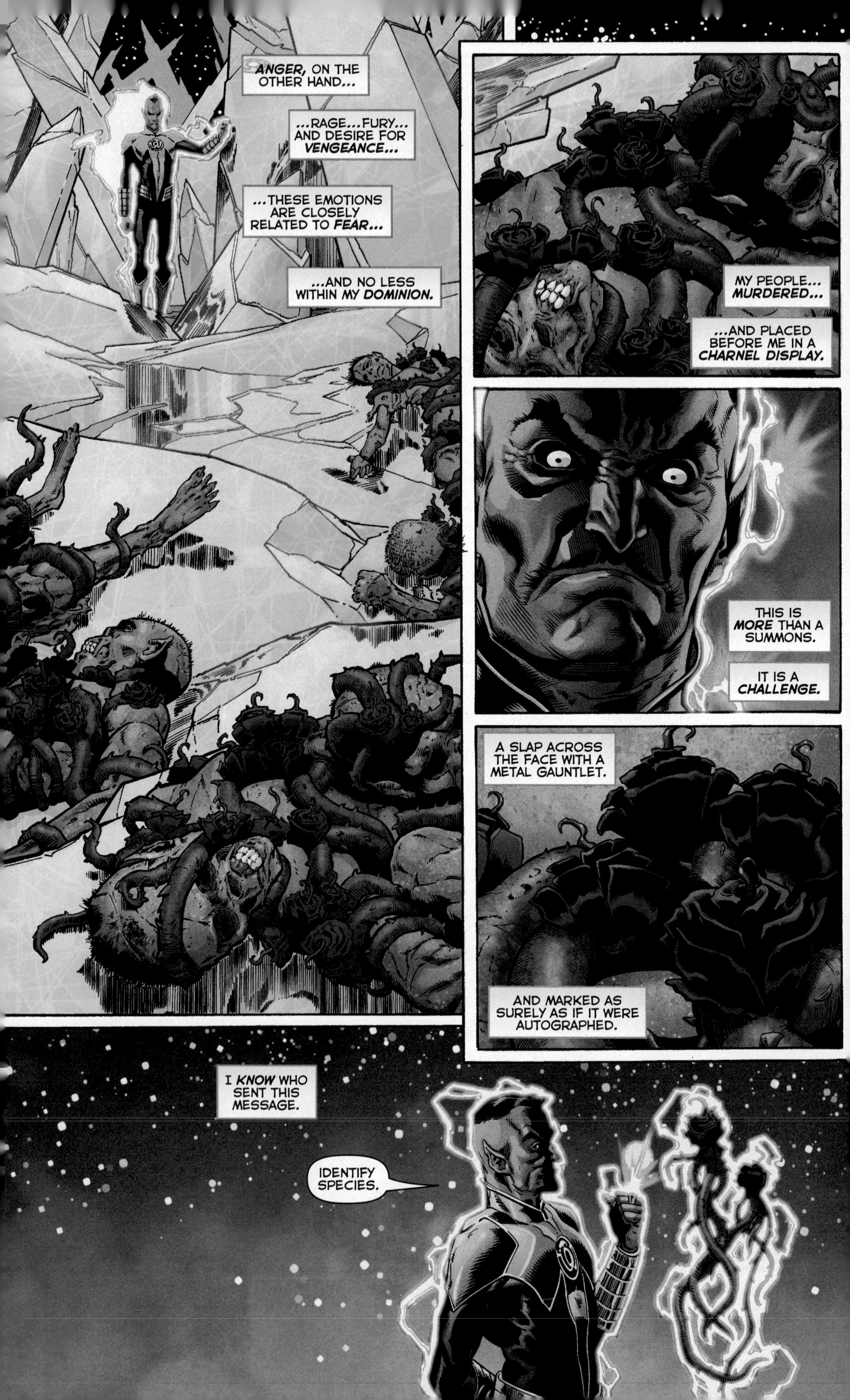
ANGER, ON THE OTHER HAND...
...RAGE...FURY... AND DESIRE FOR VENGEANCE...
...THESE EMOTIONS ARE CLOSELY RELATED TO FEAR...
...AND NO LESS WITHIN MY DOMINION.
MY PEOPLE... MURDERED...
...AND PLACED BEFORE ME IN A CHARNEL DISPLAY.
THIS IS MORE THAN A SUMMONS.
IT IS A CHALLENGE.
A SLAP ACROSS THE FACE WITH A METAL GAUNTLET.
AND MARKED AS SURELY AS IF IT WERE AUTOGRAPHED.
I KNOW WHO SENT THIS MESSAGE.
IDENTIFY SPECIES.

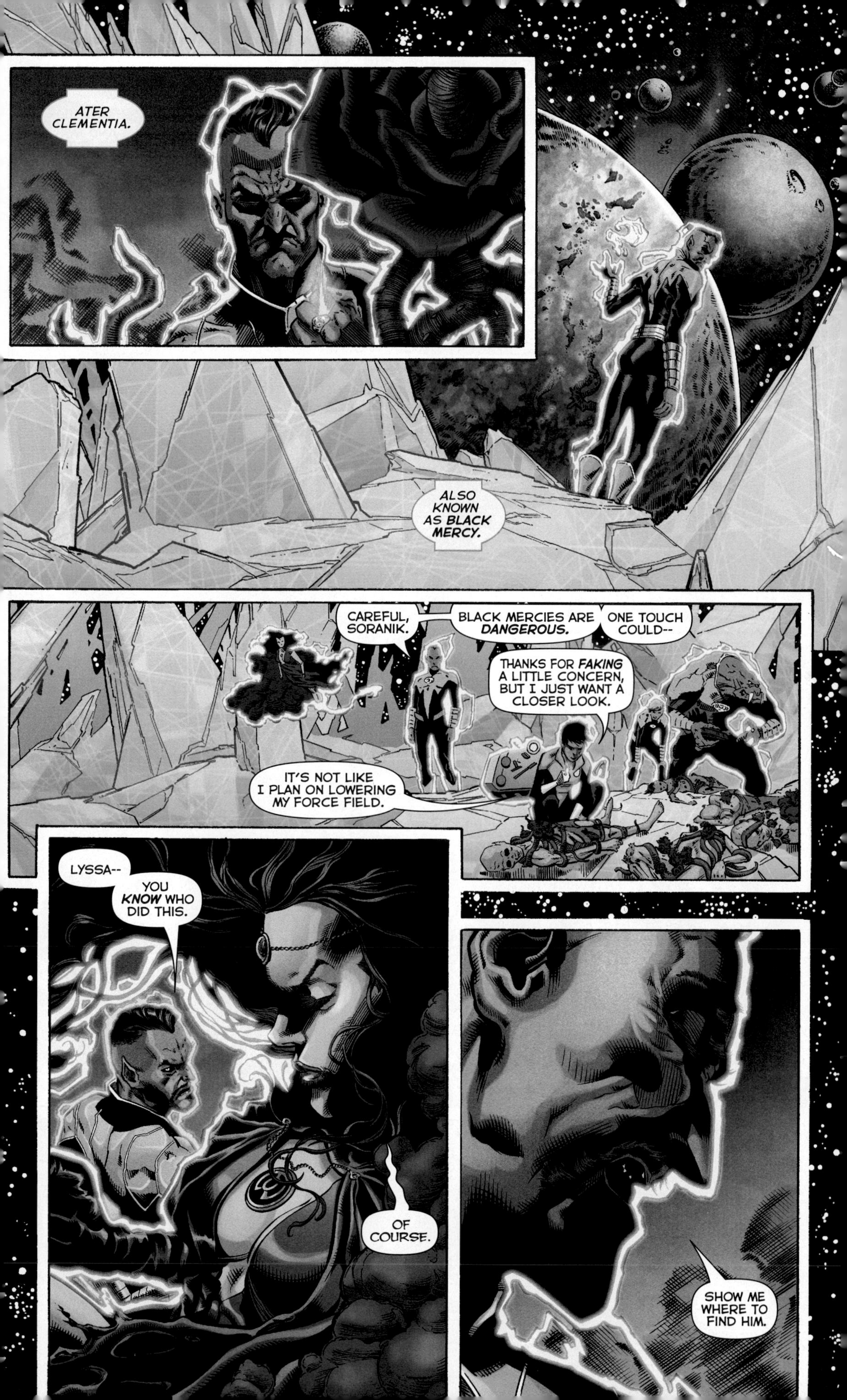
ATER CLEMENTIA.
ALSO KNOWN AS BLACK MERCY.
CAREFUL, SORANIK.
BLACK MERCIES ARE DANGEROUS.
ONE TOUCH COULD--
THANKS FOR FAKING A LITTLE CONCERN, BUT I JUST WANT A CLOSER LOOK.
IT'S NOT LIKE I PLAN ON LOWERING MY FORCE FIELD.
LYSSA--
YOU KNOW WHO DID THIS.
OF COURSE.
SHOW ME WHERE TO FIND HIM.

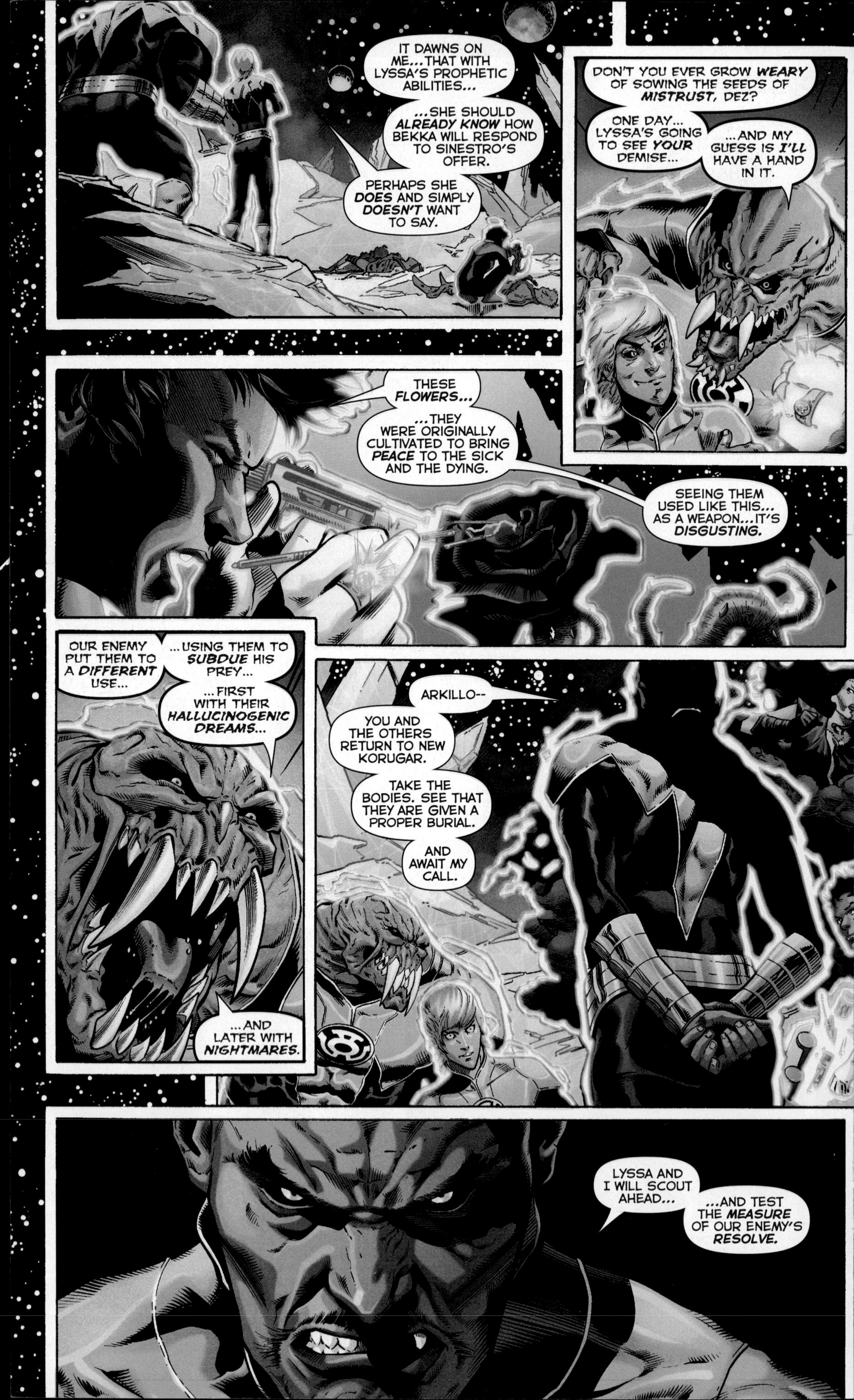
IT DAWNS ON ME...THAT WITH LYSSA'S PROPHETIC ABILITIES...
...SHE SHOULD ALREADY KNOW HOW BEKKA WILL RESPOND TO SINESTRO'S OFFER.
PERHAPS SHE DOES AND SIMPLY DOESN'T WANT TO SAY.
DON'T YOU EVER GROW WEARY OF SOWING THE SEEDS OF MISTRUST, DEZ?
ONE DAY... LYSSA'S GOING TO SEE YOUR DEMISE...
...AND MY GUESS IS I'LL HAVE A HAND IN IT.
THESE FLOWERS...
...THEY WERE ORIGINALLY CULTIVATED TO BRING PEACE TO THE SICK AND THE DYING.
SEEING THEM USED LIKE THIS... AS A WEAPON...IT'S DISGUSTING.
OUR ENEMY PUT THEM TO A DIFFERENT USE...
...USING THEM TO SUBDUE HIS PREY...
...FIRST WITH THEIR HALLUCINOGENIC DREAMS...
...AND LATER WITH NIGHTMARES.
ARKILLO--
YOU AND THE OTHERS RETURN TO NEW KORUGAR.
TAKE THE BODIES. SEE THAT THEY ARE GIVEN A PROPER BURIAL.
AND AWAIT MY CALL.
LYSSA AND I WILL SCOUT AHEAD...
...AND TEST THE MEASURE OF OUR ENEMY'S RESOLVE.

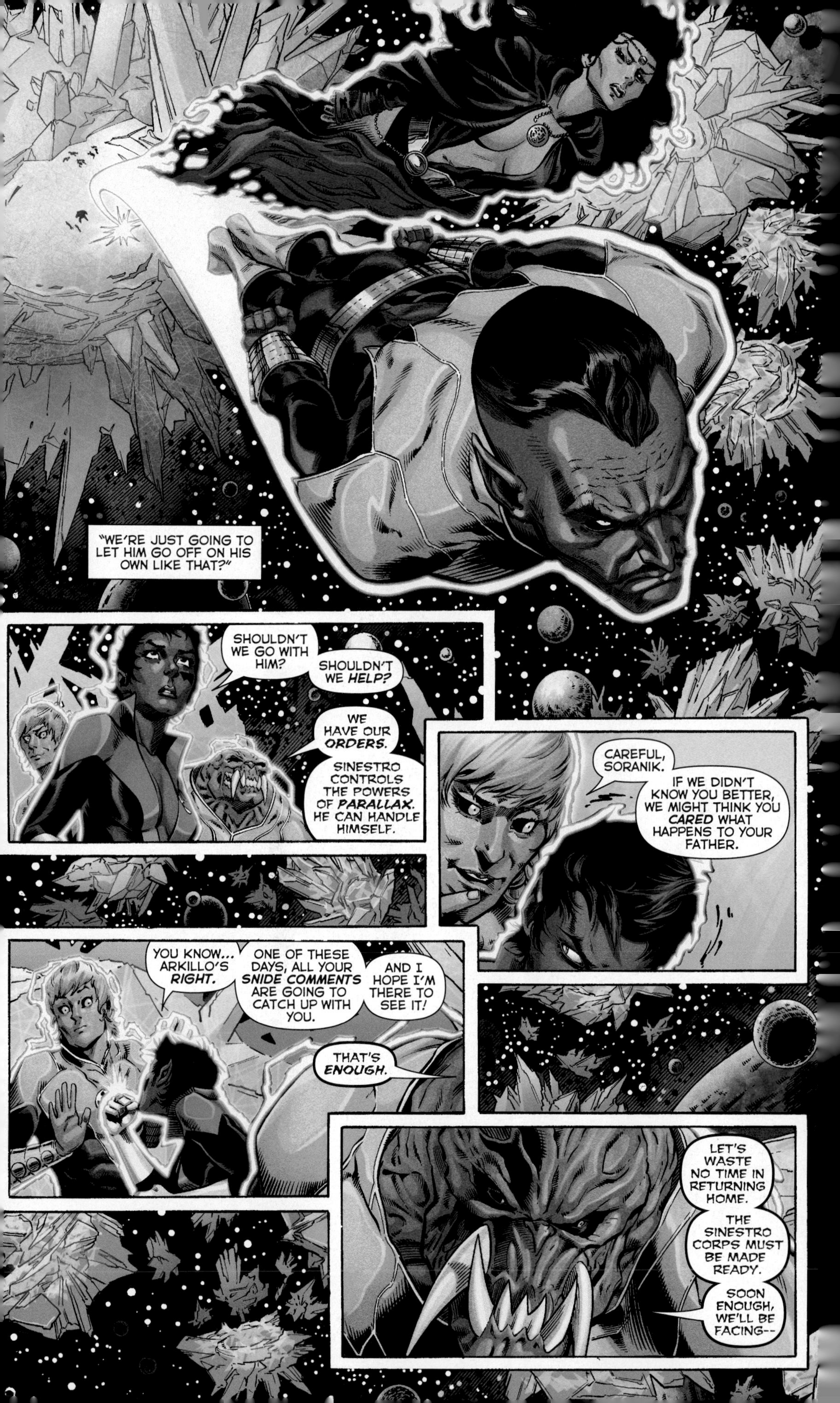
"WE'RE JUST GOING TO LET HIM GO OFF ON HIS OWN LIKE THAT?"
SHOULDN'T WE GO WITH HIM?
SHOULDN'T WE HELP?
WE HAVE OUR ORDERS.
SINESTRO CONTROLS THE POWERS OF PARALLAX. HE CAN HANDLE HIMSELF.
CAREFUL, SORANIK.
IF WE DIDN'T KNOW YOU BETTER, WE MIGHT THINK YOU CARED WHAT HAPPENS TO YOUR FATHER.
YOU KNOW... ARKILLO'S RIGHT.
ONE OF THESE DAYS, ALL YOUR SNIDE COMMENTS ARE GOING TO CATCH UP WITH YOU.
AND I HOPE I'M THERE TO SEE IT!
THAT'S ENOUGH.
LET'S WASTE NO TIME IN RETURNING HOME.
THE SINESTRO CORPS MUST BE MADE READY.
SOON ENOUGH, WE'LL BE FACING--

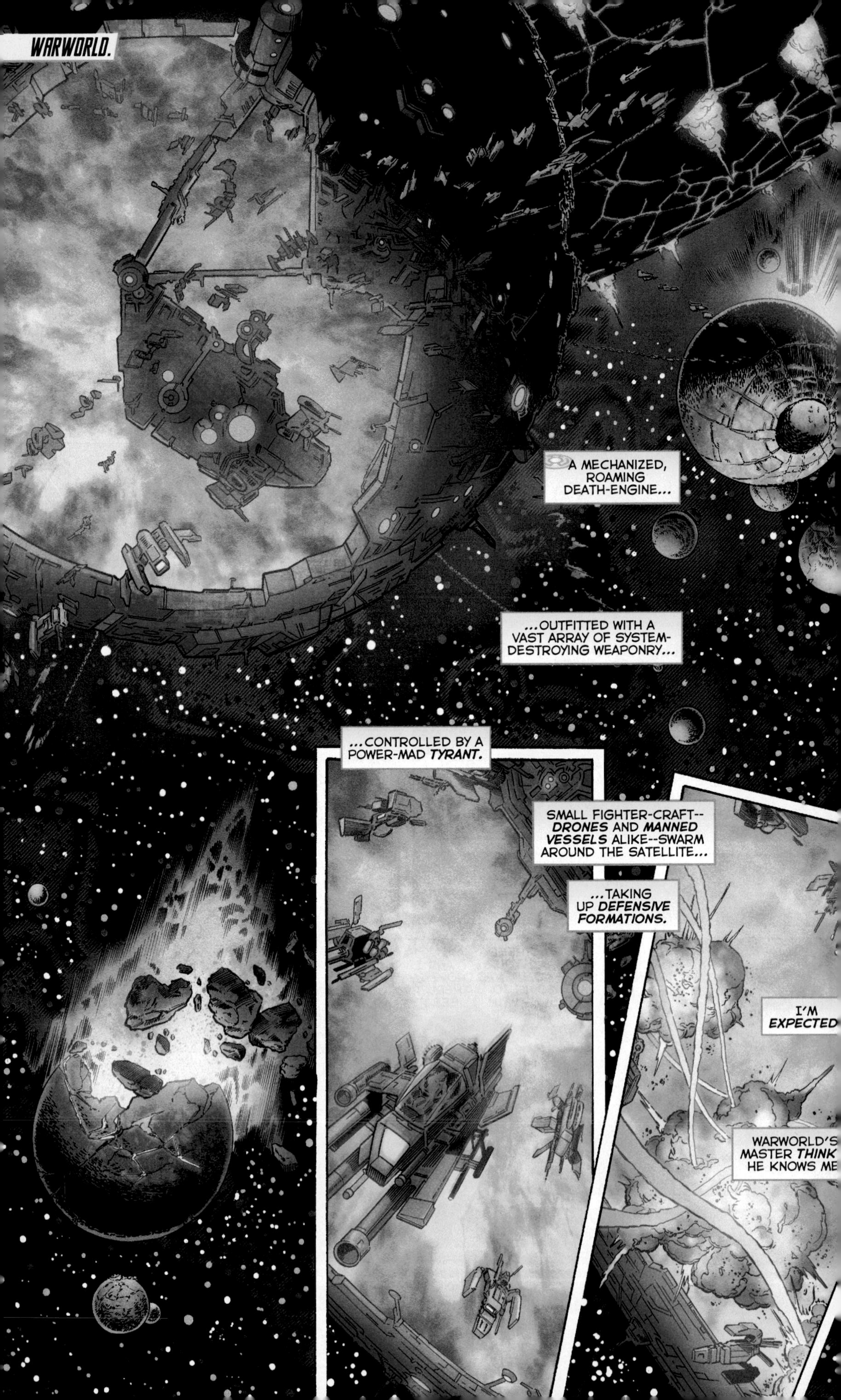
WARWORLD.
A MECHANIZED, ROAMING DEATH-ENGINE...
...OUTFITTED WITH A VAST ARRAY OF SYSTEM-DESTROYING WEAPONRY...
...CONTROLLED BY A POWER-MAD TYRANT.
SMALL FIGHTER-CRAFT-- DRONES AND MANNED VESSELS ALIKE--SWARM AROUND THE SATELLITE...
...TAKING UP DEFENSIVE FORMATIONS.
I'M EXPECTED
WARWORLD'S MASTER THINK HE KNOWS ME

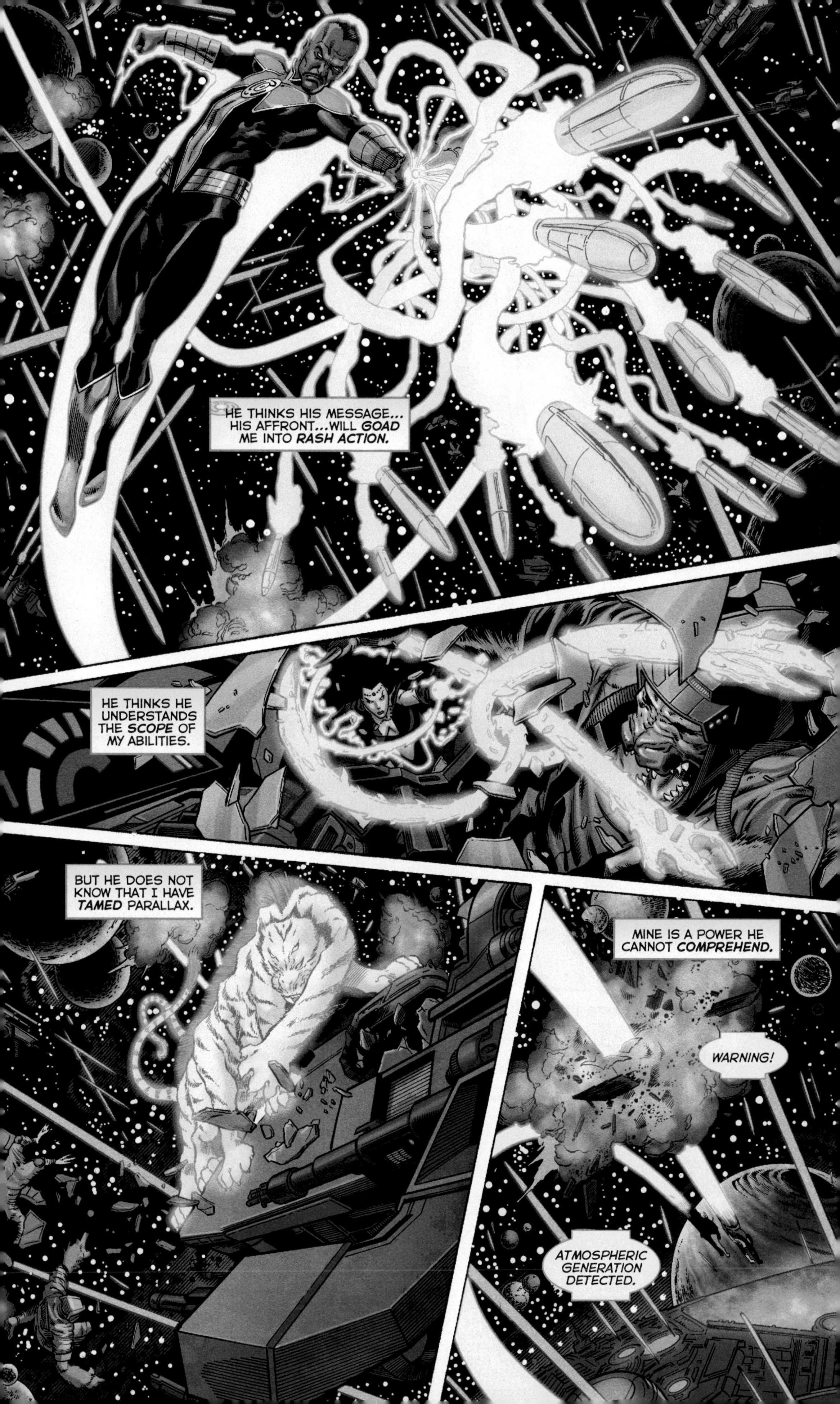
HE THINKS HIS MESSAGE... HIS AFFRONT...WILL GOAD ME INTO RASH ACTION.
HE THINKS HE UNDERSTANDS THE SCOPE OF MY ABILITIES.
BUT HE DOES NOT KNOW THAT I HAVE TAMED PARALLAX.
MINE IS A POWER HE CANNOT COMPREHEND.
WARNING!
ATMOSPHERIC GENERATION DETECTED.

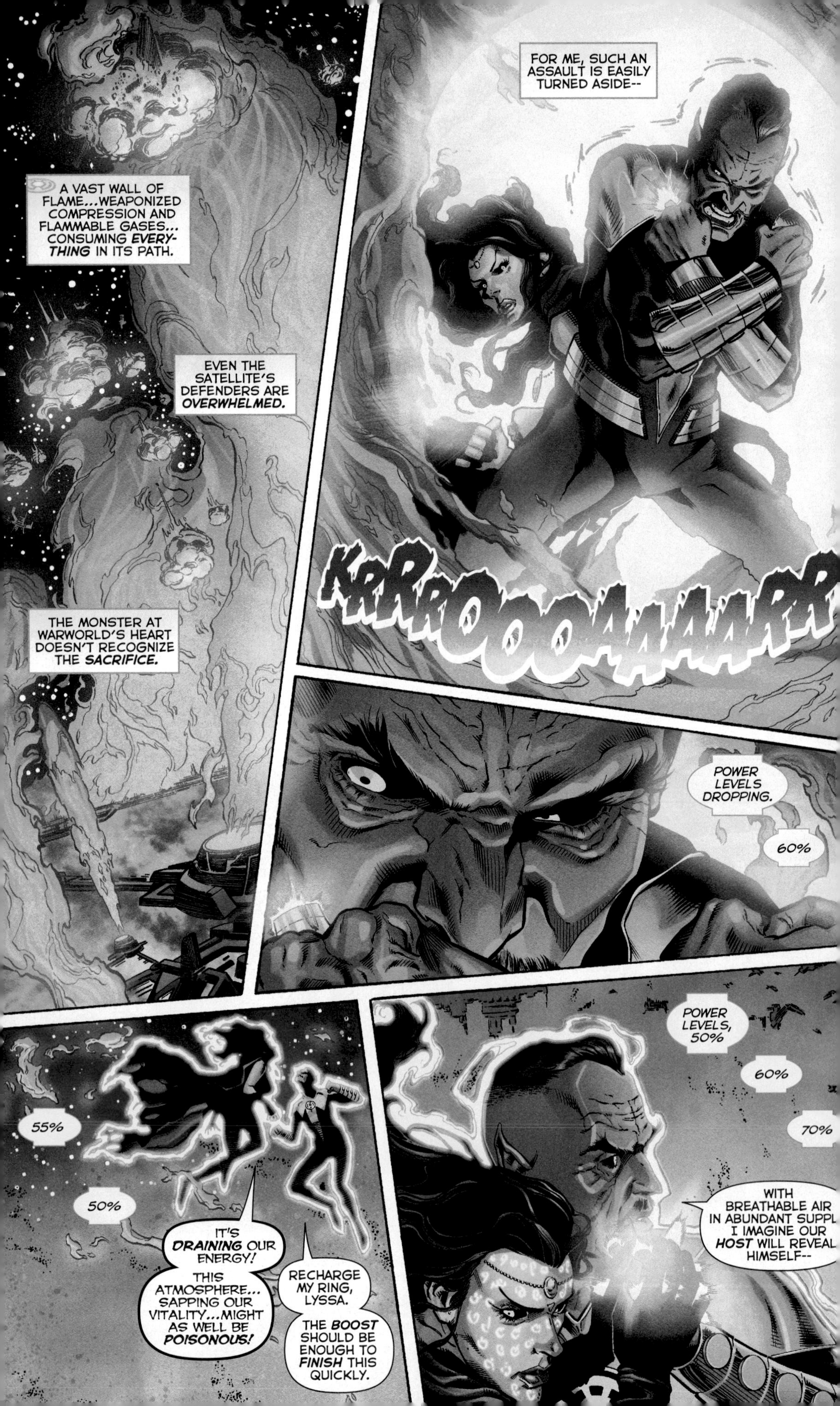
A VAST WALL OF FLAME...WEAPONIZED COMPRESSION AND FLAMMABLE GASES... CONSUMING EVERY-THING IN ITS PATH.
EVEN THE SATELLITE'S DEFENDERS ARE OVERWHELMED.
THE MONSTER AT WARWORLD'S HEART DOESN'T RECOGNIZE THE SACRIFICE.
FOR ME, SUCH AN ASSAULT IS EASILY TURNED ASIDE--
KRRROOOAAAARR
POWER LEVELS DROPPING.
60%
55%
50%
IT'S DRAINING OUR ENERGY!
THIS ATMOSPHERE... SAPPING OUR VITALITY...MIGHT AS WELL BE POISONOUS!
RECHARGE MY RING, LYSSA.
THE BOOST SHOULD BE ENOUGH TO FINISH THIS QUICKLY.
POWER LEVELS, 50%
60%
70%
WITH BREATHABLE AIR IN ABUNDANT SUPPL
I IMAGINE OUR HOST WILL REVEAL HIMSELF--

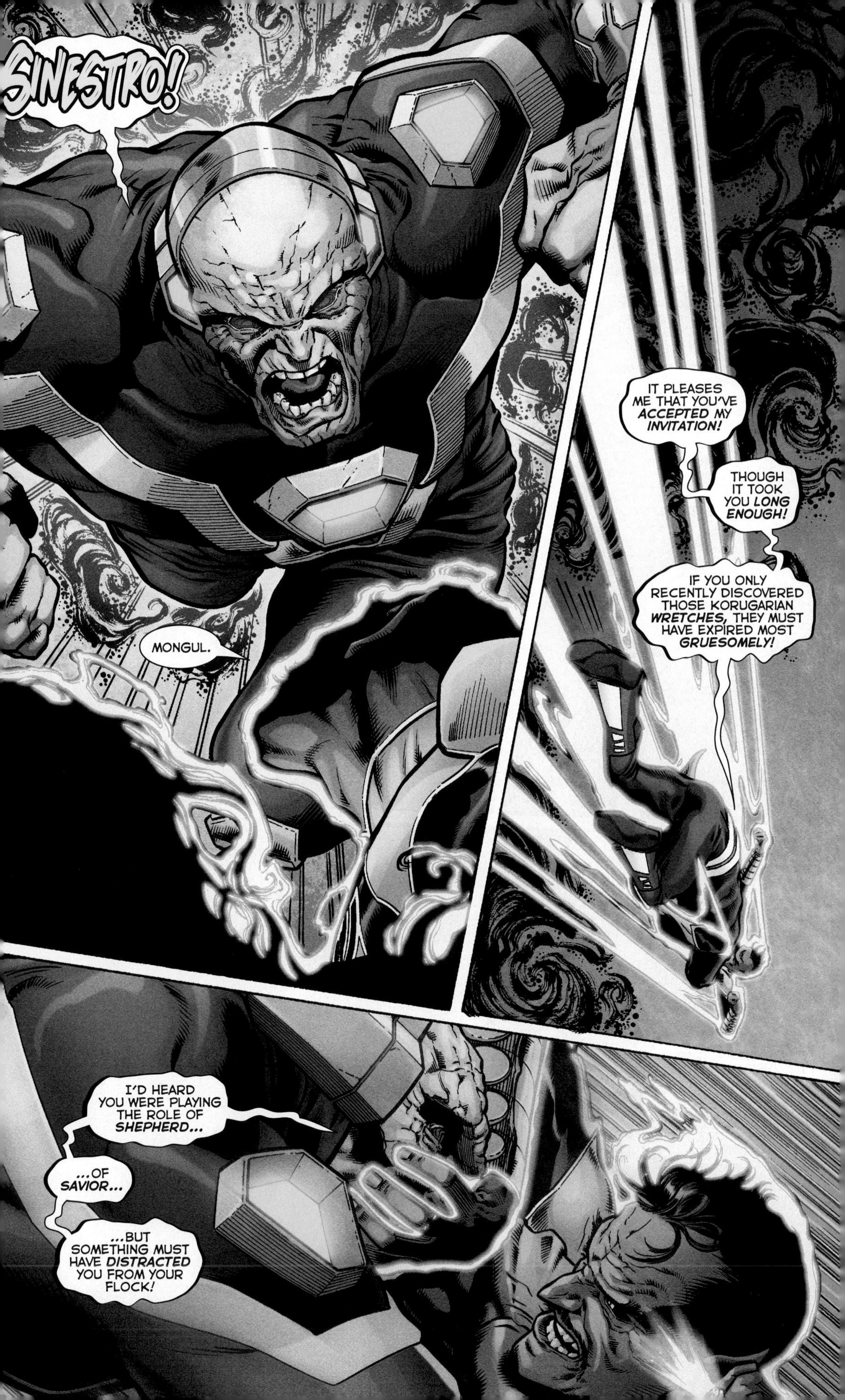
SINESTRO!
MONGUL.
IT PLEASES ME THAT YOU'VE ACCEPTED MY INVITATION!
THOUGH IT TOOK YOU LONG ENOUGH!
IF YOU ONLY RECENTLY DISCOVERED THOSE KORUGARIAN WRETCHES, THEY MUST HAVE EXPIRED MOST GRUESOMELY!
I'D HEARD YOU WERE PLAYING THE ROLE OF SHEPHERD...
...OF SAVIOR...
...BUT SOMETHING MUST HAVE DISTRACTED YOU FROM YOUR FLOCK!

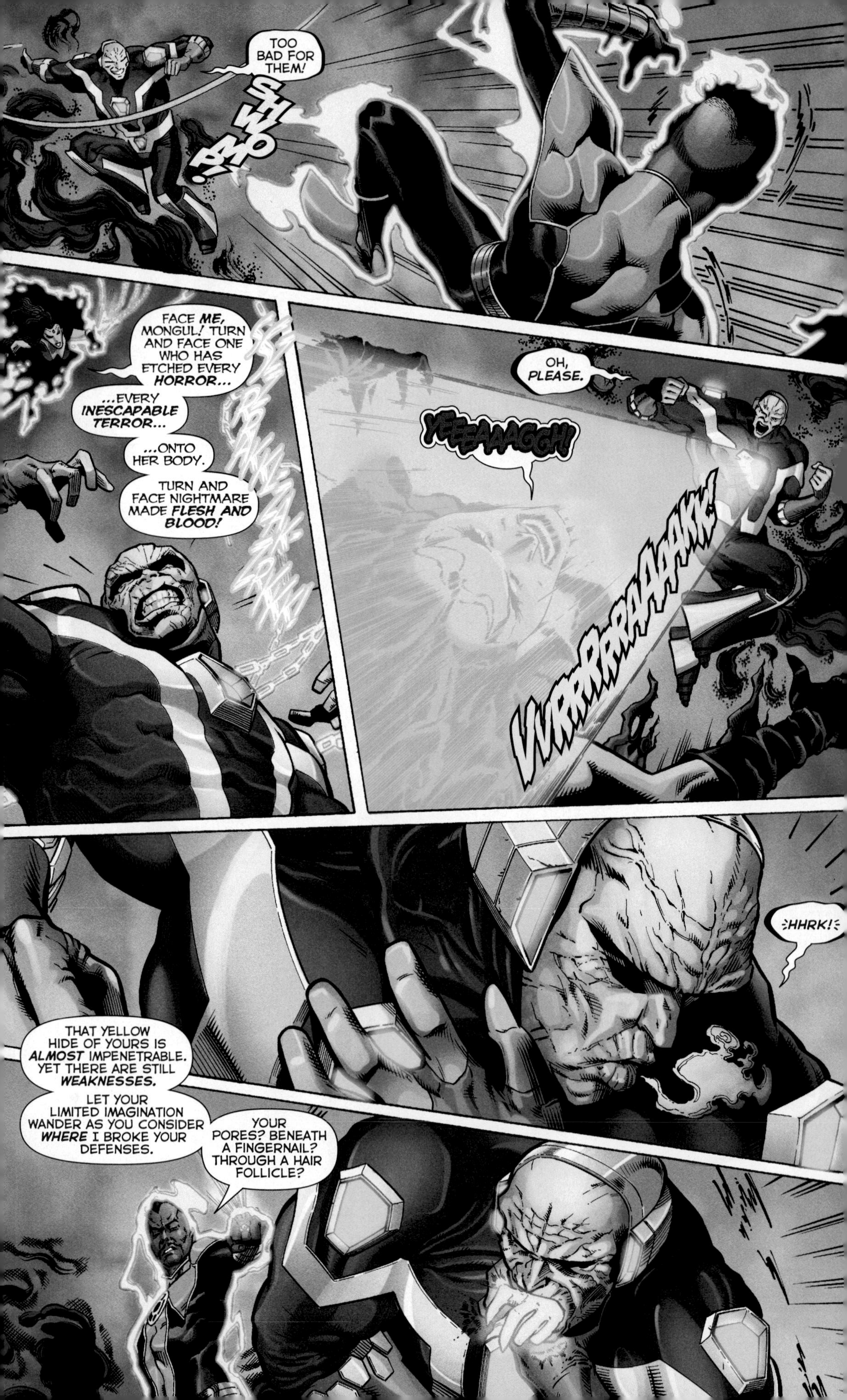
TOO BAD FOR THEM!
SHWOMP!
FACE ME, MONGUL! TURN AND FACE ONE WHO HAS ETCHED EVERY HORROR...
...EVERY INESCAPABLE TERROR...
...ONTO HER BODY.
TURN AND FACE NIGHTMARE MADE FLESH AND BLOOD!
OH, PLEASE.
YEEEAAAAGGH!
VVRRRRRAAAAKK!
HHRK!
THAT YELLOW HIDE OF YOURS IS ALMOST IMPENETRABLE. YET THERE ARE STILL WEAKNESSES.
LET YOUR LIMITED IMAGINATION WANDER AS YOU CONSIDER WHERE I BROKE YOUR DEFENSES.
YOUR PORES? BENEATH A FINGERNAIL? THROUGH A HAIR FOLLICLE?

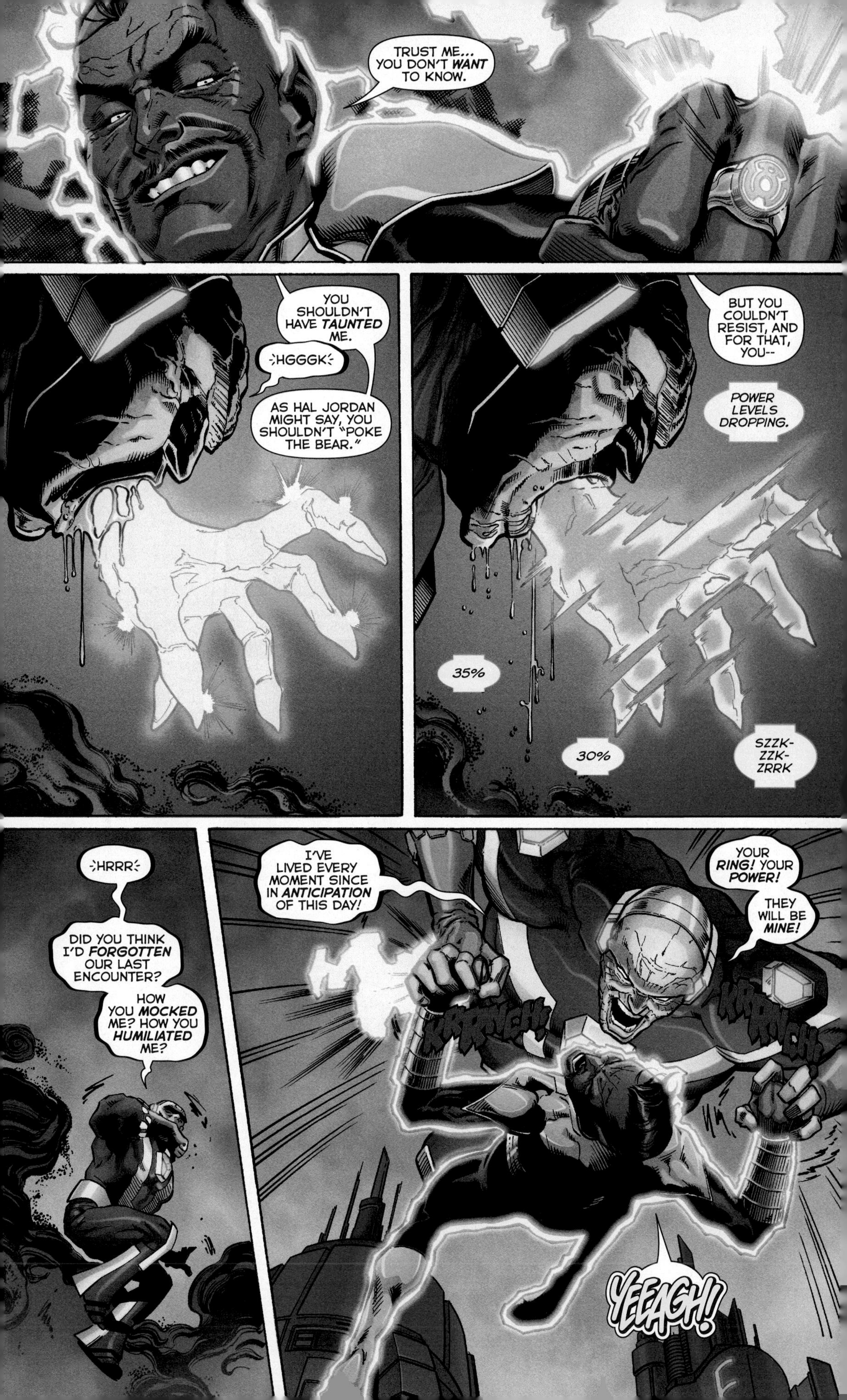

TRUST ME... YOU DON'T WANT TO KNOW.
YOU SHOULDN'T HAVE TAUNTED ME.
HGGGK
AS HAL JORDAN MIGHT SAY, YOU SHOULDN'T "POKE THE BEAR."
BUT YOU COULDN'T RESIST, AND FOR THAT, YOU--
POWER LEVELS DROPPING.
35%
30%
SZZK-ZZK-ZRRK
HRRR
DID YOU THINK I'D FORGOTTEN OUR LAST ENCOUNTER?
HOW YOU MOCKED ME? HOW YOU HUMILIATED ME?
I'VE LIVED EVERY MOMENT SINCE IN ANTICIPATION OF THIS DAY!
YOUR RING! YOUR POWER!
THEY WILL BE MINE!
KRRNCH!
KRRNCH!
YEEAGH!

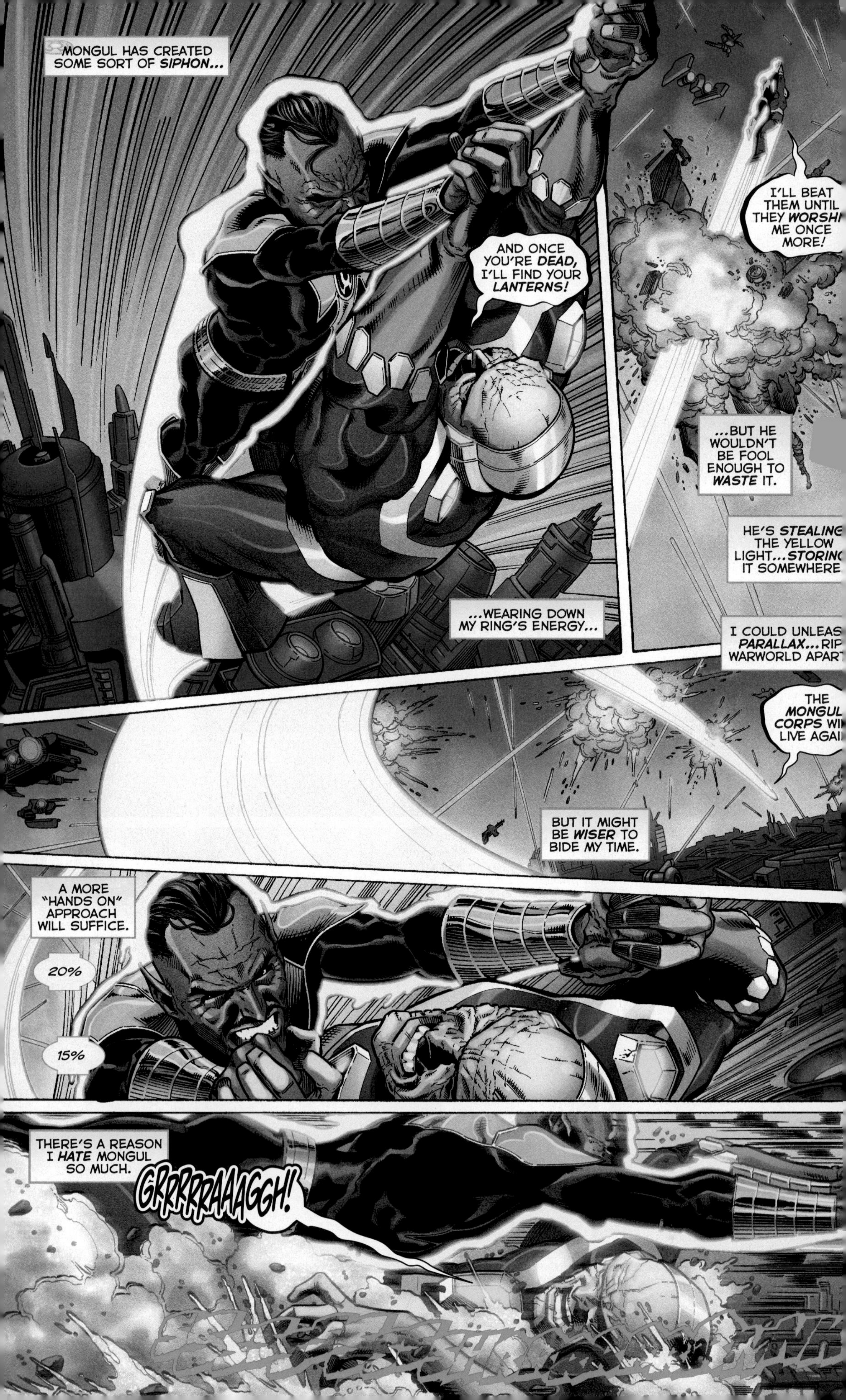
MONGUL HAS CREATED SOME SORT OF SIPHON...
AND ONCE YOU'RE DEAD, I'LL FIND YOUR LANTERNS!
...WEARING DOWN MY RING'S ENERGY...
I'LL BEAT THEM UNTIL THEY WORSHI ME ONCE MORE!
...BUT HE WOULDN'T BE FOOL ENOUGH TO WASTE IT.
HE'S STEALING THE YELLOW LIGHT...STORING IT SOMEWHERE
I COULD UNLEAS PARALLAX...RIP WARWORLD APART
THE MONGUL CORPS WI LIVE AGAI
BUT IT MIGHT BE WISER TO BIDE MY TIME.
A MORE "HANDS ON" APPROACH WILL SUFFICE.
20%
15%
THERE'S A REASON I HATE MONGUL SO MUCH.
GRRRRRAAAGGH!

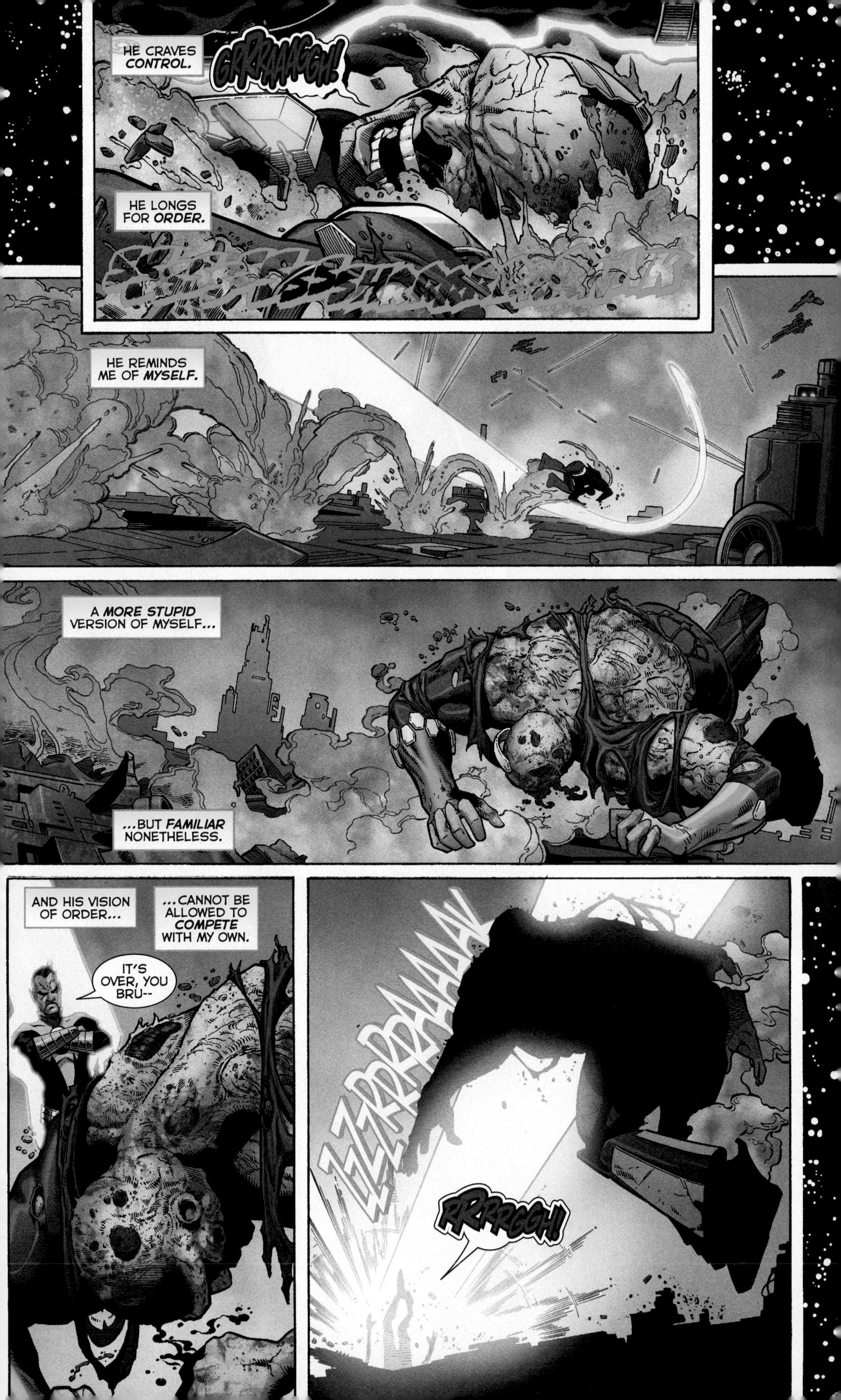

HE CRAVES CONTROL.
GRRRAAAGGH!
HE LONGS FOR ORDER.
HE REMINDS ME OF MYSELF.
A MORE STUPID VERSION OF MYSELF...
...BUT FAMILIAR NONETHELESS.
AND HIS VISION OF ORDER...
...CANNOT BE ALLOWED TO COMPETE WITH MY OWN.
IT'S OVER, YOU BRU--
RRRRGGH!

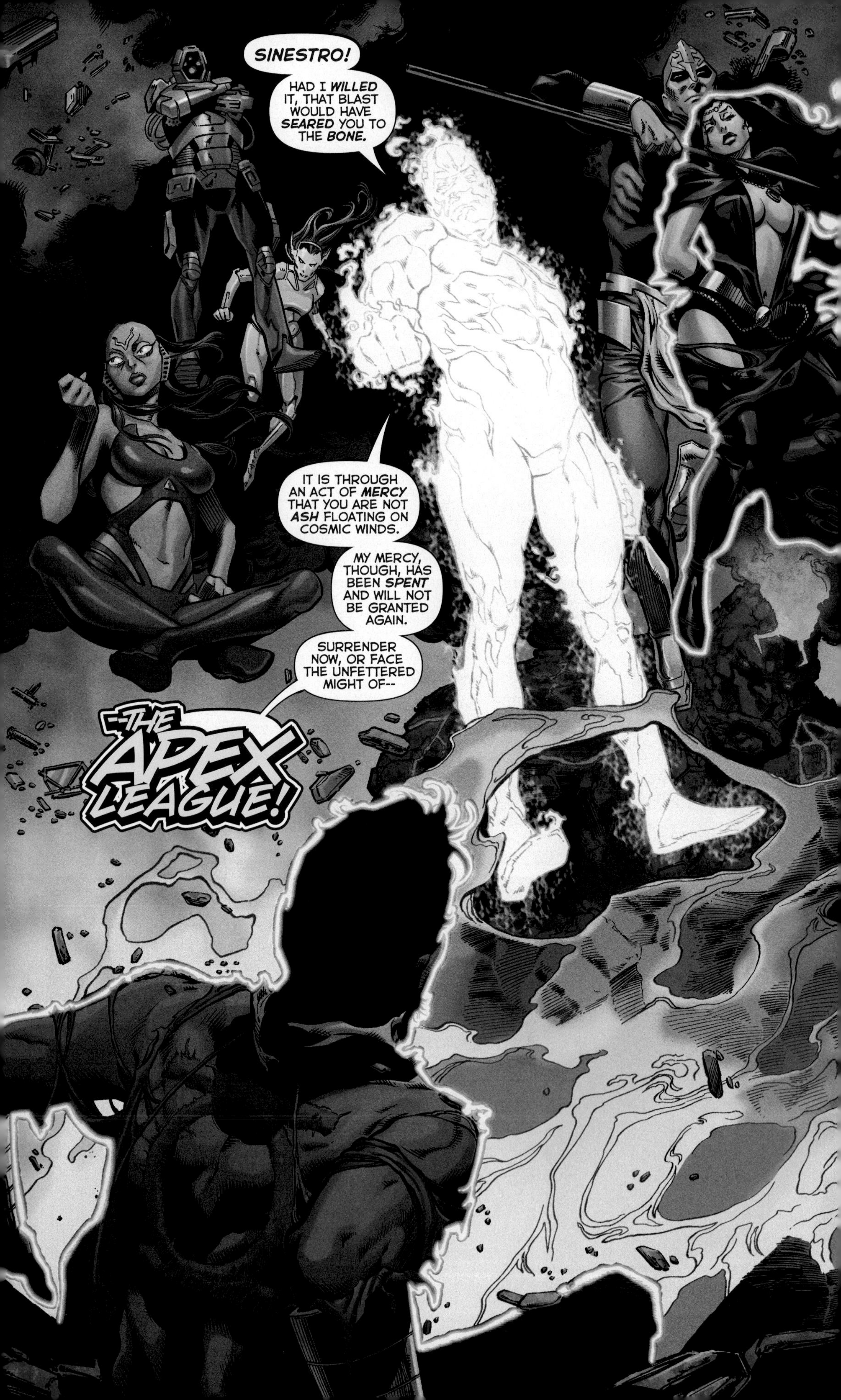
SINESTRO!
HAD I WILLED IT, THAT BLAST WOULD HAVE SEARED YOU TO THE BONE.
IT IS THROUGH AN ACT OF MERCY THAT YOU ARE NOT ASH FLOATING ON COSMIC WINDS.
MY MERCY, THOUGH, HAS BEEN SPENT AND WILL NOT BE GRANTED AGAIN.
SURRENDER NOW, OR FACE THE UNFETTERED MIGHT OF--
--THE APEX LEAGUE!

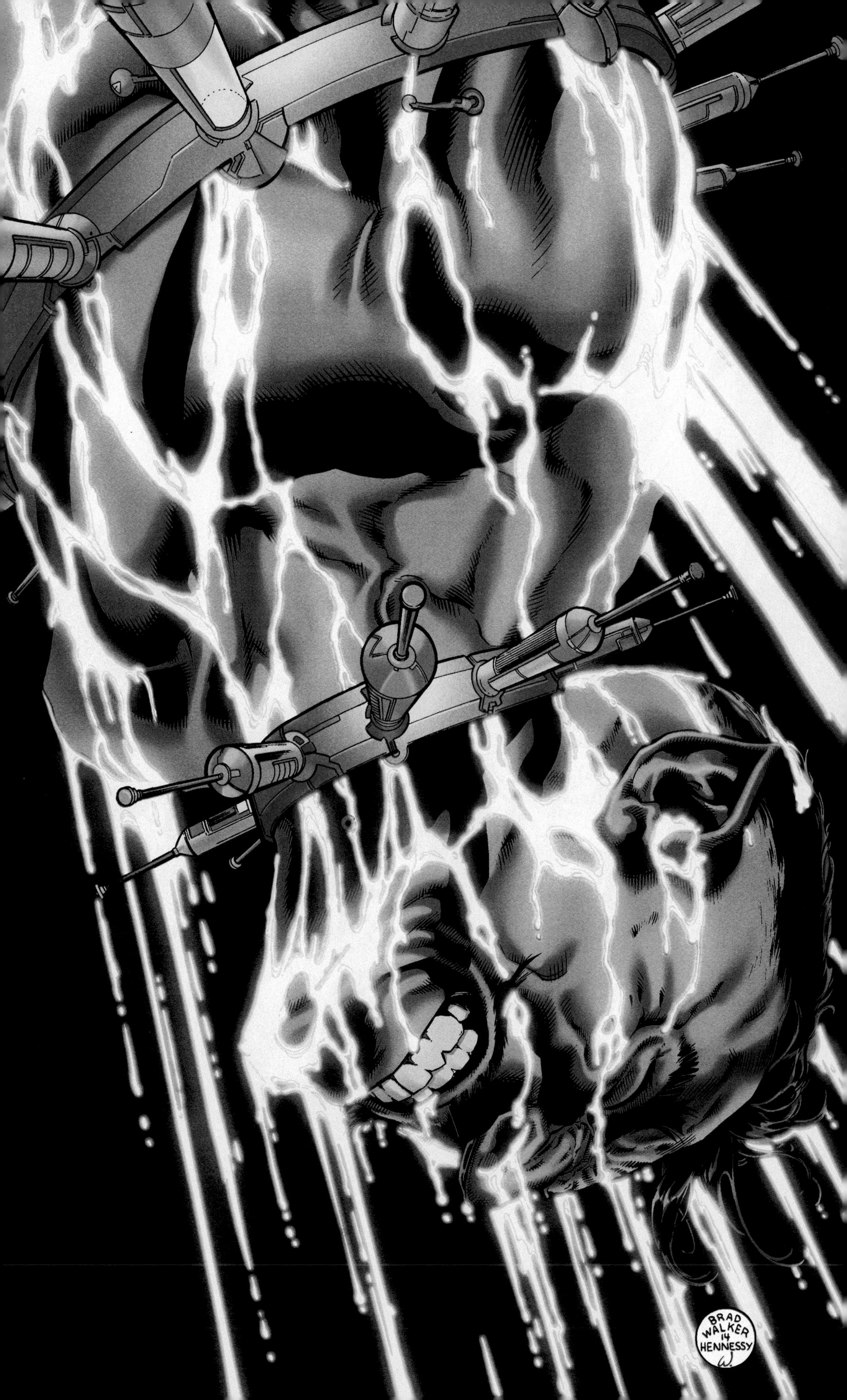
BRAD WALKER 14 HENNESSY

PRISONERS OF WARWORLD

CULLEN BUNN writer BRAD WALKER penciller ANDREW HENNESSY inker JASON WRIGHT colorist DAVE SHARPE letterer

cover art by BRAD WALKER, ANDREW HENNESSY & JASON WRIGHT

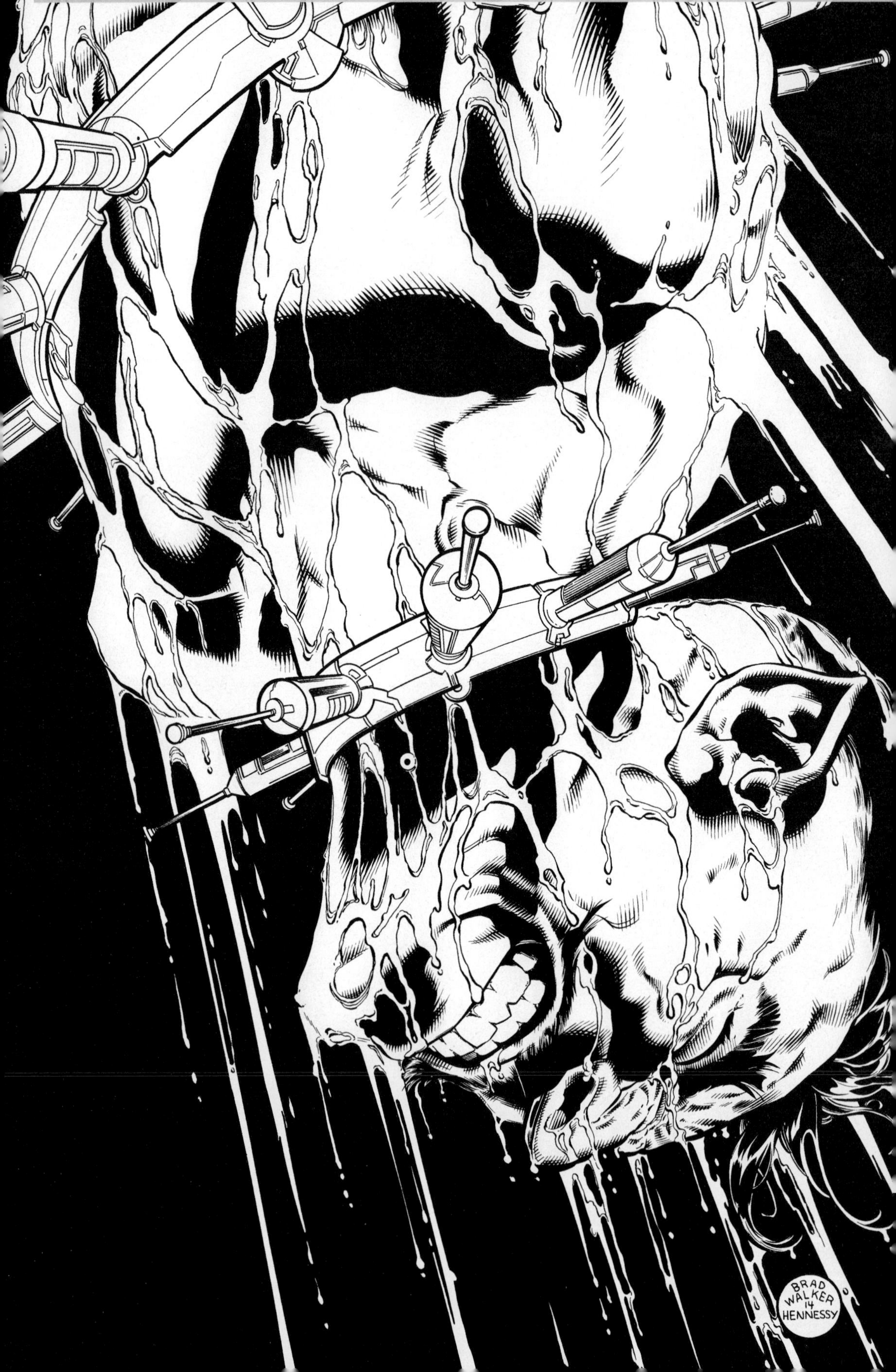
BRAD WALKER 14 HENNESSY

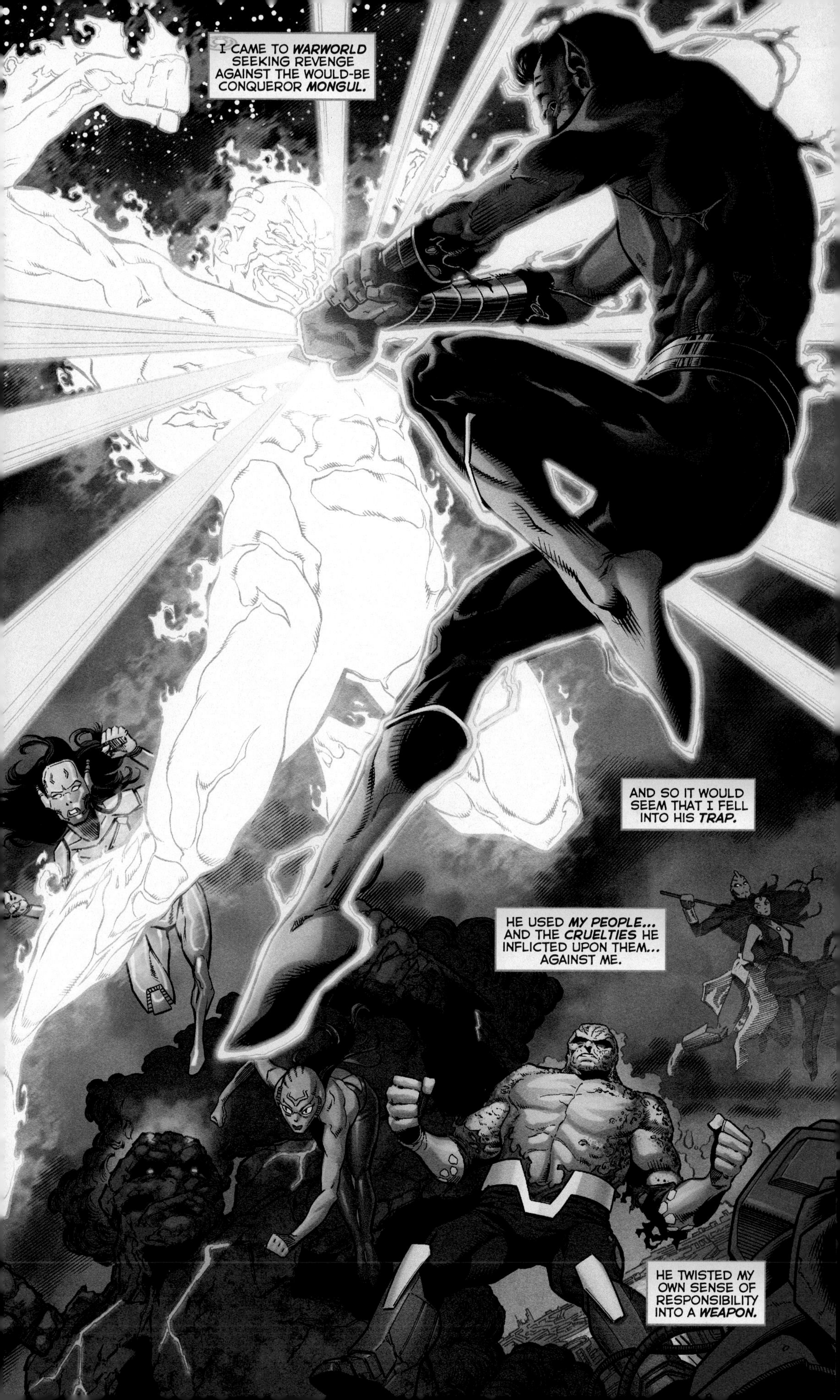
I CAME TO *WARWORLD* SEEKING REVENGE AGAINST THE WOULD-BE CONQUEROR *MONGUL.*
AND SO IT WOULD SEEM THAT I FELL INTO HIS *TRAP.*
HE USED *MY PEOPLE...* AND THE *CRUELTIES* HE INFLICTED UPON THEM... AGAINST ME.
HE TWISTED MY OWN SENSE OF RESPONSIBILITY INTO A *WEAPON.*

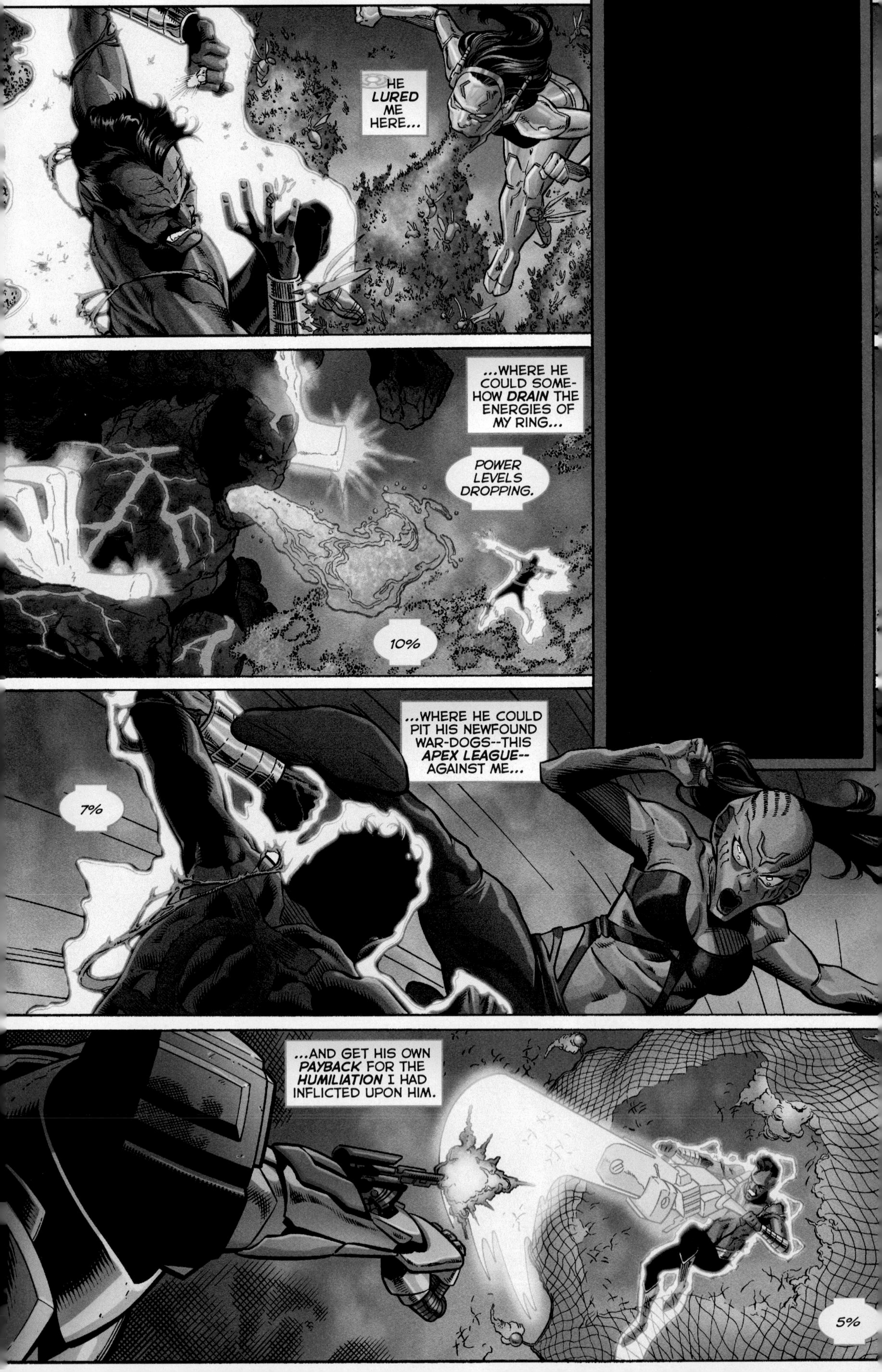
HE LURED ME HERE...
...WHERE HE COULD SOMEHOW DRAIN THE ENERGIES OF MY RING...
POWER LEVELS DROPPING.
10%
...WHERE HE COULD PIT HIS NEWFOUND WAR-DOGS--THIS APEX LEAGUE--AGAINST ME...
7%
...AND GET HIS OWN PAYBACK FOR THE HUMILIATION I HAD INFLICTED UPON HIM.
5%

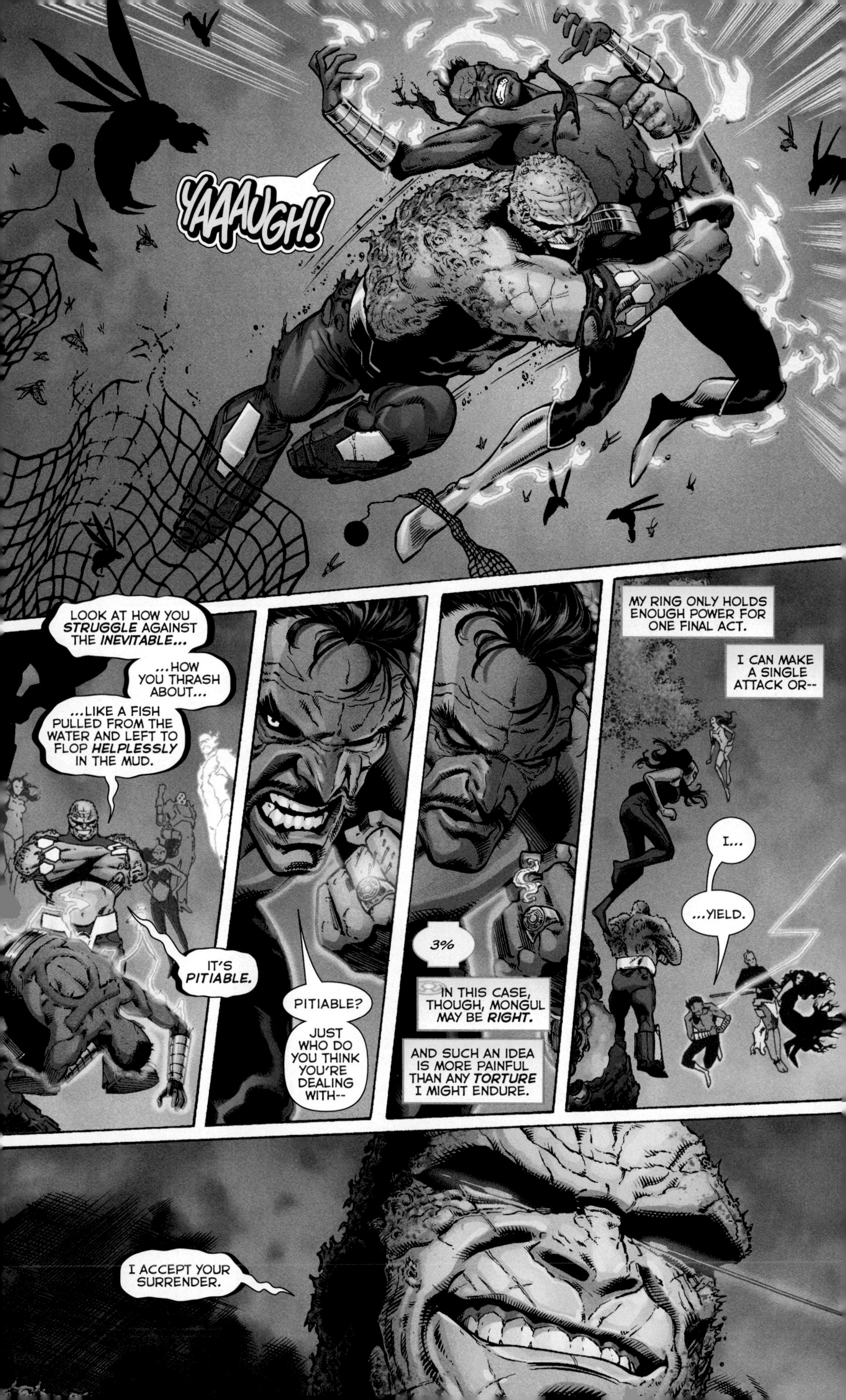

YAAAUGH!
LOOK AT HOW YOU STRUGGLE AGAINST THE INEVITABLE...
...HOW YOU THRASH ABOUT...
...LIKE A FISH PULLED FROM THE WATER AND LEFT TO FLOP HELPLESSLY IN THE MUD.
IT'S PITIABLE.
PITIABLE?
JUST WHO DO YOU THINK YOU'RE DEALING WITH--
3%
IN THIS CASE, THOUGH, MONGUL MAY BE RIGHT.
AND SUCH AN IDEA IS MORE PAINFUL THAN ANY TORTURE I MIGHT ENDURE.
MY RING ONLY HOLDS ENOUGH POWER FOR ONE FINAL ACT.
I CAN MAKE A SINGLE ATTACK OR--
I...
...YIELD.
I ACCEPT YOUR SURRENDER.

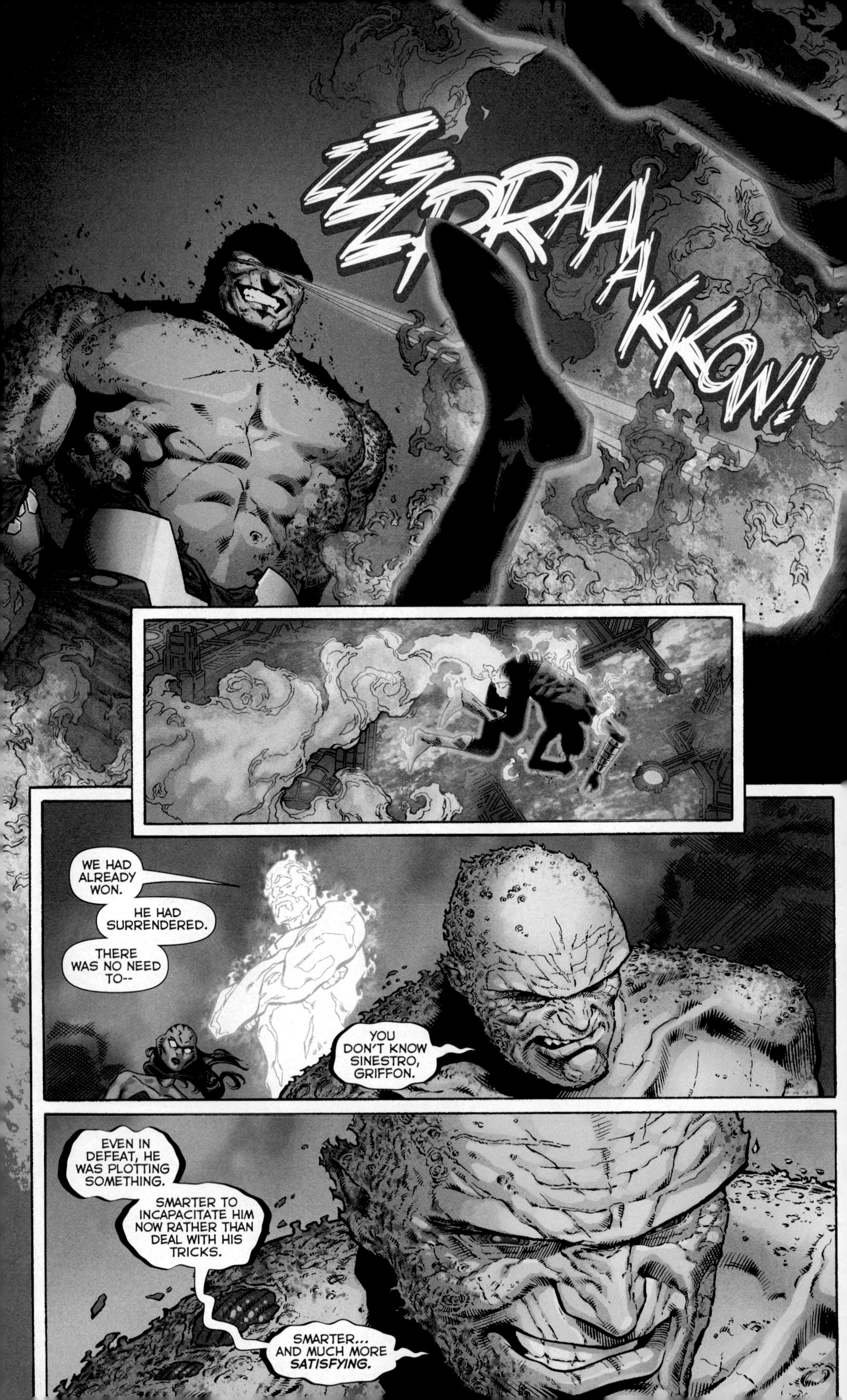
ZZZDRAAAKKOW!
WE HAD ALREADY WON.
HE HAD SURRENDERED.
THERE WAS NO NEED TO--
YOU DON'T KNOW SINESTRO, GRIFFON.
EVEN IN DEFEAT, HE WAS PLOTTING SOMETHING.
SMARTER TO INCAPACITATE HIM NOW RATHER THAN DEAL WITH HIS TRICKS.
SMARTER... AND MUCH MORE SATISFYING.

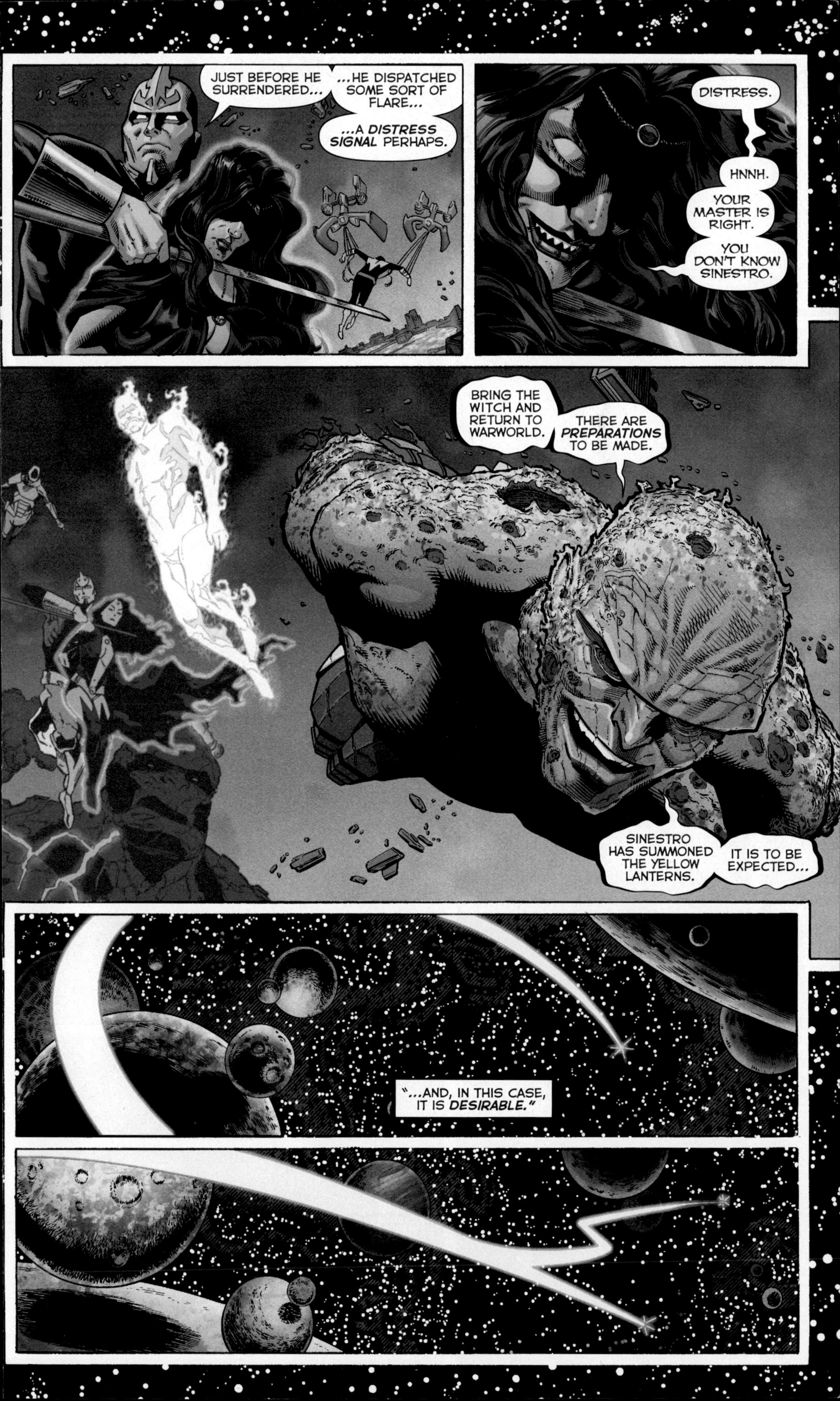
JUST BEFORE HE SURRENDERED...
...HE DISPATCHED SOME SORT OF FLARE...
...A *DISTRESS SIGNAL* PERHAPS.
DISTRESS.
HNNH.
YOUR MASTER IS RIGHT.
YOU DON'T KNOW SINESTRO.
BRING THE WITCH AND RETURN TO WARWORLD.
THERE ARE *PREPARATIONS* TO BE MADE.
SINESTRO HAS SUMMONED THE YELLOW LANTERNS.
IT IS TO BE EXPECTED...
"...AND, IN THIS CASE, IT IS *DESIRABLE.*"

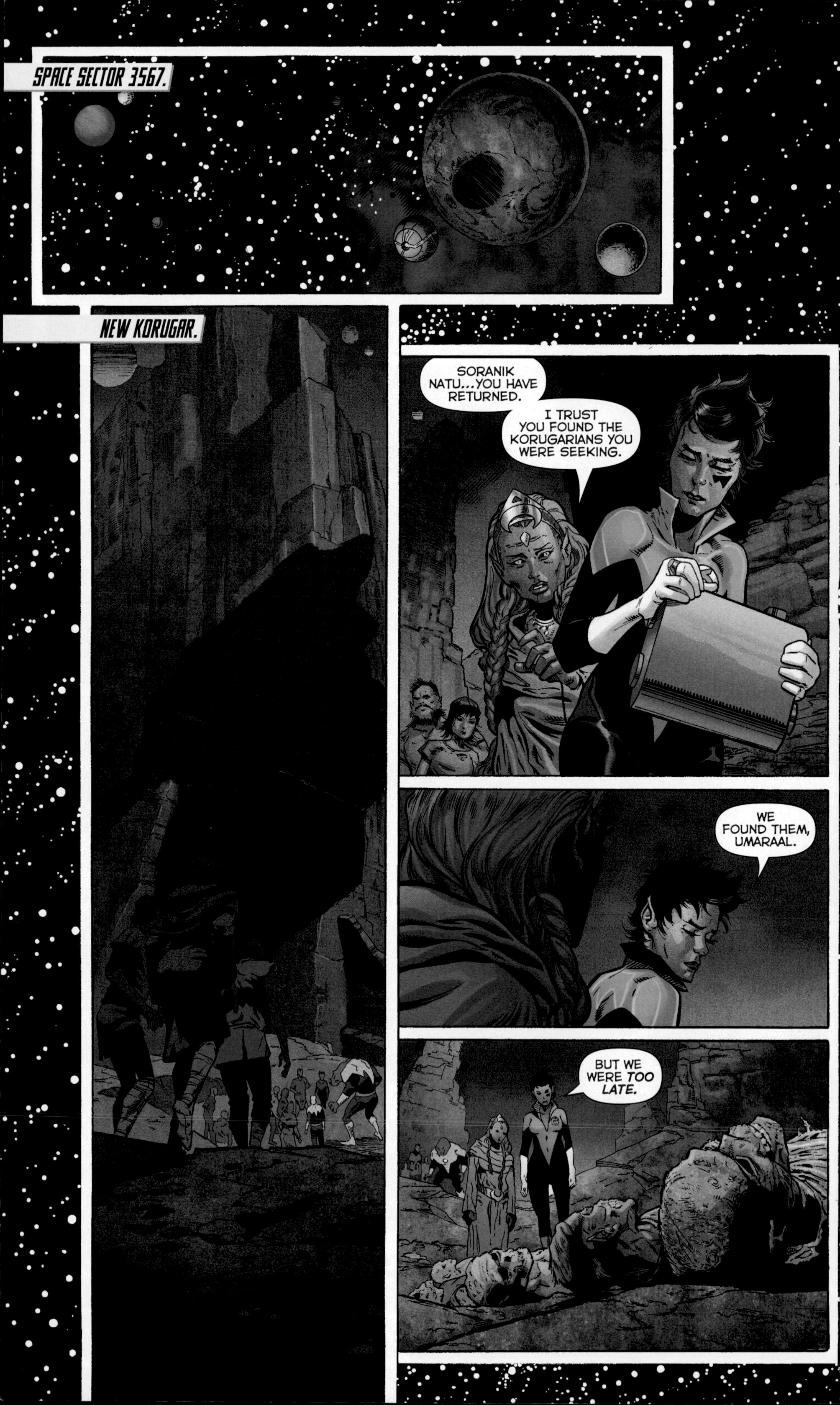
SPACE SECTOR 3567.
NEW KORUGAR.
SORANIK NATU...YOU HAVE RETURNED.
I TRUST YOU FOUND THE KORUGARIANS YOU WERE SEEKING.
WE FOUND THEM, UMARAAL.
BUT WE WERE *TOO LATE.*

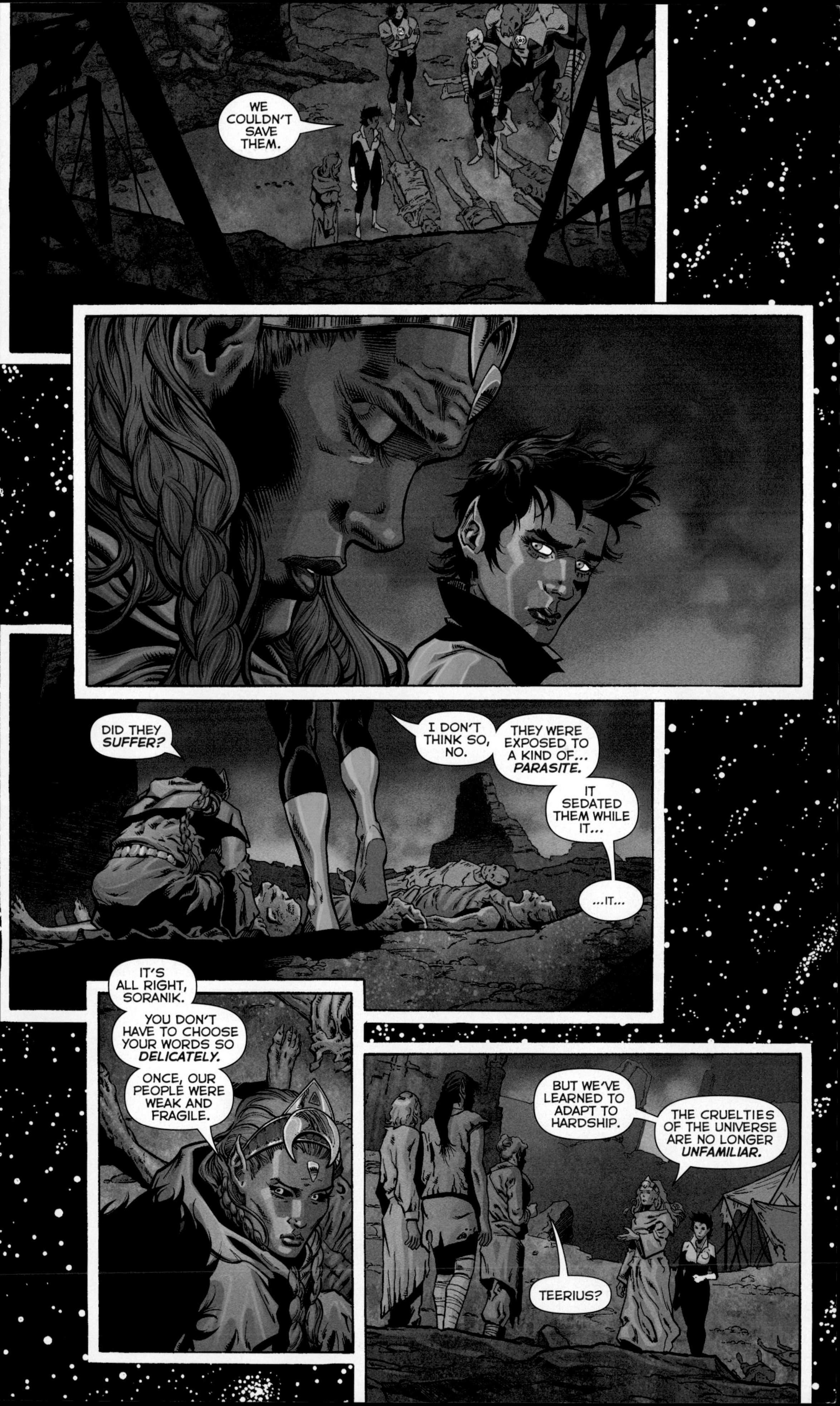

WE COULDN'T SAVE THEM.
DID THEY *SUFFER?*
I DON'T THINK SO, NO.
THEY WERE EXPOSED TO A KIND OF... *PARASITE.*
IT SEDATED THEM WHILE IT...
...IT...
IT'S ALL RIGHT, SORANIK.
YOU DON'T HAVE TO CHOOSE YOUR WORDS SO *DELICATELY.*
ONCE, OUR PEOPLE WERE WEAK AND FRAGILE.
BUT WE'VE LEARNED TO ADAPT TO HARDSHIP.
THE CRUELTIES OF THE UNIVERSE ARE NO LONGER *UNFAMILIAR.*
TEERIUS?

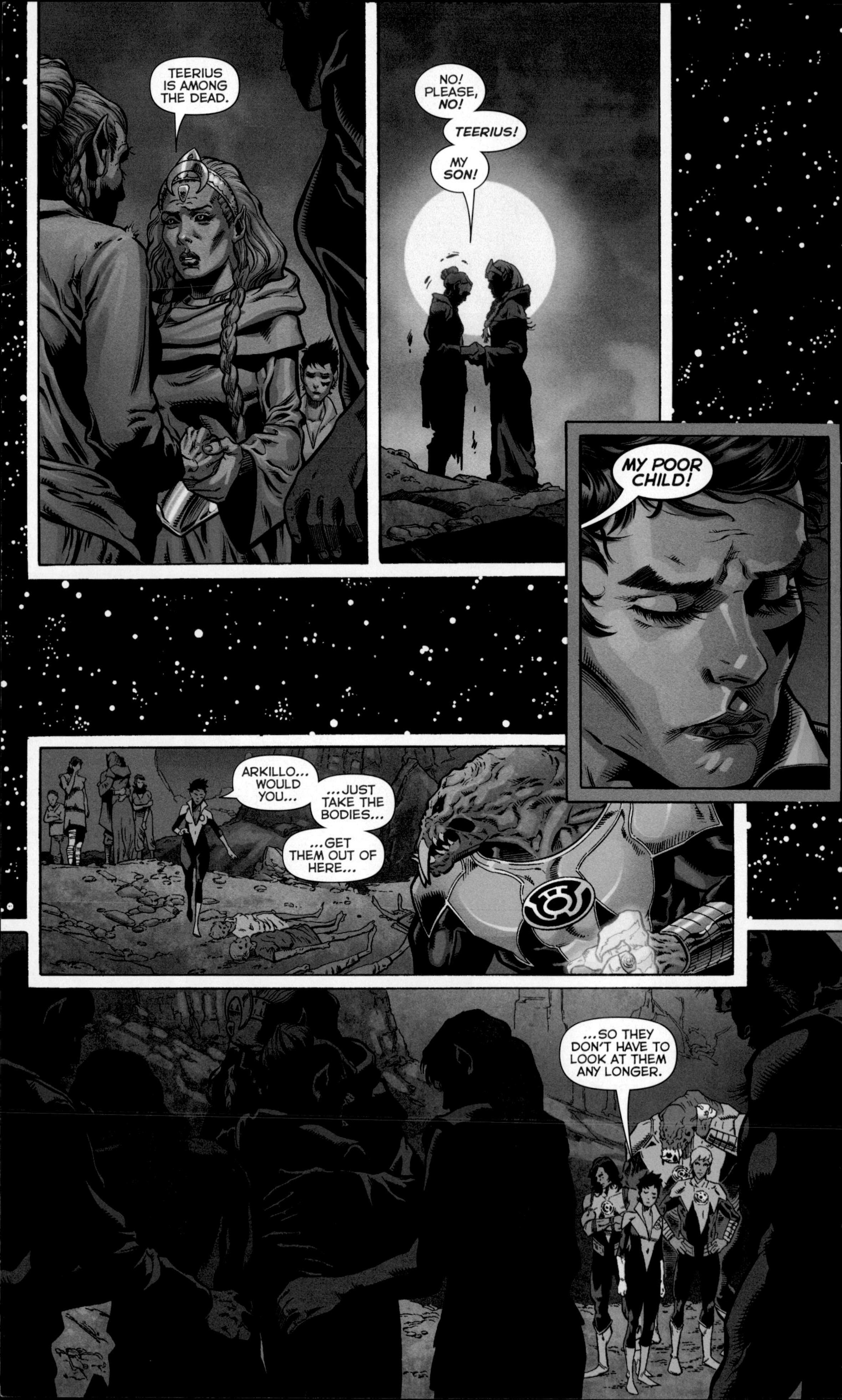

TEERIUS IS AMONG THE DEAD.
NO! PLEASE, NO!
TEERIUS!
MY SON!
MY POOR CHILD!
ARKILLO... WOULD YOU...
...JUST TAKE THE BODIES...
...GET THEM OUT OF HERE...
...SO THEY DON'T HAVE TO LOOK AT THEM ANY LONGER.

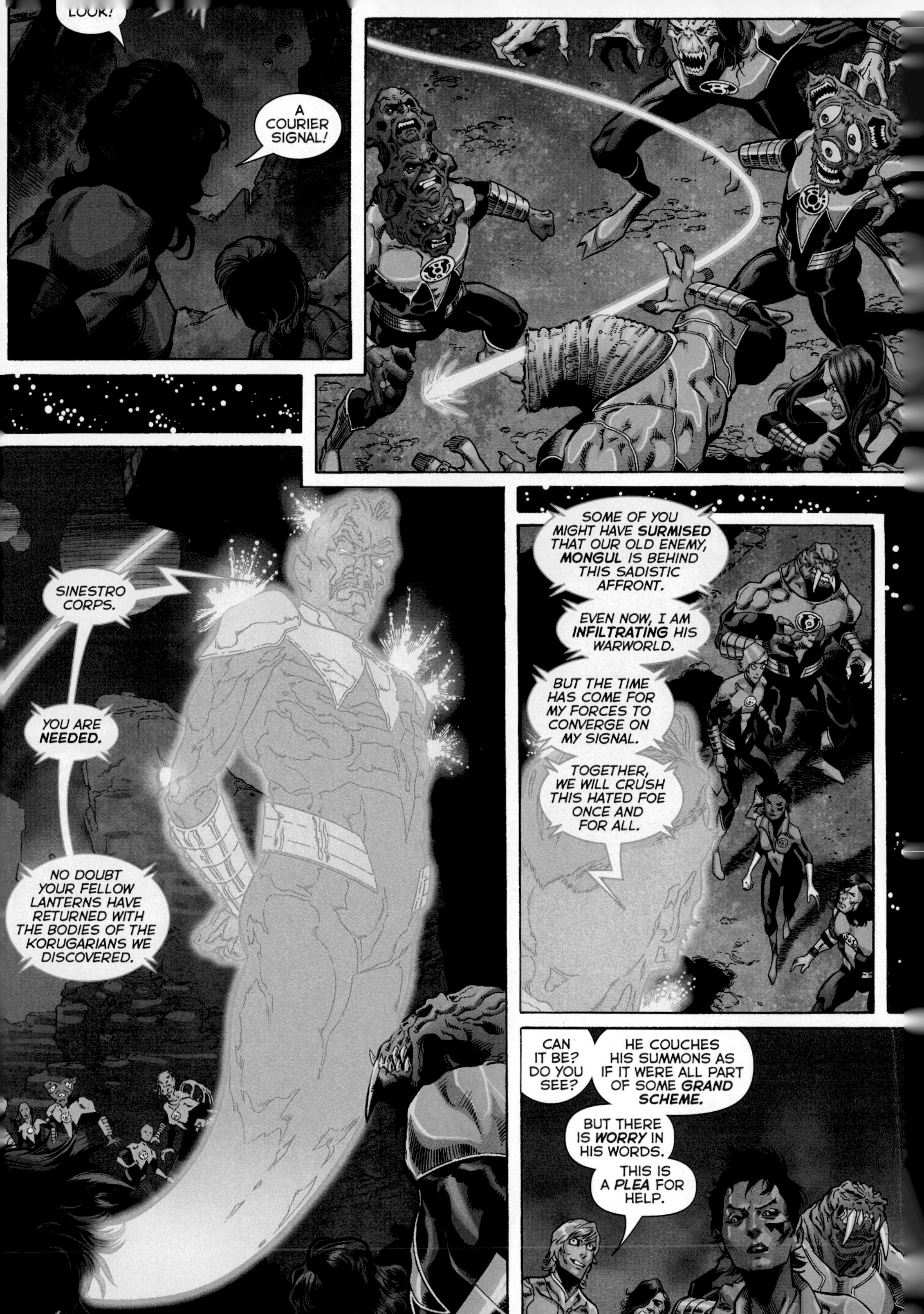
LOOK!
A COURIER SIGNAL!
SINESTRO CORPS.
YOU ARE NEEDED.
NO DOUBT YOUR FELLOW LANTERNS HAVE RETURNED WITH THE BODIES OF THE KORUGARIANS WE DISCOVERED.
SOME OF YOU MIGHT HAVE SURMISED THAT OUR OLD ENEMY, MONGUL IS BEHIND THIS SADISTIC AFFRONT.
EVEN NOW, I AM INFILTRATING HIS WARWORLD.
BUT THE TIME HAS COME FOR MY FORCES TO CONVERGE ON MY SIGNAL.
TOGETHER, WE WILL CRUSH THIS HATED FOE ONCE AND FOR ALL.
CAN IT BE? DO YOU SEE?
HE COUCHES HIS SUMMONS AS IF IT WERE ALL PART OF SOME GRAND SCHEME.
BUT THERE IS WORRY IN HIS WORDS.
THIS IS A PLEA FOR HELP.

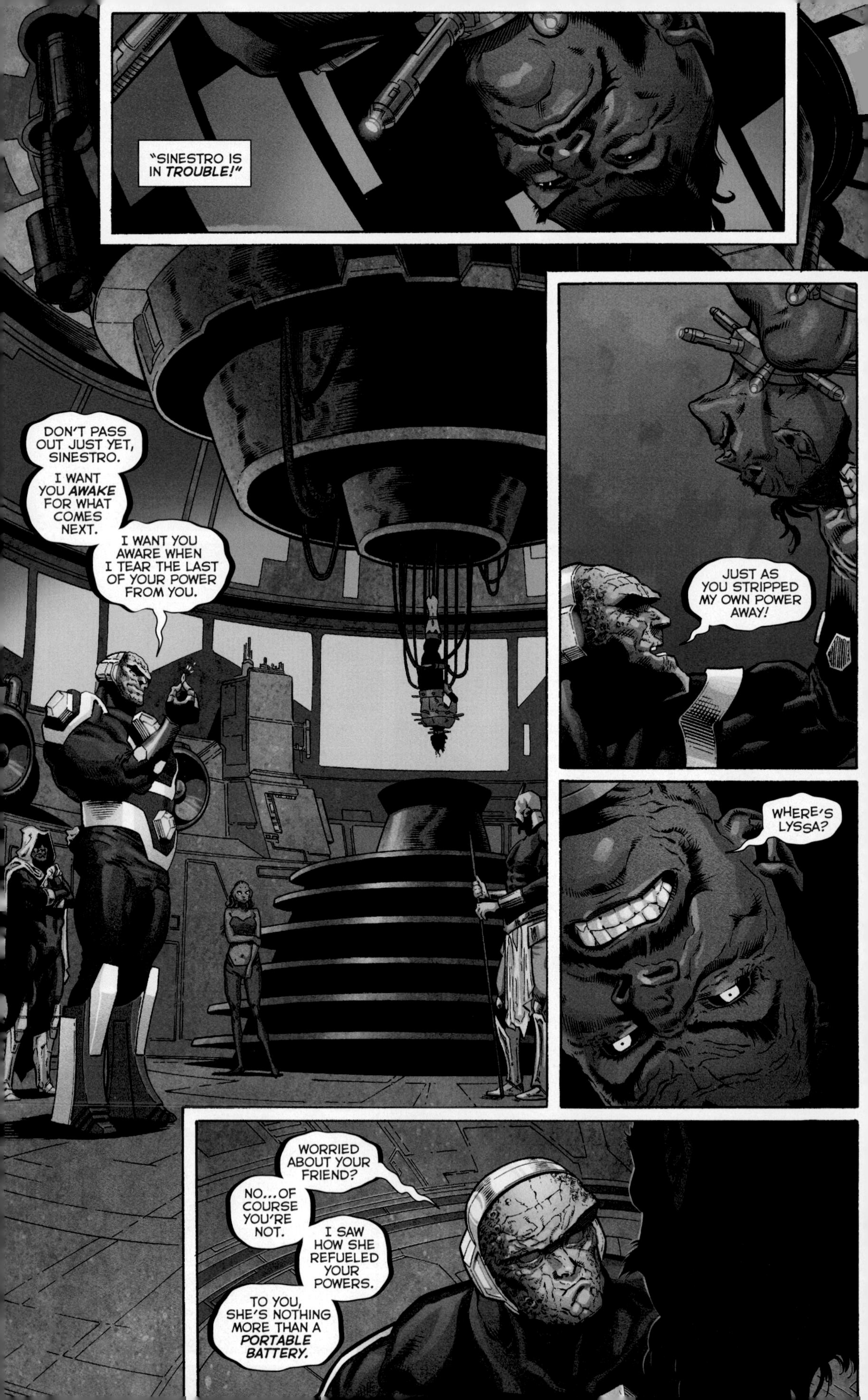

"SINESTRO IS IN *TROUBLE!*"
DON'T PASS OUT JUST YET, SINESTRO.
I WANT YOU *AWAKE* FOR WHAT COMES NEXT.
I WANT YOU AWARE WHEN I TEAR THE LAST OF YOUR POWER FROM YOU.
JUST AS YOU STRIPPED MY OWN POWER AWAY!
WHERE'S LYSSA?
WORRIED ABOUT YOUR FRIEND?
NO...OF COURSE YOU'RE NOT.
I SAW HOW SHE REFUELED YOUR POWERS.
TO YOU, SHE'S NOTHING MORE THAN A *PORTABLE BATTERY.*

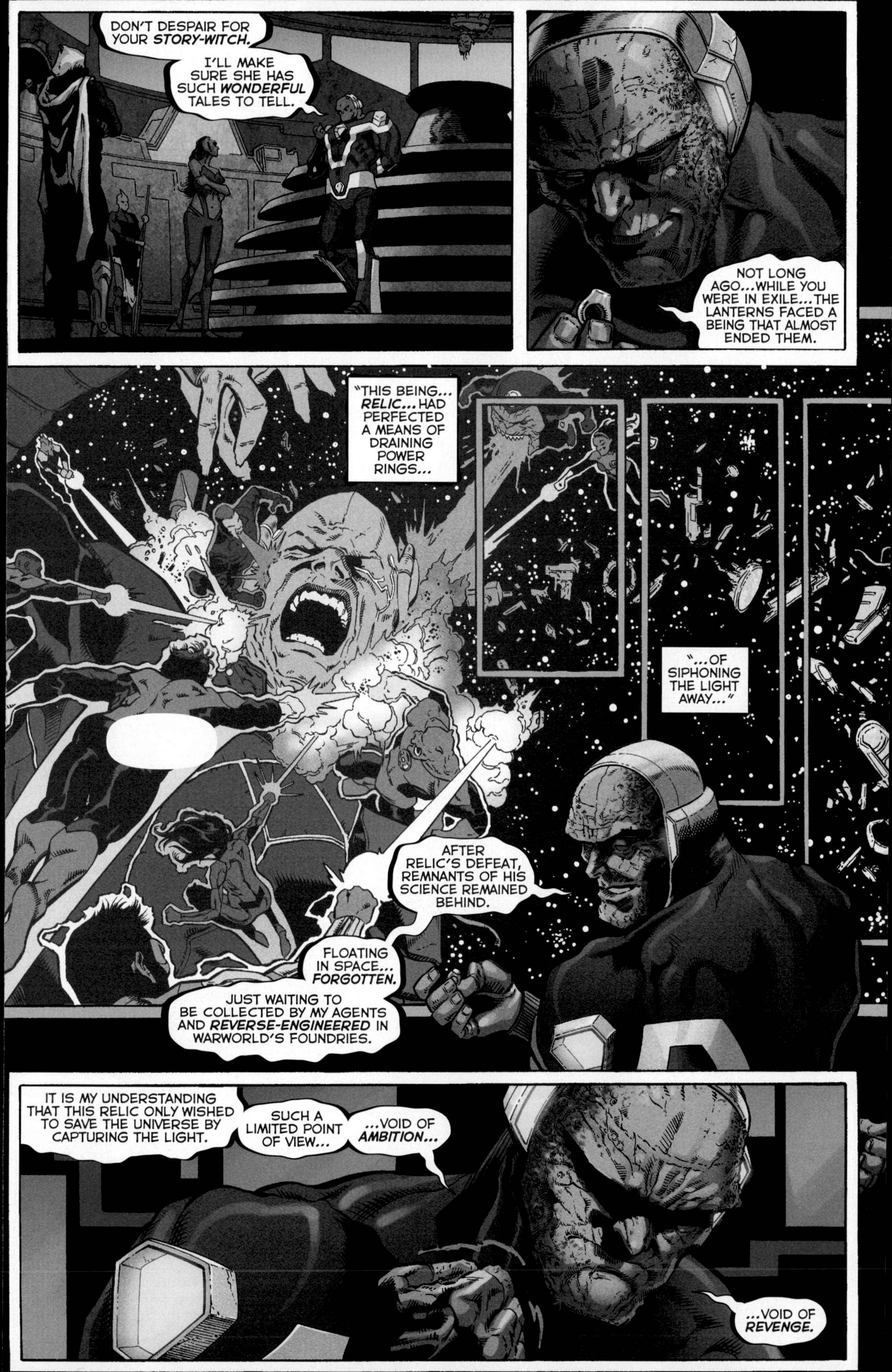

DON'T DESPAIR FOR YOUR STORY-WITCH.
I'LL MAKE SURE SHE HAS SUCH WONDERFUL TALES TO TELL.
NOT LONG AGO...WHILE YOU WERE IN EXILE...THE LANTERNS FACED A BEING THAT ALMOST ENDED THEM.
"THIS BEING... RELIC...HAD PERFECTED A MEANS OF DRAINING POWER RINGS...
"...OF SIPHONING THE LIGHT AWAY..."
AFTER RELIC'S DEFEAT, REMNANTS OF HIS SCIENCE REMAINED BEHIND.
FLOATING IN SPACE... FORGOTTEN.
JUST WAITING TO BE COLLECTED BY MY AGENTS AND REVERSE-ENGINEERED IN WARWORLD'S FOUNDRIES.
IT IS MY UNDERSTANDING THAT THIS RELIC ONLY WISHED TO SAVE THE UNIVERSE BY CAPTURING THE LIGHT.
SUCH A LIMITED POINT OF VIEW...
...VOID OF AMBITION...
...VOID OF REVENGE.

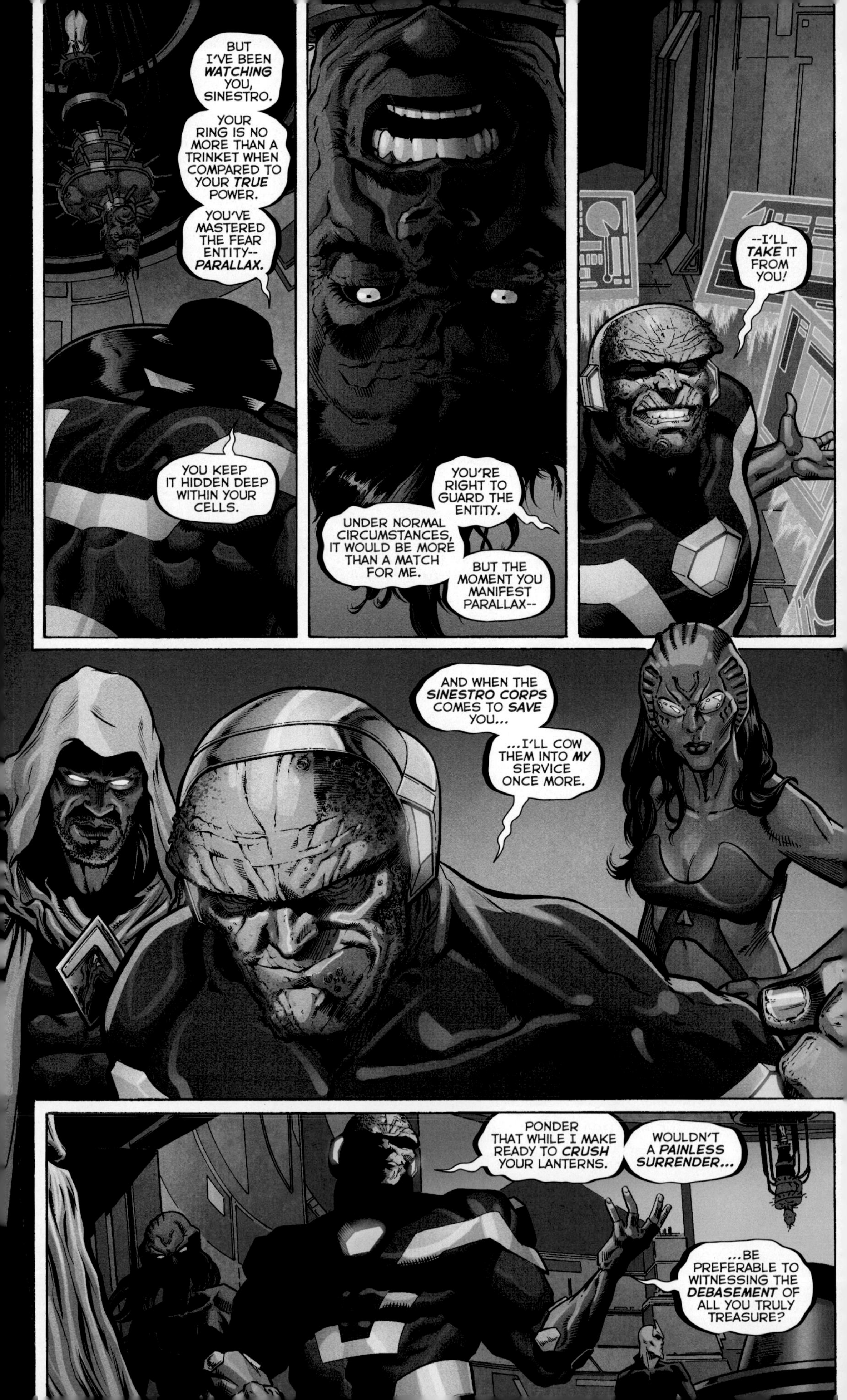
BUT I'VE BEEN WATCHING YOU, SINESTRO.
YOUR RING IS NO MORE THAN A TRINKET WHEN COMPARED TO YOUR TRUE POWER.
YOU'VE MASTERED THE FEAR ENTITY-- PARALLAX.
YOU KEEP IT HIDDEN DEEP WITHIN YOUR CELLS.
YOU'RE RIGHT TO GUARD THE ENTITY.
UNDER NORMAL CIRCUMSTANCES, IT WOULD BE MORE THAN A MATCH FOR ME.
BUT THE MOMENT YOU MANIFEST PARALLAX--
--I'LL TAKE IT FROM YOU!
AND WHEN THE SINESTRO CORPS COMES TO SAVE YOU...
...I'LL COW THEM INTO MY SERVICE ONCE MORE.
PONDER THAT WHILE I MAKE READY TO CRUSH YOUR LANTERNS.
WOULDN'T A PAINLESS SURRENDER...
...BE PREFERABLE TO WITNESSING THE DEBASEMENT OF ALL YOU TRULY TREASURE?

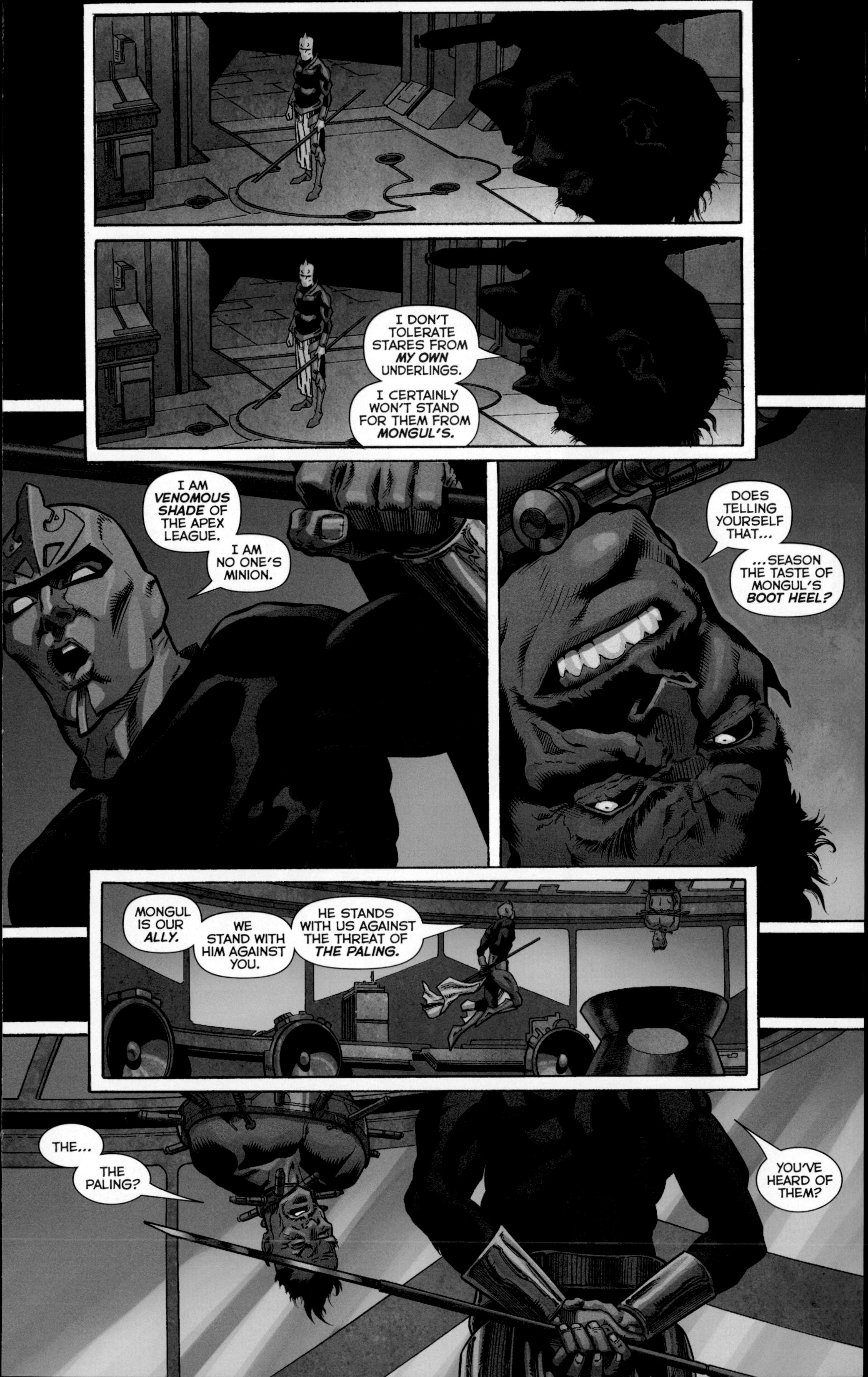
I DON'T TOLERATE STARES FROM MY OWN UNDERLINGS.
I CERTAINLY WON'T STAND FOR THEM FROM MONGUL'S.
I AM VENOMOUS SHADE OF THE APEX LEAGUE.
I AM NO ONE'S MINION.
DOES TELLING YOURSELF THAT...
...SEASON THE TASTE OF MONGUL'S BOOT HEEL?
MONGUL IS OUR ALLY.
WE STAND WITH HIM AGAINST YOU.
HE STANDS WITH US AGAINST THE THREAT OF THE PALING.
THE...
THE PALING?
YOU'VE HEARD OF THEM?

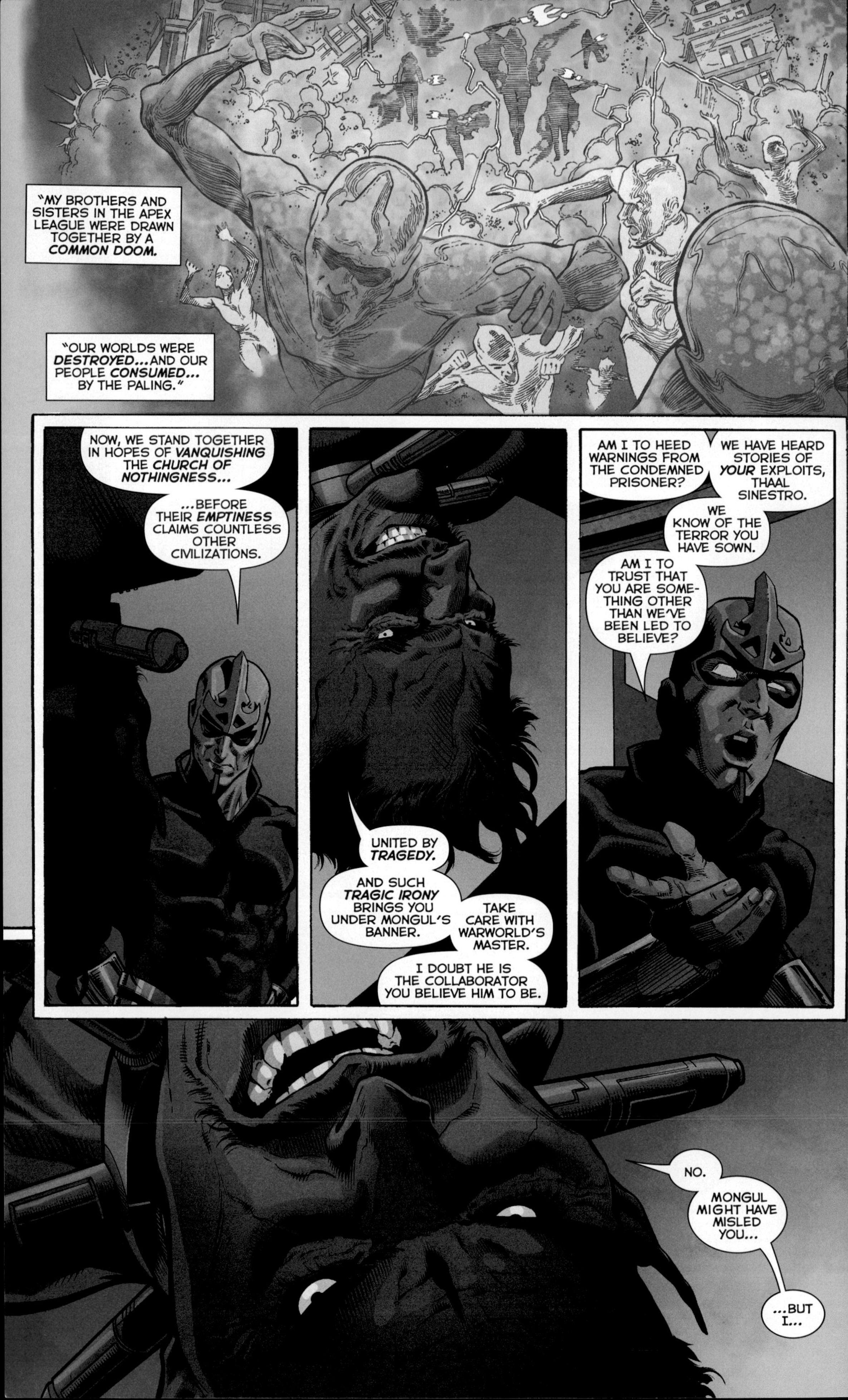
"MY BROTHERS AND SISTERS IN THE APEX LEAGUE WERE DRAWN TOGETHER BY A COMMON DOOM.
"OUR WORLDS WERE DESTROYED...AND OUR PEOPLE CONSUMED... BY THE PALING."
NOW, WE STAND TOGETHER IN HOPES OF VANQUISHING THE CHURCH OF NOTHINGNESS...
...BEFORE THEIR EMPTINESS CLAIMS COUNTLESS OTHER CIVILIZATIONS.
UNITED BY TRAGEDY.
AND SUCH TRAGIC IRONY BRINGS YOU UNDER MONGUL'S BANNER.
TAKE CARE WITH WARWORLD'S MASTER.
I DOUBT HE IS THE COLLABORATOR YOU BELIEVE HIM TO BE.
AM I TO HEED WARNINGS FROM THE CONDEMNED PRISONER?
WE HAVE HEARD STORIES OF YOUR EXPLOITS, THAAL SINESTRO.
WE KNOW OF THE TERROR YOU HAVE SOWN.
AM I TO TRUST THAT YOU ARE SOMETHING OTHER THAN WE'VE BEEN LED TO BELIEVE?
NO.
MONGUL MIGHT HAVE MISLED YOU...
...BUT I...

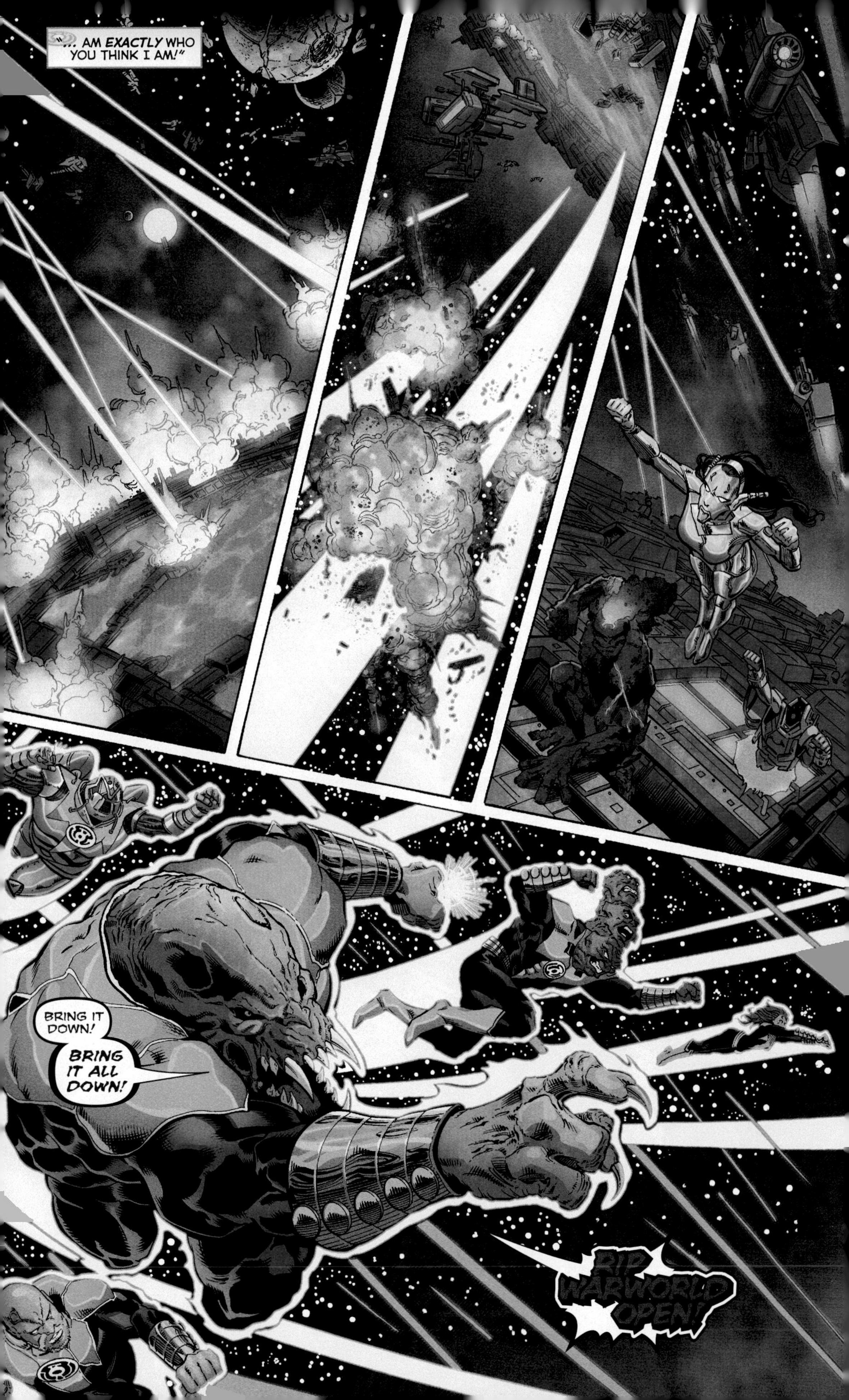
"... AM EXACTLY WHO YOU THINK I AM!"
BRING IT DOWN!
BRING IT ALL DOWN!
RIP WARWORLD OPEN!

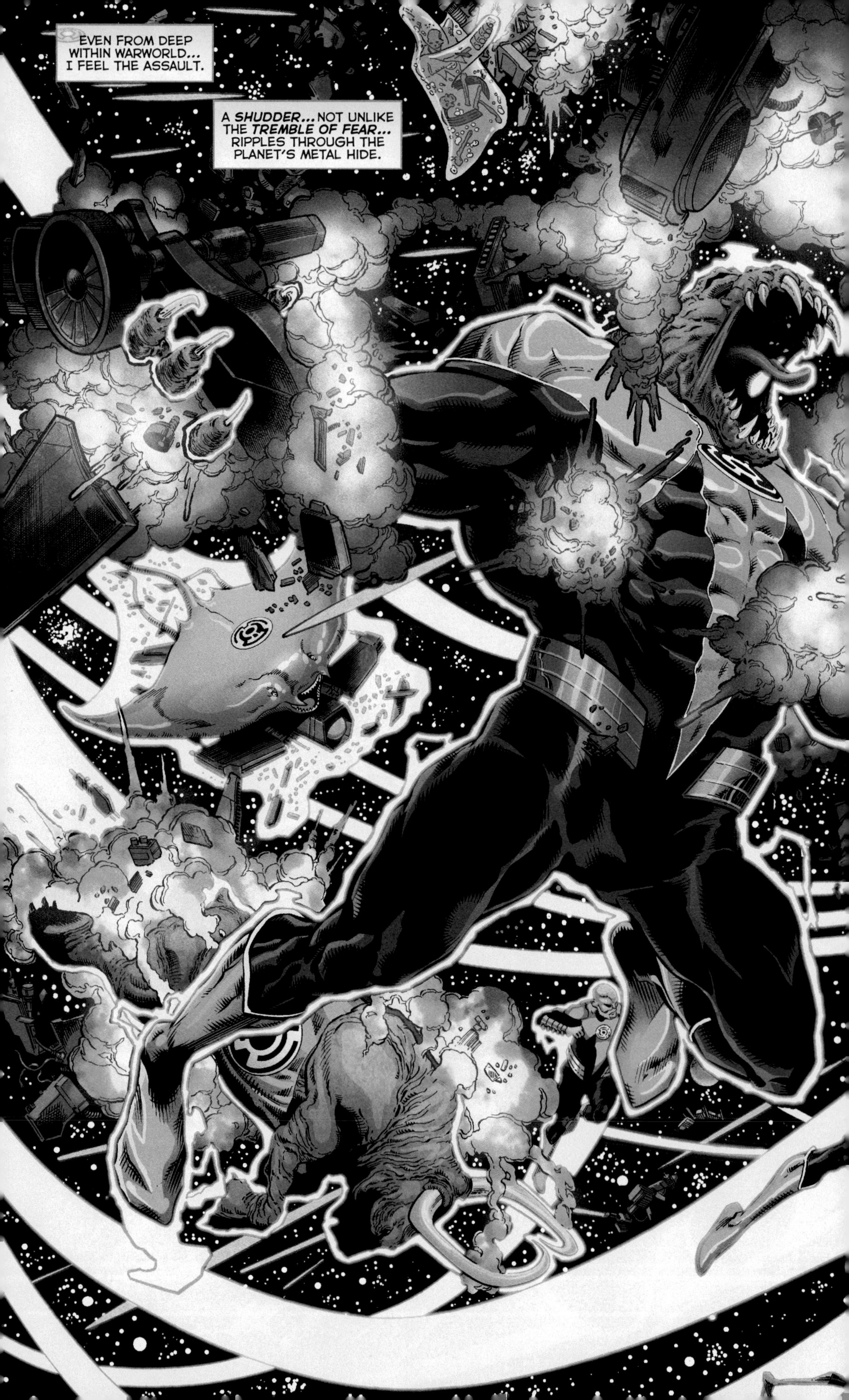
EVEN FROM DEEP WITHIN WARWORLD... I FEEL THE ASSAULT.
A *SHUDDER*... NOT UNLIKE THE *TREMBLE OF FEAR*... RIPPLES THROUGH THE PLANET'S METAL HIDE.

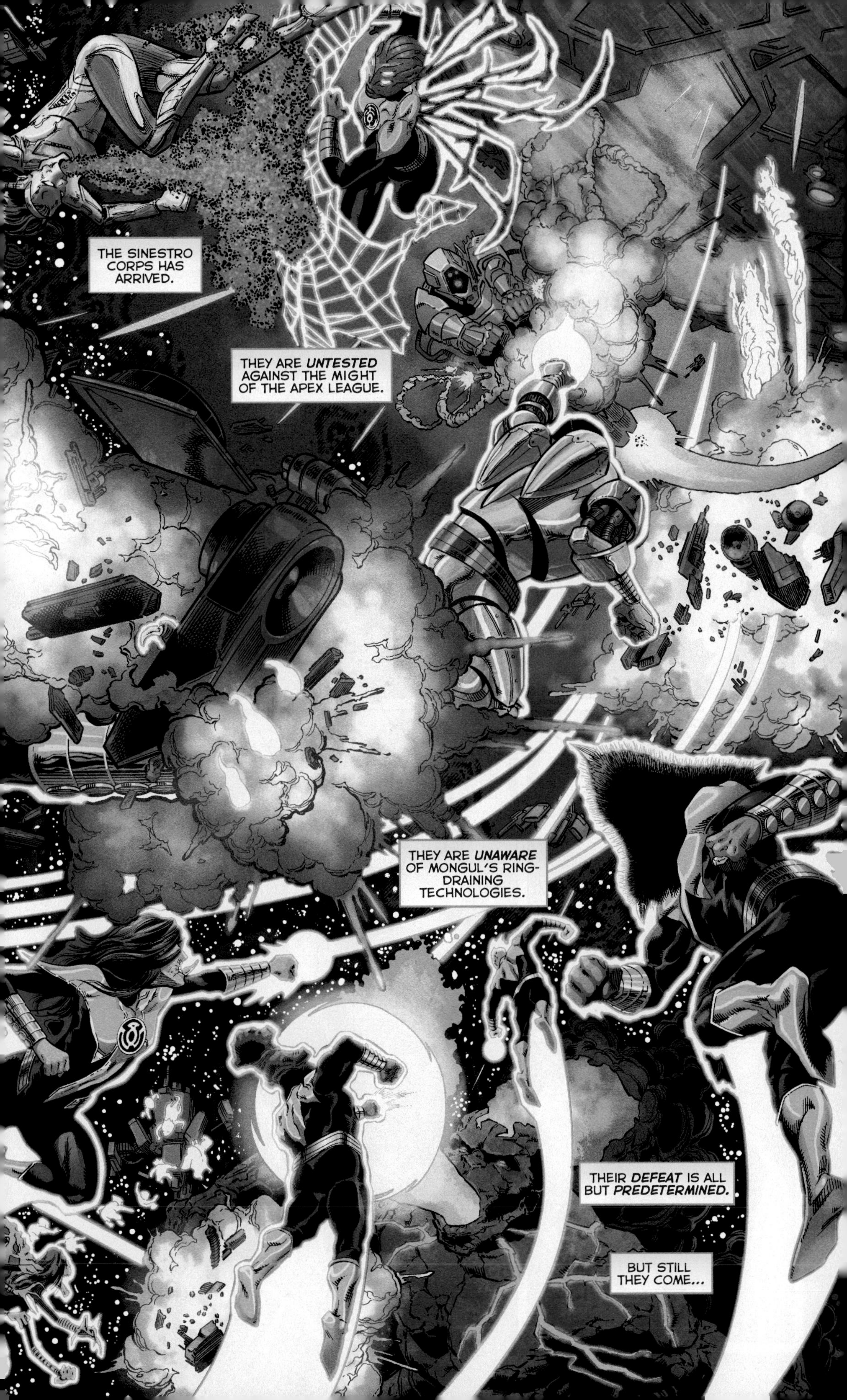
THE SINESTRO CORPS HAS ARRIVED.
THEY ARE *UNTESTED* AGAINST THE MIGHT OF THE APEX LEAGUE.
THEY ARE *UNAWARE* OF MONGUL'S RING-DRAINING TECHNOLOGIES.
THEIR *DEFEAT* IS ALL BUT *PREDETERMINED.*
BUT STILL THEY COME...

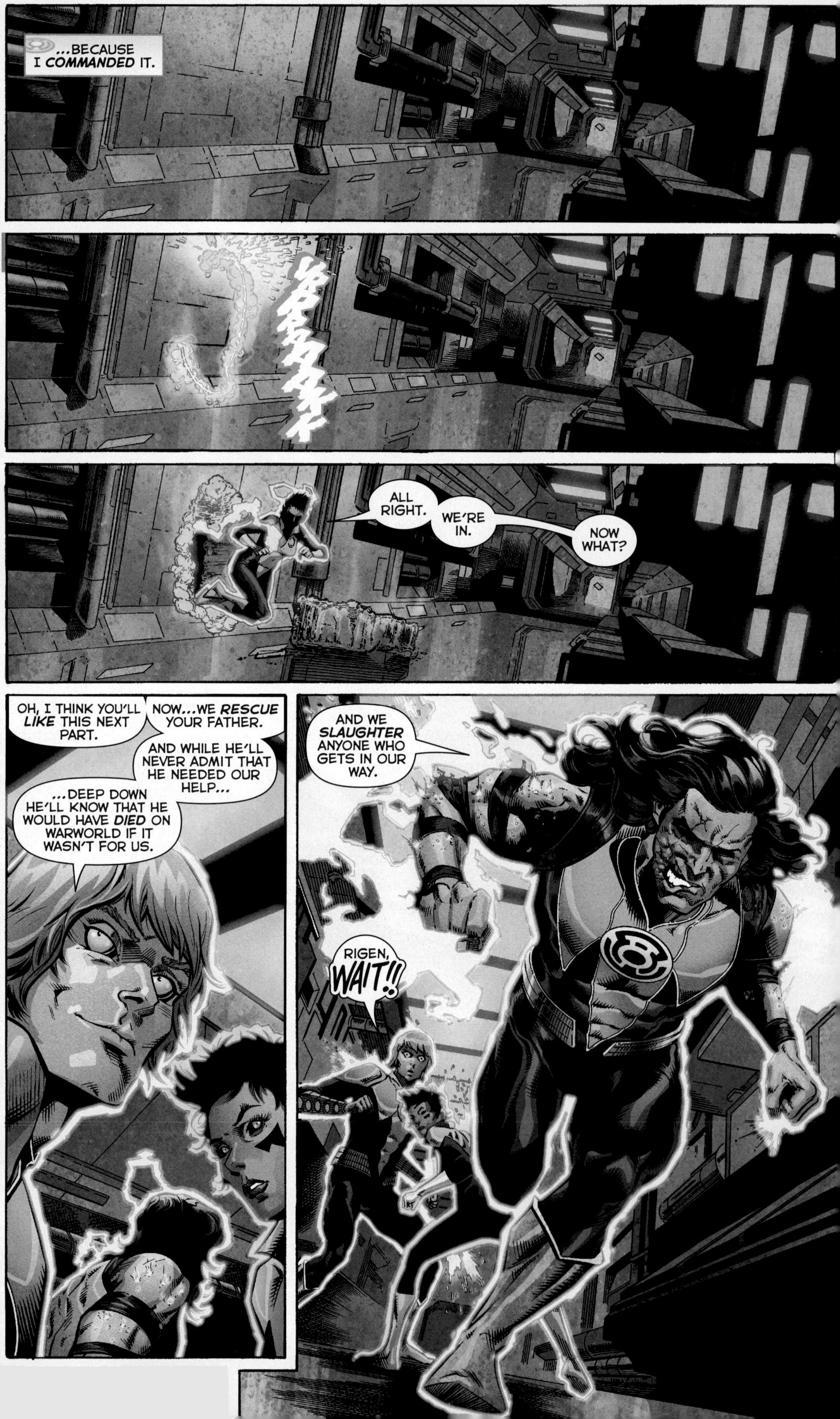
...BECAUSE I COMMANDED IT.
ALL RIGHT.
WE'RE IN.
NOW WHAT?
OH, I THINK YOU'LL LIKE THIS NEXT PART.
NOW...WE RESCUE YOUR FATHER.
AND WHILE HE'LL NEVER ADMIT THAT HE NEEDED OUR HELP...
...DEEP DOWN HE'LL KNOW THAT HE WOULD HAVE DIED ON WARWORLD IF IT WASN'T FOR US.
AND WE SLAUGHTER ANYONE WHO GETS IN OUR WAY.
RIGEN, WAIT!!

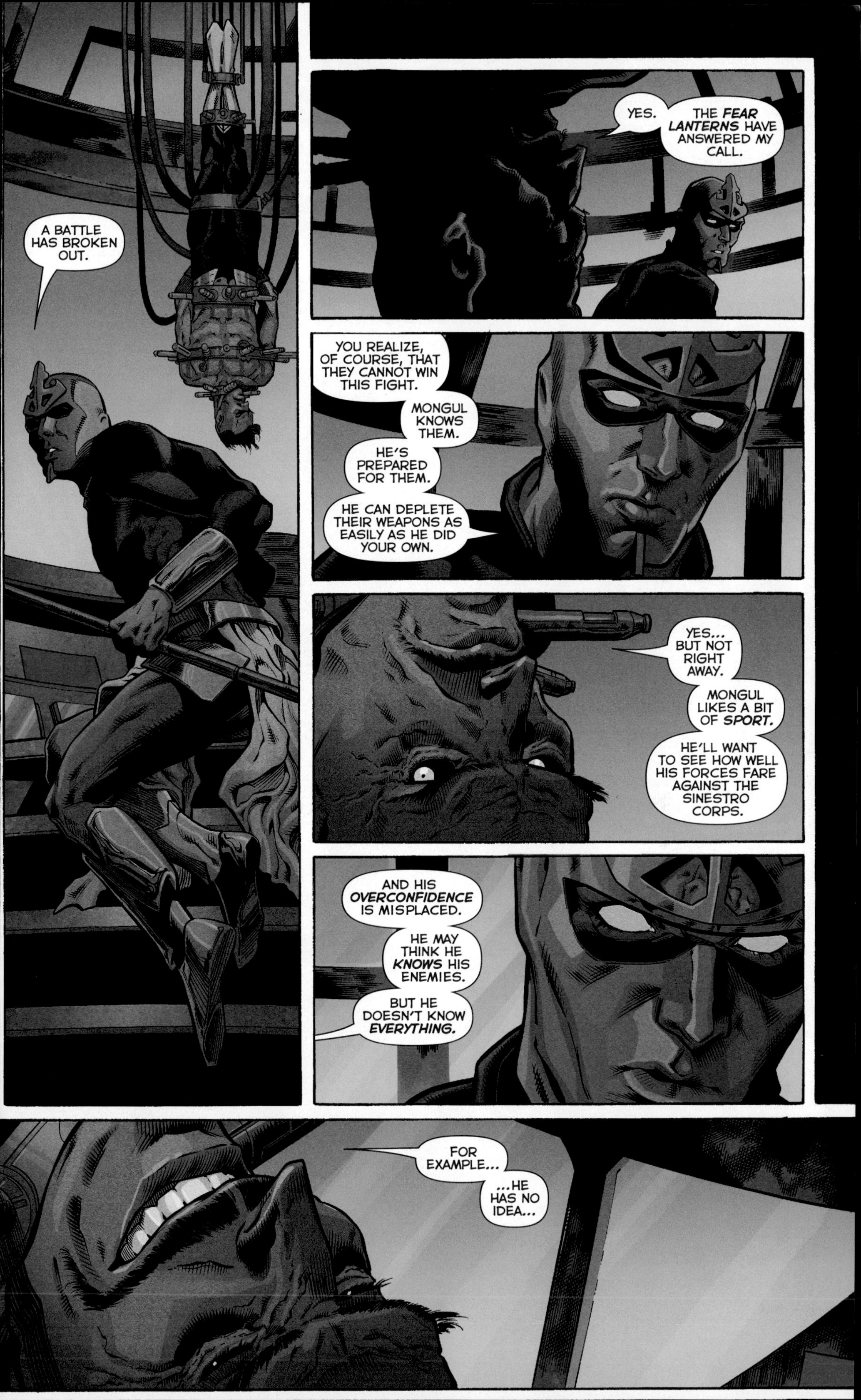
A BATTLE HAS BROKEN OUT.
YES.
THE *FEAR LANTERNS* HAVE ANSWERED MY CALL.
YOU REALIZE, OF COURSE, THAT THEY CANNOT WIN THIS FIGHT.
MONGUL KNOWS THEM.
HE'S PREPARED FOR THEM.
HE CAN DEPLETE THEIR WEAPONS AS EASILY AS HE DID YOUR OWN.
YES... BUT NOT RIGHT AWAY.
MONGUL LIKES A BIT OF *SPORT.*
HE'LL WANT TO SEE HOW WELL HIS FORCES FARE AGAINST THE SINESTRO CORPS.
AND HIS *OVERCONFIDENCE* IS MISPLACED.
HE MAY THINK HE *KNOWS* HIS ENEMIES.
BUT HE DOESN'T KNOW *EVERYTHING.*
FOR EXAMPLE...
...HE HAS NO IDEA...

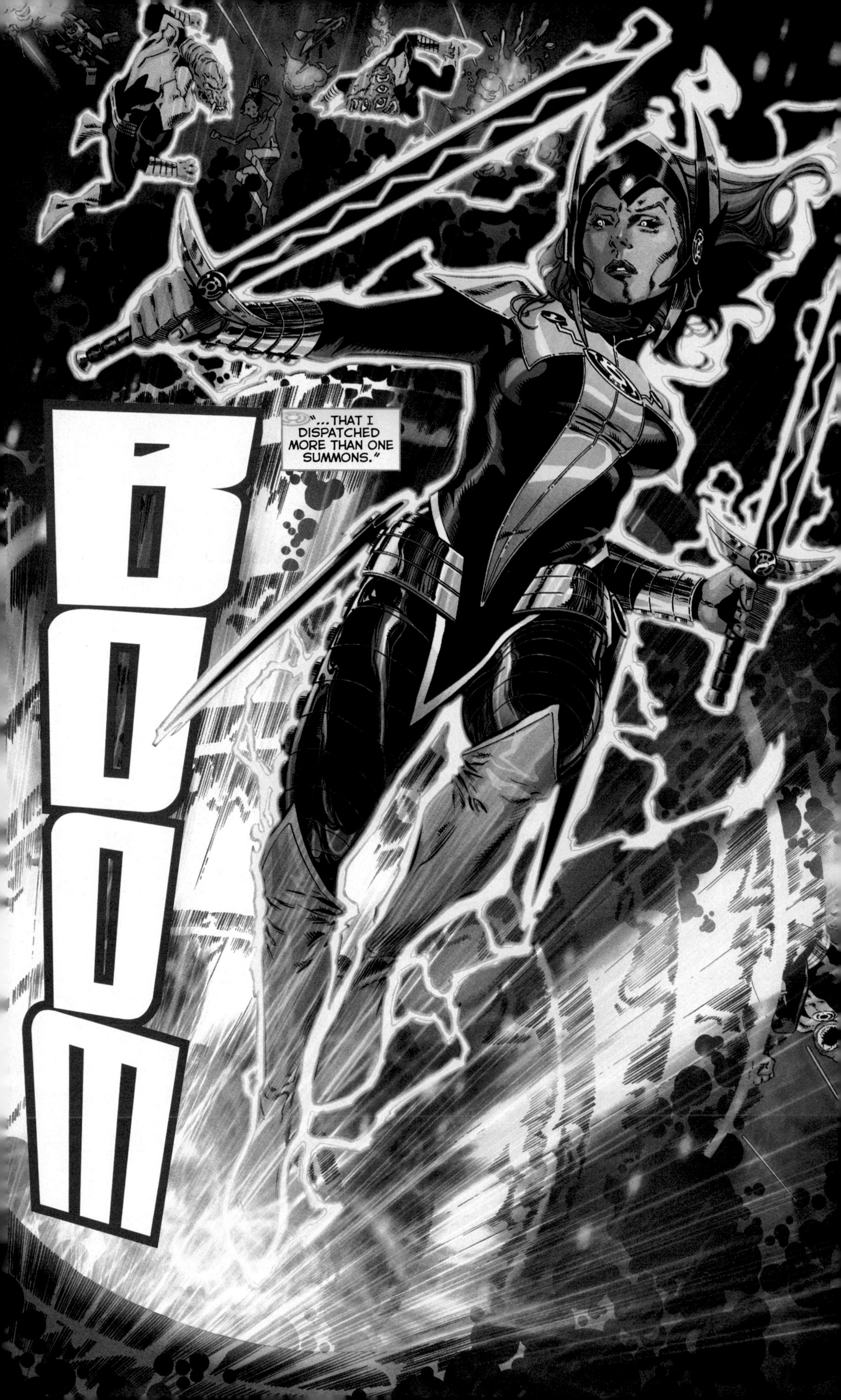
"...THAT I DISPATCHED MORE THAN ONE SUMMONS."
BOOM

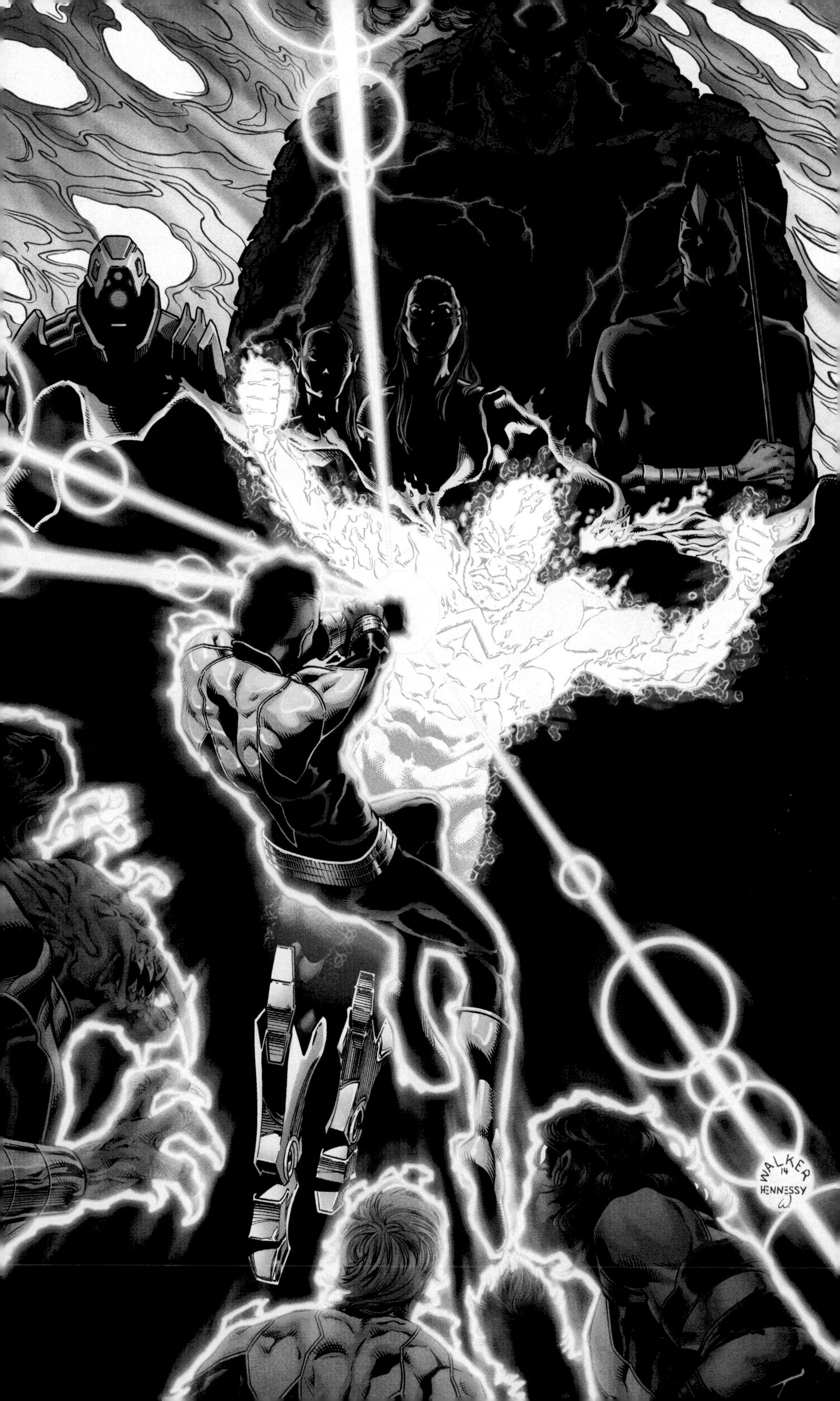
WALKER 14
HENNESSY

SPOILS OF WAR

CULLEN BUNN writer **BRAD WALKER GERALDO BORGES** pencillers **ANDREW HENNESSY OCLAIR ALBERT GERALDO BORGES** inkers **JASON WRIGHT** colorist **DAVE SHARPE** letterer
cover art by **BRAD WALKER, ANDREW HENNESSY & JASON WRIGHT**

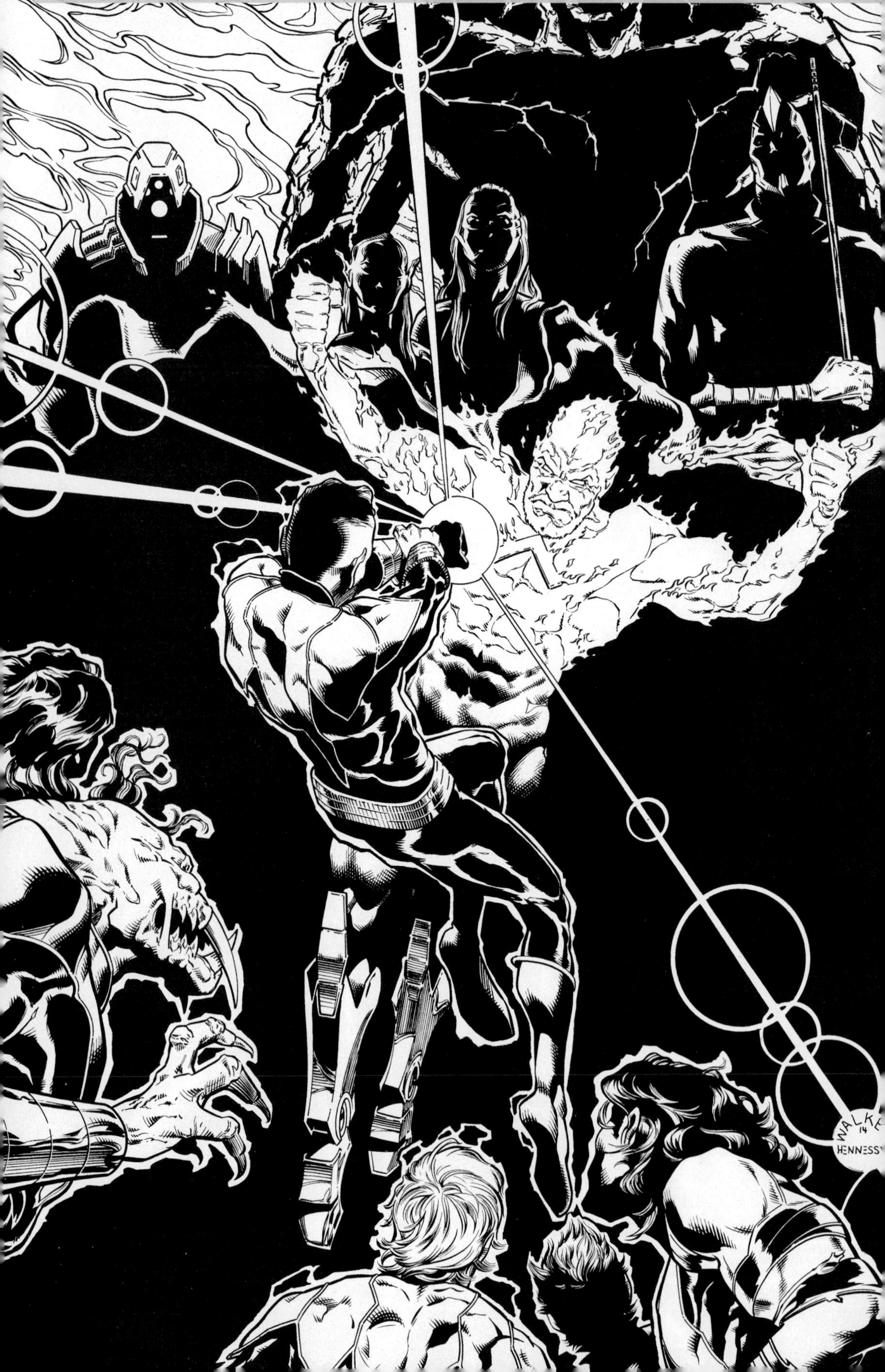
WALKER '14
HENNESSY

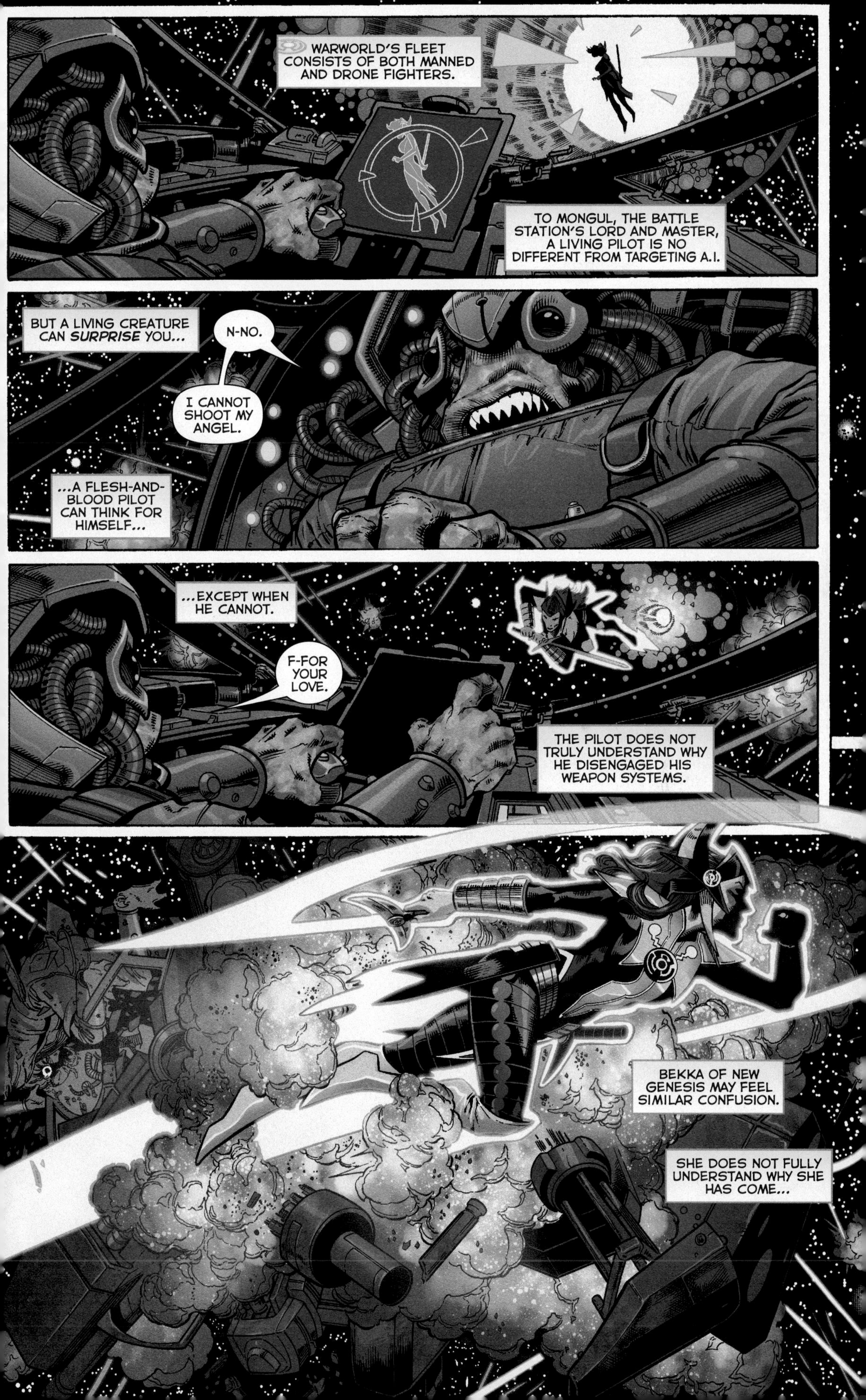
WARWORLD'S FLEET CONSISTS OF BOTH MANNED AND DRONE FIGHTERS.
TO MONGUL, THE BATTLE STATION'S LORD AND MASTER, A LIVING PILOT IS NO DIFFERENT FROM TARGETING A.I.
BUT A LIVING CREATURE CAN SURPRISE YOU...
N-NO.
I CANNOT SHOOT MY ANGEL.
...A FLESH-AND-BLOOD PILOT CAN THINK FOR HIMSELF...
...EXCEPT WHEN HE CANNOT.
F-FOR YOUR LOVE.
THE PILOT DOES NOT TRULY UNDERSTAND WHY HE DISENGAGED HIS WEAPON SYSTEMS.
BEKKA OF NEW GENESIS MAY FEEL SIMILAR CONFUSION.
SHE DOES NOT FULLY UNDERSTAND WHY SHE HAS COME...

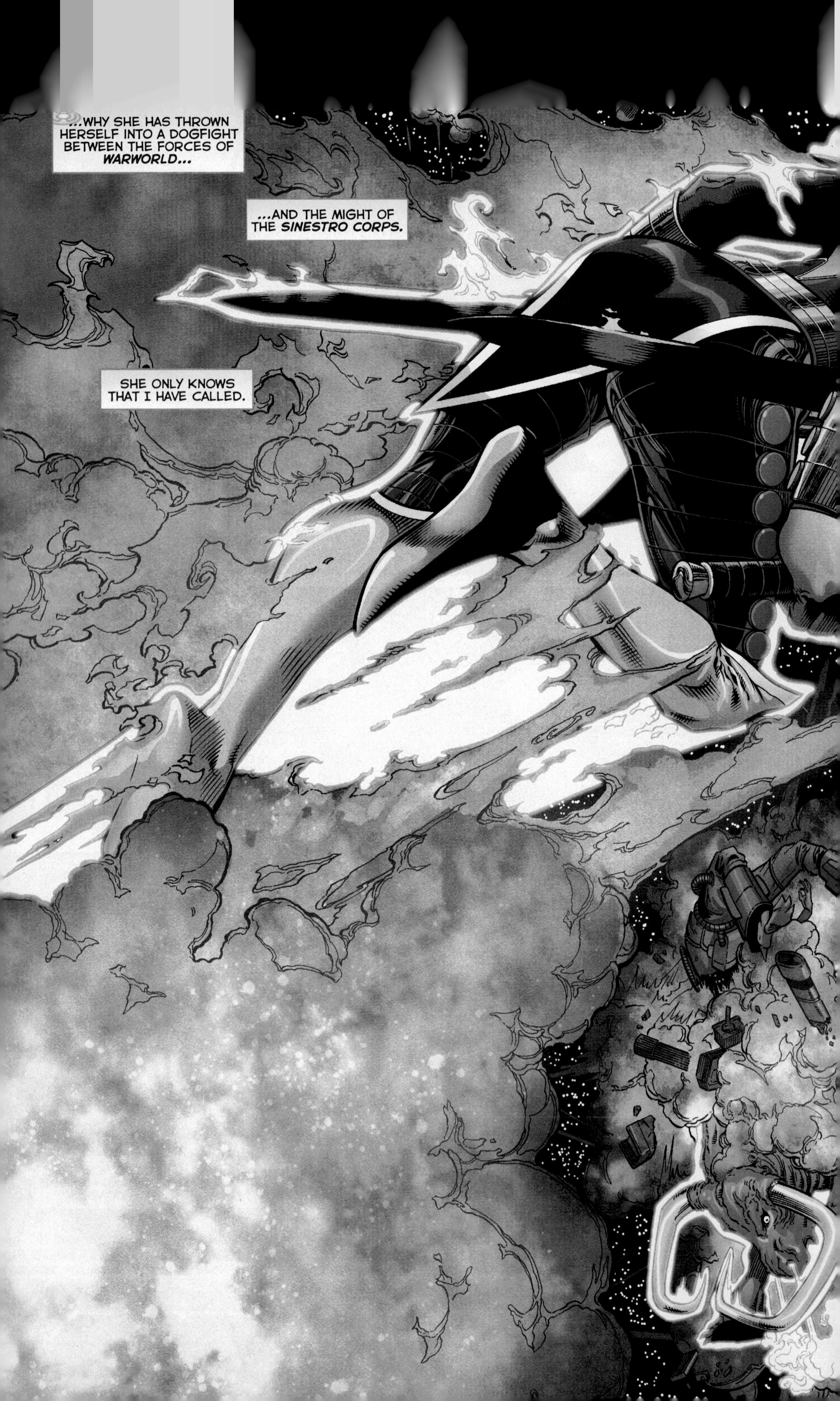
...WHY SHE HAS THROWN HERSELF INTO A DOGFIGHT BETWEEN THE FORCES OF WARWORLD...
...AND THE MIGHT OF THE SINESTRO CORPS.
SHE ONLY KNOWS THAT I HAVE CALLED.

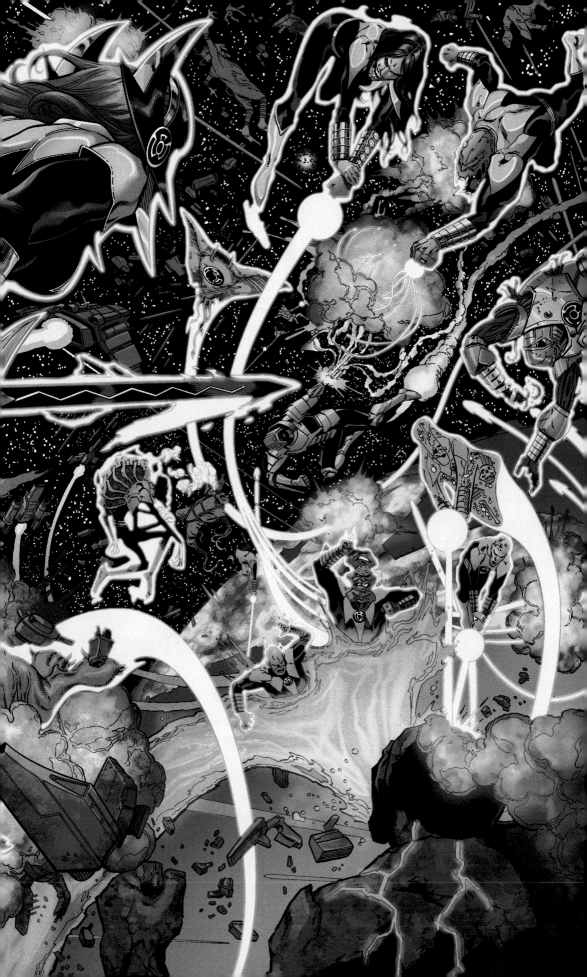

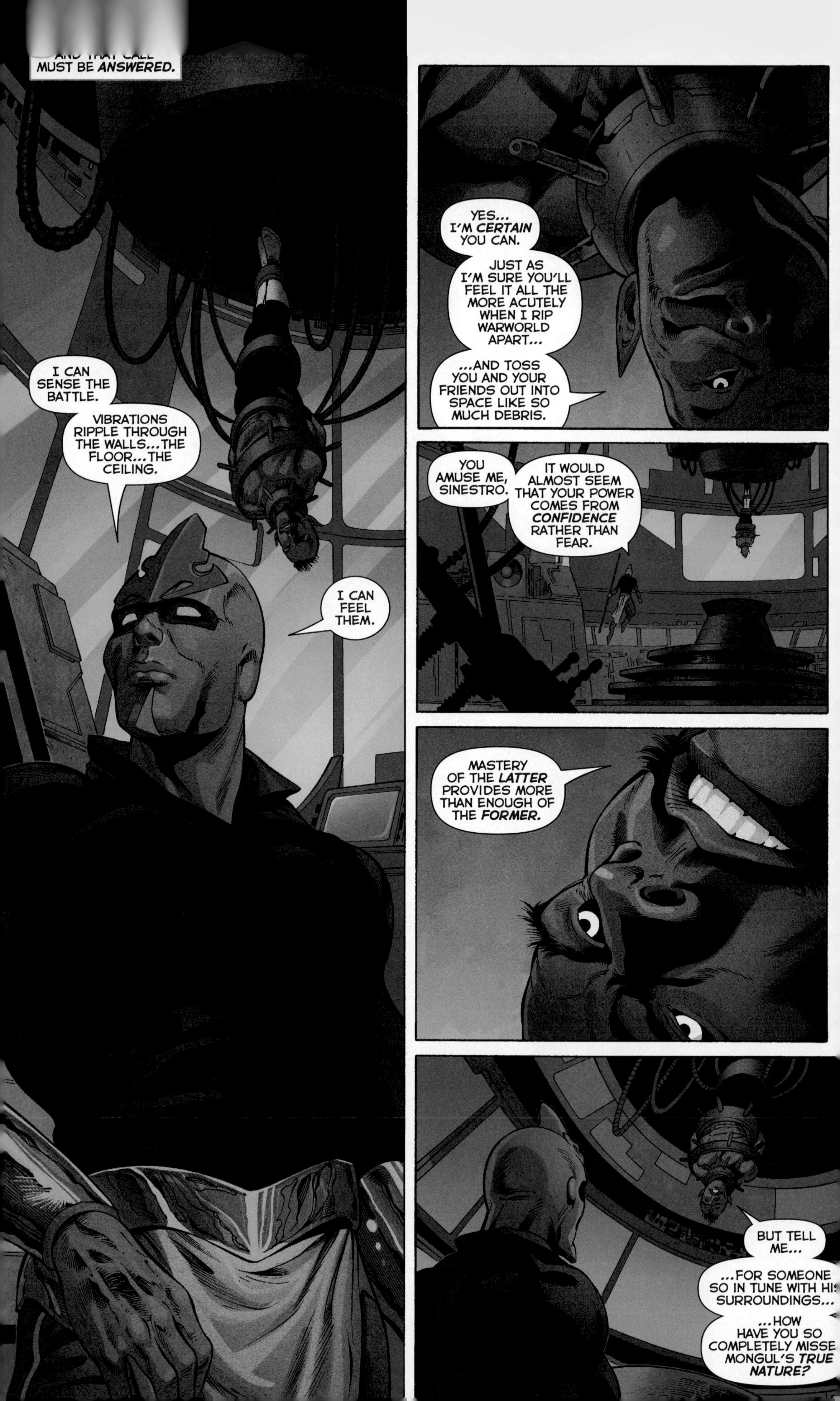

MUST BE *ANSWERED.*
I CAN SENSE THE BATTLE.
VIBRATIONS RIPPLE THROUGH THE WALLS...THE FLOOR...THE CEILING.
I CAN FEEL THEM.
YES... I'M *CERTAIN* YOU CAN.
JUST AS I'M SURE YOU'LL FEEL IT ALL THE MORE ACUTELY WHEN I RIP WARWORLD APART...
...AND TOSS YOU AND YOUR FRIENDS OUT INTO SPACE LIKE SO MUCH DEBRIS.
YOU AMUSE ME, SINESTRO.
IT WOULD ALMOST SEEM THAT YOUR POWER COMES FROM *CONFIDENCE* RATHER THAN FEAR.
MASTERY OF THE *LATTER* PROVIDES MORE THAN ENOUGH OF THE *FORMER.*
BUT TELL ME...
...FOR SOMEONE SO IN TUNE WITH HI SURROUNDINGS...
...HOW HAVE YOU SO COMPLETELY MISSE MONGUL'S *TRUE NATURE?*

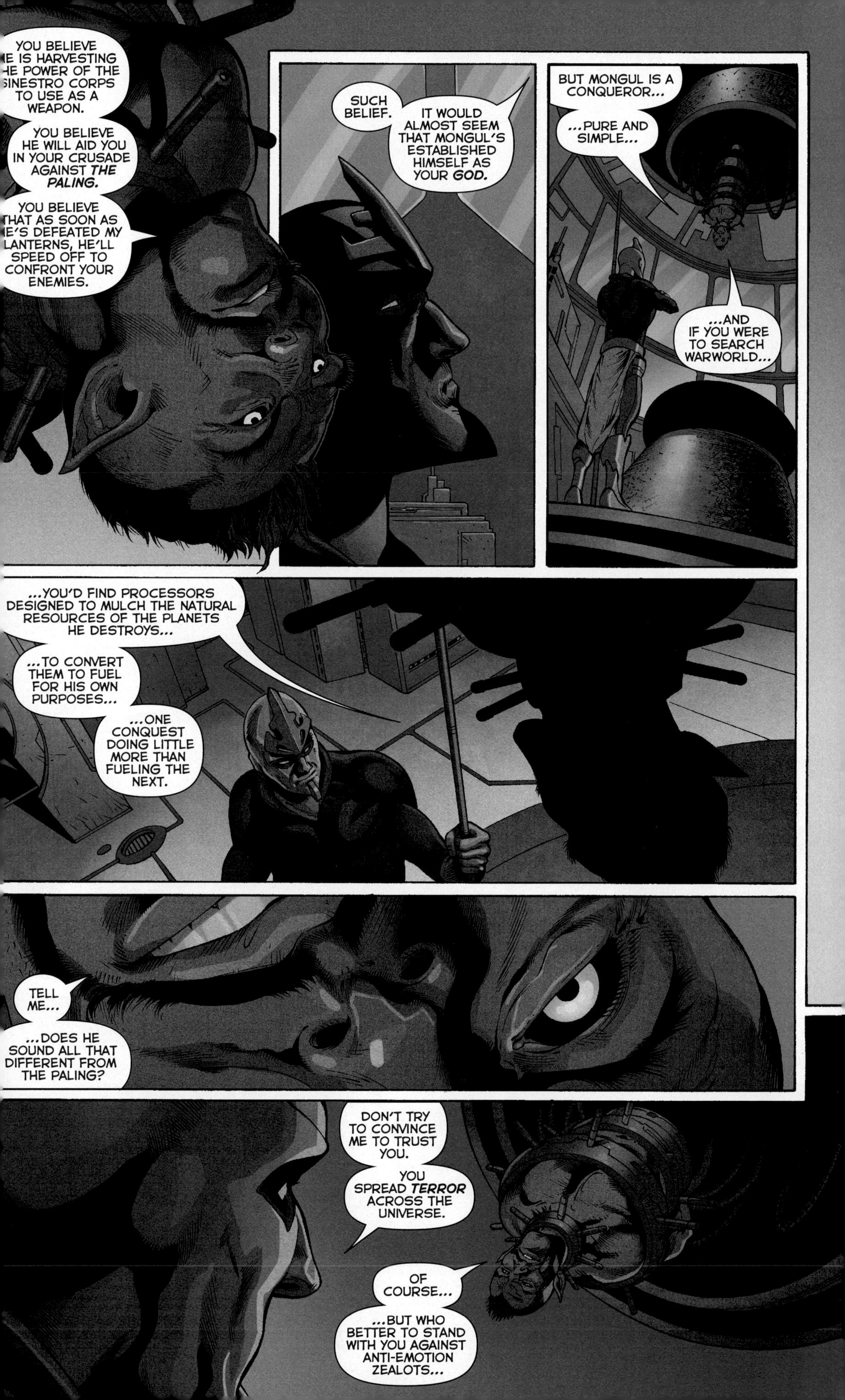
YOU BELIEVE HE IS HARVESTING THE POWER OF THE SINESTRO CORPS TO USE AS A WEAPON.
YOU BELIEVE HE WILL AID YOU IN YOUR CRUSADE AGAINST THE PALING.
YOU BELIEVE THAT AS SOON AS HE'S DEFEATED MY LANTERNS, HE'LL SPEED OFF TO CONFRONT YOUR ENEMIES.
SUCH BELIEF.
IT WOULD ALMOST SEEM THAT MONGUL'S ESTABLISHED HIMSELF AS YOUR GOD.
BUT MONGUL IS A CONQUEROR...
...PURE AND SIMPLE...
...AND IF YOU WERE TO SEARCH WARWORLD...
...YOU'D FIND PROCESSORS DESIGNED TO MULCH THE NATURAL RESOURCES OF THE PLANETS HE DESTROYS...
...TO CONVERT THEM TO FUEL FOR HIS OWN PURPOSES...
...ONE CONQUEST DOING LITTLE MORE THAN FUELING THE NEXT.
TELL ME...
...DOES HE SOUND ALL THAT DIFFERENT FROM THE PALING?
DON'T TRY TO CONVINCE ME TO TRUST YOU.
YOU SPREAD TERROR ACROSS THE UNIVERSE.
OF COURSE...
...BUT WHO BETTER TO STAND WITH YOU AGAINST ANTI-EMOTION ZEALOTS...

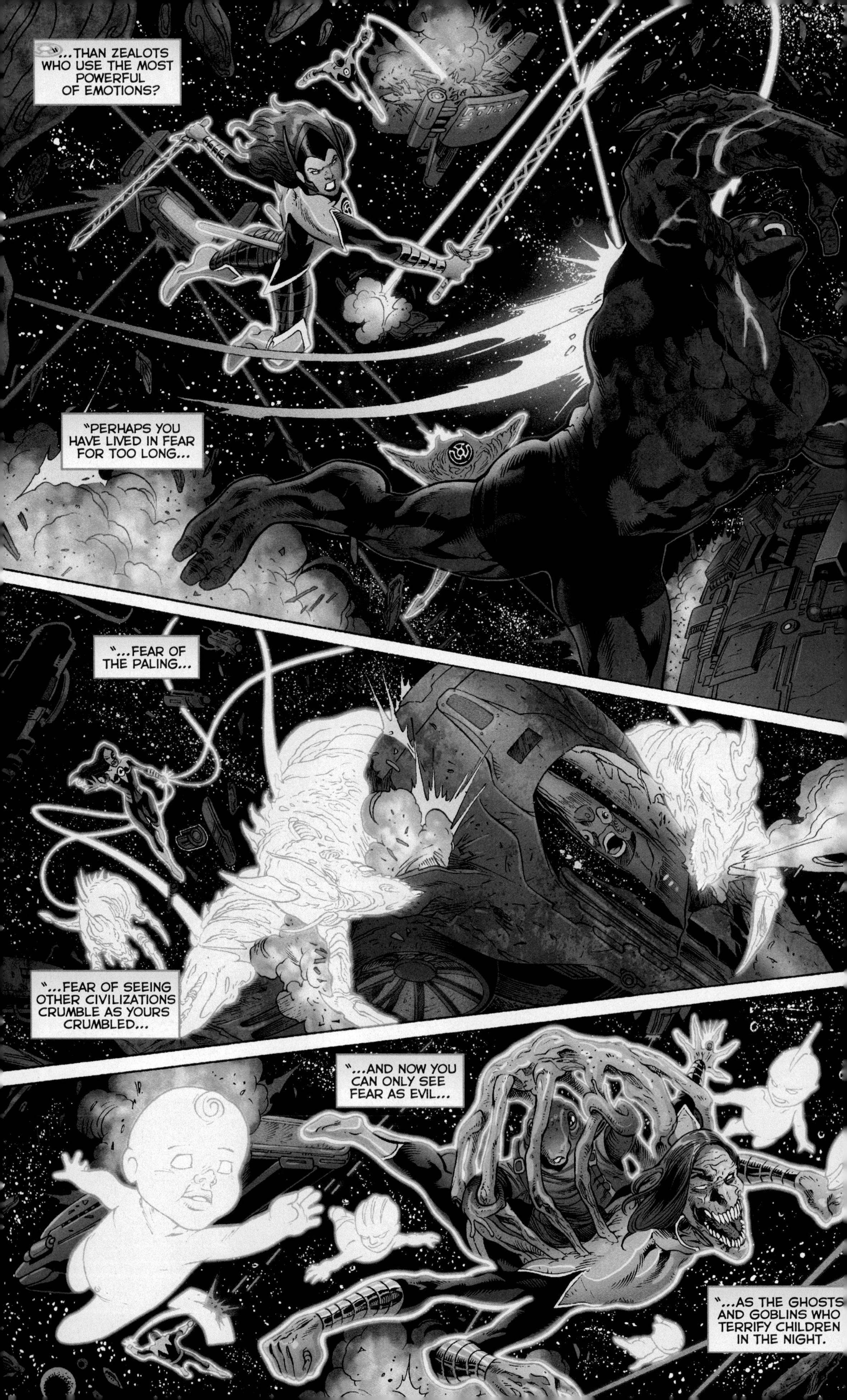
"...THAN ZEALOTS WHO USE THE MOST POWERFUL OF EMOTIONS?
"PERHAPS YOU HAVE LIVED IN FEAR FOR TOO LONG...
"...FEAR OF THE PALING...
"...FEAR OF SEEING OTHER CIVILIZATIONS CRUMBLE AS YOURS CRUMBLED...
"...AND NOW YOU CAN ONLY SEE FEAR AS EVIL...
"...AS THE GHOSTS AND GOBLINS WHO TERRIFY CHILDREN IN THE NIGHT.

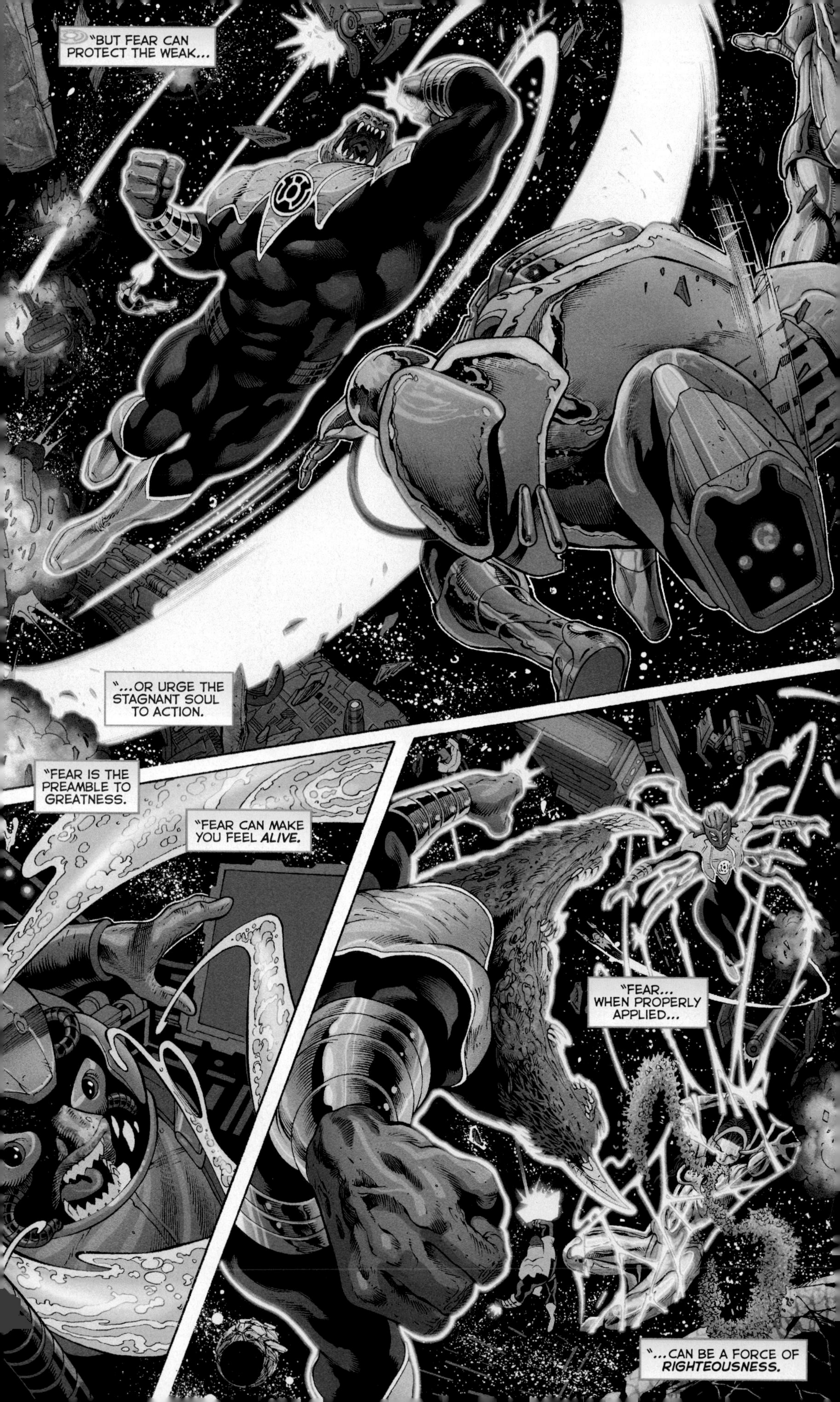
"BUT FEAR CAN PROTECT THE WEAK...
"...OR URGE THE STAGNANT SOUL TO ACTION.
"FEAR IS THE PREAMBLE TO GREATNESS.
"FEAR CAN MAKE YOU FEEL *ALIVE.*
"FEAR... WHEN PROPERLY APPLIED...
"...CAN BE A FORCE OF *RIGHTEOUSNESS.*

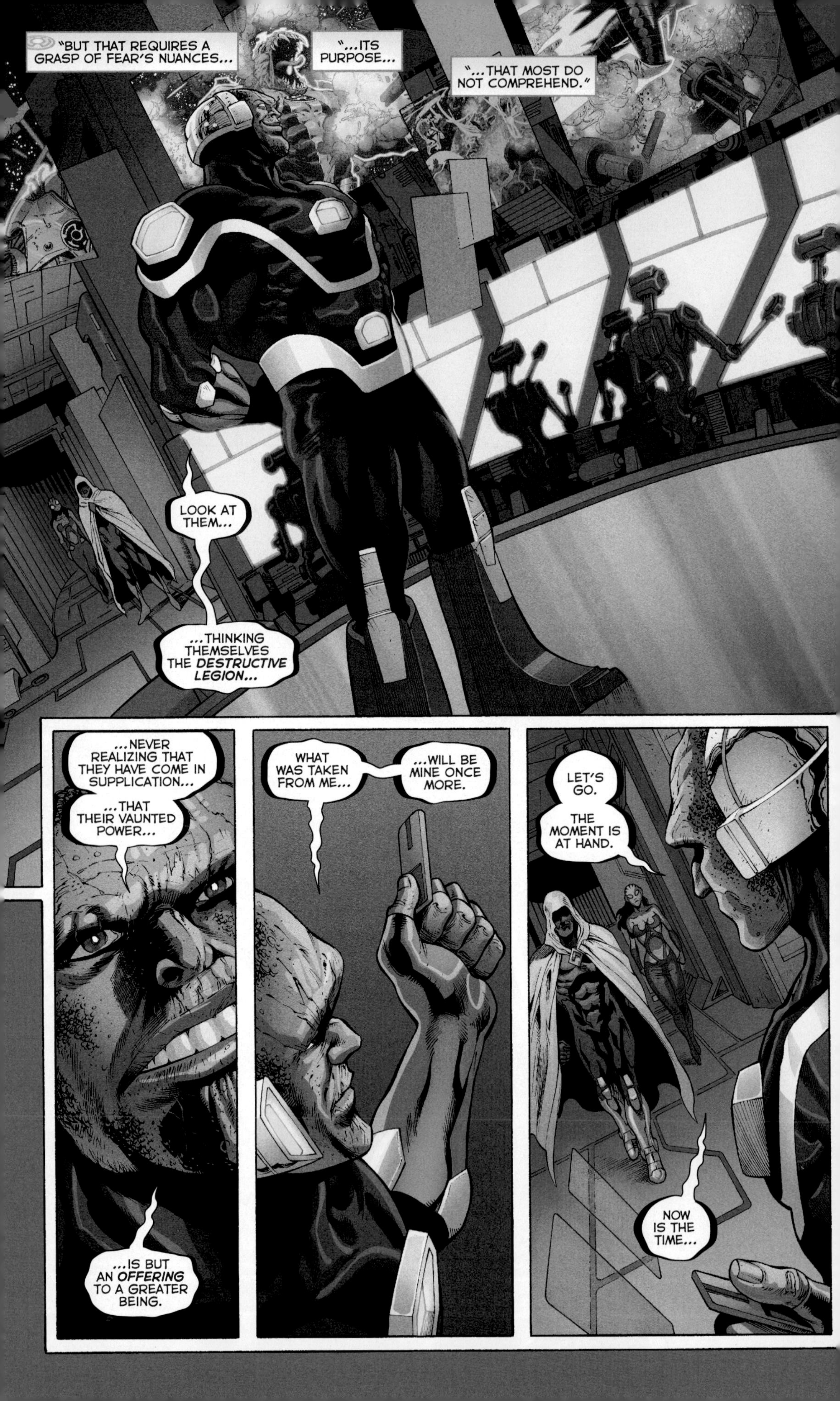
"BUT THAT REQUIRES A GRASP OF FEAR'S NUANCES...
"...ITS PURPOSE...
"...THAT MOST DO NOT COMPREHEND."
LOOK AT THEM...
...THINKING THEMSELVES THE *DESTRUCTIVE LEGION*...
...NEVER REALIZING THAT THEY HAVE COME IN SUPPLICATION...
...THAT THEIR VAUNTED POWER...
...IS BUT AN *OFFERING* TO A GREATER BEING.
WHAT WAS TAKEN FROM ME...
...WILL BE MINE ONCE MORE.
LET'S GO.
THE MOMENT IS AT HAND.
NOW IS THE TIME...

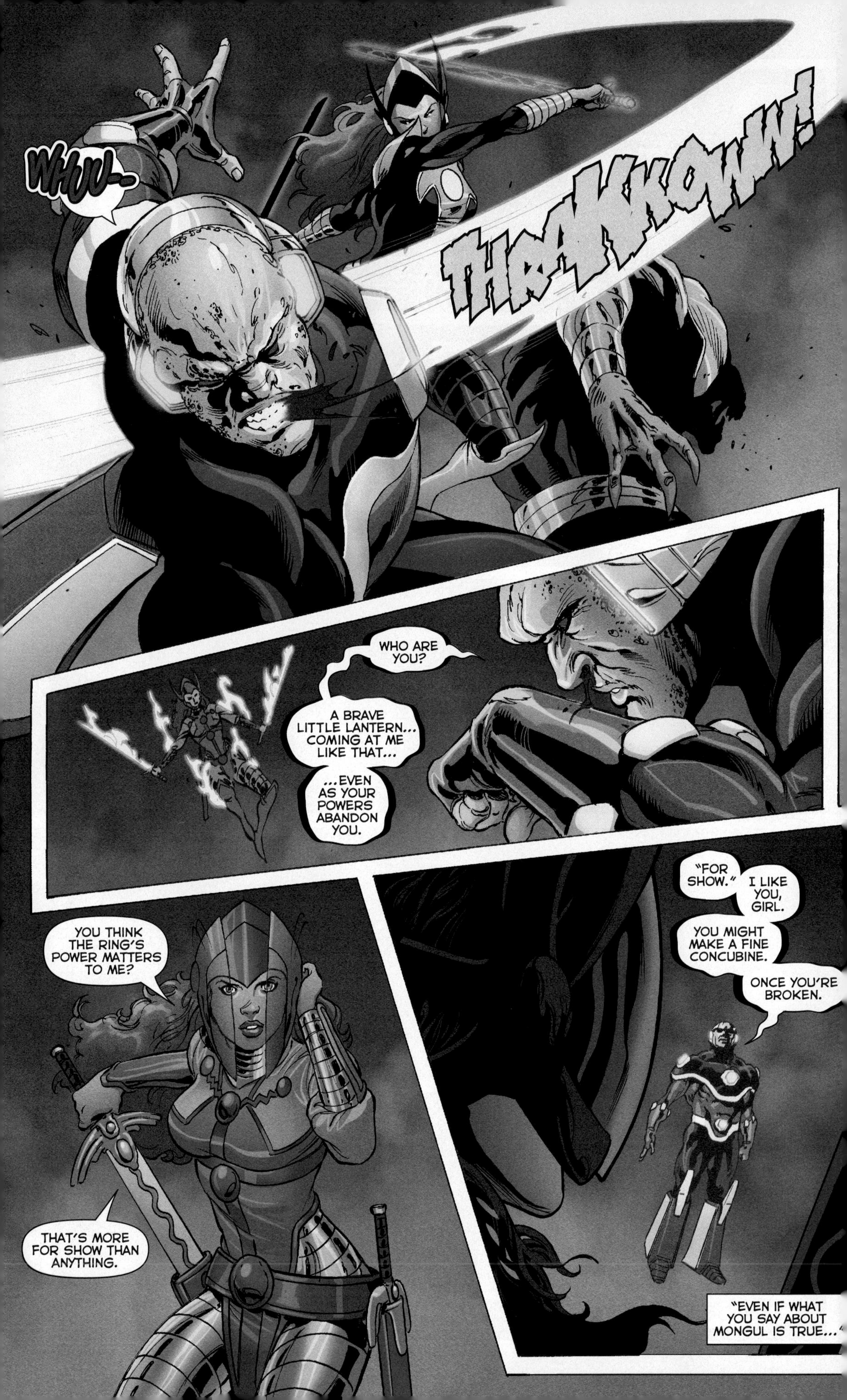
WHUU--
THRAKKOWW!
WHO ARE YOU?
A BRAVE LITTLE LANTERN... COMING AT ME LIKE THAT...
...EVEN AS YOUR POWERS ABANDON YOU.
YOU THINK THE RING'S POWER MATTERS TO ME?
THAT'S MORE FOR SHOW THAN ANYTHING.
"FOR SHOW." I LIKE YOU, GIRL.
YOU MIGHT MAKE A FINE CONCUBINE.
ONCE YOU'RE BROKEN.
"EVEN IF WHAT YOU SAY ABOUT MONGUL IS TRUE..."

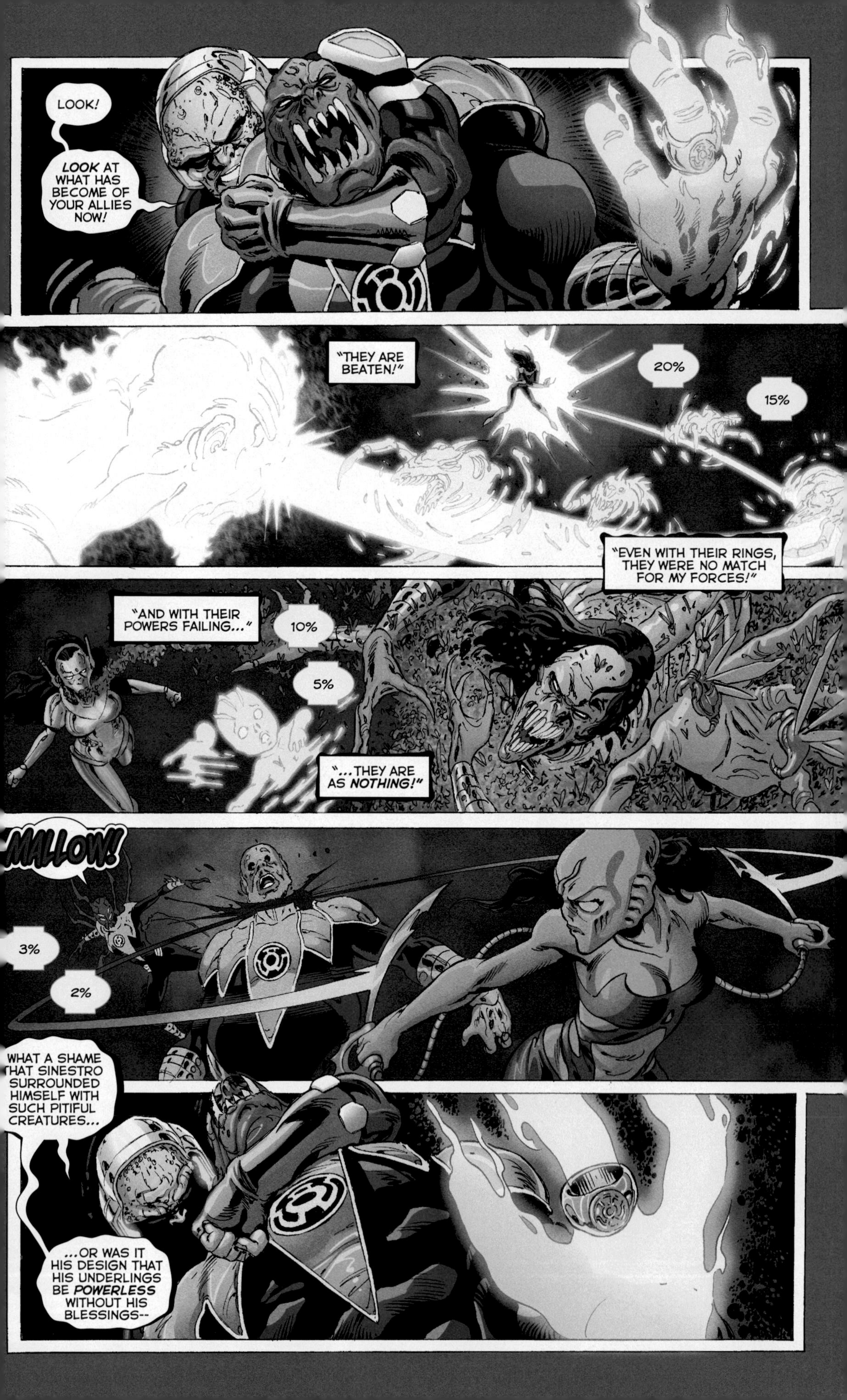
LOOK!
LOOK AT WHAT HAS BECOME OF YOUR ALLIES NOW!
"THEY ARE BEATEN!"
20%
15%
"EVEN WITH THEIR RINGS, THEY WERE NO MATCH FOR MY FORCES!"
"AND WITH THEIR POWERS FAILING..."
10%
5%
"...THEY ARE AS NOTHING!"
MALLOW!
3%
2%
WHAT A SHAME THAT SINESTRO SURROUNDED HIMSELF WITH SUCH PITIFUL CREATURES...
...OR WAS IT HIS DESIGN THAT HIS UNDERLINGS BE POWERLESS WITHOUT HIS BLESSINGS--

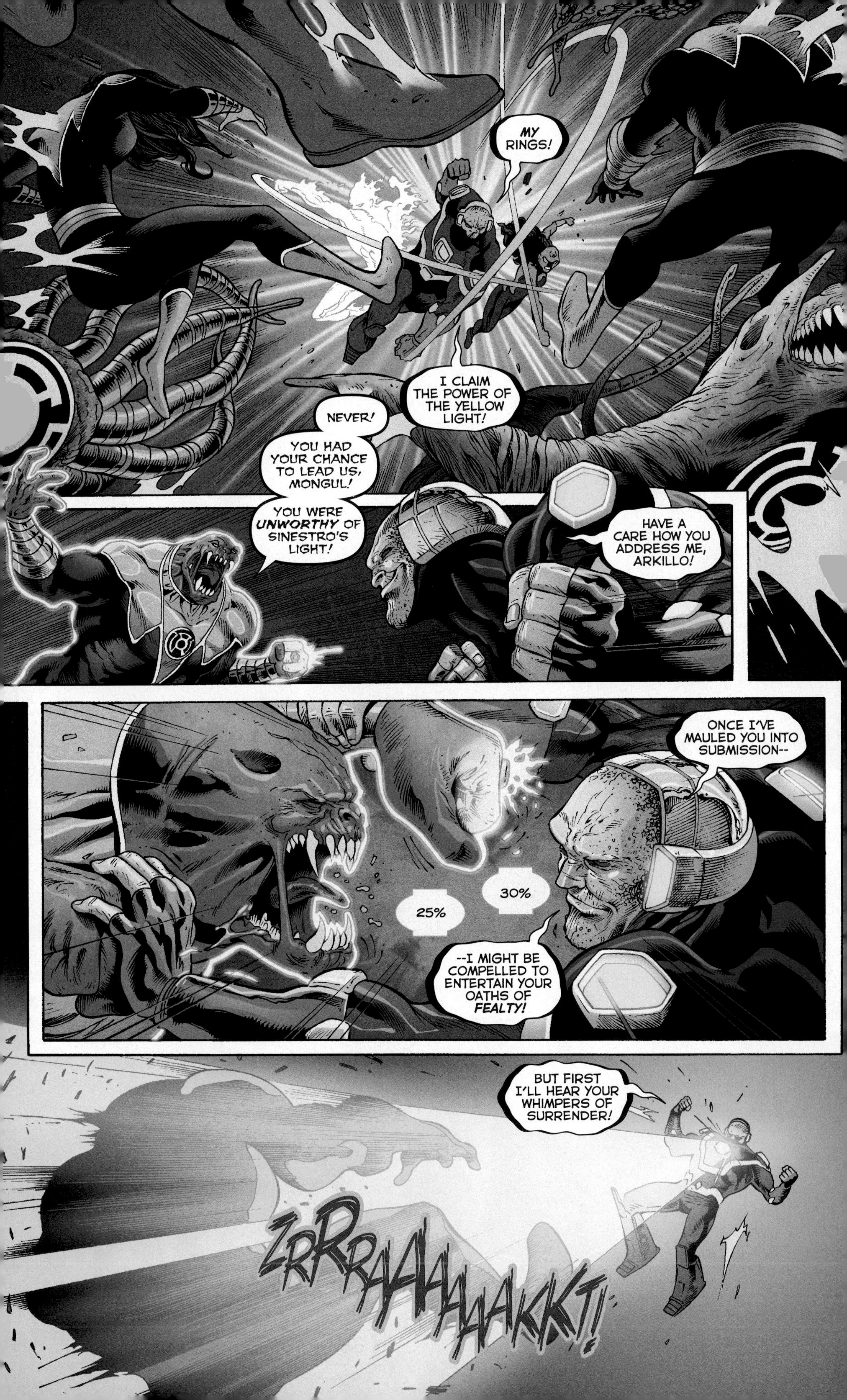
MY RINGS!
I CLAIM THE POWER OF THE YELLOW LIGHT!
NEVER!
YOU HAD YOUR CHANCE TO LEAD US, MONGUL!
YOU WERE UNWORTHY OF SINESTRO'S LIGHT!
HAVE A CARE HOW YOU ADDRESS ME, ARKILLO!
ONCE I'VE MAULED YOU INTO SUBMISSION--
30%
25%
--I MIGHT BE COMPELLED TO ENTERTAIN YOUR OATHS OF FEALTY!
BUT FIRST I'LL HEAR YOUR WHIMPERS OF SURRENDER!
ZRRRAAAAAAAKKT!

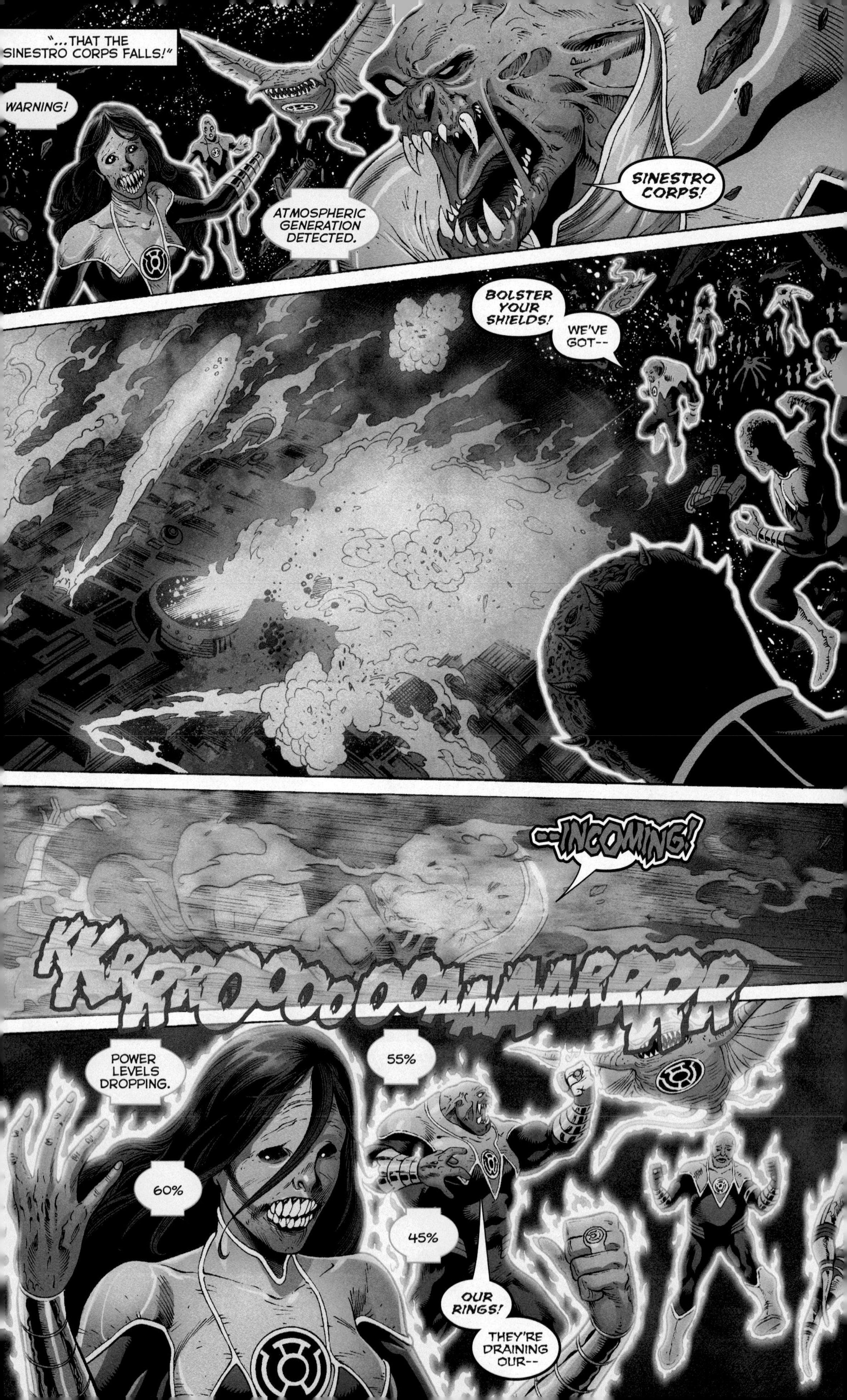
"...THAT THE SINESTRO CORPS FALLS!"
WARNING!
ATMOSPHERIC GENERATION DETECTED.
SINESTRO CORPS!
BOLSTER YOUR SHIELDS!
WE'VE GOT--
--INCOMING!
KRROOOOOOMMMRRRR
POWER LEVELS DROPPING.
55%
60%
45%
OUR RINGS!
THEY'RE DRAINING OUR--

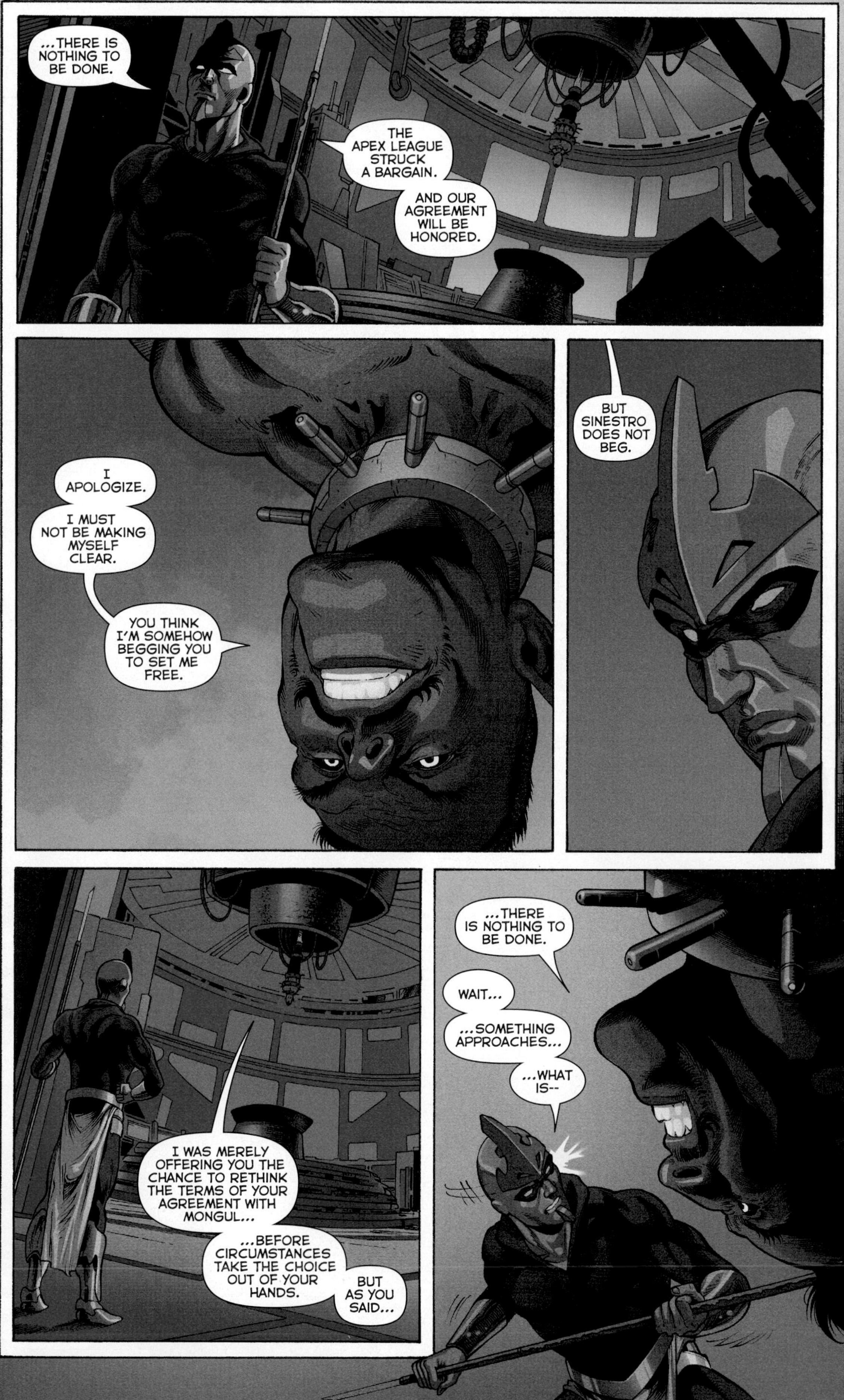

...THERE IS NOTHING TO BE DONE.
THE APEX LEAGUE STRUCK A BARGAIN.
AND OUR AGREEMENT WILL BE HONORED.
I APOLOGIZE.
I MUST NOT BE MAKING MYSELF CLEAR.
YOU THINK I'M SOMEHOW BEGGING YOU TO SET ME FREE.
BUT SINESTRO DOES NOT BEG.
I WAS MERELY OFFERING YOU THE CHANCE TO RETHINK THE TERMS OF YOUR AGREEMENT WITH MONGUL...
...BEFORE CIRCUMSTANCES TAKE THE CHOICE OUT OF YOUR HANDS.
BUT AS YOU SAID...
...THERE IS NOTHING TO BE DONE.
WAIT...
...SOMETHING APPROACHES...
...WHAT IS--

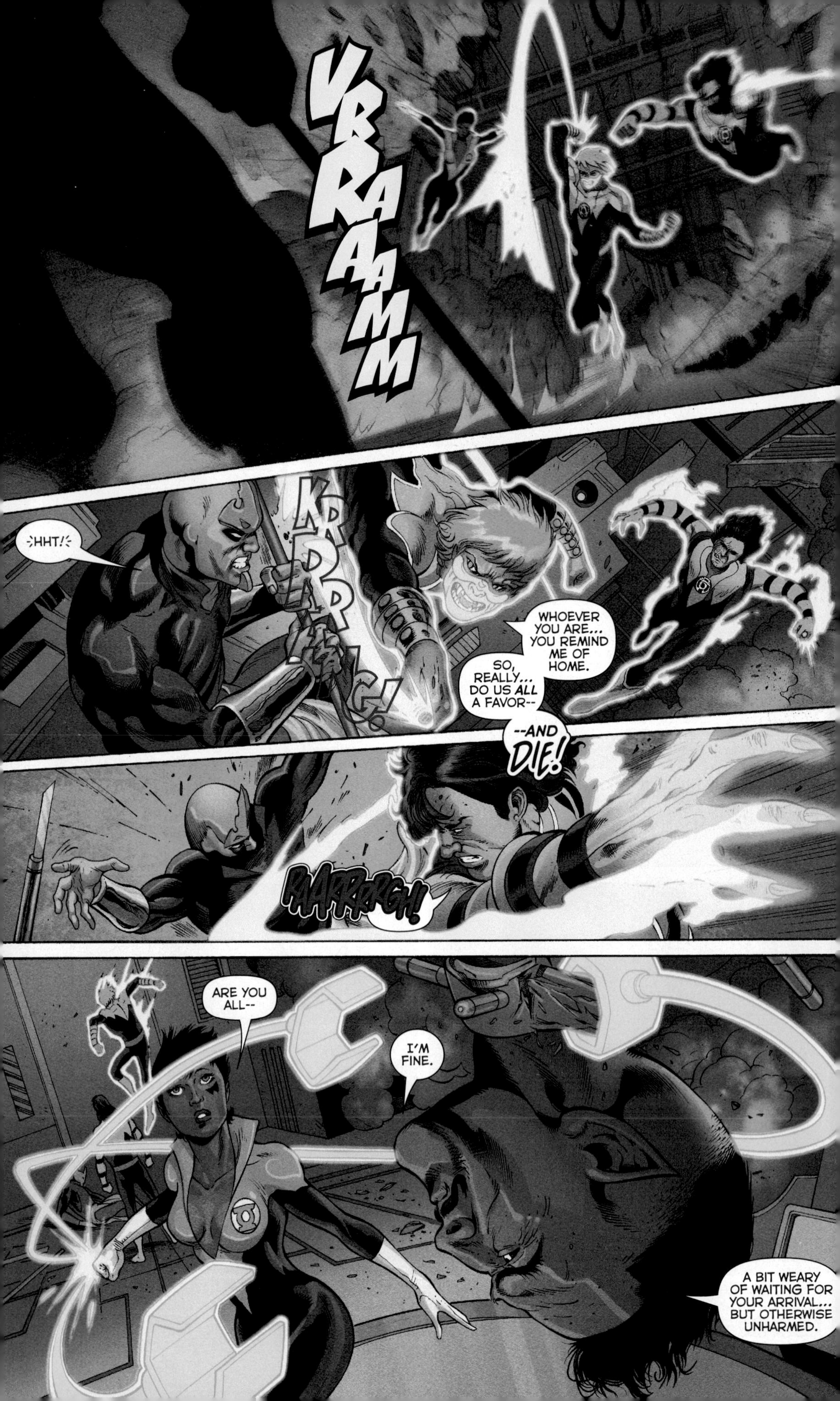
VRRAAAMMM
HHT!
KRRRANG!
WHOEVER YOU ARE... YOU REMIND ME OF HOME.
SO, REALLY... DO US ALL A FAVOR--
--AND DIE!
RAAARRRRGH!
ARE YOU ALL--
I'M FINE.
A BIT WEARY OF WAITING FOR YOUR ARRIVAL... BUT OTHERWISE UNHARMED.

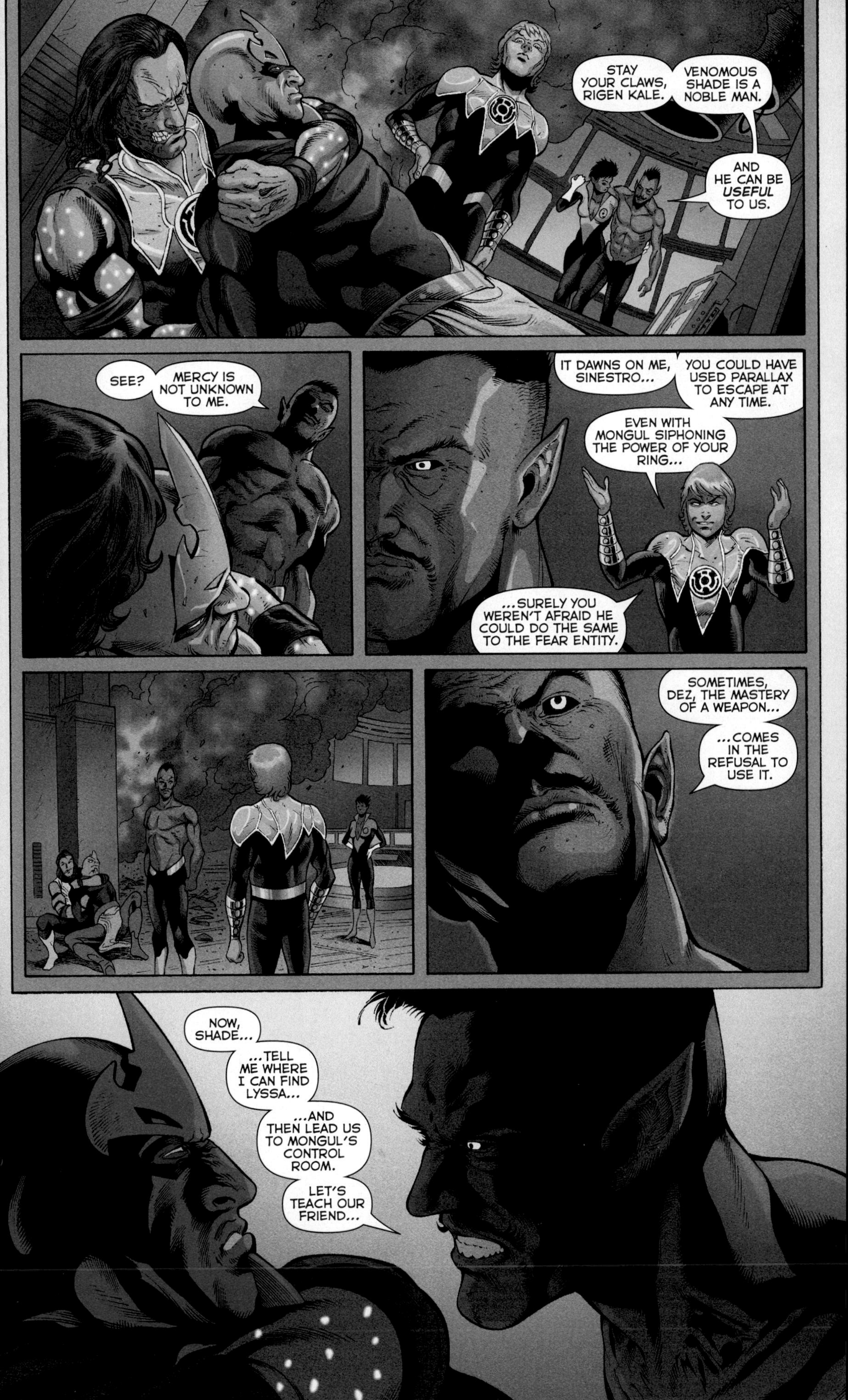
STAY YOUR CLAWS, RIGEN KALE.
VENOMOUS SHADE IS A NOBLE MAN.
AND HE CAN BE *USEFUL* TO US.
SEE?
MERCY IS NOT UNKNOWN TO ME.
IT DAWNS ON ME, SINESTRO...
YOU COULD HAVE USED PARALLAX TO ESCAPE AT ANY TIME.
EVEN WITH MONGUL SIPHONING THE POWER OF YOUR RING...
...SURELY YOU WEREN'T AFRAID HE COULD DO THE SAME TO THE FEAR ENTITY.
SOMETIMES, DEZ, THE MASTERY OF A WEAPON...
...COMES IN THE REFUSAL TO USE IT.
NOW, SHADE...
...TELL ME WHERE I CAN FIND LYSSA...
...AND THEN LEAD US TO MONGUL'S CONTROL ROOM.
LET'S TEACH OUR FRIEND...

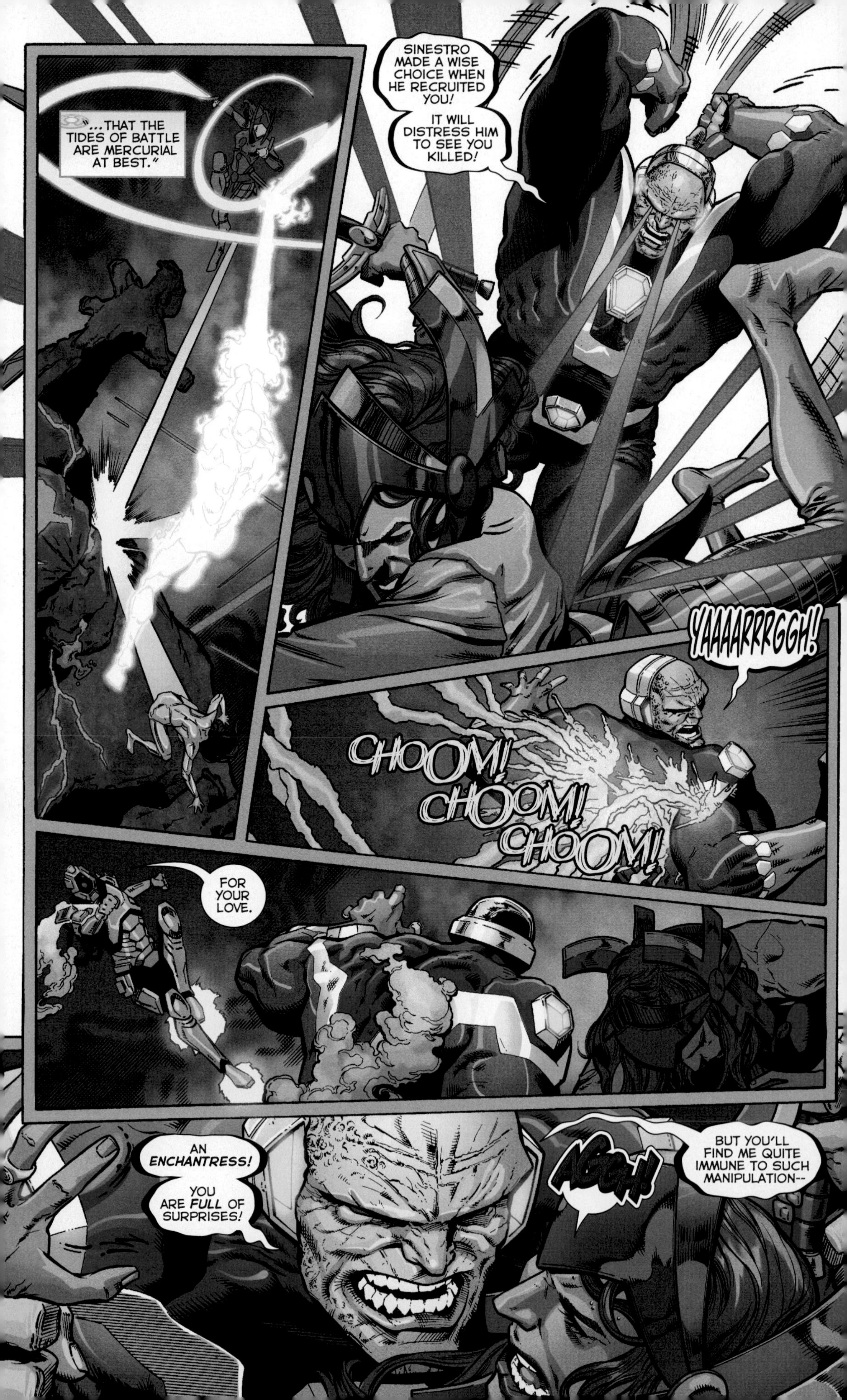
"...THAT THE TIDES OF BATTLE ARE MERCURIAL AT BEST."
SINESTRO MADE A WISE CHOICE WHEN HE RECRUITED YOU!
IT WILL DISTRESS HIM TO SEE YOU KILLED!
YAAAARRRGGH!
CHOOM! CHOOM! CHOOM!
FOR YOUR LOVE.
AN ENCHANTRESS!
YOU ARE FULL OF SURPRISES!
AGGH!
BUT YOU'LL FIND ME QUITE IMMUNE TO SUCH MANIPULATION--

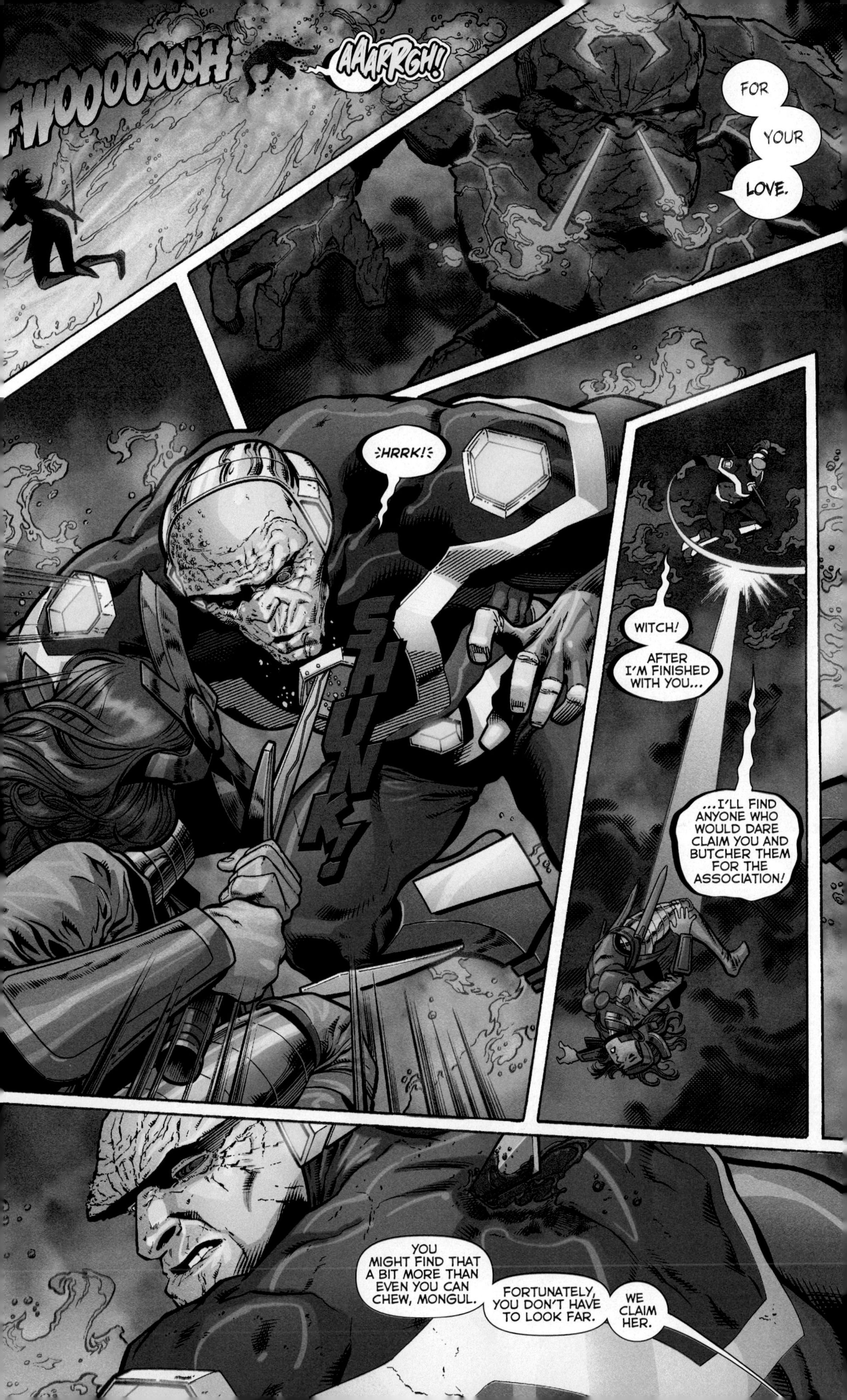
FWOOOOOOSH
AAARRGH!
FOR
YOUR
LOVE.
HRRK!
SHUNK!
WITCH!
AFTER I'M FINISHED WITH YOU...
...I'LL FIND ANYONE WHO WOULD DARE CLAIM YOU AND BUTCHER THEM FOR THE ASSOCIATION!
YOU MIGHT FIND THAT A BIT MORE THAN EVEN YOU CAN CHEW, MONGUL.
FORTUNATELY, YOU DON'T HAVE TO LOOK FAR.
WE CLAIM HER.

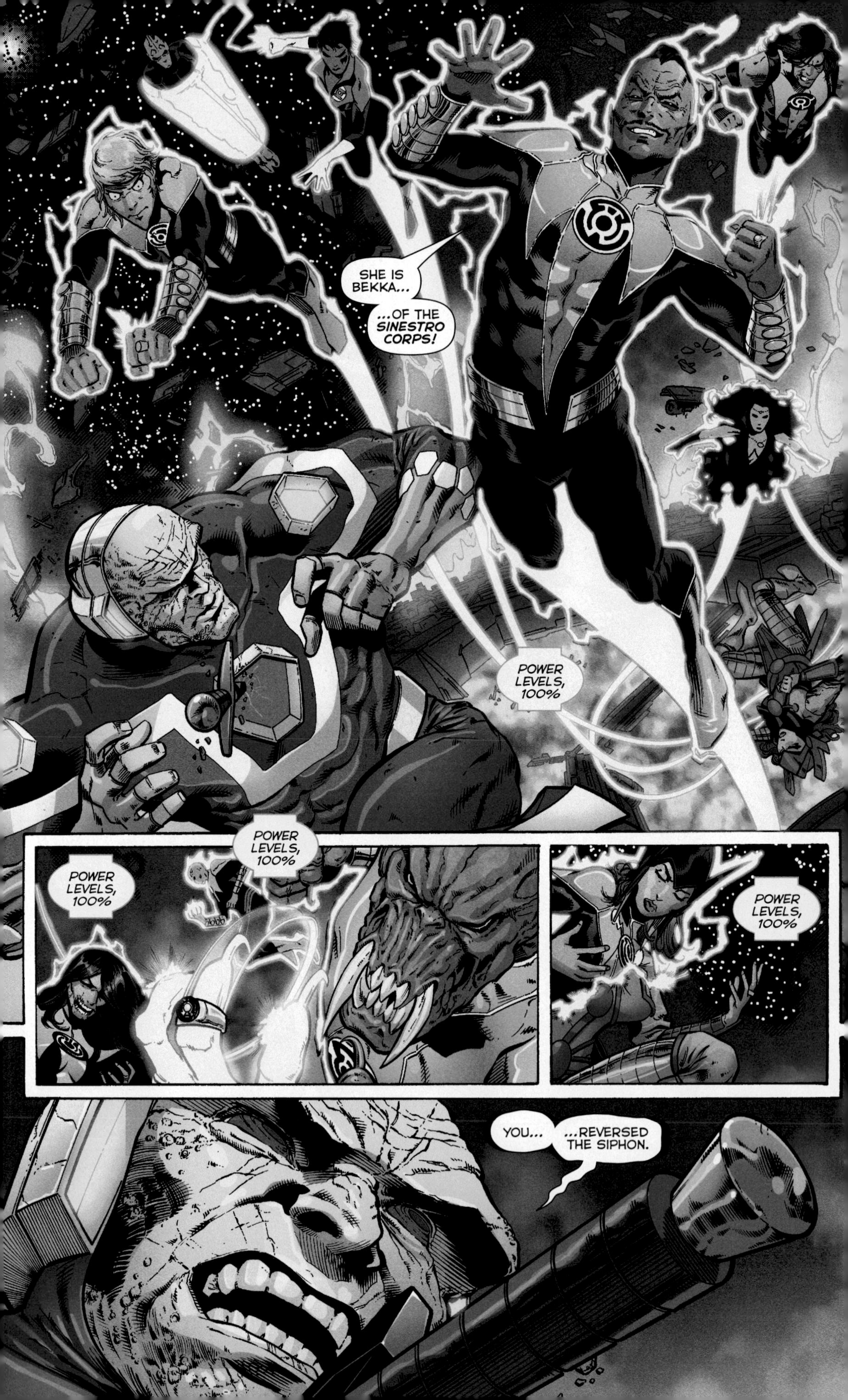
SHE IS BEKKA...
...OF THE SINESTRO CORPS!
POWER LEVELS, 100%
POWER LEVELS, 100%
POWER LEVELS, 100%
POWER LEVELS, 100%
YOU...
...REVERSED THE SIPHON.

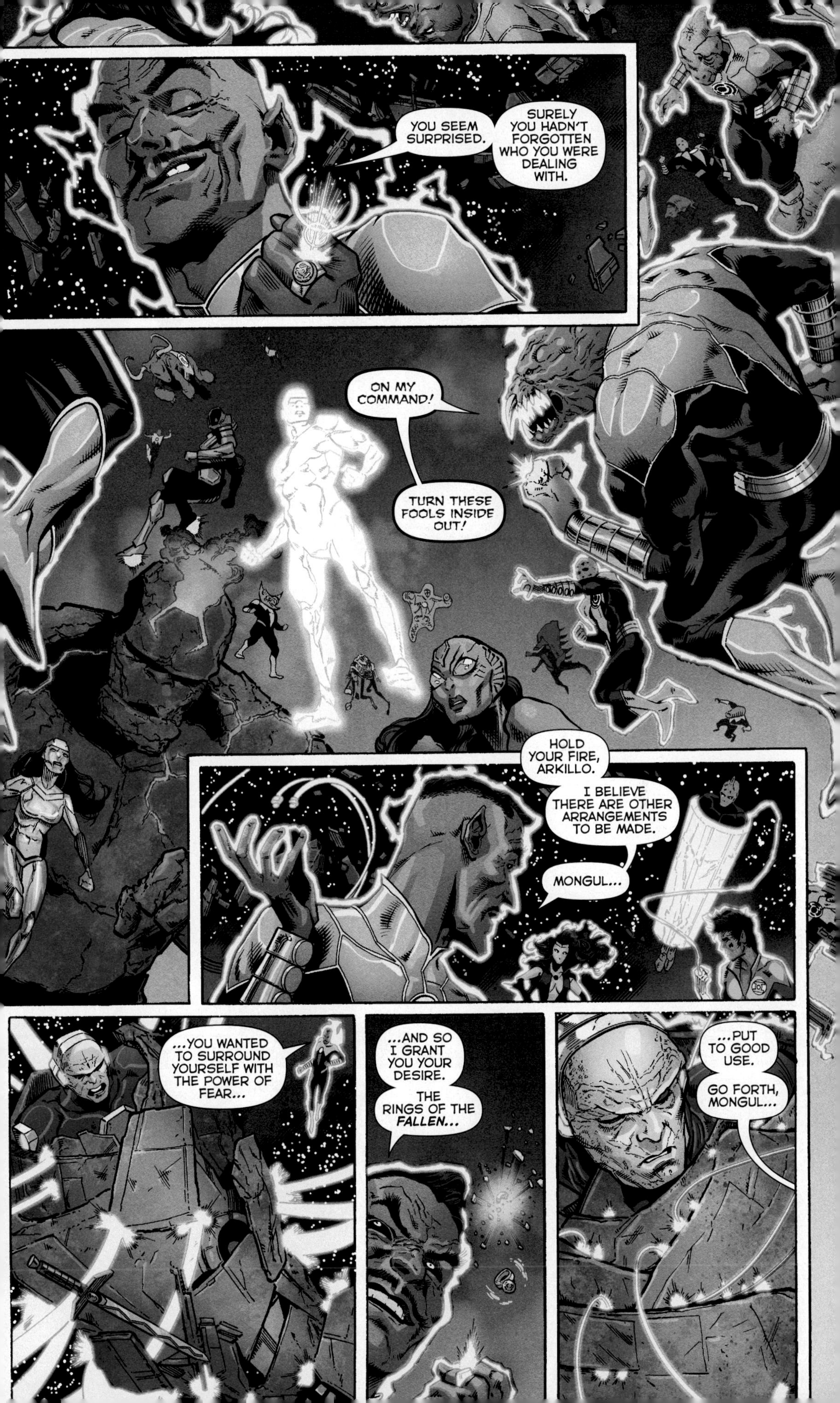
YOU SEEM SURPRISED.
SURELY YOU HADN'T FORGOTTEN WHO YOU WERE DEALING WITH.
ON MY COMMAND!
TURN THESE FOOLS INSIDE OUT!
HOLD YOUR FIRE, ARKILLO.
I BELIEVE THERE ARE OTHER ARRANGEMENTS TO BE MADE.
MONGUL...
...YOU WANTED TO SURROUND YOURSELF WITH THE POWER OF FEAR...
...AND SO I GRANT YOU YOUR DESIRE.
THE RINGS OF THE *FALLEN*...
...PUT TO GOOD USE.
GO FORTH, MONGUL...

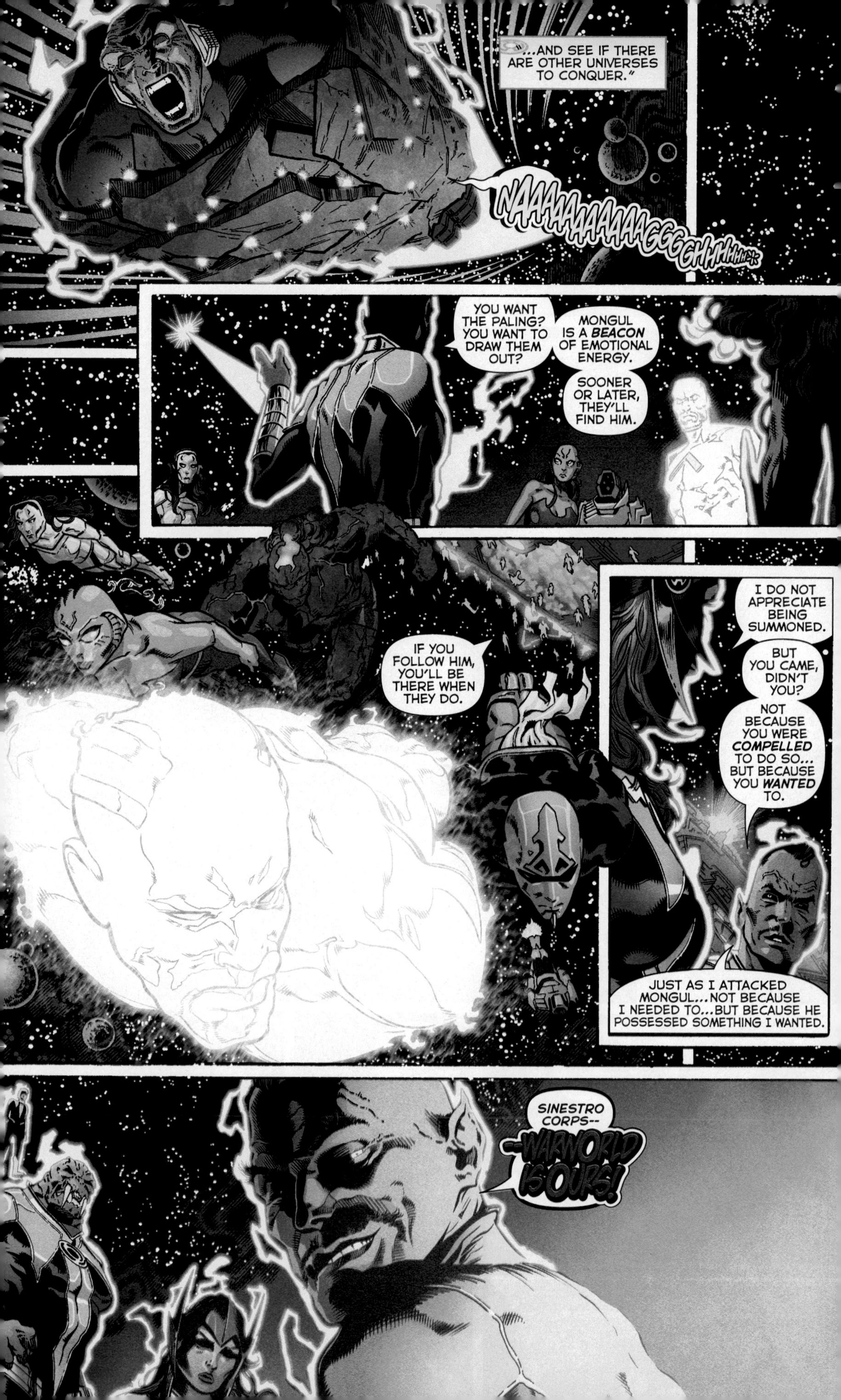

"...AND SEE IF THERE ARE OTHER UNIVERSES TO CONQUER."
NAAAAAAAAAAAAGGGGHHHHHHH!
YOU WANT THE PALING? YOU WANT TO DRAW THEM OUT?
MONGUL IS A BEACON OF EMOTIONAL ENERGY.
SOONER OR LATER, THEY'LL FIND HIM.
IF YOU FOLLOW HIM, YOU'LL BE THERE WHEN THEY DO.
I DO NOT APPRECIATE BEING SUMMONED.
BUT YOU CAME, DIDN'T YOU?
NOT BECAUSE YOU WERE COMPELLED TO DO SO... BUT BECAUSE YOU WANTED TO.
JUST AS I ATTACKED MONGUL...NOT BECAUSE I NEEDED TO...BUT BECAUSE HE POSSESSED SOMETHING I WANTED.
SINESTRO CORPS--
--WARWORLD IS OURS!

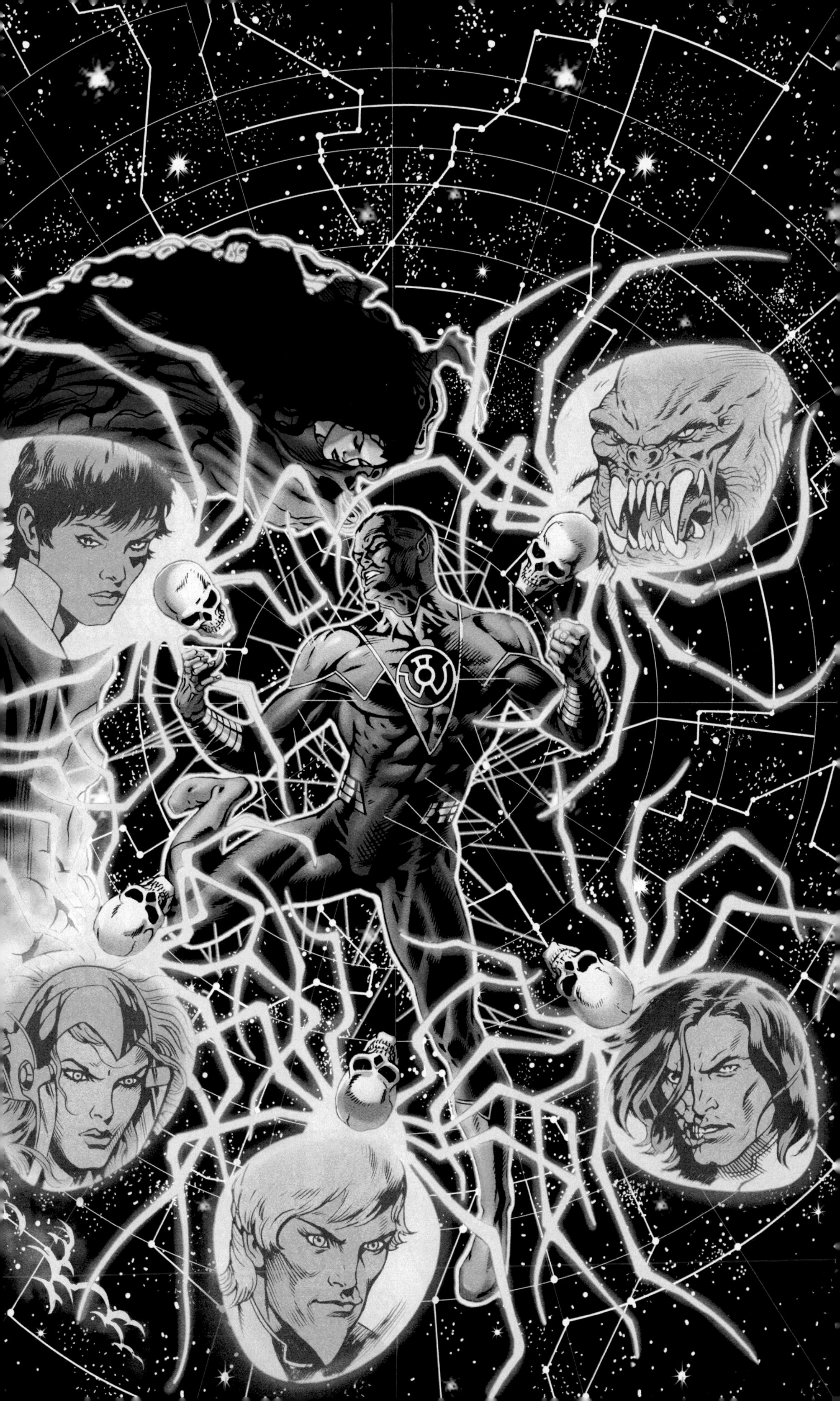

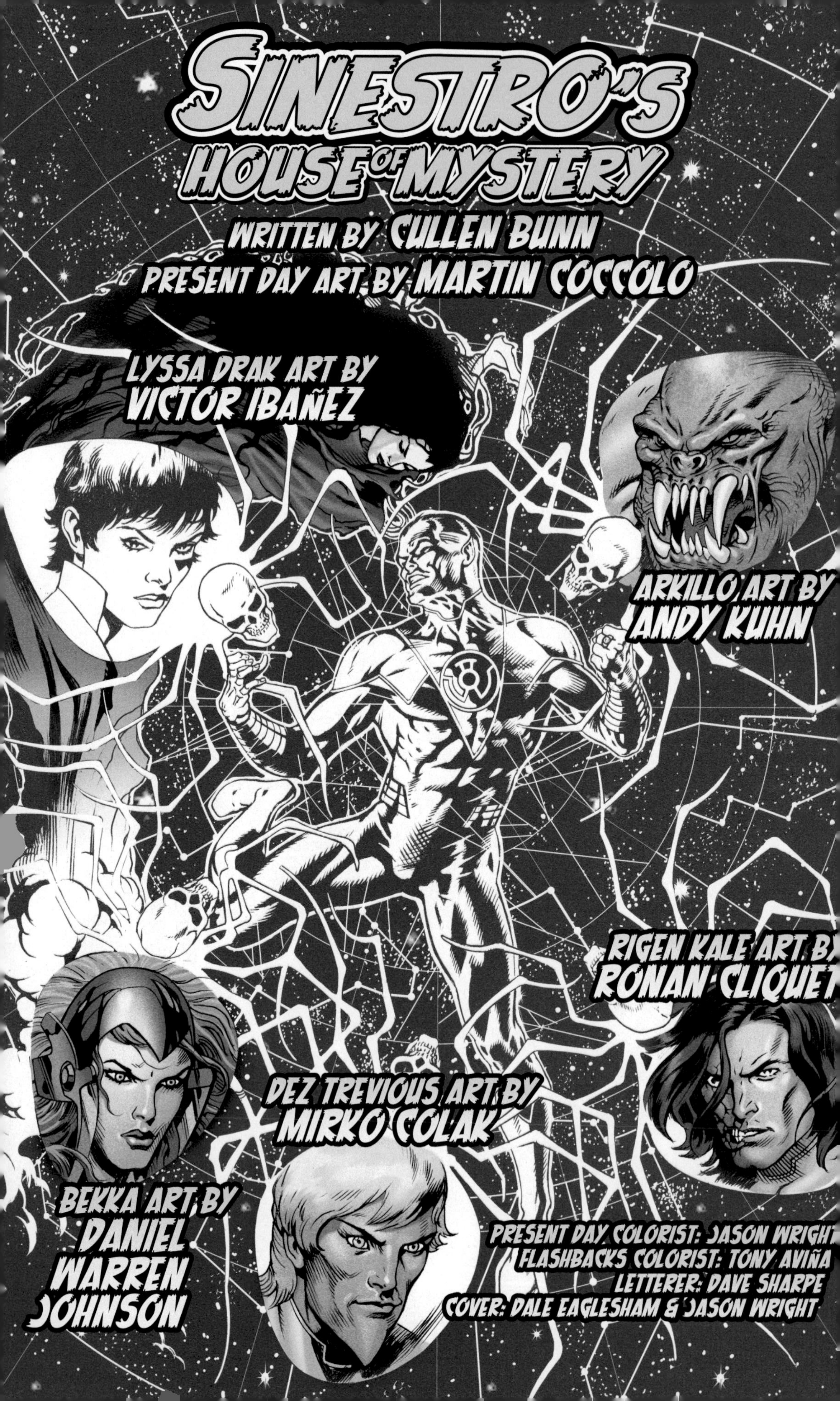
SINESTRO'S HOUSE OF MYSTERY
WRITTEN BY CULLEN BUNN
PRESENT DAY ART BY MARTIN COCCOLO
LYSSA DRAK ART BY VICTOR IBAÑEZ
ARKILLO ART BY ANDY KUHN
RIGEN KALE ART BY RONAN CLIQUET
DEZ TREVIOUS ART BY MIRKO COLAK
BEKKA ART BY DANIEL WARREN JOHNSON
PRESENT DAY COLORIST: JASON WRIGHT
FLASHBACKS COLORIST: TONY AVIÑA
LETTERER: DAVE SHARPE
COVER: DALE EAGLESHAM & JASON WRIGHT

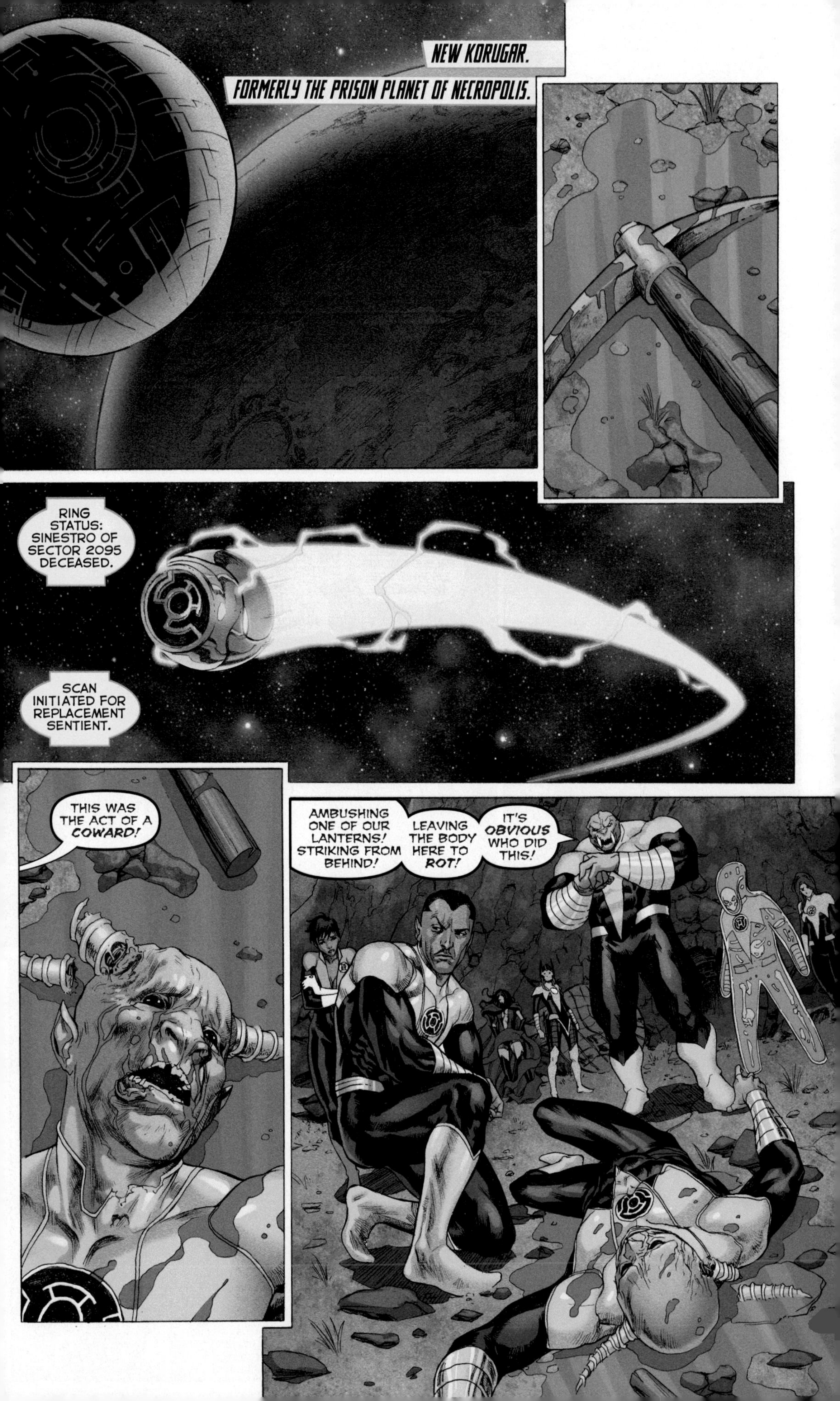
NEW KORUGAR.
FORMERLY THE PRISON PLANET OF NECROPOLIS.
RING STATUS: SINESTRO OF SECTOR 2095 DECEASED.
SCAN INITIATED FOR REPLACEMENT SENTIENT.
THIS WAS THE ACT OF A COWARD!
AMBUSHING ONE OF OUR LANTERNS! STRIKING FROM BEHIND!
LEAVING THE BODY HERE TO ROT!
IT'S OBVIOUS WHO DID THIS!

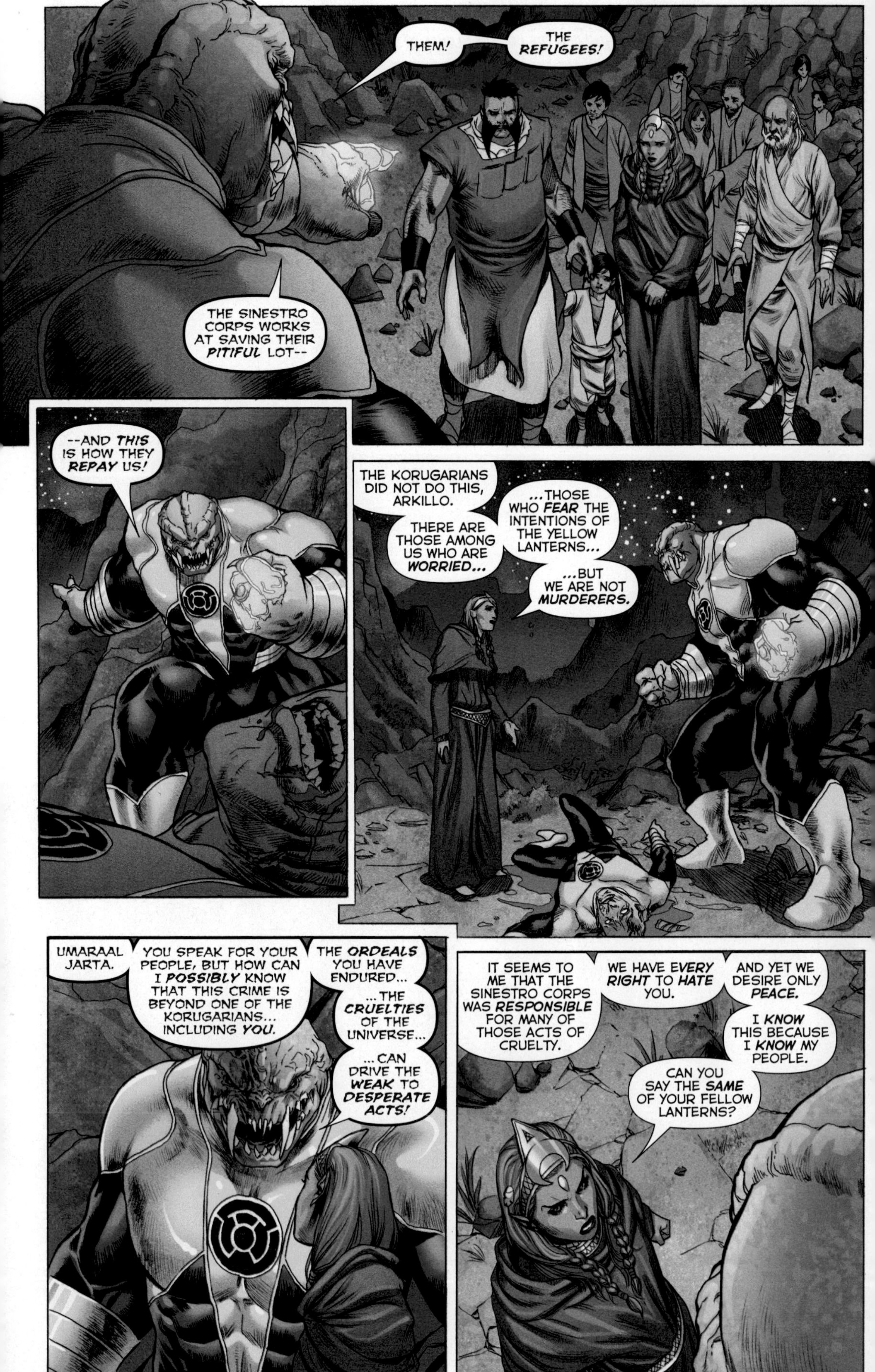
THEM!
THE REFUGEES!
THE SINESTRO CORPS WORKS AT SAVING THEIR PITIFUL LOT--
--AND THIS IS HOW THEY REPAY US!
THE KORUGARIANS DID NOT DO THIS, ARKILLO.
THERE ARE THOSE AMONG US WHO ARE WORRIED...
...THOSE WHO FEAR THE INTENTIONS OF THE YELLOW LANTERNS...
...BUT WE ARE NOT MURDERERS.
UMARAAL JARTA.
YOU SPEAK FOR YOUR PEOPLE, BUT HOW CAN I POSSIBLY KNOW THAT THIS CRIME IS BEYOND ONE OF THE KORUGARIANS... INCLUDING YOU.
THE ORDEALS YOU HAVE ENDURED...
...THE CRUELTIES OF THE UNIVERSE...
...CAN DRIVE THE WEAK TO DESPERATE ACTS!
IT SEEMS TO ME THAT THE SINESTRO CORPS WAS RESPONSIBLE FOR MANY OF THOSE ACTS OF CRUELTY.
WE HAVE EVERY RIGHT TO HATE YOU.
AND YET WE DESIRE ONLY PEACE.
I KNOW THIS BECAUSE I KNOW MY PEOPLE.
CAN YOU SAY THE SAME OF YOUR FELLOW LANTERNS?

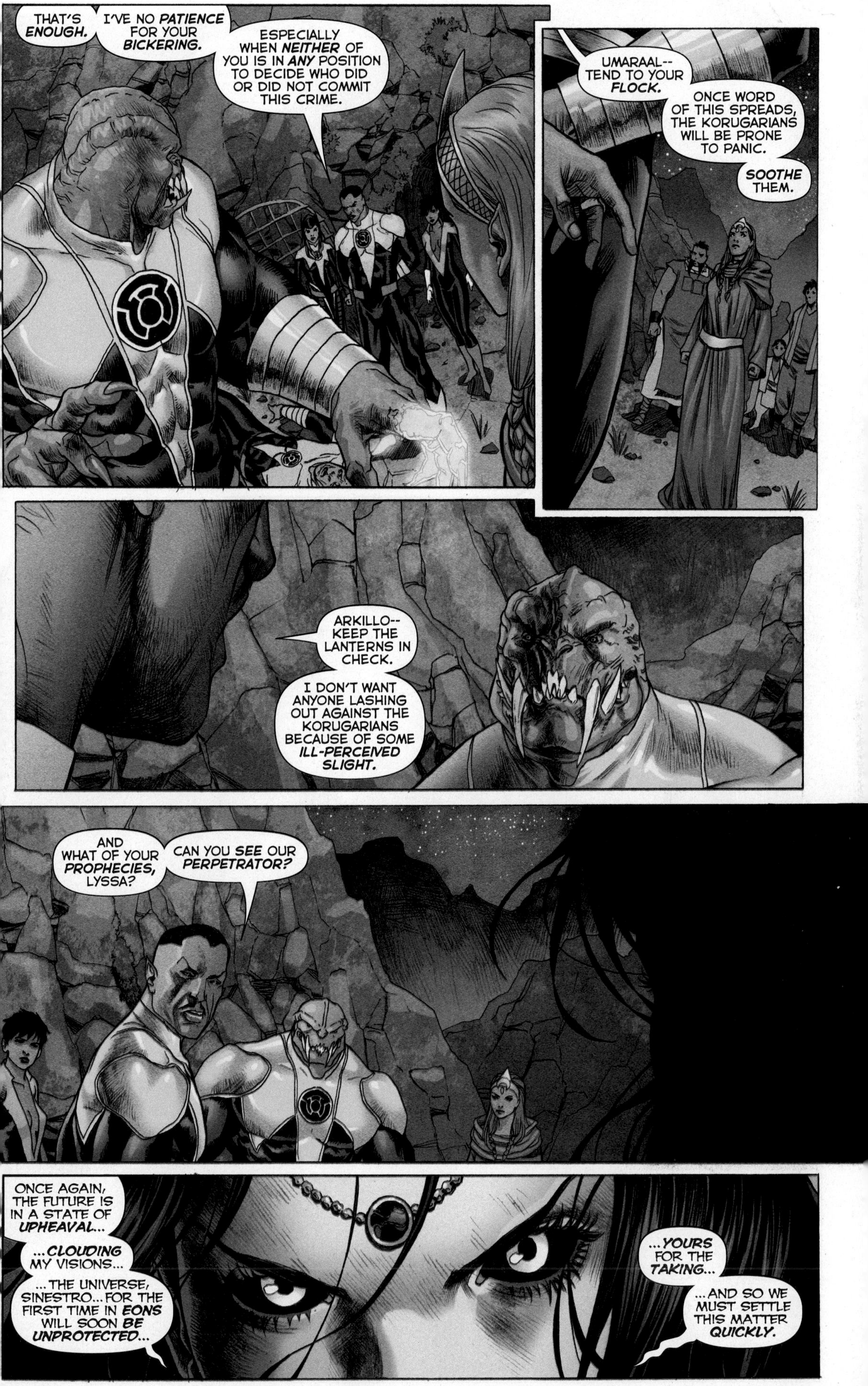
THAT'S ENOUGH.
I'VE NO PATIENCE FOR YOUR BICKERING.
ESPECIALLY WHEN NEITHER OF YOU IS IN ANY POSITION TO DECIDE WHO DID OR DID NOT COMMIT THIS CRIME.
UMARAAL-- TEND TO YOUR FLOCK.
ONCE WORD OF THIS SPREADS, THE KORUGARIANS WILL BE PRONE TO PANIC.
SOOTHE THEM.
ARKILLO-- KEEP THE LANTERNS IN CHECK.
I DON'T WANT ANYONE LASHING OUT AGAINST THE KORUGARIANS BECAUSE OF SOME ILL-PERCEIVED SLIGHT.
AND WHAT OF YOUR PROPHECIES, LYSSA?
CAN YOU SEE OUR PERPETRATOR?
ONCE AGAIN, THE FUTURE IS IN A STATE OF UPHEAVAL...
...CLOUDING MY VISIONS...
...THE UNIVERSE, SINESTRO...FOR THE FIRST TIME IN EONS WILL SOON BE UNPROTECTED...
...YOURS FOR THE TAKING...
...AND SO WE MUST SETTLE THIS MATTER QUICKLY.

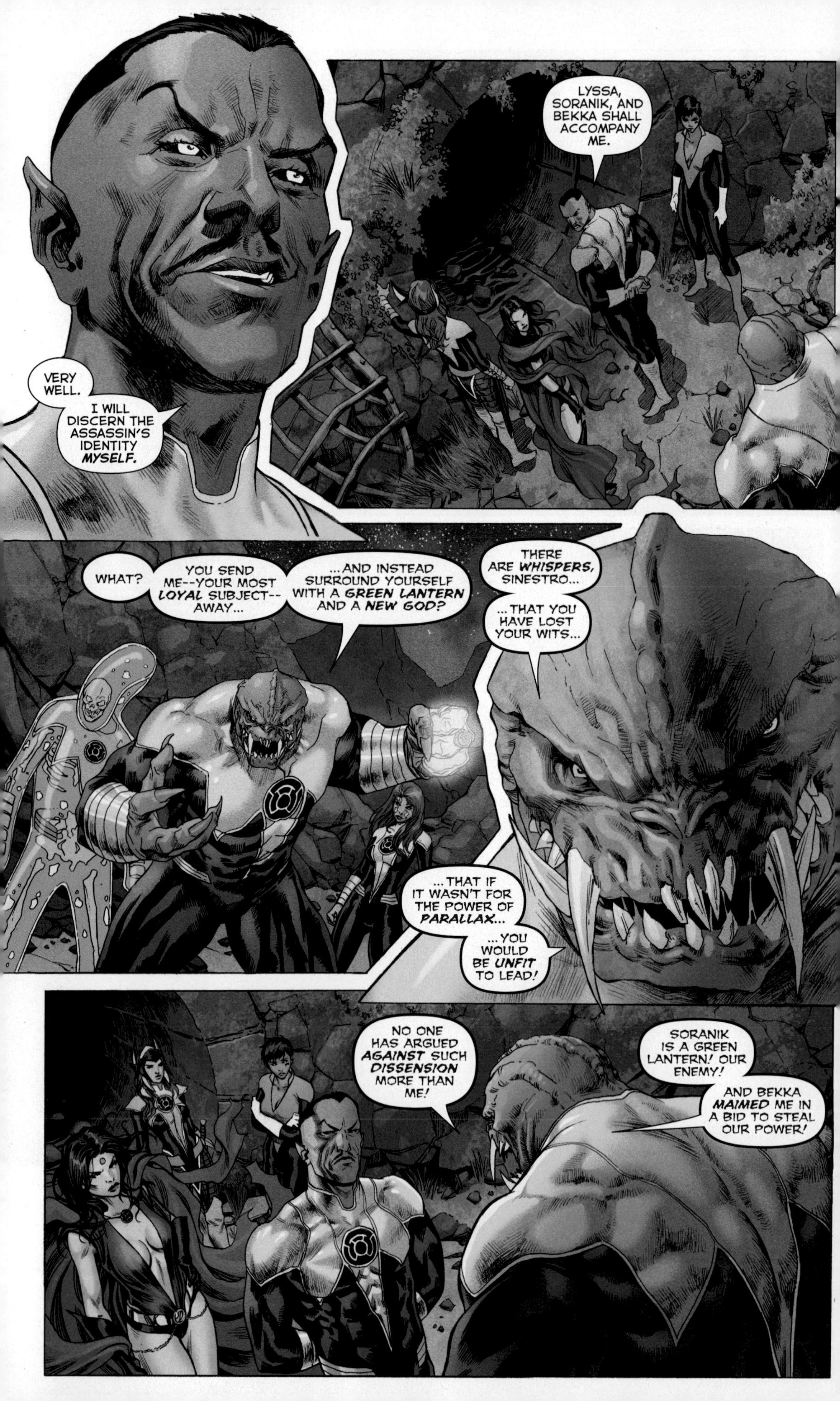
LYSSA, SORANIK, AND BEKKA SHALL ACCOMPANY ME.
VERY WELL.
I WILL DISCERN THE ASSASSIN'S IDENTITY MYSELF.
WHAT?
YOU SEND ME--YOUR MOST LOYAL SUBJECT--AWAY...
...AND INSTEAD SURROUND YOURSELF WITH A GREEN LANTERN AND A NEW GOD?
THERE ARE WHISPERS, SINESTRO...
...THAT YOU HAVE LOST YOUR WITS...
...THAT IF IT WASN'T FOR THE POWER OF PARALLAX...
...YOU WOULD BE UNFIT TO LEAD!
SORANIK IS A GREEN LANTERN! OUR ENEMY!
AND BEKKA MAIMED ME IN A BID TO STEAL OUR POWER!
NO ONE HAS ARGUED AGAINST SUCH DISSENSION MORE THAN ME!

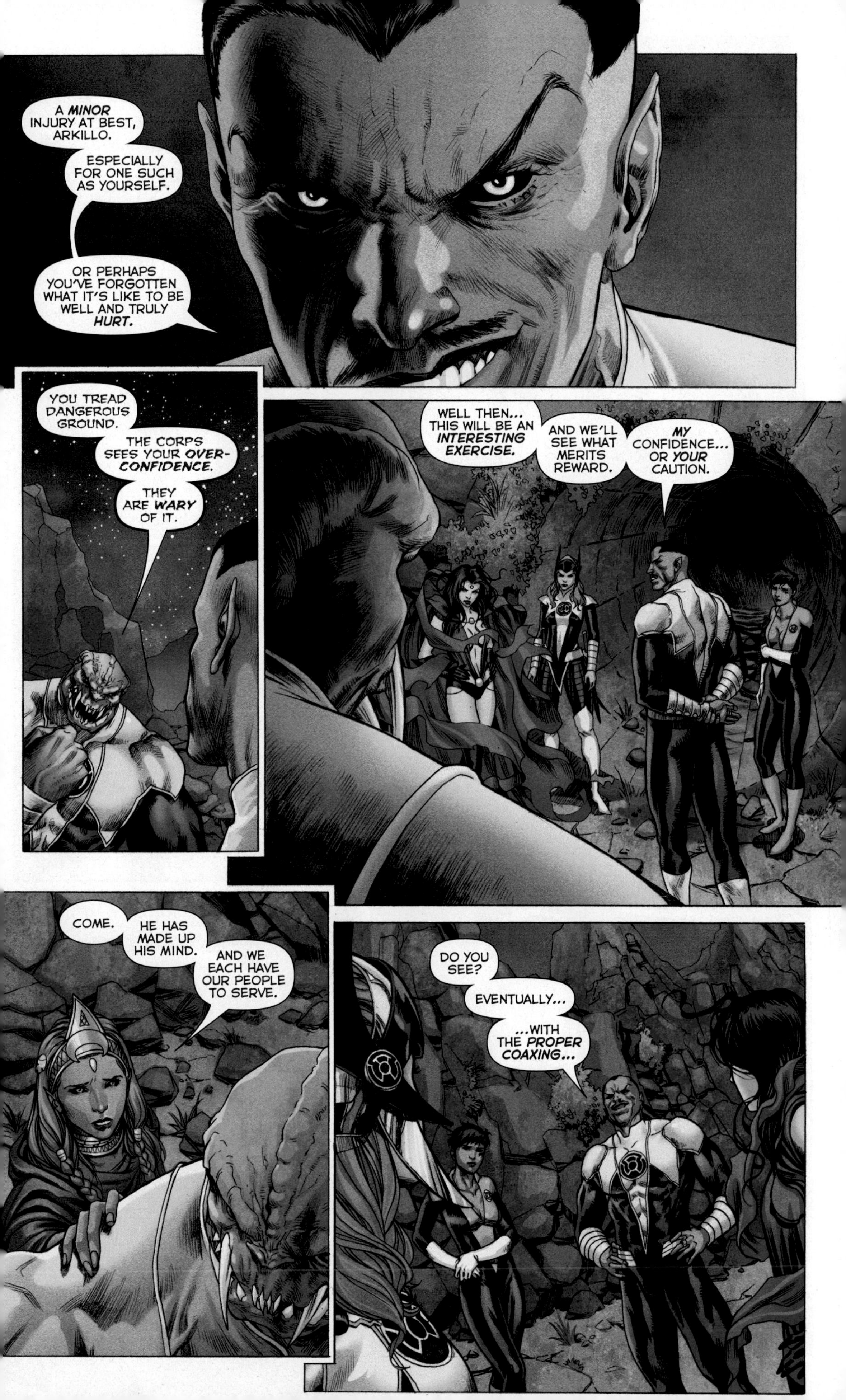
A MINOR INJURY AT BEST, ARKILLO.
ESPECIALLY FOR ONE SUCH AS YOURSELF.
OR PERHAPS YOU'VE FORGOTTEN WHAT IT'S LIKE TO BE WELL AND TRULY HURT.
YOU TREAD DANGEROUS GROUND.
THE CORPS SEES YOUR OVER-CONFIDENCE.
THEY ARE WARY OF IT.
WELL THEN... THIS WILL BE AN INTERESTING EXERCISE.
AND WE'LL SEE WHAT MERITS REWARD.
MY CONFIDENCE... OR YOUR CAUTION.
COME.
HE HAS MADE UP HIS MIND.
AND WE EACH HAVE OUR PEOPLE TO SERVE.
DO YOU SEE?
EVENTUALLY...
...WITH THE PROPER COAXING...

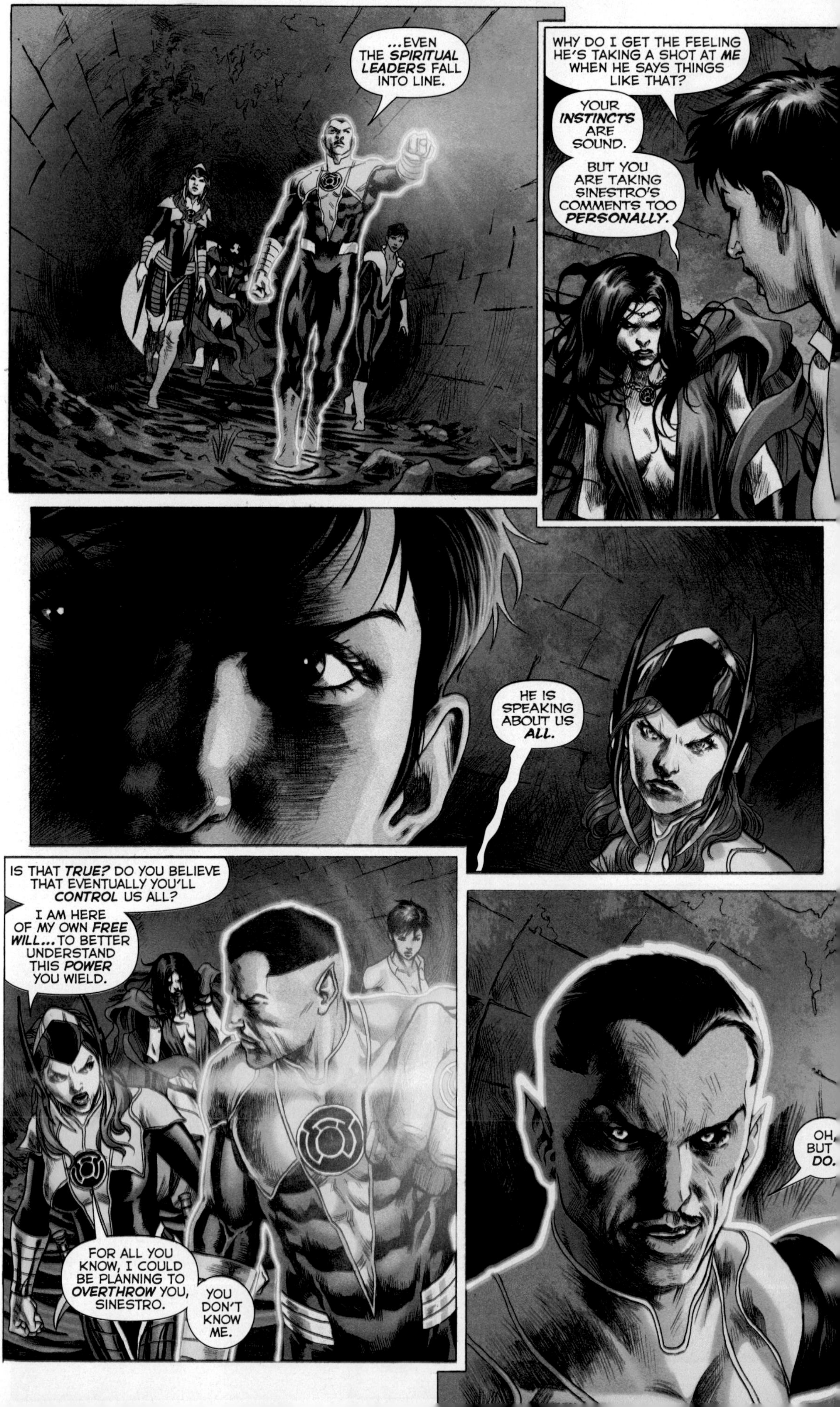
...EVEN THE SPIRITUAL LEADERS FALL INTO LINE.
WHY DO I GET THE FEELING HE'S TAKING A SHOT AT ME WHEN HE SAYS THINGS LIKE THAT?
YOUR INSTINCTS ARE SOUND.
BUT YOU ARE TAKING SINESTRO'S COMMENTS TOO PERSONALLY.
HE IS SPEAKING ABOUT US ALL.
IS THAT TRUE? DO YOU BELIEVE THAT EVENTUALLY YOU'LL CONTROL US ALL?
I AM HERE OF MY OWN FREE WILL... TO BETTER UNDERSTAND THIS POWER YOU WIELD.
FOR ALL YOU KNOW, I COULD BE PLANNING TO OVERTHROW YOU, SINESTRO.
YOU DON'T KNOW ME.
OH, BUT I DO.

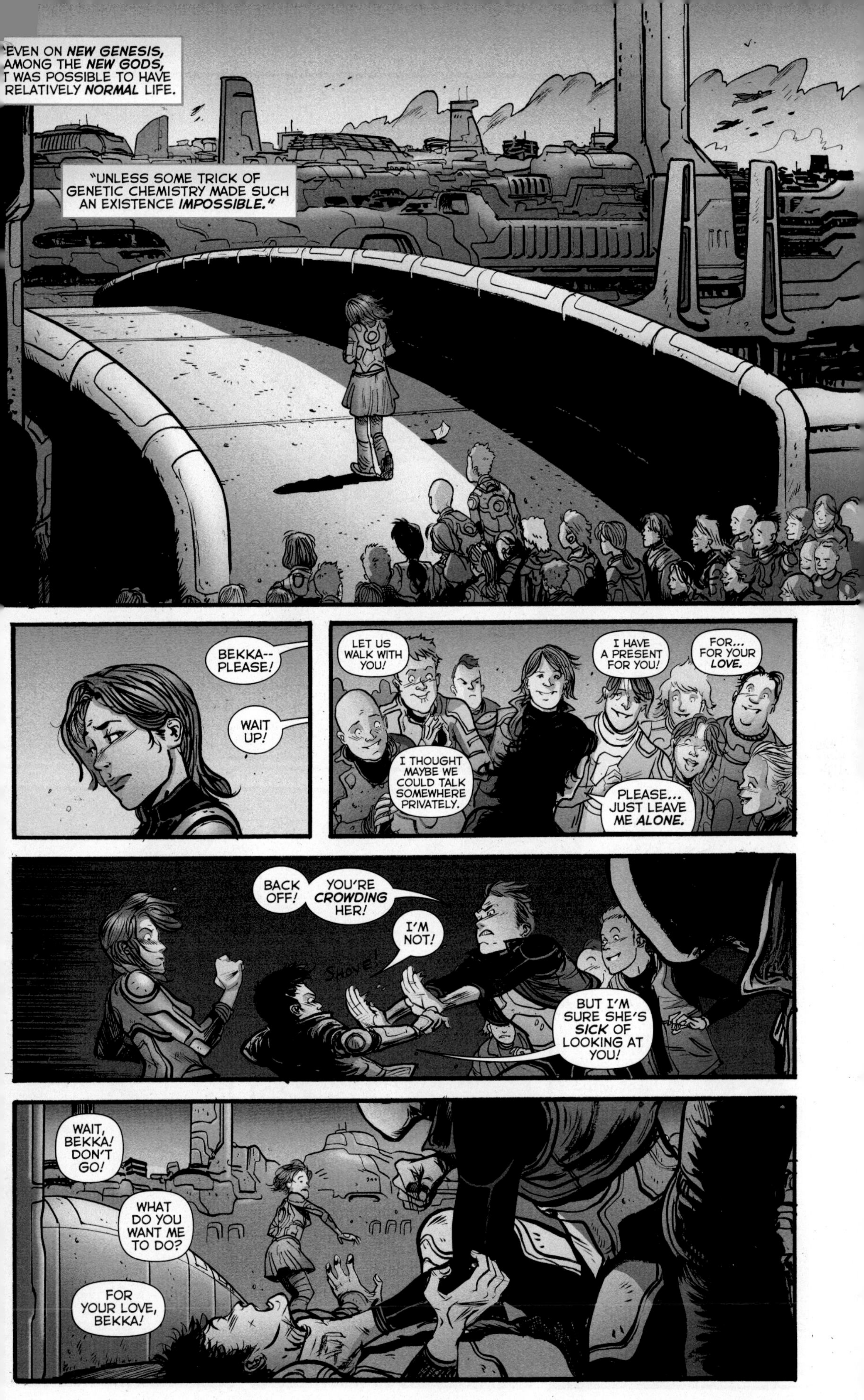
EVEN ON NEW GENESIS, AMONG THE NEW GODS, IT WAS POSSIBLE TO HAVE RELATIVELY NORMAL LIFE.
"UNLESS SOME TRICK OF GENETIC CHEMISTRY MADE SUCH AN EXISTENCE IMPOSSIBLE."
BEKKA-- PLEASE!
WAIT UP!
LET US WALK WITH YOU!
I THOUGHT MAYBE WE COULD TALK SOMEWHERE PRIVATELY.
I HAVE A PRESENT FOR YOU!
FOR... FOR YOUR LOVE.
PLEASE... JUST LEAVE ME ALONE.
BACK OFF!
YOU'RE CROWDING HER!
I'M NOT!
SHOVE!
BUT I'M SURE SHE'S SICK OF LOOKING AT YOU!
WAIT, BEKKA! DON'T GO!
WHAT DO YOU WANT ME TO DO?
FOR YOUR LOVE, BEKKA!

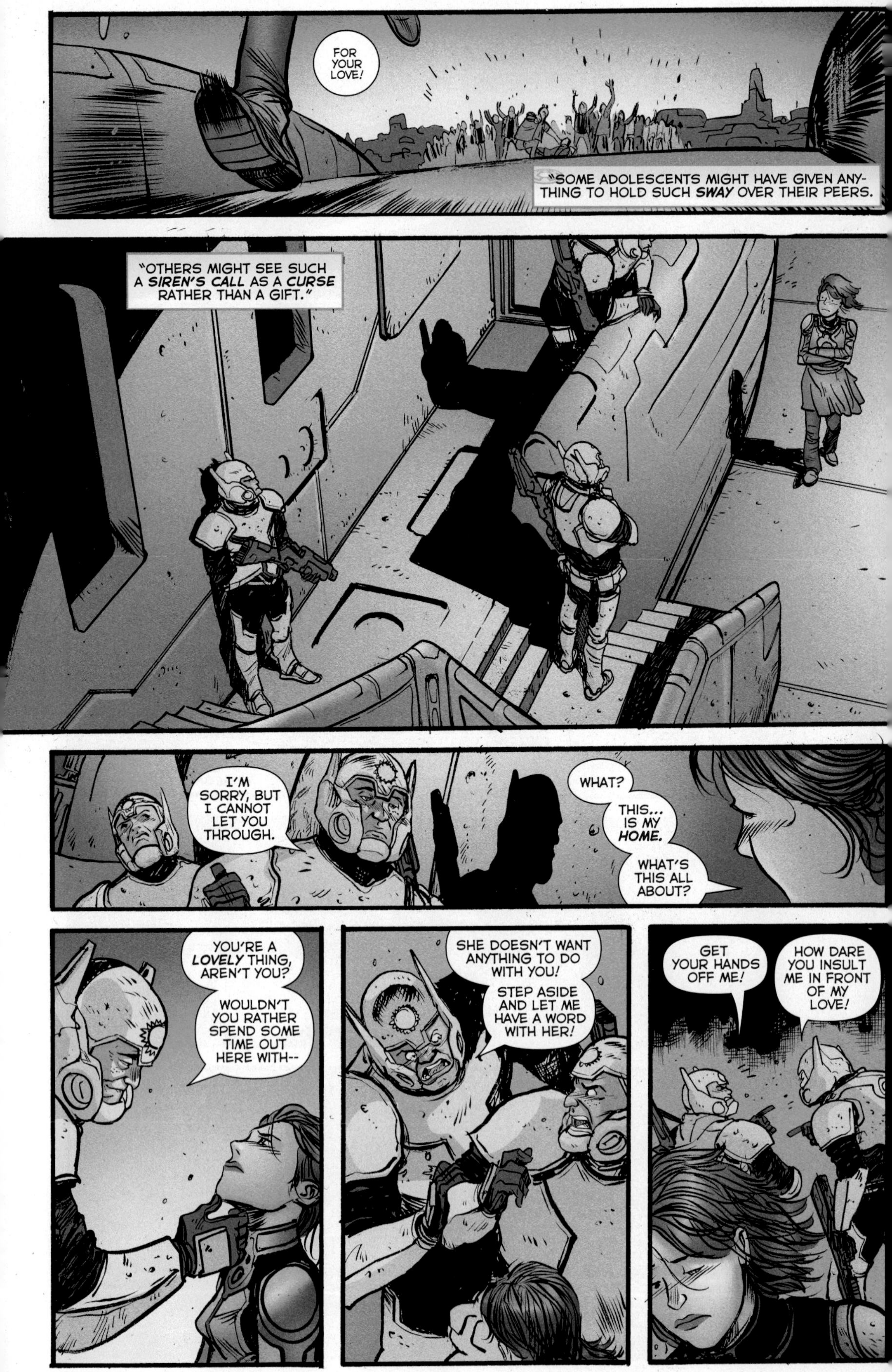
FOR YOUR LOVE!
"SOME ADOLESCENTS MIGHT HAVE GIVEN ANYTHING TO HOLD SUCH SWAY OVER THEIR PEERS.
"OTHERS MIGHT SEE SUCH A SIREN'S CALL AS A CURSE RATHER THAN A GIFT."
I'M SORRY, BUT I CANNOT LET YOU THROUGH.
WHAT?
THIS... IS MY HOME.
WHAT'S THIS ALL ABOUT?
YOU'RE A LOVELY THING, AREN'T YOU?
WOULDN'T YOU RATHER SPEND SOME TIME OUT HERE WITH--
SHE DOESN'T WANT ANYTHING TO DO WITH YOU!
STEP ASIDE AND LET ME HAVE A WORD WITH HER!
GET YOUR HANDS OFF ME!
HOW DARE YOU INSULT ME IN FRONT OF MY LOVE!

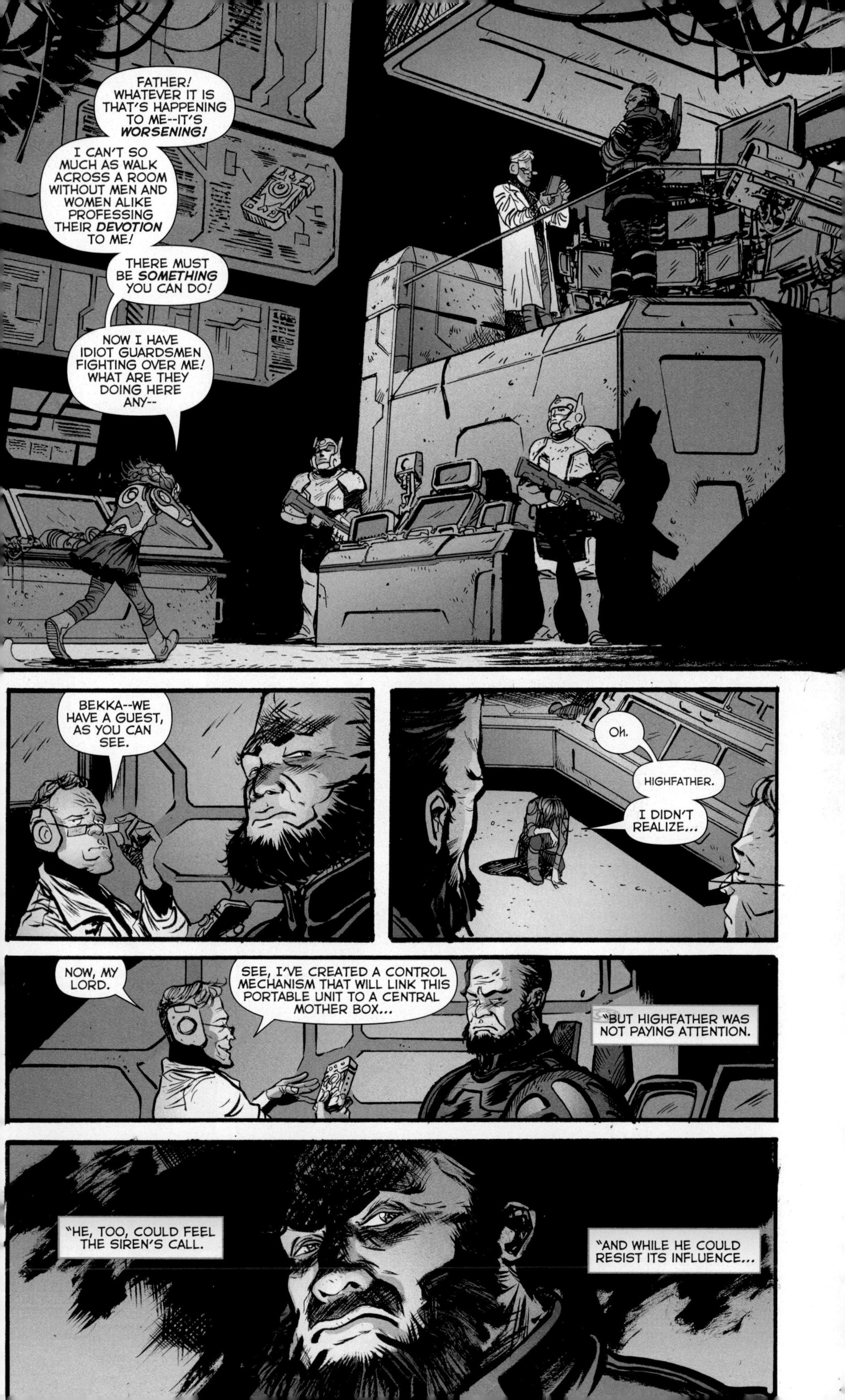
FATHER! WHATEVER IT IS THAT'S HAPPENING TO ME--IT'S WORSENING!
I CAN'T SO MUCH AS WALK ACROSS A ROOM WITHOUT MEN AND WOMEN ALIKE PROFESSING THEIR DEVOTION TO ME!
THERE MUST BE SOMETHING YOU CAN DO!
NOW I HAVE IDIOT GUARDSMEN FIGHTING OVER ME! WHAT ARE THEY DOING HERE ANY--
BEKKA--WE HAVE A GUEST, AS YOU CAN SEE.
Oh.
HIGHFATHER.
I DIDN'T REALIZE...
NOW, MY LORD.
SEE, I'VE CREATED A CONTROL MECHANISM THAT WILL LINK THIS PORTABLE UNIT TO A CENTRAL MOTHER BOX...
"BUT HIGHFATHER WAS NOT PAYING ATTENTION.
"HE, TOO, COULD FEEL THE SIREN'S CALL.
"AND WHILE HE COULD RESIST ITS INFLUENCE...

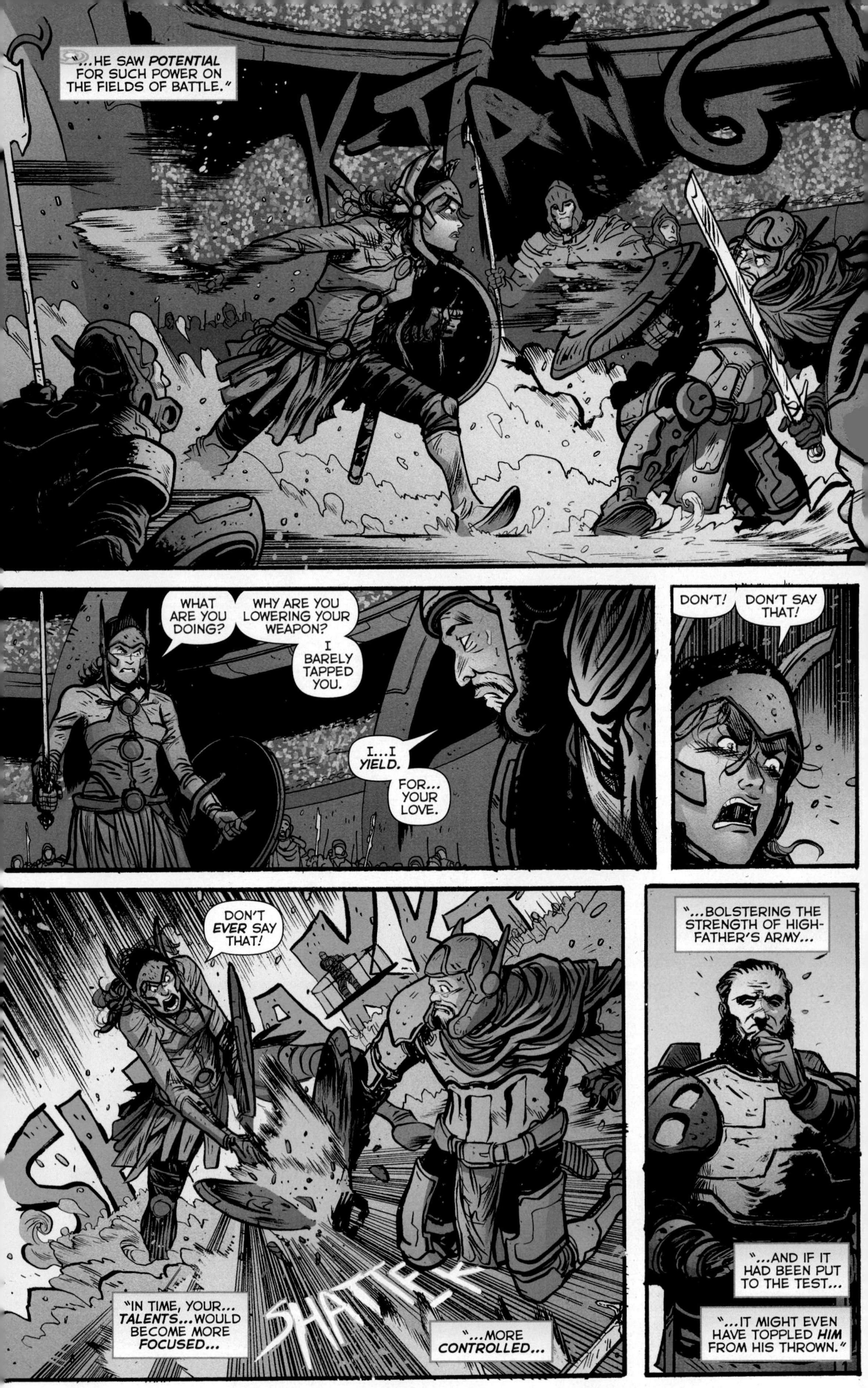
"...HE SAW POTENTIAL FOR SUCH POWER ON THE FIELDS OF BATTLE."
K-TANG!
WHAT ARE YOU DOING?
WHY ARE YOU LOWERING YOUR WEAPON?
I BARELY TAPPED YOU.
I...I YIELD.
FOR... YOUR LOVE.
DON'T!
DON'T SAY THAT!
DON'T EVER SAY THAT!
"IN TIME, YOUR... TALENTS...WOULD BECOME MORE FOCUSED...
SHATTER
"...MORE CONTROLLED...
"...BOLSTERING THE STRENGTH OF HIGH-FATHER'S ARMY...
"...AND IF IT HAD BEEN PUT TO THE TEST...
"...IT MIGHT EVEN HAVE TOPPLED HIM FROM HIS THROWN."

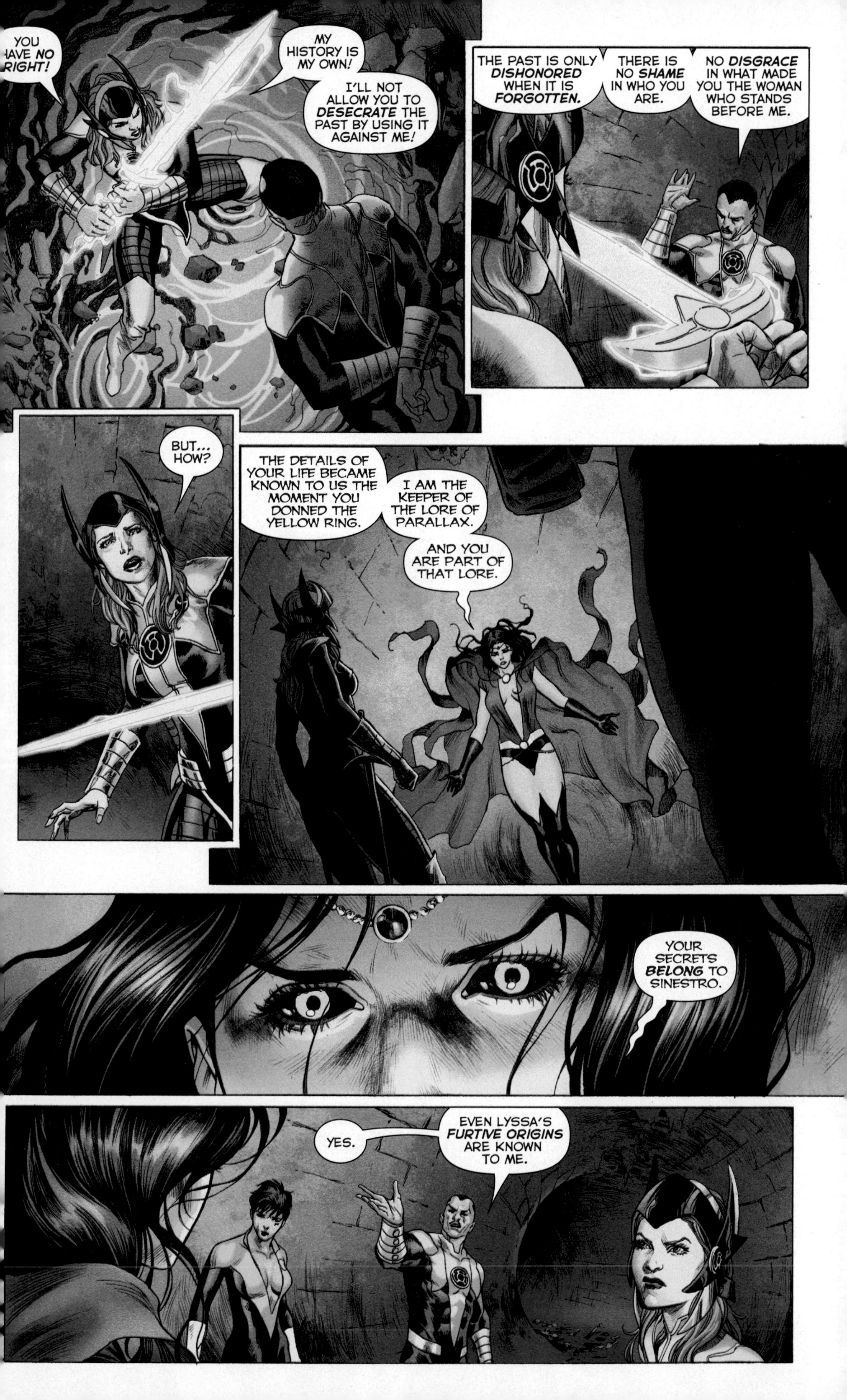

YOU HAVE **NO RIGHT!**
MY HISTORY IS MY OWN!
I'LL NOT ALLOW YOU TO ***DESECRATE*** THE PAST BY USING IT AGAINST ME!
THE PAST IS ONLY ***DISHONORED*** WHEN IT IS ***FORGOTTEN.***
THERE IS NO ***SHAME*** IN WHO YOU ARE.
NO ***DISGRACE*** IN WHAT MADE YOU THE WOMAN WHO STANDS BEFORE ME.
BUT... HOW?
THE DETAILS OF YOUR LIFE BECAME KNOWN TO US THE MOMENT YOU DONNED THE YELLOW RING.
I AM THE KEEPER OF THE LORE OF PARALLAX.
AND YOU ARE PART OF THAT LORE.
YOUR SECRETS ***BELONG*** TO SINESTRO.
YES.
EVEN LYSSA'S ***FURTIVE ORIGINS*** ARE KNOWN TO ME.

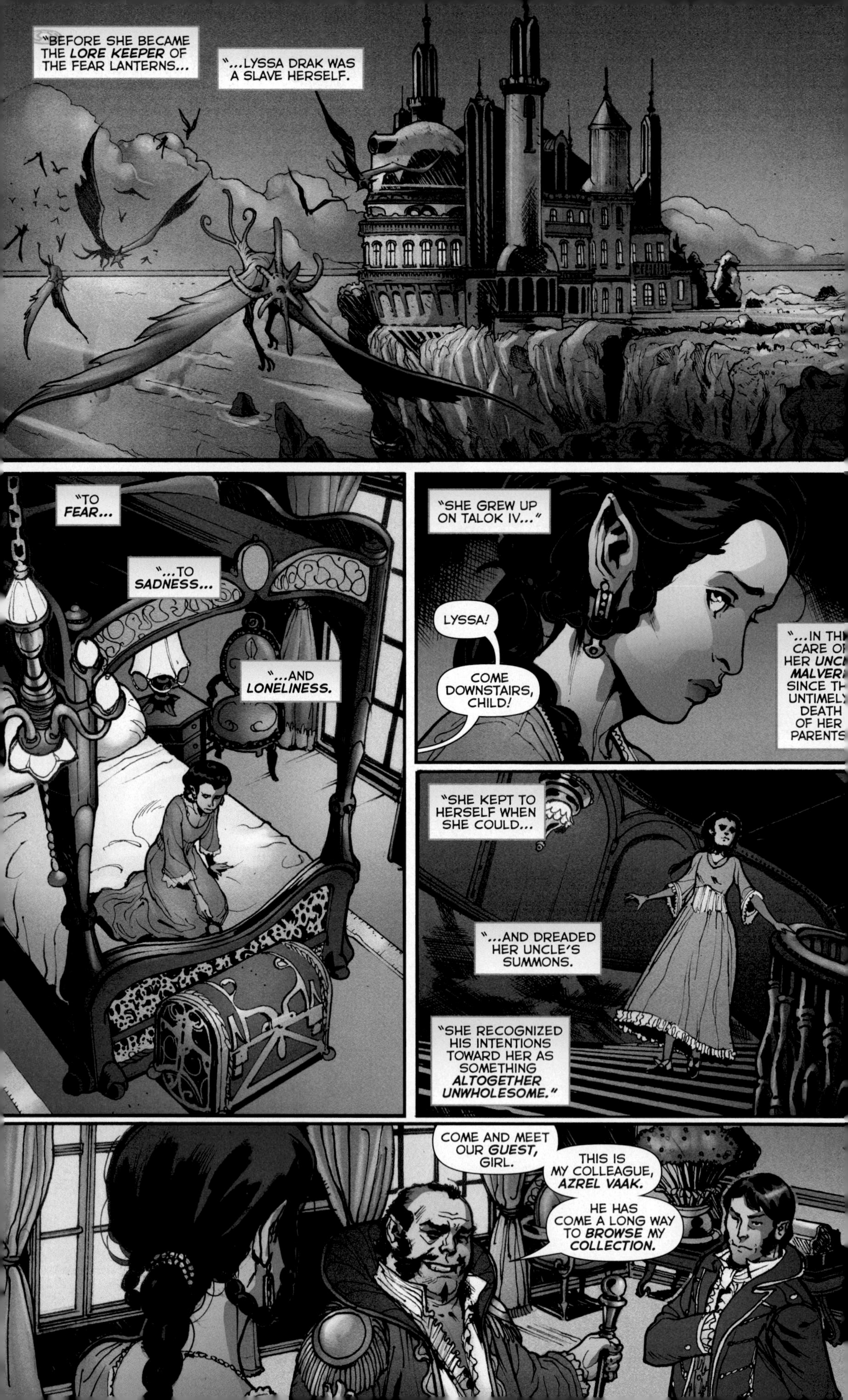

"BEFORE SHE BECAME THE LORE KEEPER OF THE FEAR LANTERNS...
"...LYSSA DRAK WAS A SLAVE HERSELF.
"TO FEAR...
"...TO SADNESS...
"...AND LONELINESS.
"SHE GREW UP ON TALOK IV..."
LYSSA!
COME DOWNSTAIRS, CHILD!
"...IN TH CARE OF HER UNC MALVER SINCE TH UNTIMEL DEATH OF HER PARENTS
"SHE KEPT TO HERSELF WHEN SHE COULD...
"...AND DREADED HER UNCLE'S SUMMONS.
"SHE RECOGNIZED HIS INTENTIONS TOWARD HER AS SOMETHING ALTOGETHER UNWHOLESOME."
COME AND MEET OUR GUEST, GIRL.
THIS IS MY COLLEAGUE, AZREL VAAK.
HE HAS COME A LONG WAY TO BROWSE MY COLLECTION.

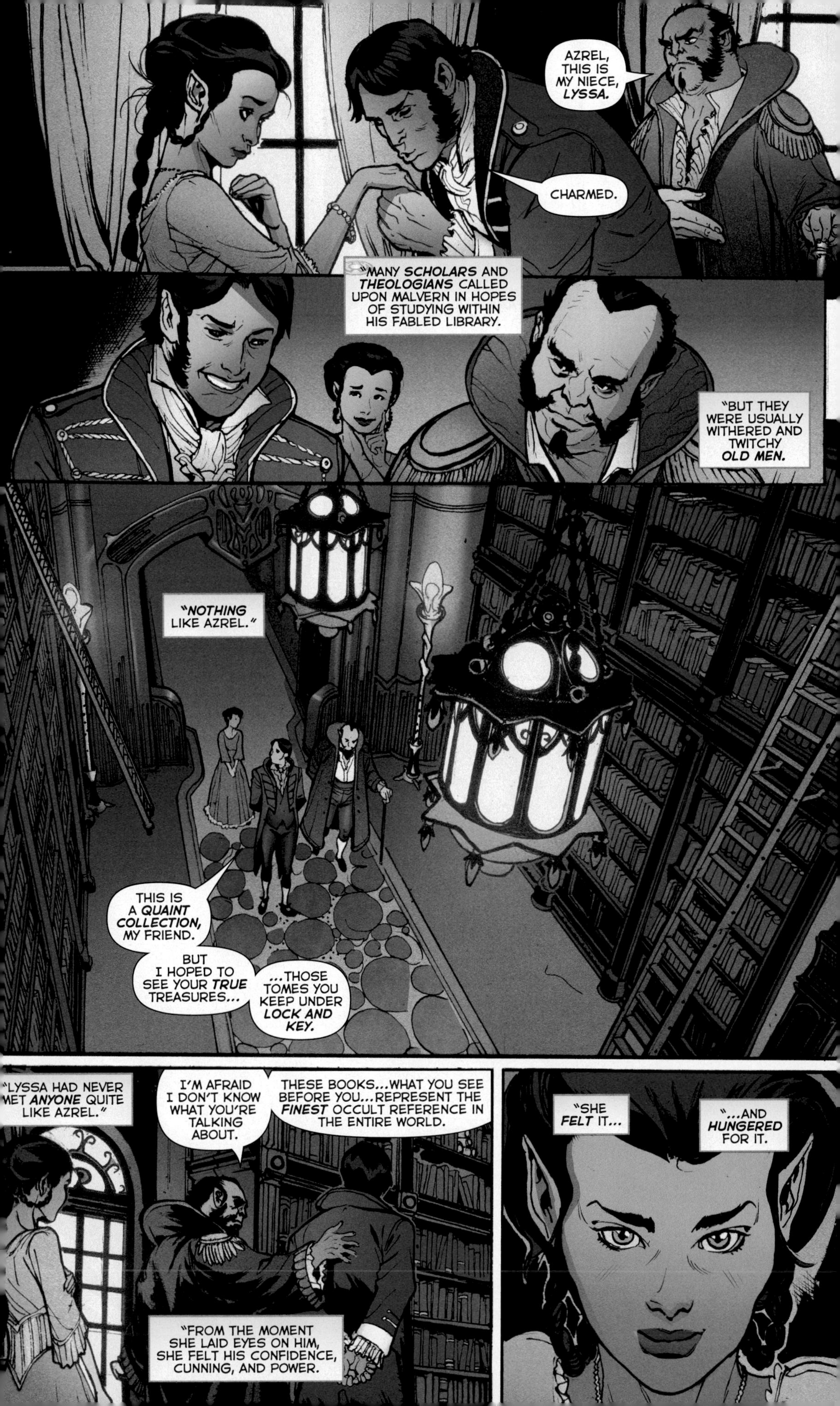
AZREL, THIS IS MY NIECE, LYSSA.
CHARMED.
"MANY SCHOLARS AND THEOLOGIANS CALLED UPON MALVERN IN HOPES OF STUDYING WITHIN HIS FABLED LIBRARY.
"BUT THEY WERE USUALLY WITHERED AND TWITCHY OLD MEN.
"NOTHING LIKE AZREL."
THIS IS A QUAINT COLLECTION, MY FRIEND.
BUT I HOPED TO SEE YOUR TRUE TREASURES...
...THOSE TOMES YOU KEEP UNDER LOCK AND KEY.
"LYSSA HAD NEVER MET ANYONE QUITE LIKE AZREL."
I'M AFRAID I DON'T KNOW WHAT YOU'RE TALKING ABOUT.
THESE BOOKS...WHAT YOU SEE BEFORE YOU...REPRESENT THE FINEST OCCULT REFERENCE IN THE ENTIRE WORLD.
"FROM THE MOMENT SHE LAID EYES ON HIM, SHE FELT HIS CONFIDENCE, CUNNING, AND POWER.
"SHE FELT IT...
"...AND HUNGERED FOR IT.

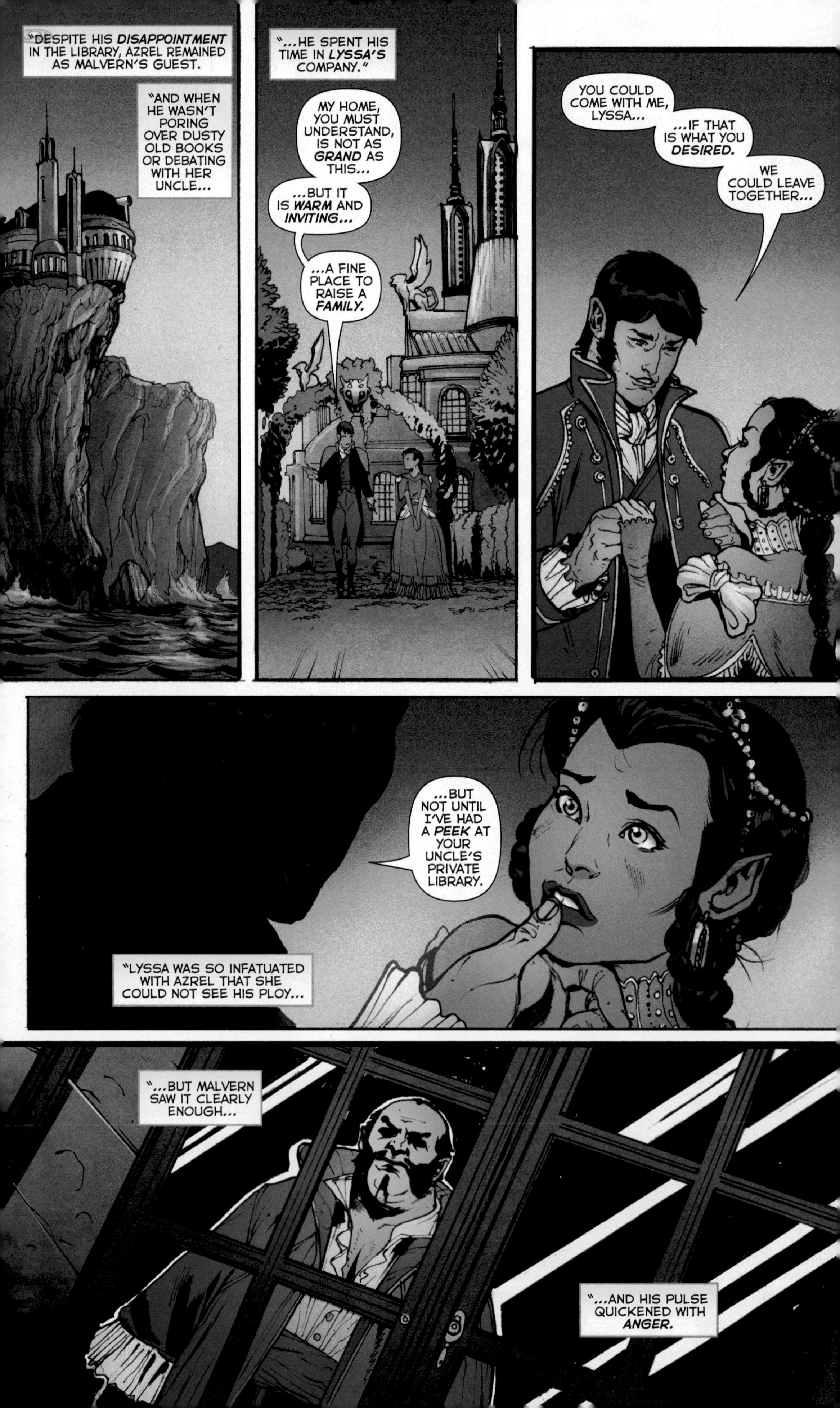
"DESPITE HIS DISAPPOINTMENT IN THE LIBRARY, AZREL REMAINED AS MALVERN'S GUEST.
"AND WHEN HE WASN'T PORING OVER DUSTY OLD BOOKS OR DEBATING WITH HER UNCLE...
"...HE SPENT HIS TIME IN LYSSA'S COMPANY."
MY HOME, YOU MUST UNDERSTAND, IS NOT AS GRAND AS THIS...
...BUT IT IS WARM AND INVITING...
...A FINE PLACE TO RAISE A FAMILY.
YOU COULD COME WITH ME, LYSSA...
...IF THAT IS WHAT YOU DESIRED.
WE COULD LEAVE TOGETHER...
...BUT NOT UNTIL I'VE HAD A PEEK AT YOUR UNCLE'S PRIVATE LIBRARY.
"LYSSA WAS SO INFATUATED WITH AZREL THAT SHE COULD NOT SEE HIS PLOY...
"...BUT MALVERN SAW IT CLEARLY ENOUGH...
"...AND HIS PULSE QUICKENED WITH ANGER.

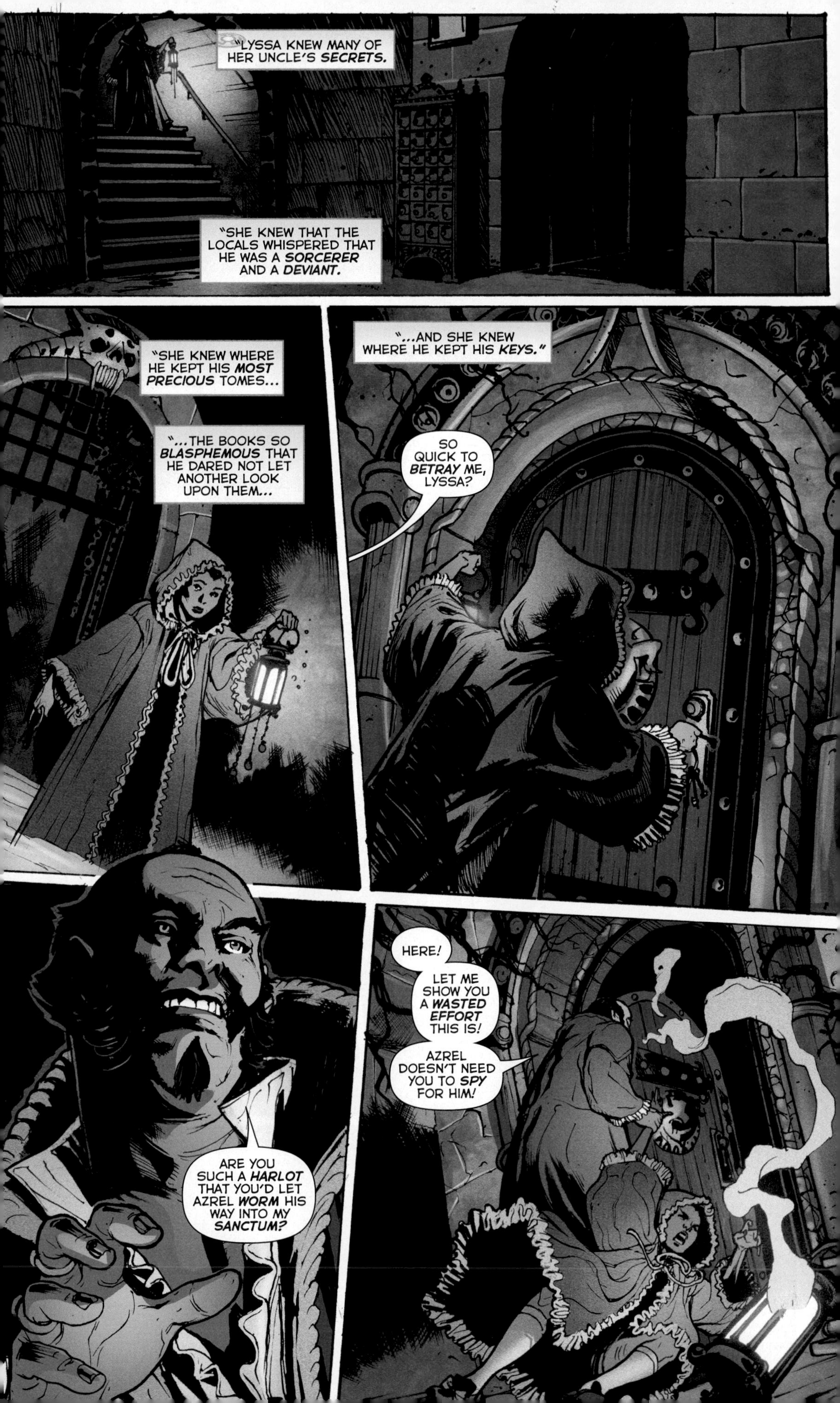
"LYSSA KNEW MANY OF HER UNCLE'S SECRETS.
"SHE KNEW THAT THE LOCALS WHISPERED THAT HE WAS A SORCERER AND A DEVIANT.
"SHE KNEW WHERE HE KEPT HIS MOST PRECIOUS TOMES...
"...THE BOOKS SO BLASPHEMOUS THAT HE DARED NOT LET ANOTHER LOOK UPON THEM...
"...AND SHE KNEW WHERE HE KEPT HIS KEYS."
SO QUICK TO BETRAY ME, LYSSA?
ARE YOU SUCH A HARLOT THAT YOU'D LET AZREL WORM HIS WAY INTO MY SANCTUM?
HERE!
LET ME SHOW YOU A WASTED EFFORT THIS IS!
AZREL DOESN'T NEED YOU TO SPY FOR HIM!

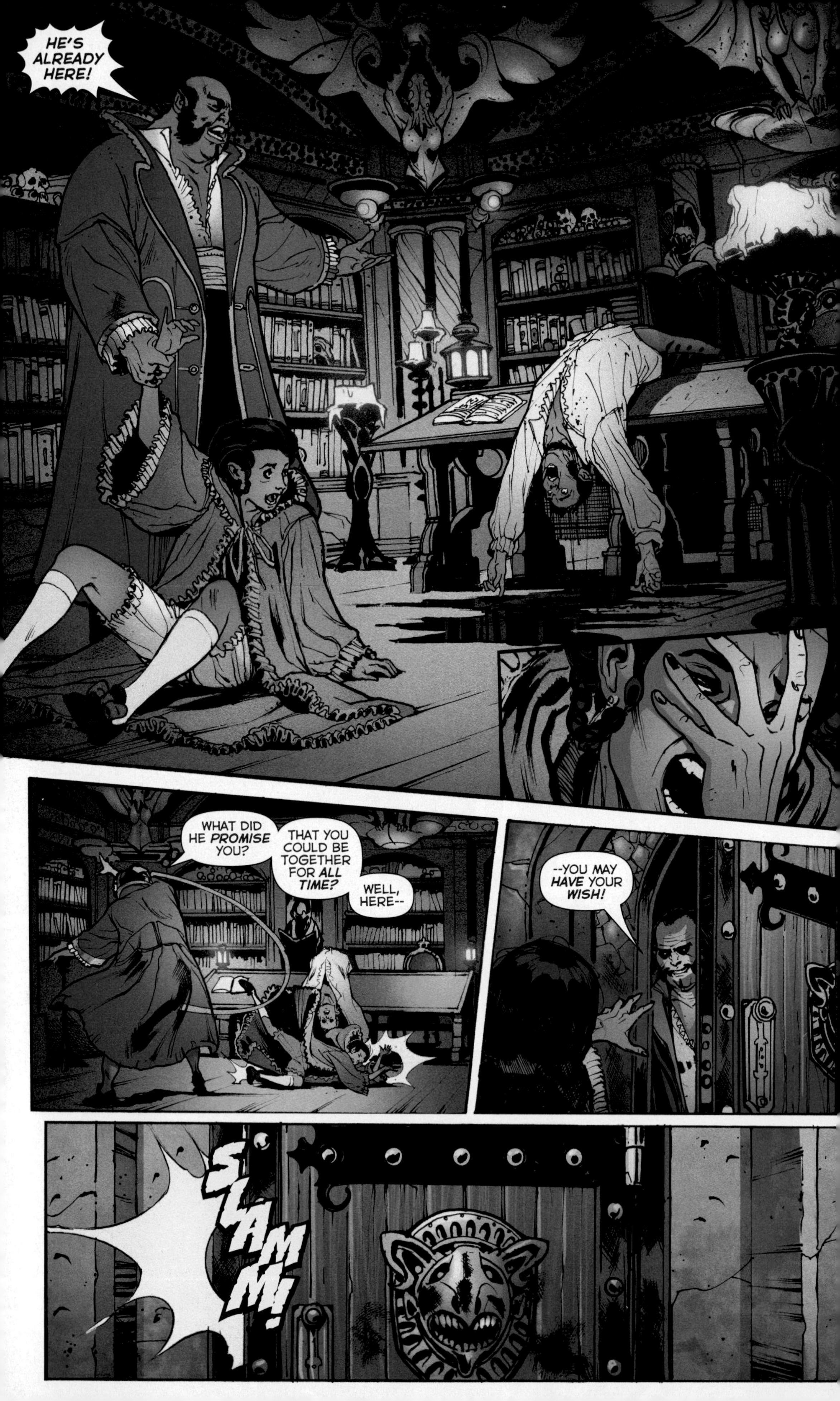

HE'S ALREADY HERE!
WHAT DID HE PROMISE YOU?
THAT YOU COULD BE TOGETHER FOR ALL TIME?
WELL, HERE--
--YOU MAY HAVE YOUR WISH!
SLAMM!

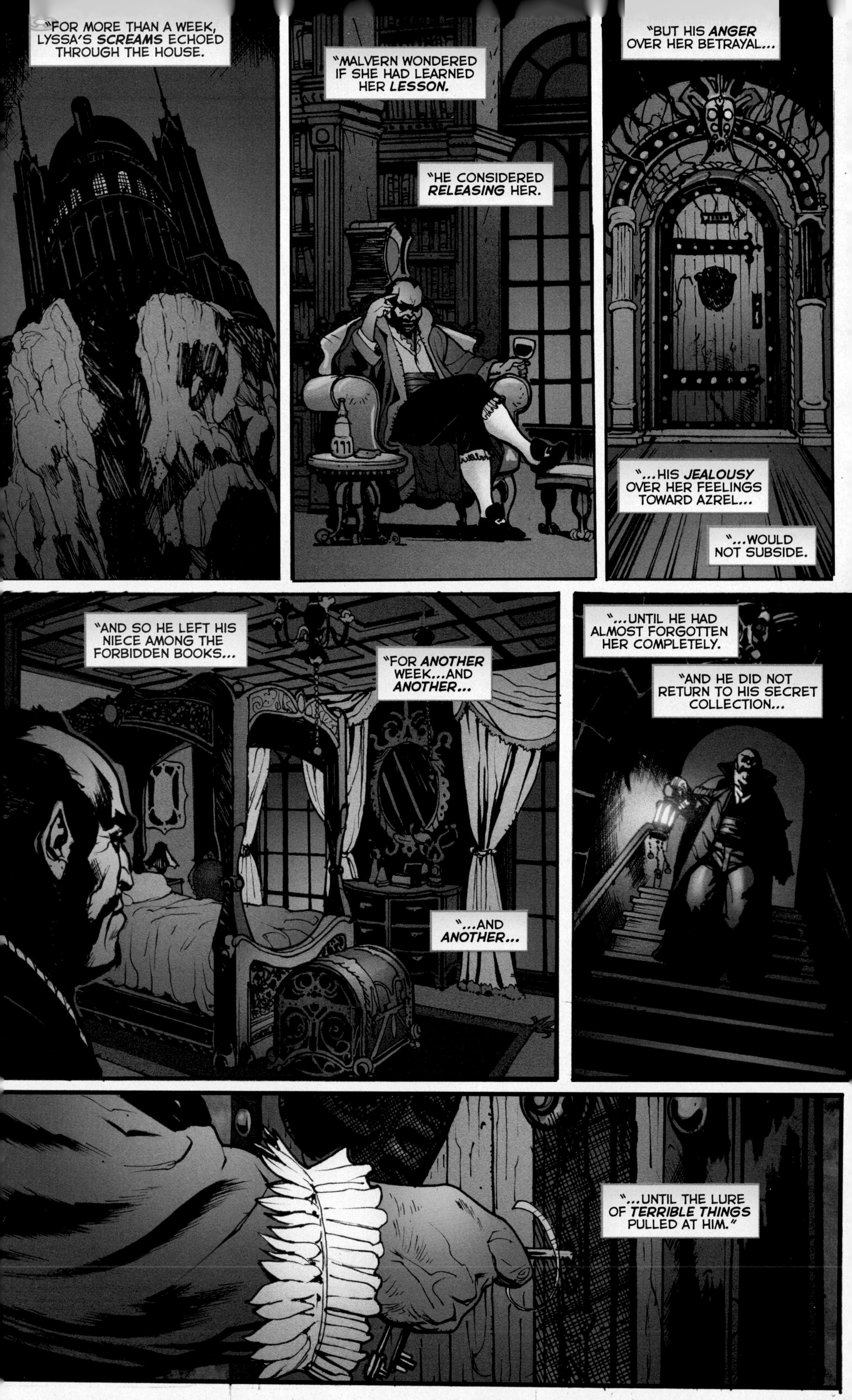
"FOR MORE THAN A WEEK, LYSSA'S SCREAMS ECHOED THROUGH THE HOUSE.
"MALVERN WONDERED IF SHE HAD LEARNED HER LESSON.
"HE CONSIDERED RELEASING HER.
"BUT HIS ANGER OVER HER BETRAYAL...
"...HIS JEALOUSY OVER HER FEELINGS TOWARD AZREL...
"...WOULD NOT SUBSIDE.
"AND SO HE LEFT HIS NIECE AMONG THE FORBIDDEN BOOKS...
"FOR ANOTHER WEEK...AND ANOTHER...
"...AND ANOTHER...
"...UNTIL HE HAD ALMOST FORGOTTEN HER COMPLETELY.
"AND HE DID NOT RETURN TO HIS SECRET COLLECTION...
"...UNTIL THE LURE OF TERRIBLE THINGS PULLED AT HIM."

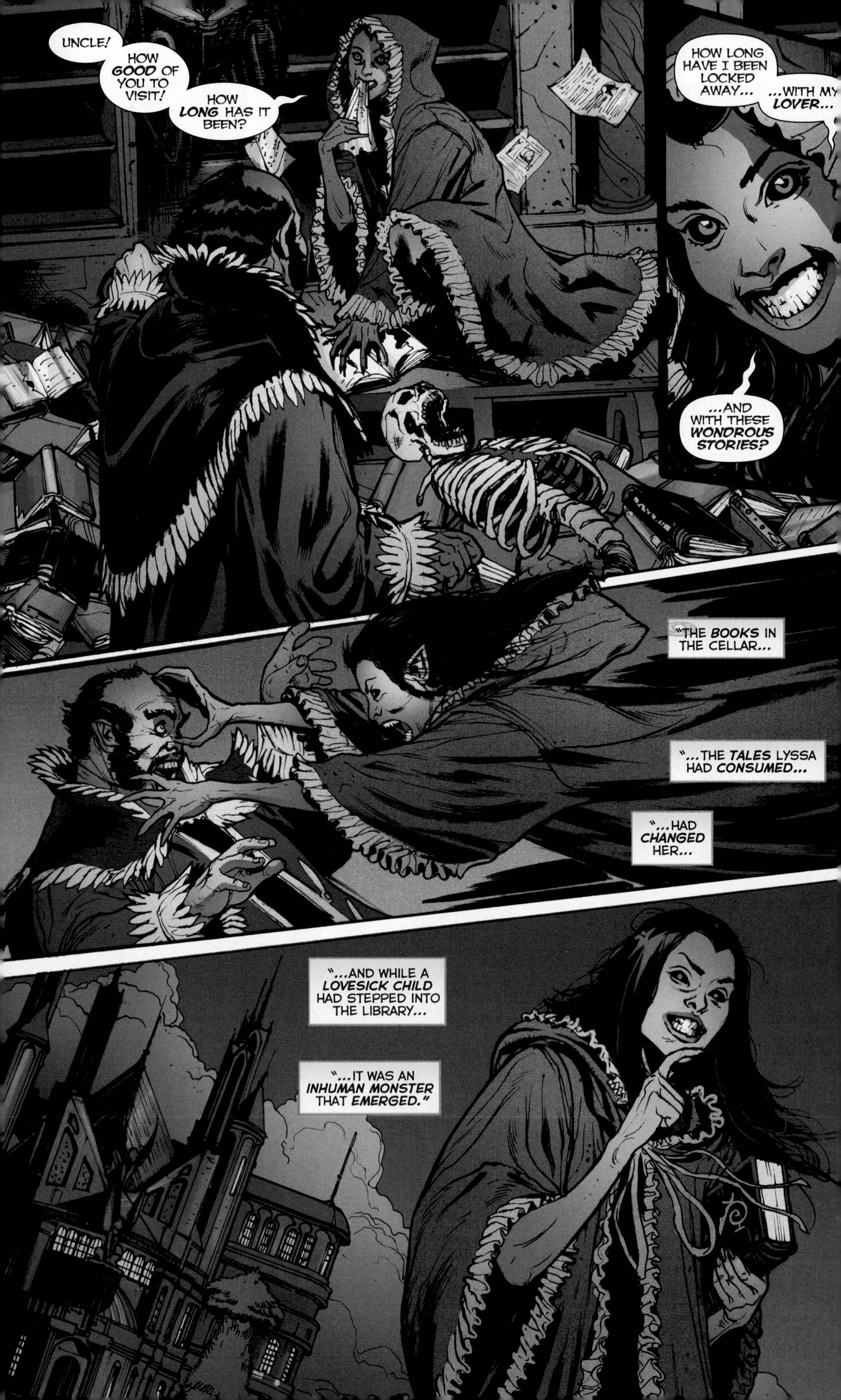
UNCLE!
HOW GOOD OF YOU TO VISIT!
HOW LONG HAS IT BEEN?
HOW LONG HAVE I BEEN LOCKED AWAY...
...WITH MY LOVER...
...AND WITH THESE WONDROUS STORIES?
"THE BOOKS IN THE CELLAR...
"...THE TALES LYSSA HAD CONSUMED...
"...HAD CHANGED HER...
"...AND WHILE A LOVESICK CHILD HAD STEPPED INTO THE LIBRARY...
"...IT WAS AN INHUMAN MONSTER THAT EMERGED."

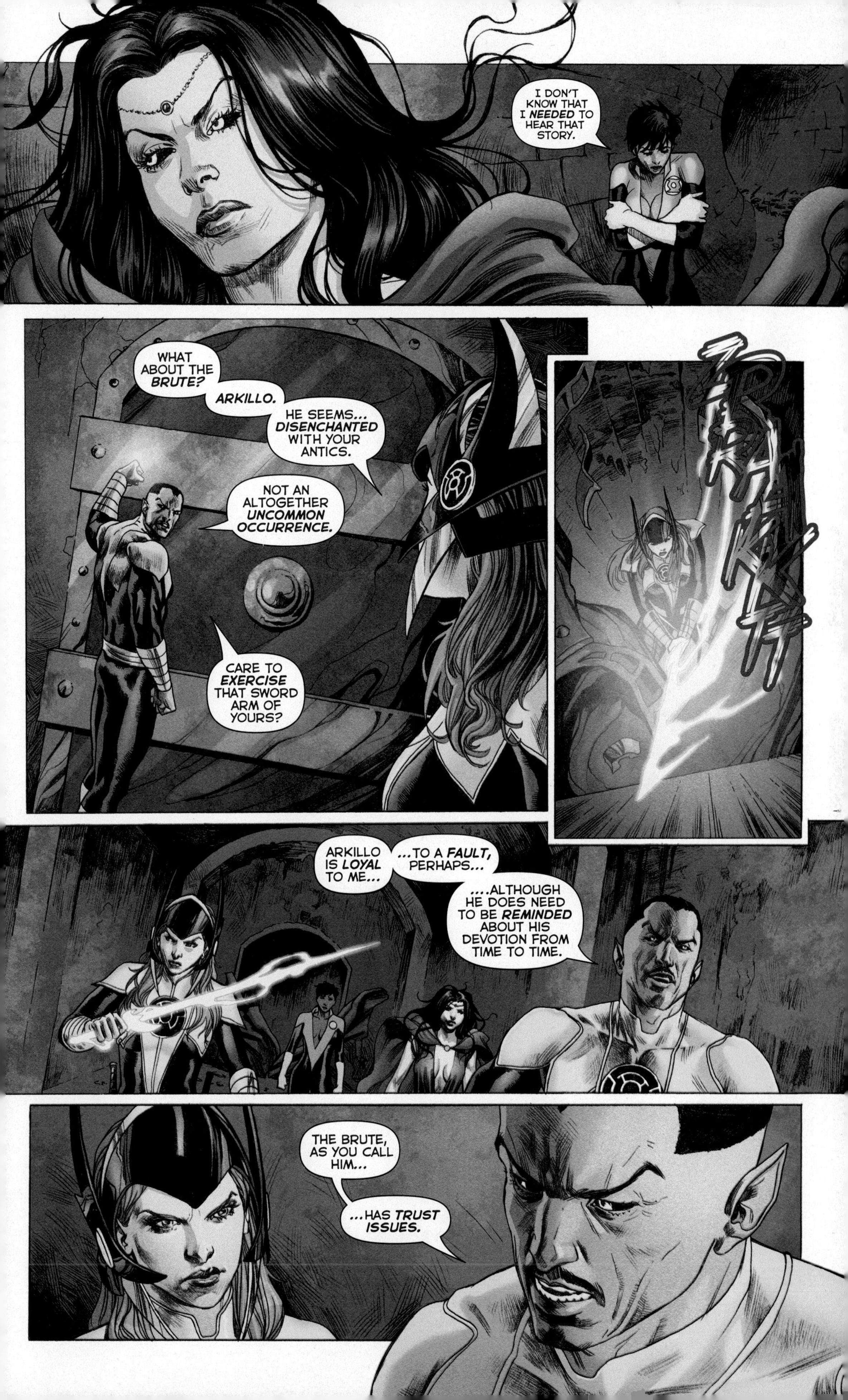
I DON'T KNOW THAT I *NEEDED* TO HEAR THAT STORY.
WHAT ABOUT THE *BRUTE?*
ARKILLO.
HE SEEMS... *DISENCHANTED* WITH YOUR ANTICS.
NOT AN ALTOGETHER *UNCOMMON OCCURRENCE.*
CARE TO *EXERCISE* THAT SWORD ARM OF YOURS?
ARKILLO IS *LOYAL* TO ME...
...TO A *FAULT,* PERHAPS...
....ALTHOUGH HE DOES NEED TO BE *REMINDED* ABOUT HIS DEVOTION FROM TIME TO TIME.
THE BRUTE, AS YOU CALL HIM...
...HAS *TRUST ISSUES.*

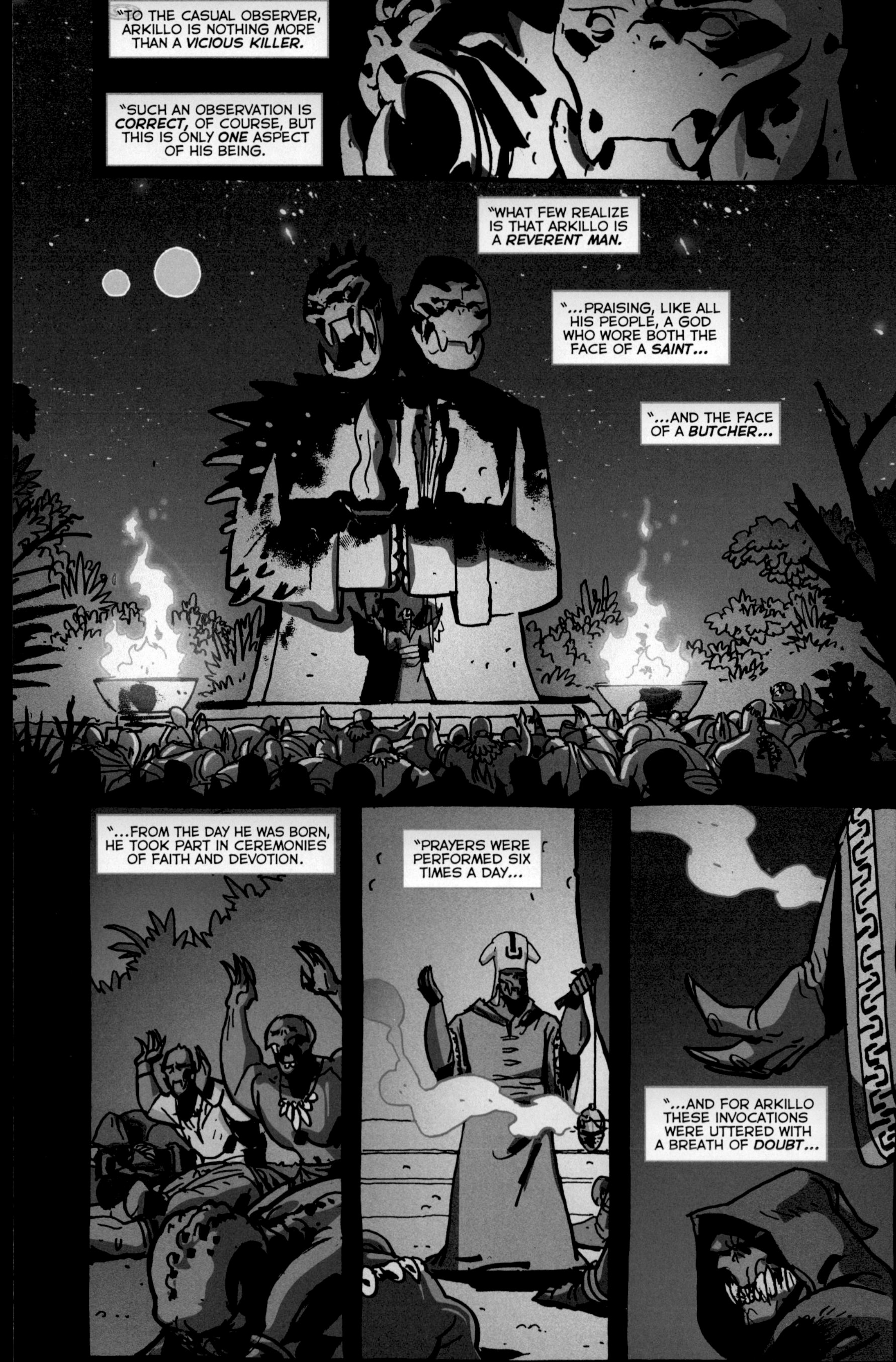
"TO THE CASUAL OBSERVER, ARKILLO IS NOTHING MORE THAN A VICIOUS KILLER.
"SUCH AN OBSERVATION IS CORRECT, OF COURSE, BUT THIS IS ONLY ONE ASPECT OF HIS BEING.
"WHAT FEW REALIZE IS THAT ARKILLO IS A REVERENT MAN.
"...PRAISING, LIKE ALL HIS PEOPLE, A GOD WHO WORE BOTH THE FACE OF A SAINT...
"...AND THE FACE OF A BUTCHER...
"...FROM THE DAY HE WAS BORN, HE TOOK PART IN CEREMONIES OF FAITH AND DEVOTION.
"PRAYERS WERE PERFORMED SIX TIMES A DAY...
"...AND FOR ARKILLO THESE INVOCATIONS WERE UTTERED WITH A BREATH OF DOUBT...

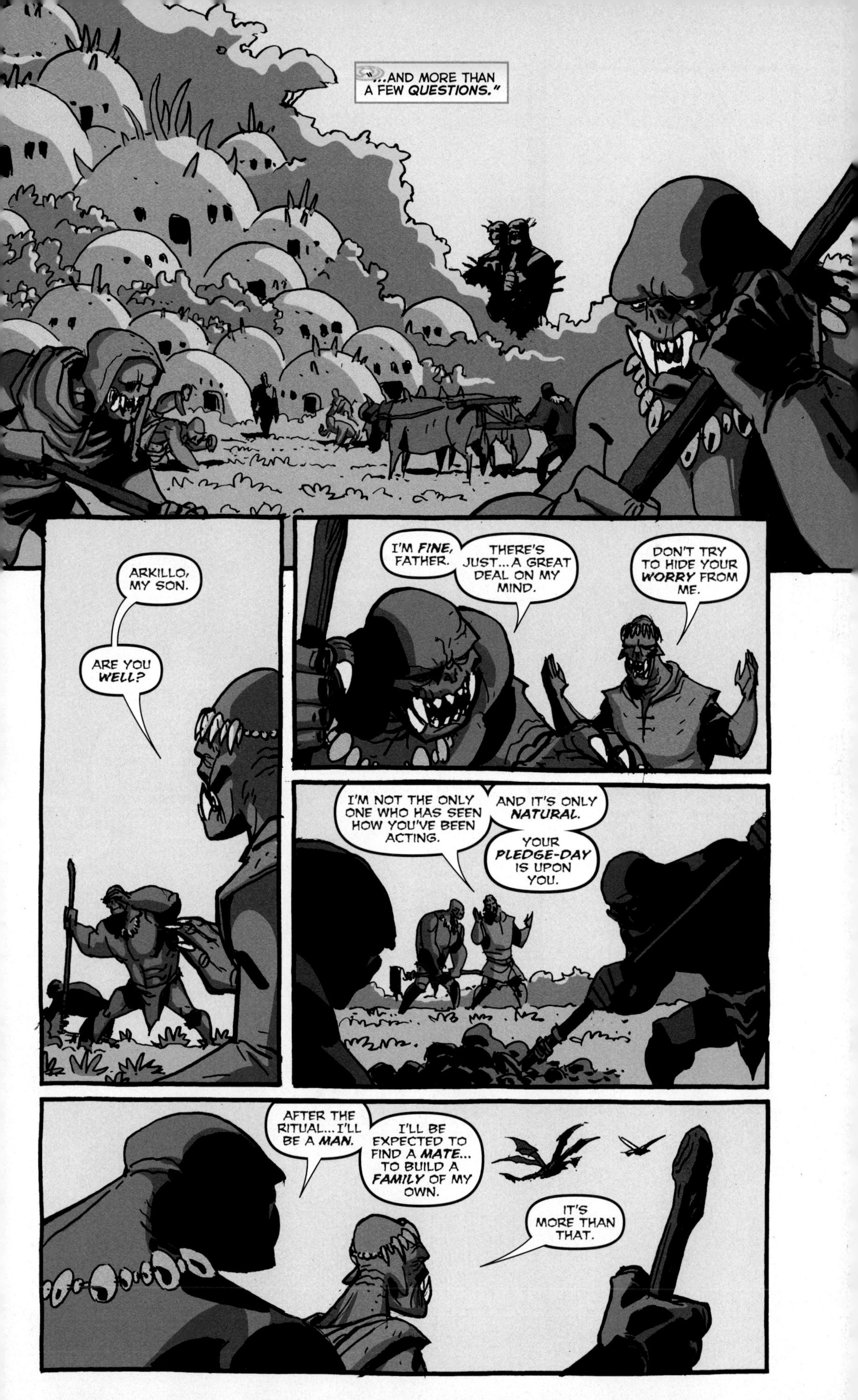
"...AND MORE THAN A FEW QUESTIONS."
ARKILLO, MY SON.
ARE YOU WELL?
I'M FINE, FATHER.
THERE'S JUST... A GREAT DEAL ON MY MIND.
DON'T TRY TO HIDE YOUR WORRY FROM ME.
I'M NOT THE ONLY ONE WHO HAS SEEN HOW YOU'VE BEEN ACTING.
AND IT'S ONLY NATURAL.
YOUR PLEDGE-DAY IS UPON YOU.
AFTER THE RITUAL... I'LL BE A MAN.
I'LL BE EXPECTED TO FIND A MATE... TO BUILD A FAMILY OF MY OWN.
IT'S MORE THAN THAT.

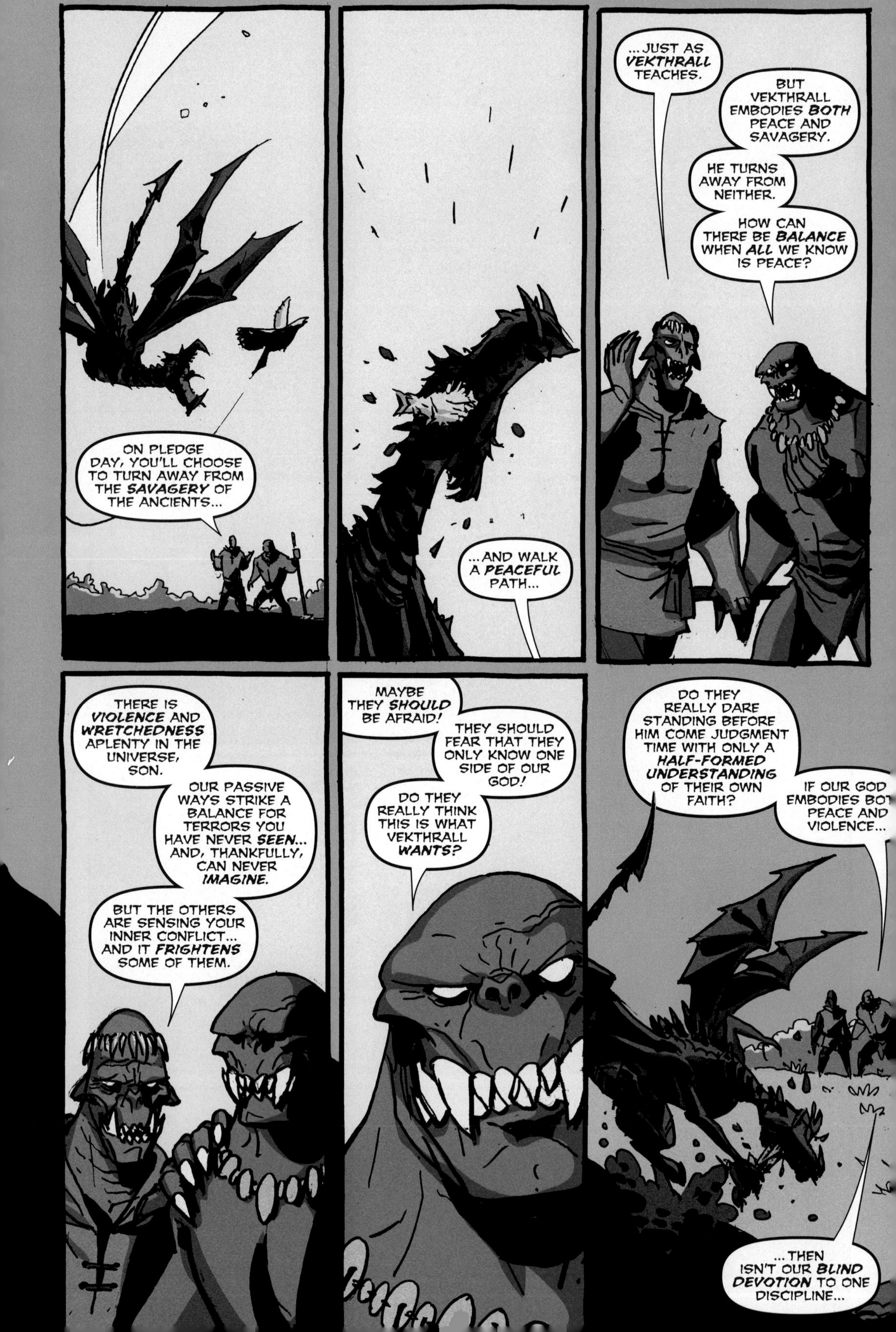
ON PLEDGE DAY, YOU'LL CHOOSE TO TURN AWAY FROM THE *SAVAGERY* OF THE ANCIENTS...
...AND WALK A *PEACEFUL* PATH...
...JUST AS *VEKTHRALL* TEACHES.
BUT VEKTHRALL EMBODIES *BOTH* PEACE AND SAVAGERY.
HE TURNS AWAY FROM NEITHER.
HOW CAN THERE BE *BALANCE* WHEN *ALL* WE KNOW IS PEACE?
THERE IS *VIOLENCE* AND *WRETCHEDNESS* APLENTY IN THE UNIVERSE, SON.
OUR PASSIVE WAYS STRIKE A BALANCE FOR TERRORS YOU HAVE NEVER *SEEN*... AND, THANKFULLY, CAN NEVER *IMAGINE*.
BUT THE OTHERS ARE SENSING YOUR INNER CONFLICT... AND IT *FRIGHTENS* SOME OF THEM.
MAYBE THEY *SHOULD* BE AFRAID!
THEY SHOULD FEAR THAT THEY ONLY KNOW ONE SIDE OF OUR GOD!
DO THEY REALLY THINK THIS IS WHAT VEKTHRALL *WANTS?*
DO THEY REALLY DARE STANDING BEFORE HIM COME JUDGMENT TIME WITH ONLY A *HALF-FORMED UNDERSTANDING* OF THEIR OWN FAITH?
IF OUR GOD EMBODIES BOT PEACE AND VIOLENCE...
...THEN ISN'T OUR *BLIND DEVOTION* TO ONE DISCIPLINE...

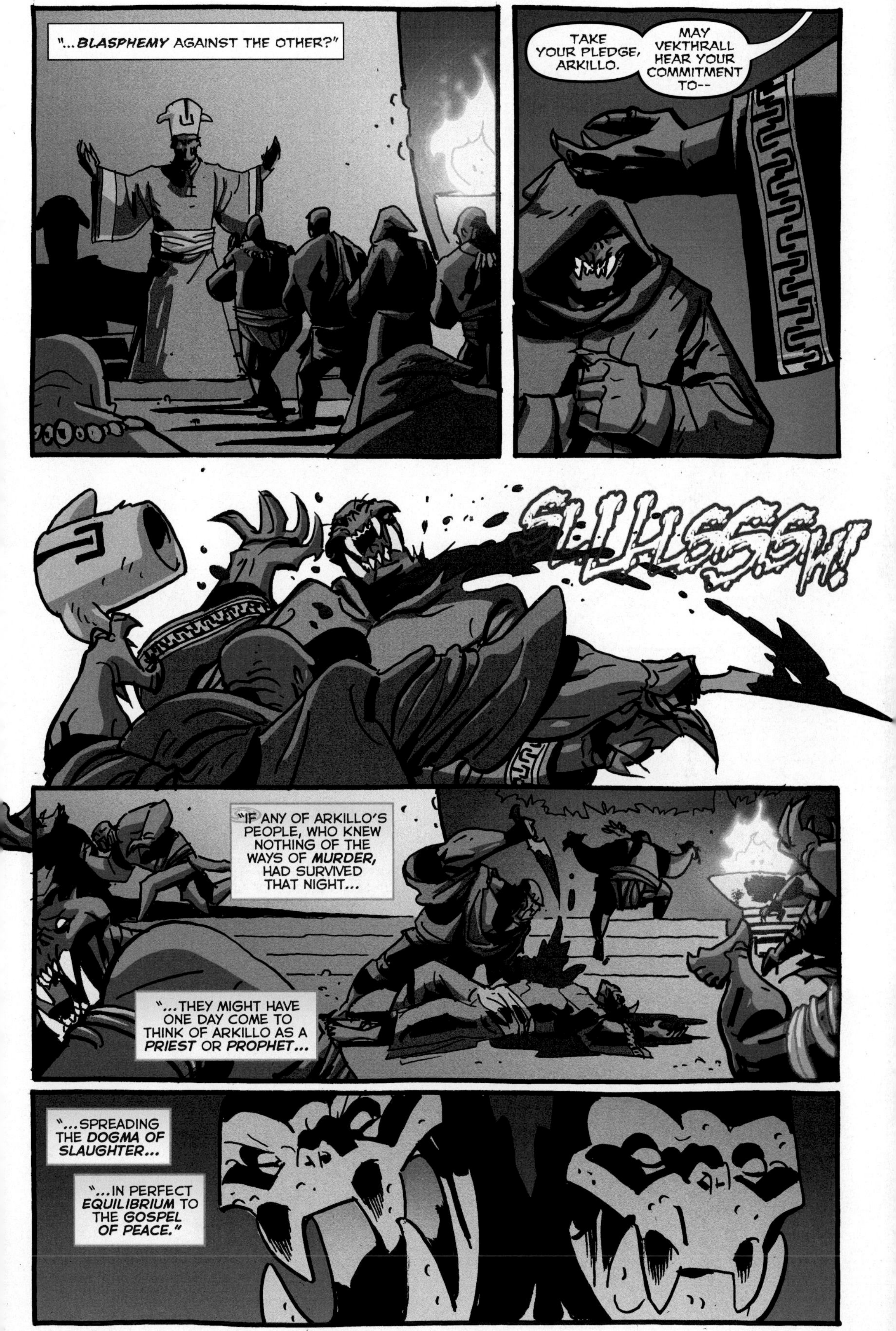
"...BLASPHEMY AGAINST THE OTHER?"
TAKE YOUR PLEDGE, ARKILLO.
MAY VEKTHRALL HEAR YOUR COMMITMENT TO--
SLLHSSSH!
"IF ANY OF ARKILLO'S PEOPLE, WHO KNEW NOTHING OF THE WAYS OF MURDER, HAD SURVIVED THAT NIGHT...
"...THEY MIGHT HAVE ONE DAY COME TO THINK OF ARKILLO AS A PRIEST OR PROPHET...
"...SPREADING THE DOGMA OF SLAUGHTER...
"...IN PERFECT EQUILIBRIUM TO THE GOSPEL OF PEACE."

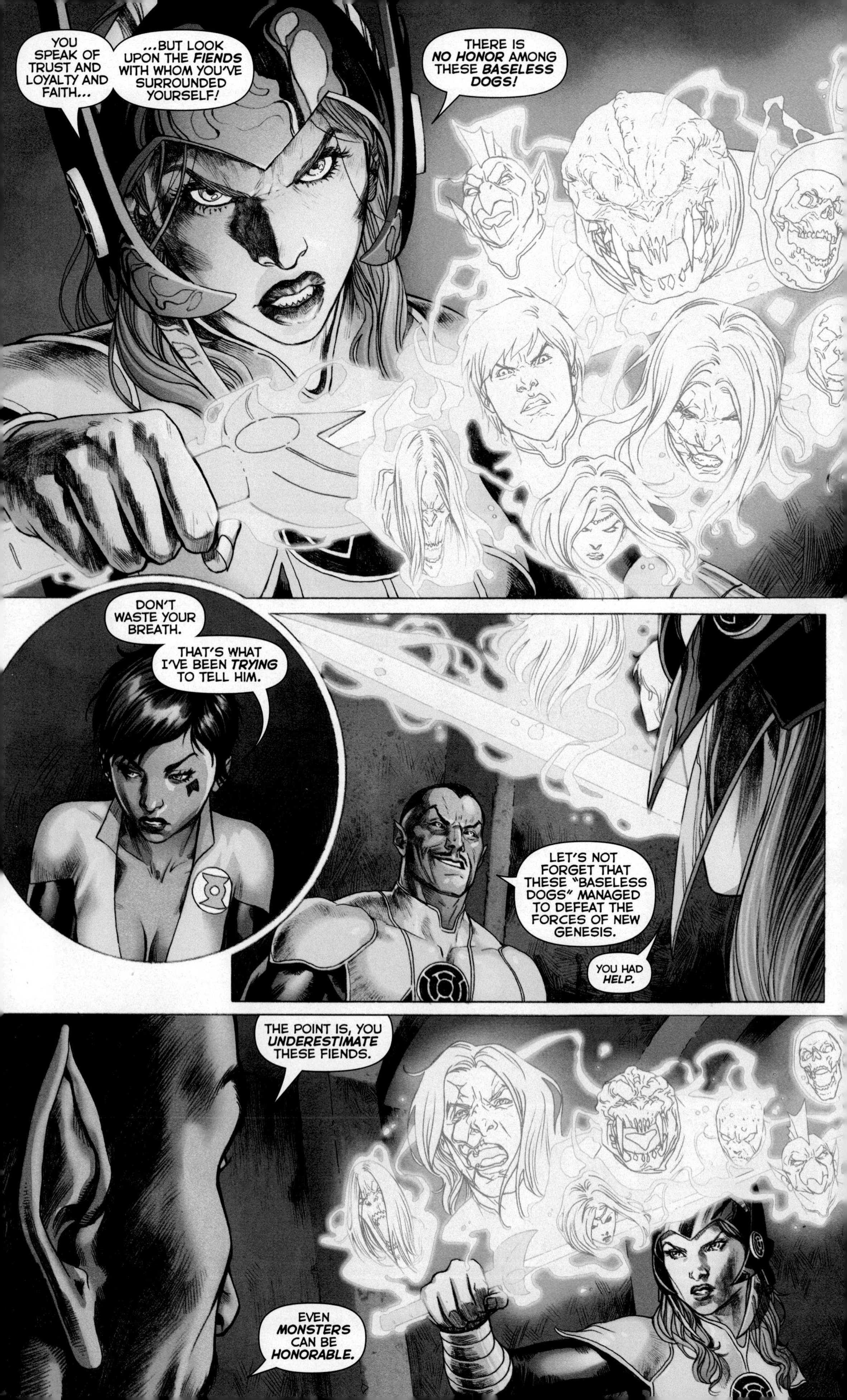
YOU SPEAK OF TRUST AND LOYALTY AND FAITH...
...BUT LOOK UPON THE *FIENDS* WITH WHOM YOU'VE SURROUNDED YOURSELF!
THERE IS *NO HONOR* AMONG THESE *BASELESS DOGS!*
DON'T WASTE YOUR BREATH.
THAT'S WHAT I'VE BEEN *TRYING* TO TELL HIM.
LET'S NOT FORGET THAT THESE "BASELESS DOGS" MANAGED TO DEFEAT THE FORCES OF NEW GENESIS.
YOU HAD *HELP.*
THE POINT IS, YOU *UNDERESTIMATE* THESE FIENDS.
EVEN *MONSTERS* CAN BE *HONORABLE.*

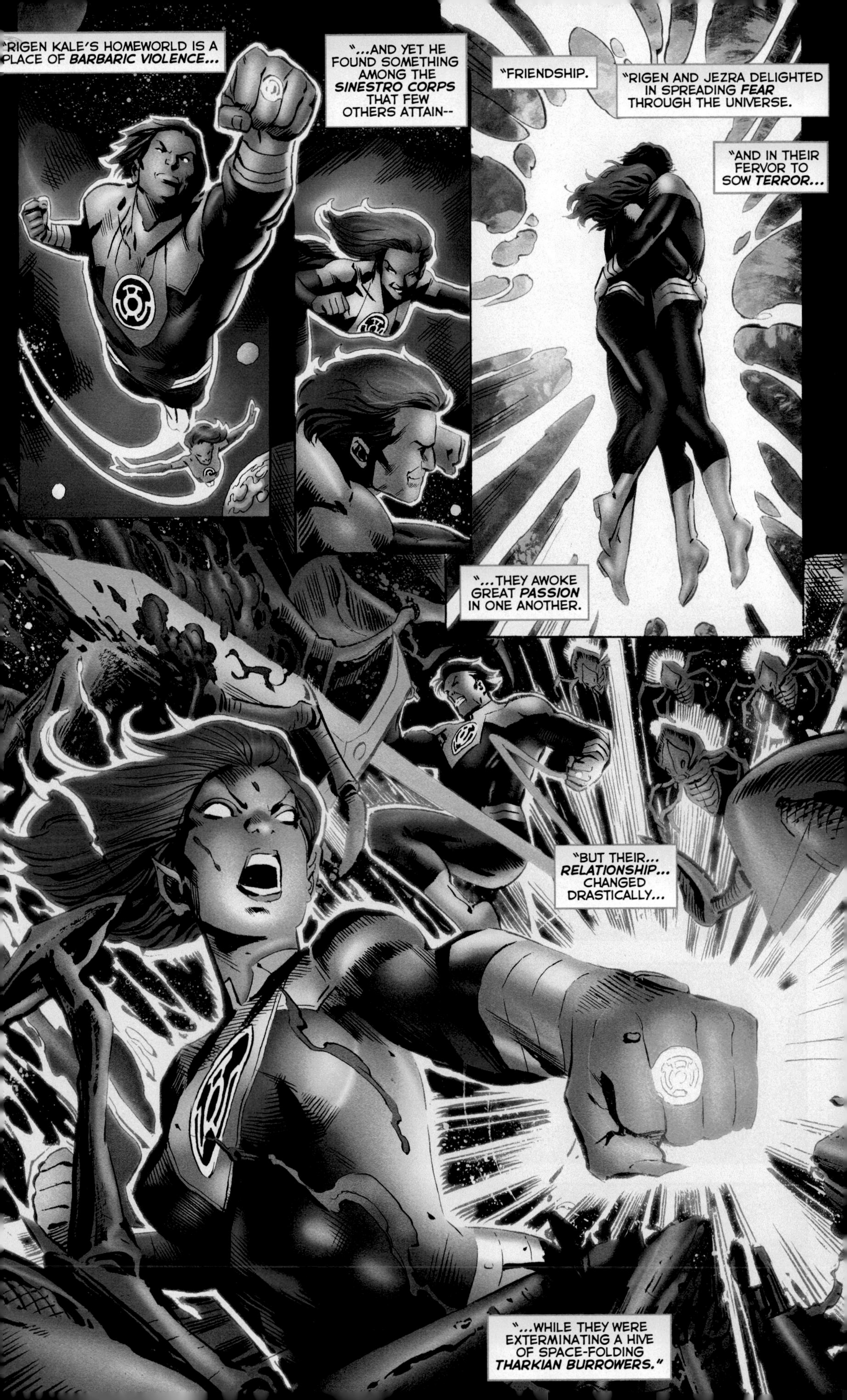
"RIGEN KALE'S HOMEWORLD IS A PLACE OF BARBARIC VIOLENCE...
"...AND YET HE FOUND SOMETHING AMONG THE SINESTRO CORPS THAT FEW OTHERS ATTAIN--
"FRIENDSHIP.
"RIGEN AND JEZRA DELIGHTED IN SPREADING FEAR THROUGH THE UNIVERSE.
"AND IN THEIR FERVOR TO SOW TERROR...
"...THEY AWOKE GREAT PASSION IN ONE ANOTHER.
"BUT THEIR... RELATIONSHIP... CHANGED DRASTICALLY...
"...WHILE THEY WERE EXTERMINATING A HIVE OF SPACE-FOLDING THARKIAN BURROWERS."

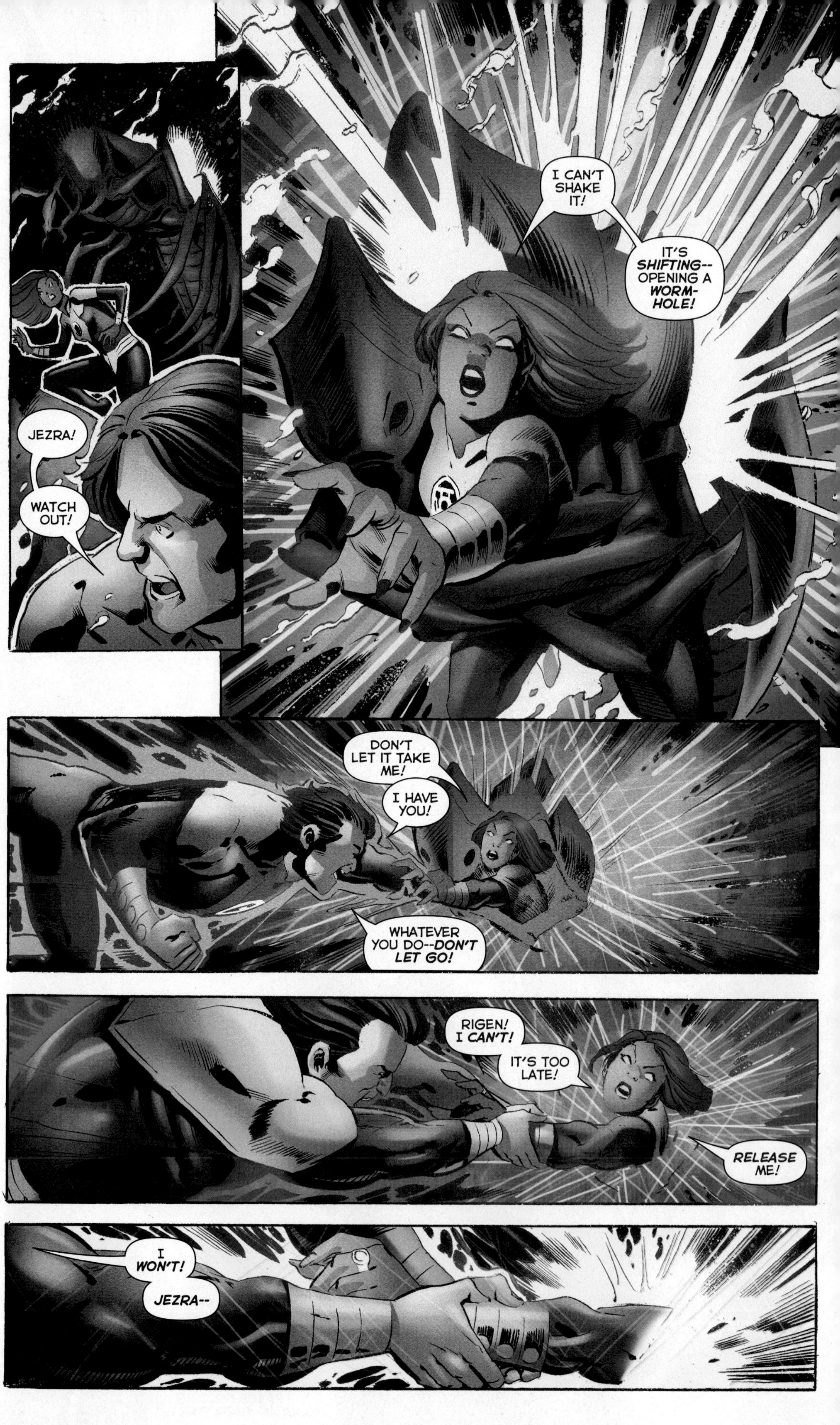
JEZRA!
WATCH OUT!
I CAN'T SHAKE IT!
IT'S SHIFTING-- OPENING A WORM-HOLE!
DON'T LET IT TAKE ME!
I HAVE YOU!
WHATEVER YOU DO--DON'T LET GO!
RIGEN! I CAN'T!
IT'S TOO LATE!
RELEASE ME!
I WON'T!
JEZRA--

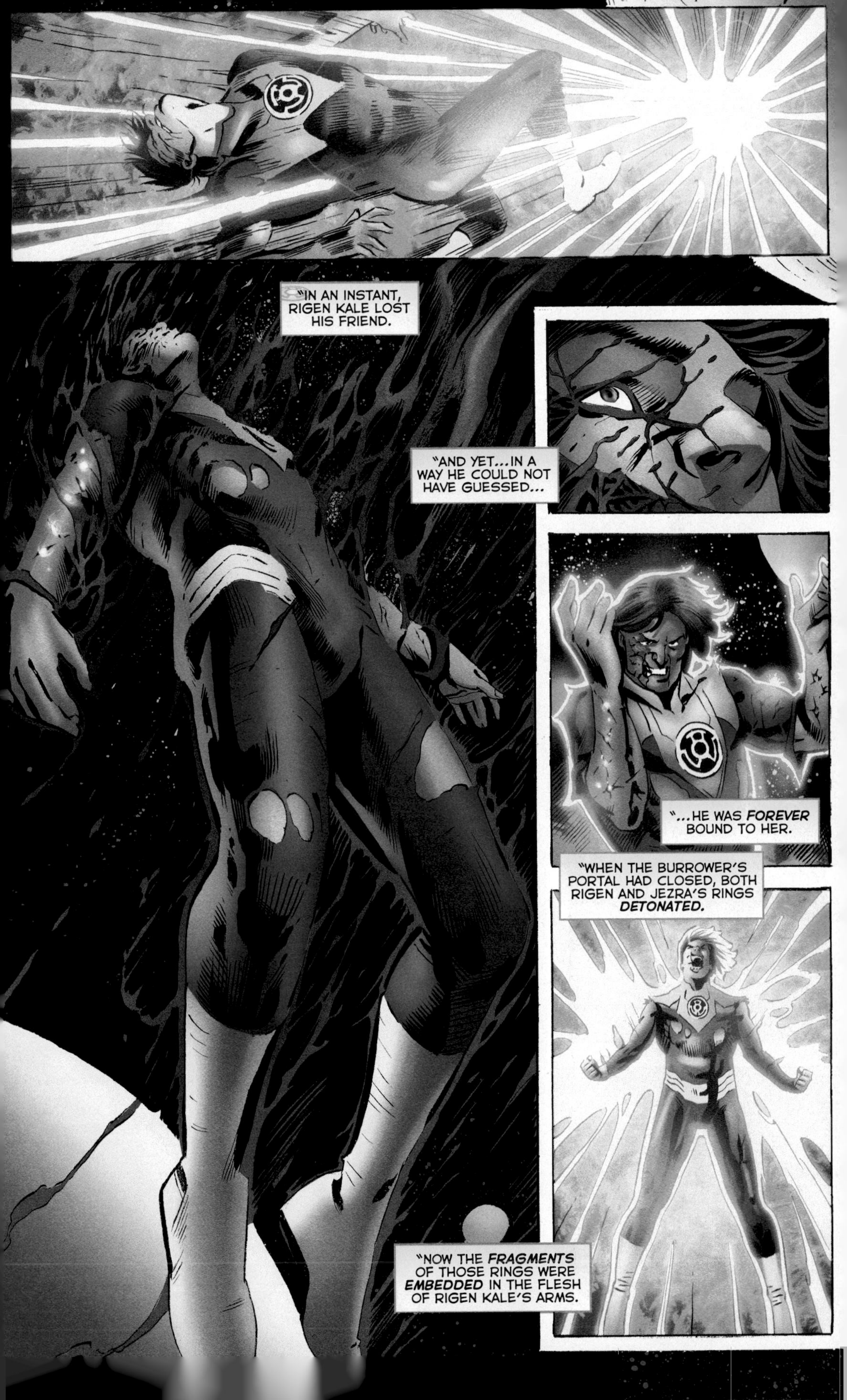
"IN AN INSTANT, RIGEN KALE LOST HIS FRIEND.
"AND YET...IN A WAY HE COULD NOT HAVE GUESSED...
"...HE WAS *FOREVER* BOUND TO HER.
"WHEN THE BURROWER'S PORTAL HAD CLOSED, BOTH RIGEN AND JEZRA'S RINGS *DETONATED.*
"NOW THE *FRAGMENTS* OF THOSE RINGS WERE *EMBEDDED* IN THE FLESH OF RIGEN KALE'S ARMS.

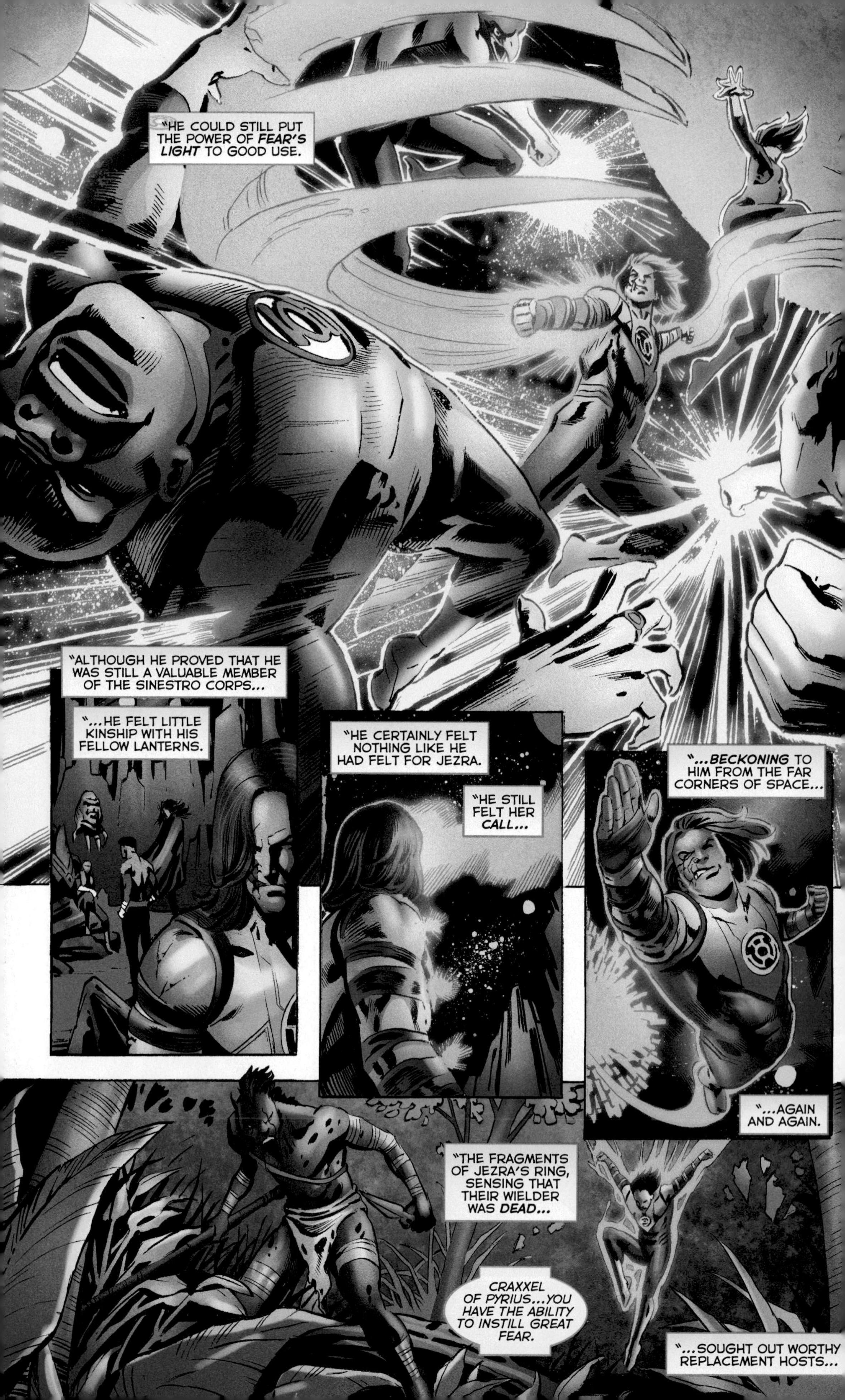
"HE COULD STILL PUT THE POWER OF FEAR'S LIGHT TO GOOD USE.
"ALTHOUGH HE PROVED THAT HE WAS STILL A VALUABLE MEMBER OF THE SINESTRO CORPS...
"...HE FELT LITTLE KINSHIP WITH HIS FELLOW LANTERNS.
"HE CERTAINLY FELT NOTHING LIKE HE HAD FELT FOR JEZRA.
"HE STILL FELT HER CALL...
"...BECKONING TO HIM FROM THE FAR CORNERS OF SPACE...
"...AGAIN AND AGAIN.
"THE FRAGMENTS OF JEZRA'S RING, SENSING THAT THEIR WIELDER WAS DEAD...
CRAXXEL OF PYRIUS...YOU HAVE THE ABILITY TO INSTILL GREAT FEAR.
"...SOUGHT OUT WORTHY REPLACEMENT HOSTS...

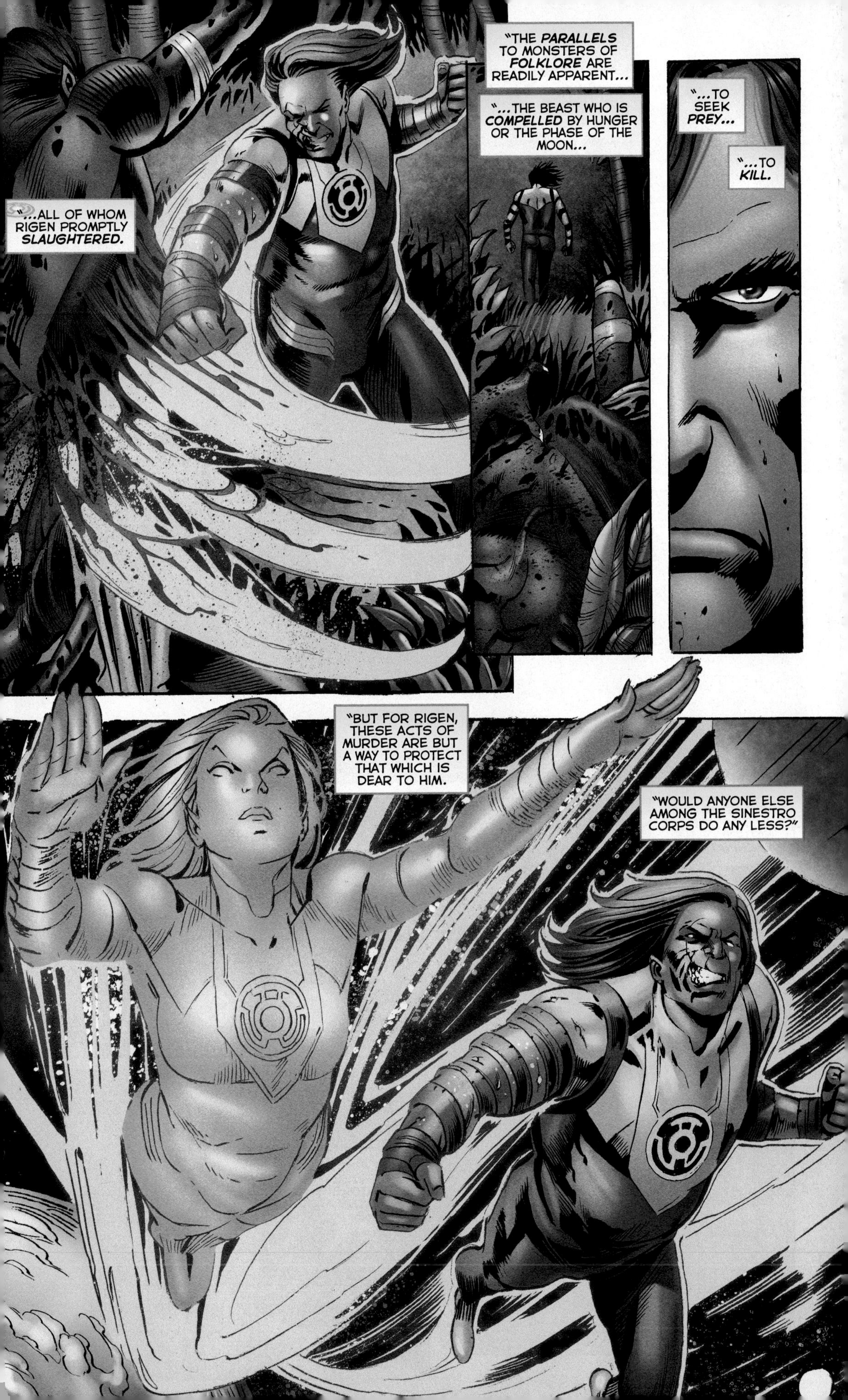
"...ALL OF WHOM RIGEN PROMPTLY SLAUGHTERED.
"THE PARALLELS TO MONSTERS OF FOLKLORE ARE READILY APPARENT...
"...THE BEAST WHO IS COMPELLED BY HUNGER OR THE PHASE OF THE MOON...
"...TO SEEK PREY...
"...TO KILL.
"BUT FOR RIGEN, THESE ACTS OF MURDER ARE BUT A WAY TO PROTECT THAT WHICH IS DEAR TO HIM.
"WOULD ANYONE ELSE AMONG THE SINESTRO CORPS DO ANY LESS?"

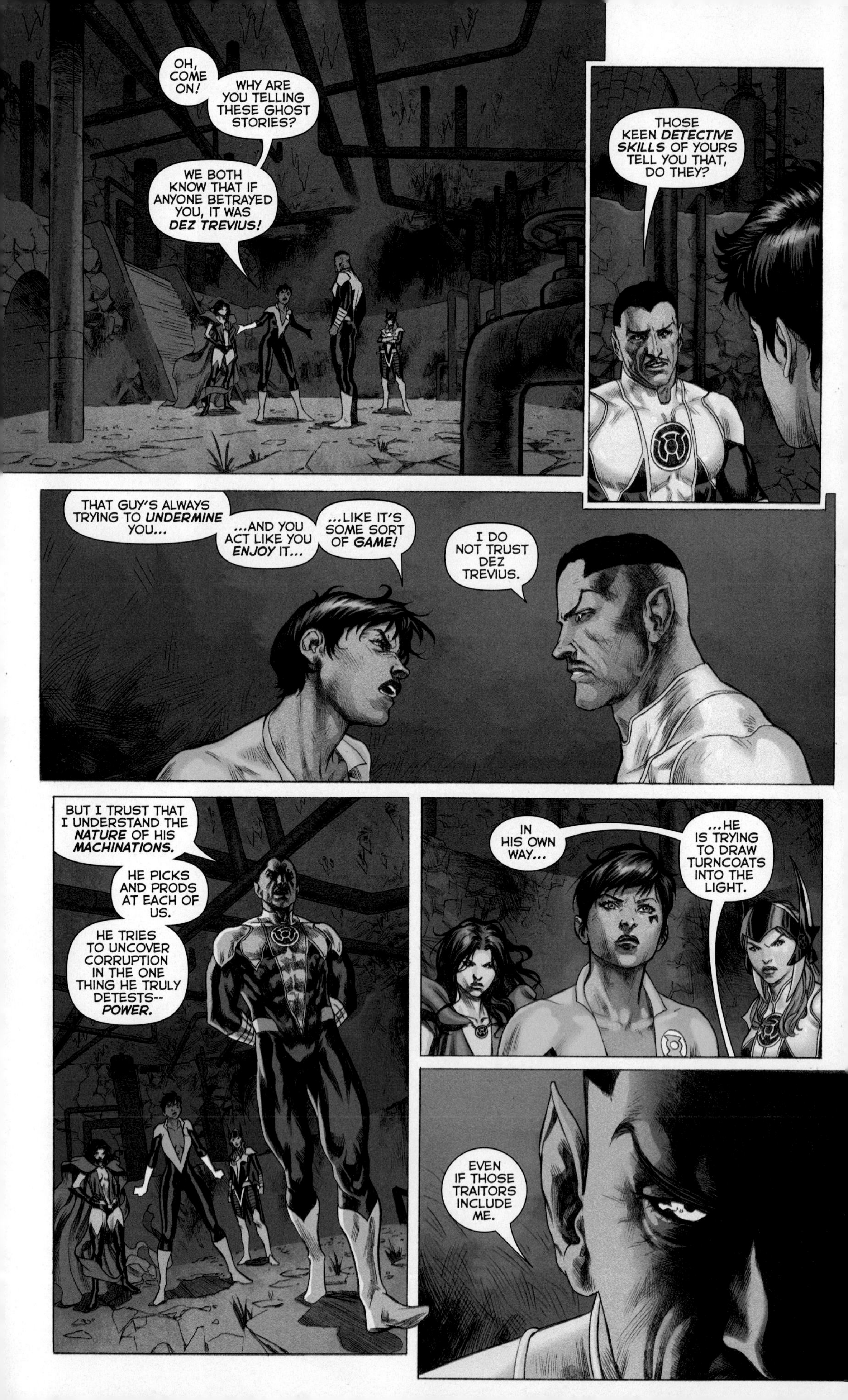
OH, COME ON!
WHY ARE YOU TELLING THESE GHOST STORIES?
WE BOTH KNOW THAT IF ANYONE BETRAYED YOU, IT WAS DEZ TREVIUS!
THOSE KEEN DETECTIVE SKILLS OF YOURS TELL YOU THAT, DO THEY?
THAT GUY'S ALWAYS TRYING TO UNDERMINE YOU...
...AND YOU ACT LIKE YOU ENJOY IT...
...LIKE IT'S SOME SORT OF GAME!
I DO NOT TRUST DEZ TREVIUS.
BUT I TRUST THAT I UNDERSTAND THE NATURE OF HIS MACHINATIONS.
HE PICKS AND PRODS AT EACH OF US.
HE TRIES TO UNCOVER CORRUPTION IN THE ONE THING HE TRULY DETESTS--POWER.
IN HIS OWN WAY...
...HE IS TRYING TO DRAW TURNCOATS INTO THE LIGHT.
EVEN IF THOSE TRAITORS INCLUDE ME.

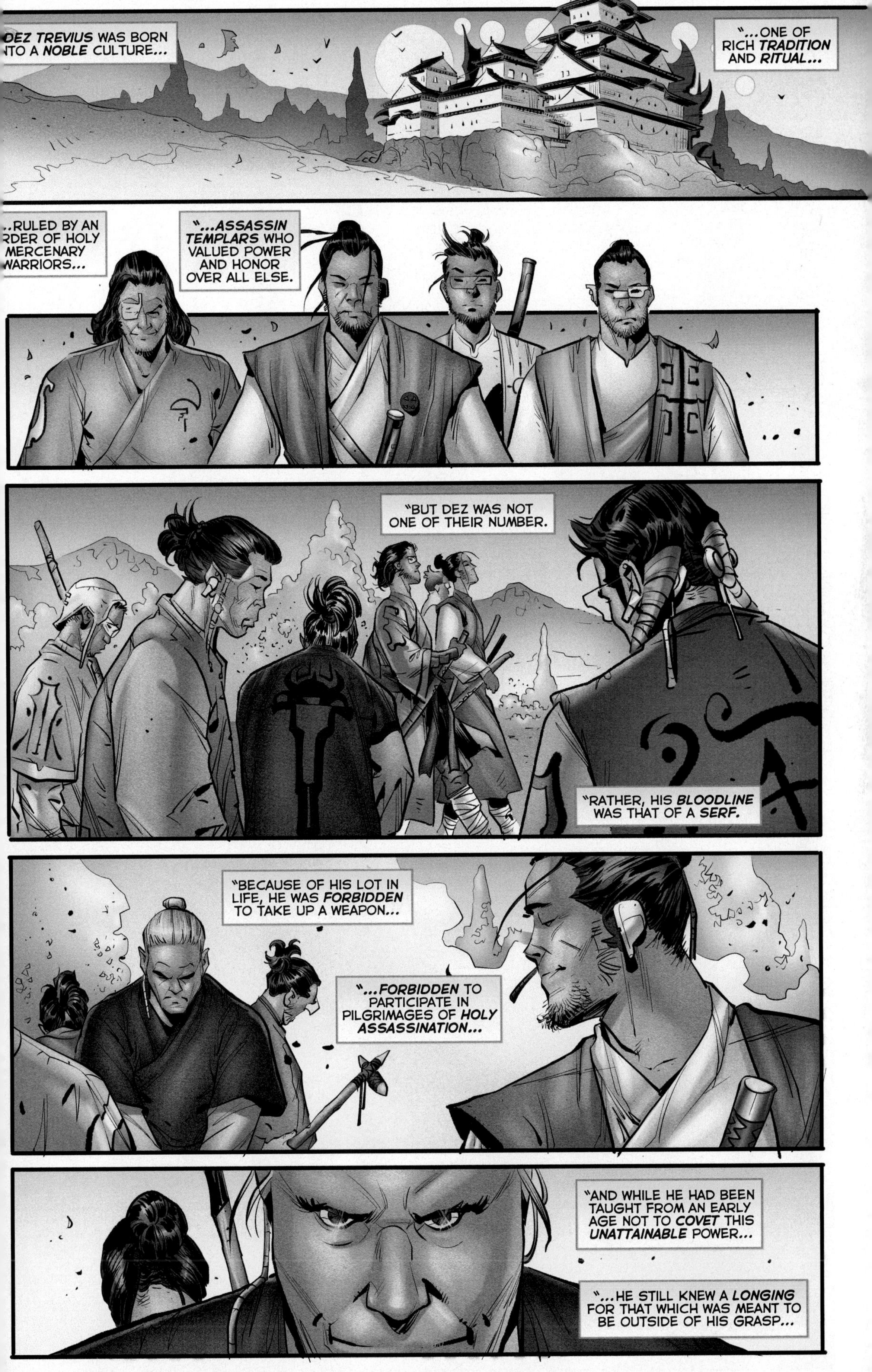
DEZ TREVIUS WAS BORN
NTO A NOBLE CULTURE...
"...ONE OF RICH TRADITION AND RITUAL...
..RULED BY AN RDER OF HOLY MERCENARY WARRIORS...
"...ASSASSIN TEMPLARS WHO VALUED POWER AND HONOR OVER ALL ELSE.
"BUT DEZ WAS NOT ONE OF THEIR NUMBER.
"RATHER, HIS BLOODLINE WAS THAT OF A SERF.
"BECAUSE OF HIS LOT IN LIFE, HE WAS FORBIDDEN TO TAKE UP A WEAPON...
"...FORBIDDEN TO PARTICIPATE IN PILGRIMAGES OF HOLY ASSASSINATION...
"AND WHILE HE HAD BEEN TAUGHT FROM AN EARLY AGE NOT TO COVET THIS UNATTAINABLE POWER...
"...HE STILL KNEW A LONGING FOR THAT WHICH WAS MEANT TO BE OUTSIDE OF HIS GRASP...

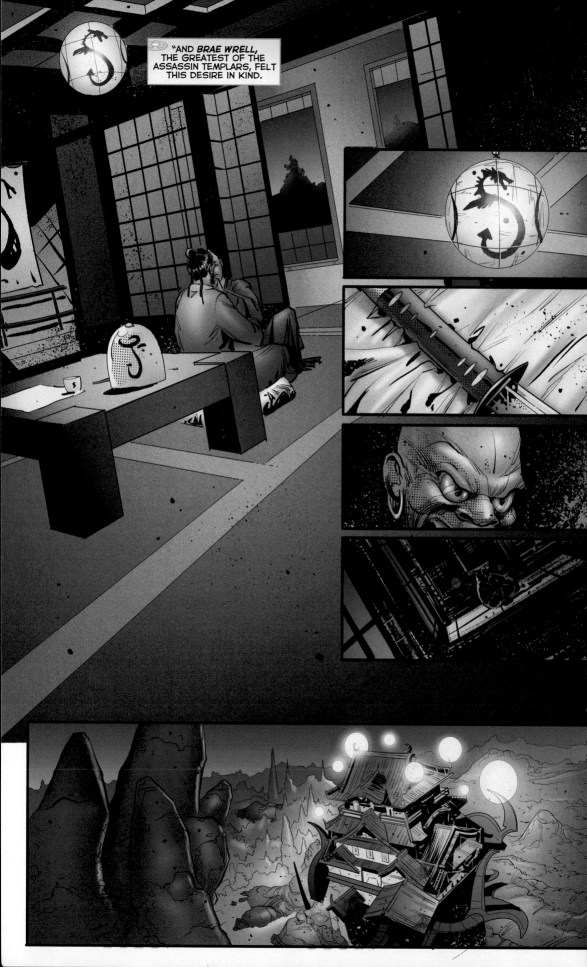

"AND *BRAE WRELL,*
THE GREATEST OF THE
ASSASSIN TEMPLARS, FELT
THIS DESIRE IN KIND.

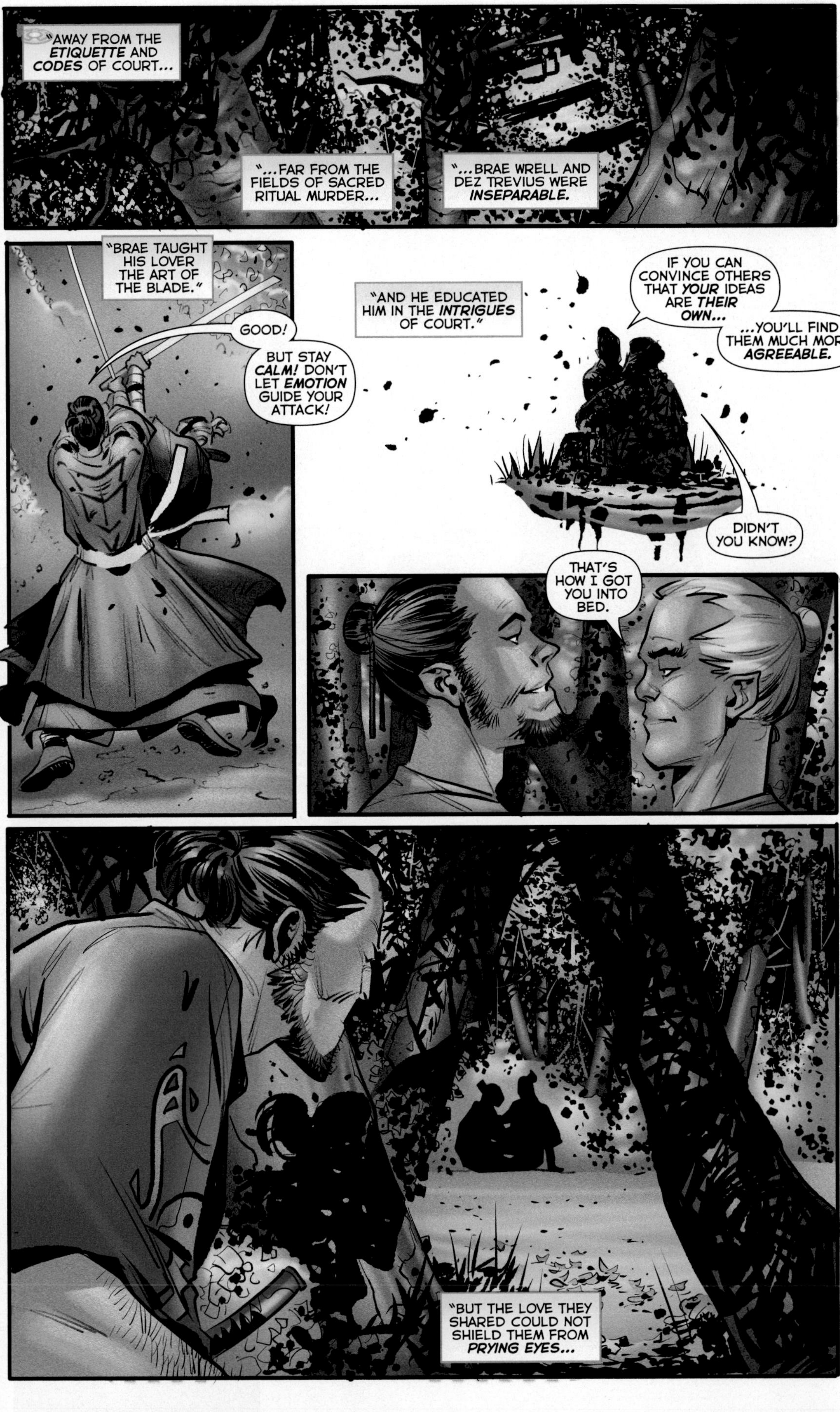

"AWAY FROM THE *ETIQUETTE* AND *CODES* OF COURT...
"...FAR FROM THE FIELDS OF SACRED RITUAL MURDER...
"...BRAE WRELL AND DEZ TREVIUS WERE *INSEPARABLE.*
"BRAE TAUGHT HIS LOVER THE ART OF THE BLADE."
GOOD!
BUT STAY *CALM!* DON'T LET *EMOTION* GUIDE YOUR ATTACK!
"AND HE EDUCATED HIM IN THE *INTRIGUES* OF COURT."
IF YOU CAN CONVINCE OTHERS THAT *YOUR* IDEAS ARE *THEIR OWN*...
...YOU'LL FIND THEM MUCH MORE *AGREEABLE.*
DIDN'T YOU KNOW?
THAT'S HOW I GOT YOU INTO BED.
"BUT THE LOVE THEY SHARED COULD NOT SHIELD THEM FROM *PRYING EYES*...

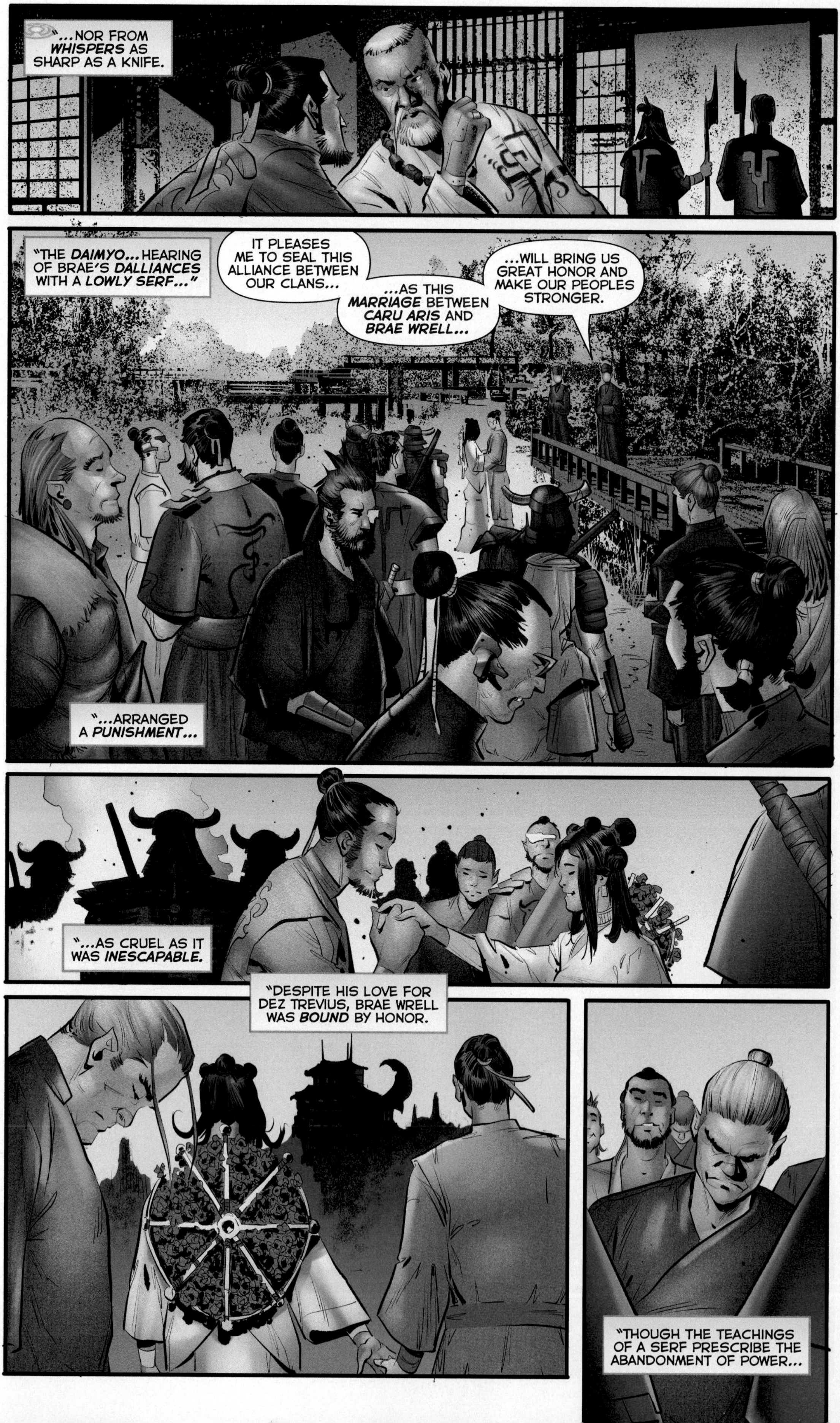
"...NOR FROM WHISPERS AS SHARP AS A KNIFE.
"THE DAIMYO...HEARING OF BRAE'S DALLIANCES WITH A LOWLY SERF..."
IT PLEASES ME TO SEAL THIS ALLIANCE BETWEEN OUR CLANS...
...AS THIS MARRIAGE BETWEEN CARU ARIS AND BRAE WRELL...
...WILL BRING US GREAT HONOR AND MAKE OUR PEOPLES STRONGER.
"...ARRANGED A PUNISHMENT...
"...AS CRUEL AS IT WAS INESCAPABLE.
"DESPITE HIS LOVE FOR DEZ TREVIUS, BRAE WRELL WAS BOUND BY HONOR.
"THOUGH THE TEACHINGS OF A SERF PRESCRIBE THE ABANDONMENT OF POWER...

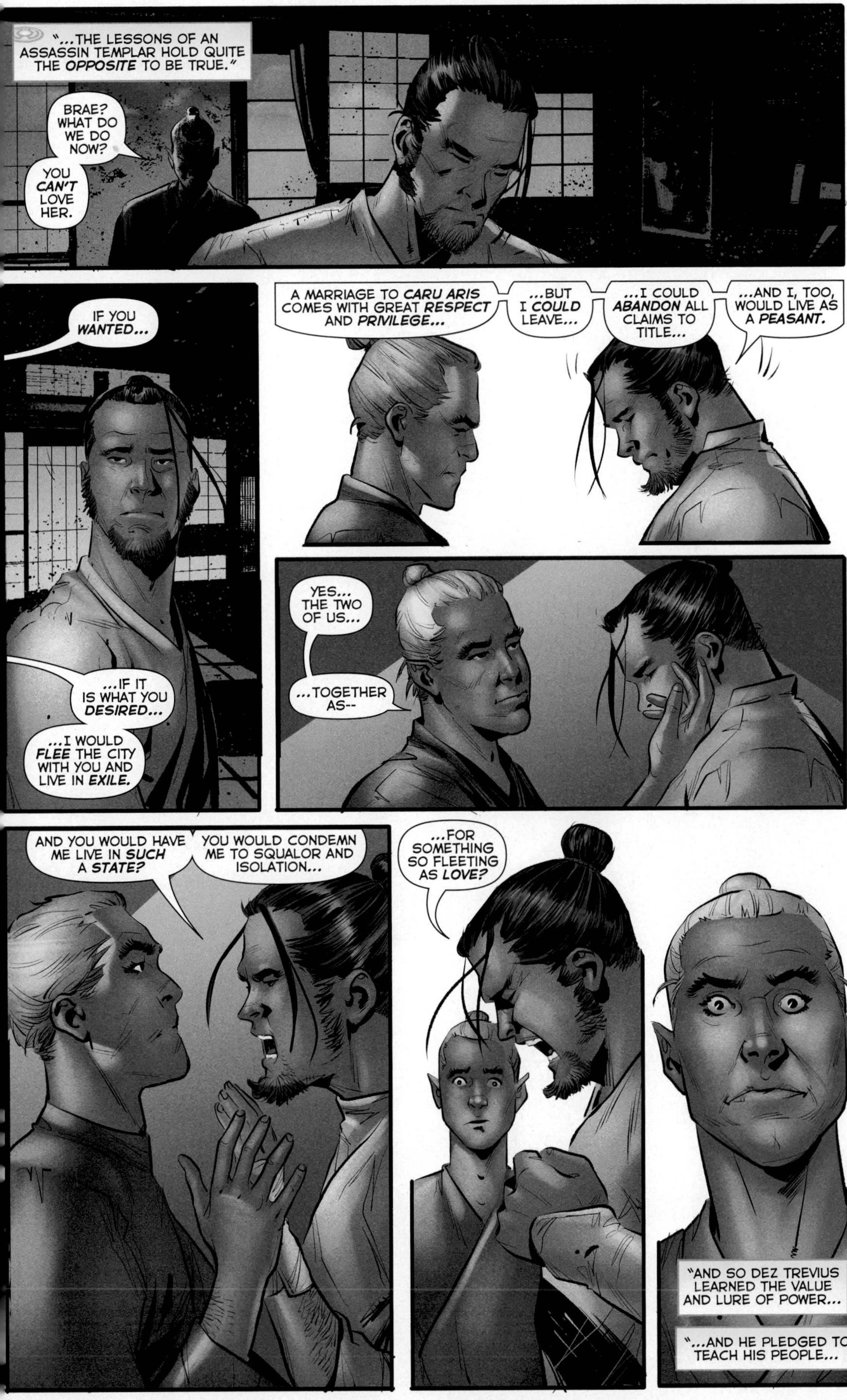
"...THE LESSONS OF AN ASSASSIN TEMPLAR HOLD QUITE THE OPPOSITE TO BE TRUE."
BRAE? WHAT DO WE DO NOW?
YOU CAN'T LOVE HER.
IF YOU WANTED...
...IF IT IS WHAT YOU DESIRED...
...I WOULD FLEE THE CITY WITH YOU AND LIVE IN EXILE.
A MARRIAGE TO CARU ARIS COMES WITH GREAT RESPECT AND PRIVILEGE...
...BUT I COULD LEAVE...
...I COULD ABANDON ALL CLAIMS TO TITLE...
...AND I, TOO, WOULD LIVE AS A PEASANT.
YES... THE TWO OF US...
...TOGETHER AS--
AND YOU WOULD HAVE ME LIVE IN SUCH A STATE?
YOU WOULD CONDEMN ME TO SQUALOR AND ISOLATION...
...FOR SOMETHING SO FLEETING AS LOVE?
"AND SO DEZ TREVIUS LEARNED THE VALUE AND LURE OF POWER...
"...AND HE PLEDGED TO TEACH HIS PEOPLE...

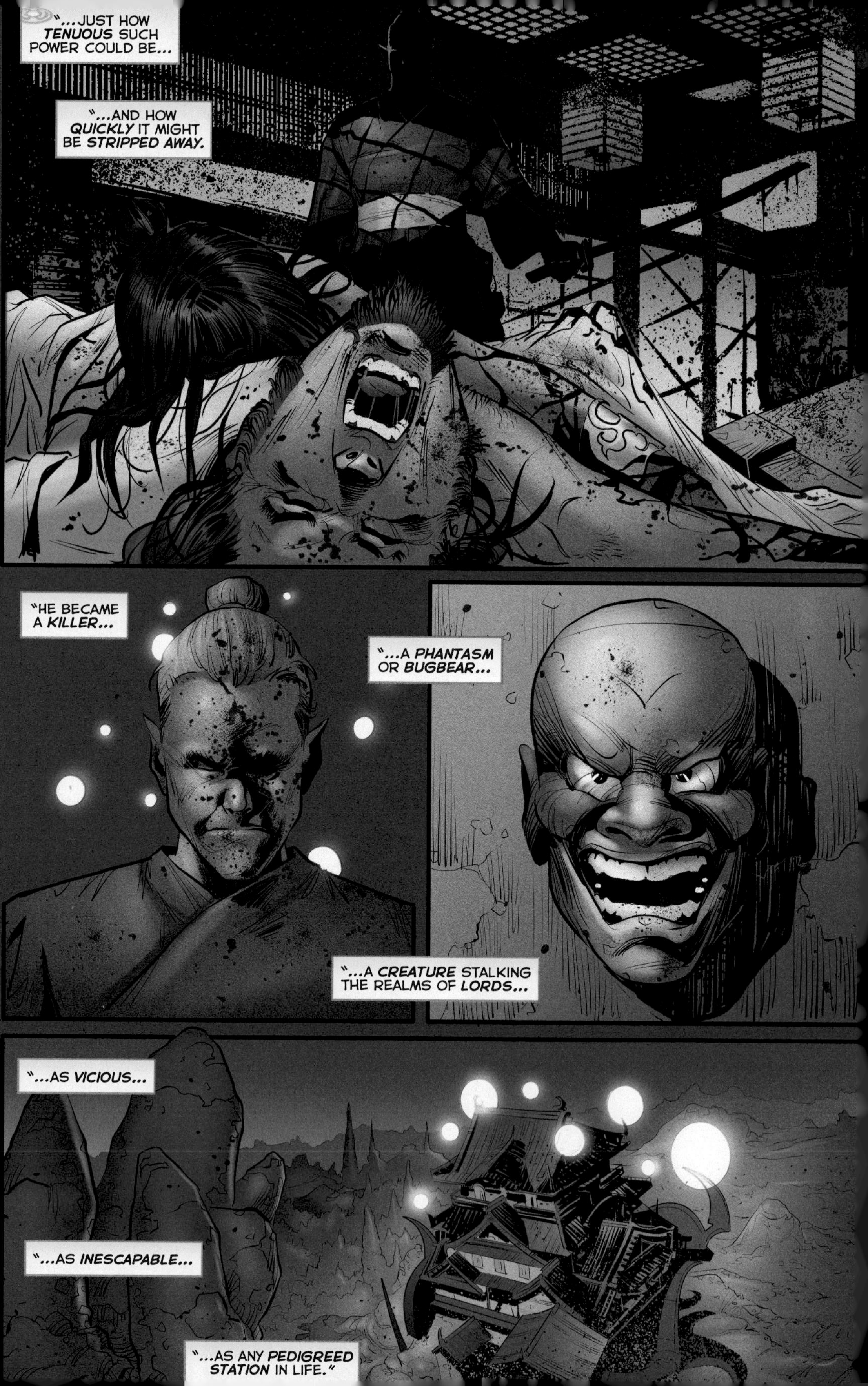
"...JUST HOW TENUOUS SUCH POWER COULD BE...
"...AND HOW QUICKLY IT MIGHT BE STRIPPED AWAY.
"HE BECAME A KILLER...
"...A PHANTASM OR BUGBEAR...
"...A CREATURE STALKING THE REALMS OF LORDS...
"...AS VICIOUS...
"...AS INESCAPABLE...
"...AS ANY PEDIGREED STATION IN LIFE."

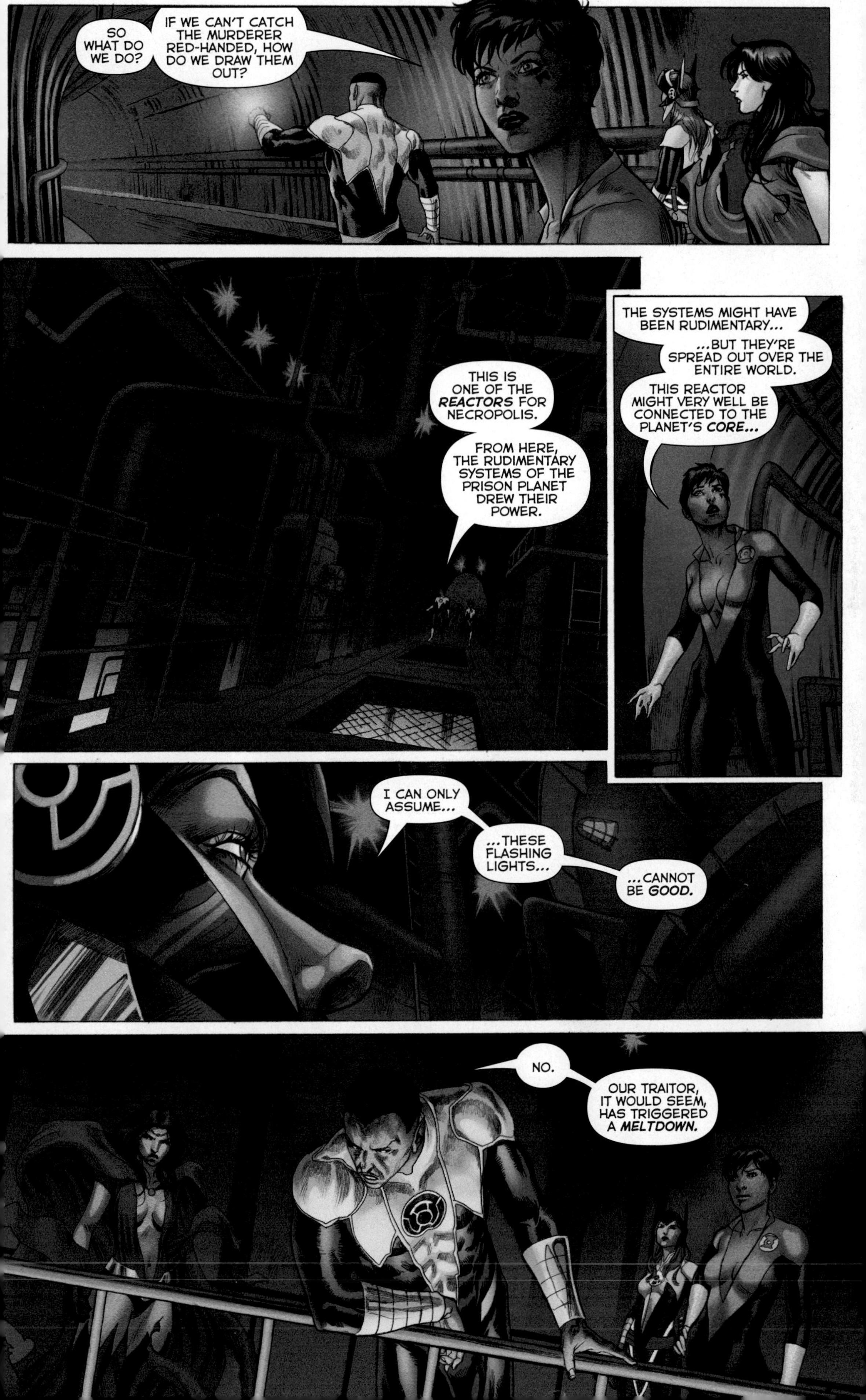
SO WHAT DO WE DO?
IF WE CAN'T CATCH THE MURDERER RED-HANDED, HOW DO WE DRAW THEM OUT?
THIS IS ONE OF THE *REACTORS* FOR NECROPOLIS.
FROM HERE, THE RUDIMENTARY SYSTEMS OF THE PRISON PLANET DREW THEIR POWER.
THE SYSTEMS MIGHT HAVE BEEN RUDIMENTARY...
...BUT THEY'RE SPREAD OUT OVER THE ENTIRE WORLD.
THIS REACTOR MIGHT VERY WELL BE CONNECTED TO THE PLANET'S *CORE*...
I CAN ONLY ASSUME...
...THESE FLASHING LIGHTS...
...CANNOT BE *GOOD.*
NO.
OUR TRAITOR, IT WOULD SEEM, HAS TRIGGERED A *MELTDOWN.*

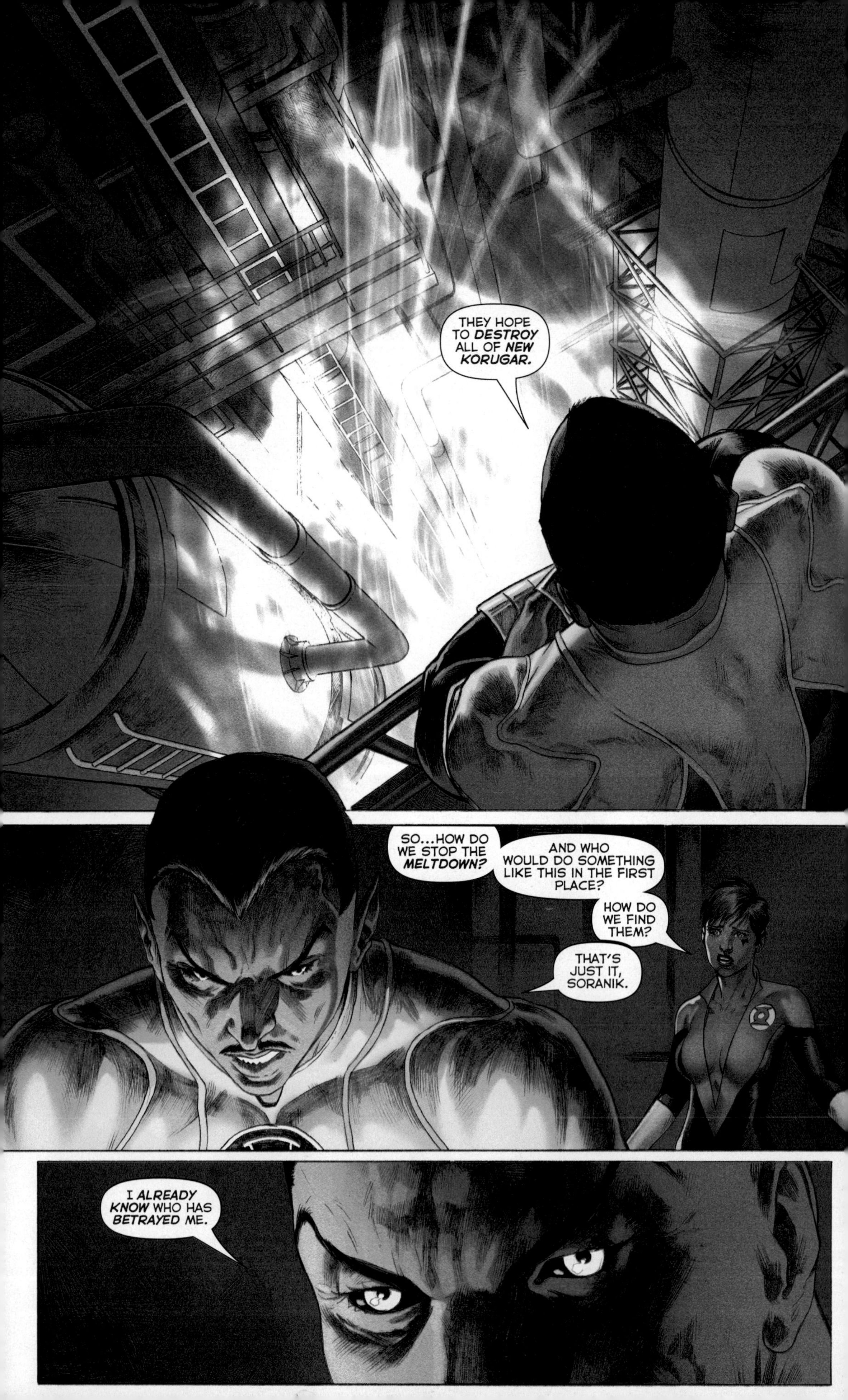
THEY HOPE TO DESTROY ALL OF NEW KORUGAR.
SO...HOW DO WE STOP THE MELTDOWN?
AND WHO WOULD DO SOMETHING LIKE THIS IN THE FIRST PLACE?
HOW DO WE FIND THEM?
THAT'S JUST IT, SORANIK.
I ALREADY KNOW WHO HAS BETRAYED ME.

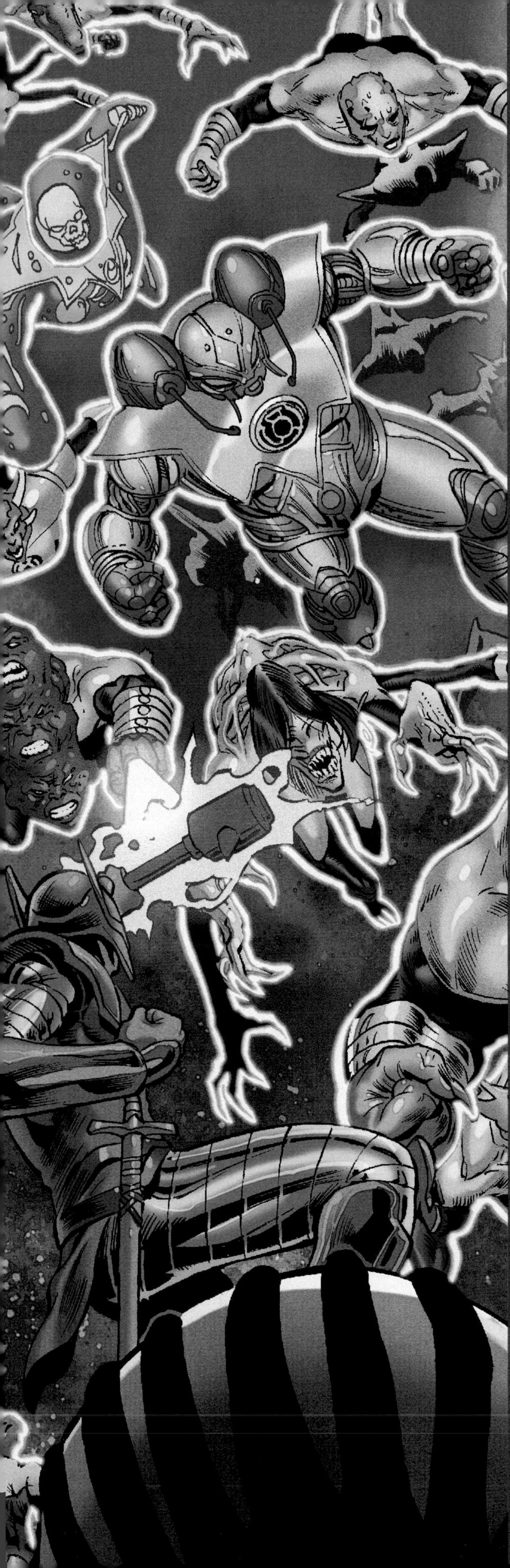

VARIANT COVER GALLERY

SINESTRO #6
MONSTER OF THE MONTH
VARIANT COVER ART
BY BART SEARS AND
MICHAEL ATIYEH

SINESTRO #7
LEGO MONTH VARIANT COVER

SINESTRO #8
VARIANT COVER ART
BY DARWYN COOKE

SINESTRO #9
FLASH 75TH ANNIVERSARY
VARIANT COVER ART
BY ETHAN VAN SCIVER
AND ALEX SINCLAIR

SINESTRO #10
HARLEY QUINN VARIANT COVER
ART BY IAN BERTRAM
AND MATT HOLLINGSWORTH

SINESTRO #11
MOVIE POSTER VARIANT COVER
ART BY DAVE JOHNSON

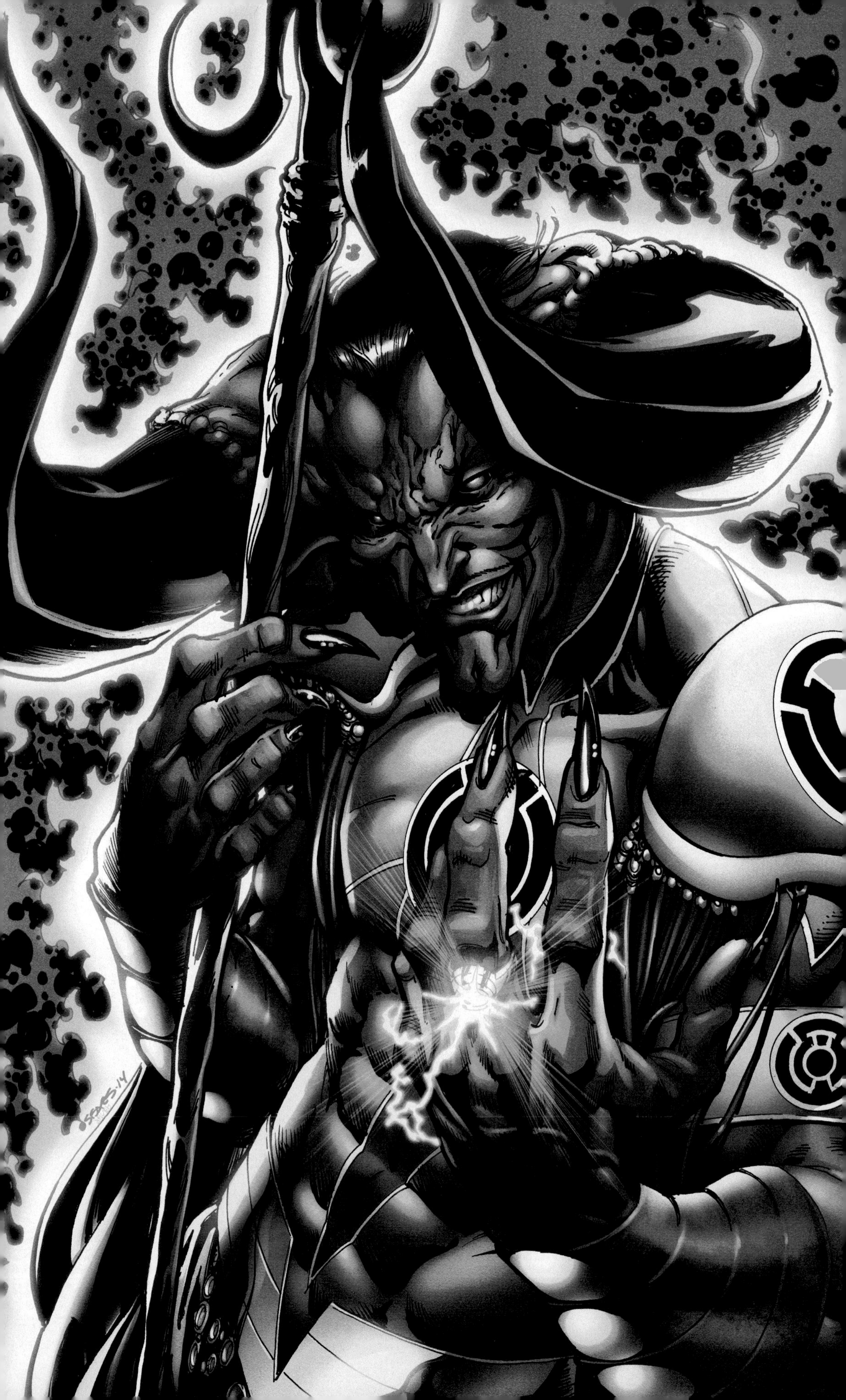

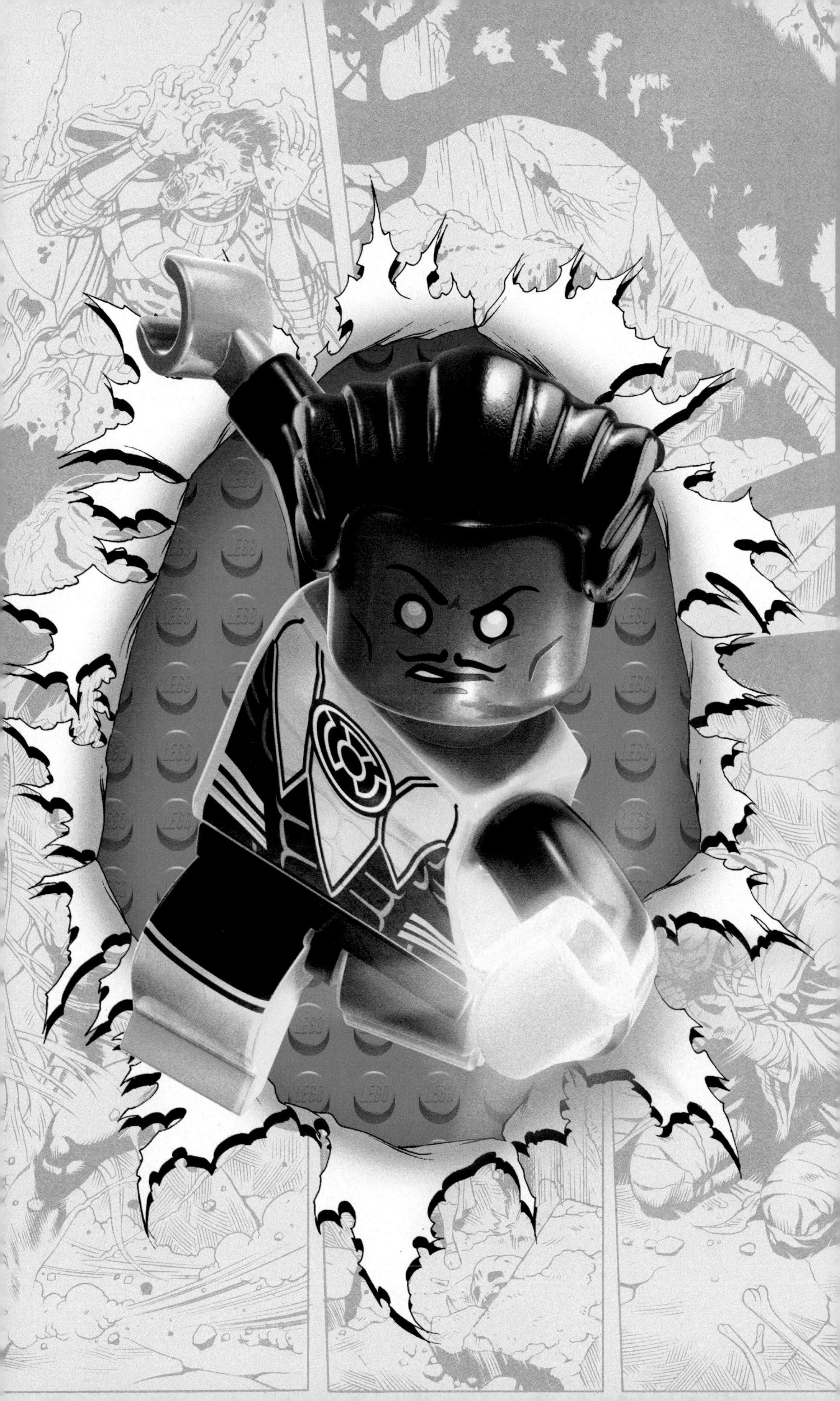

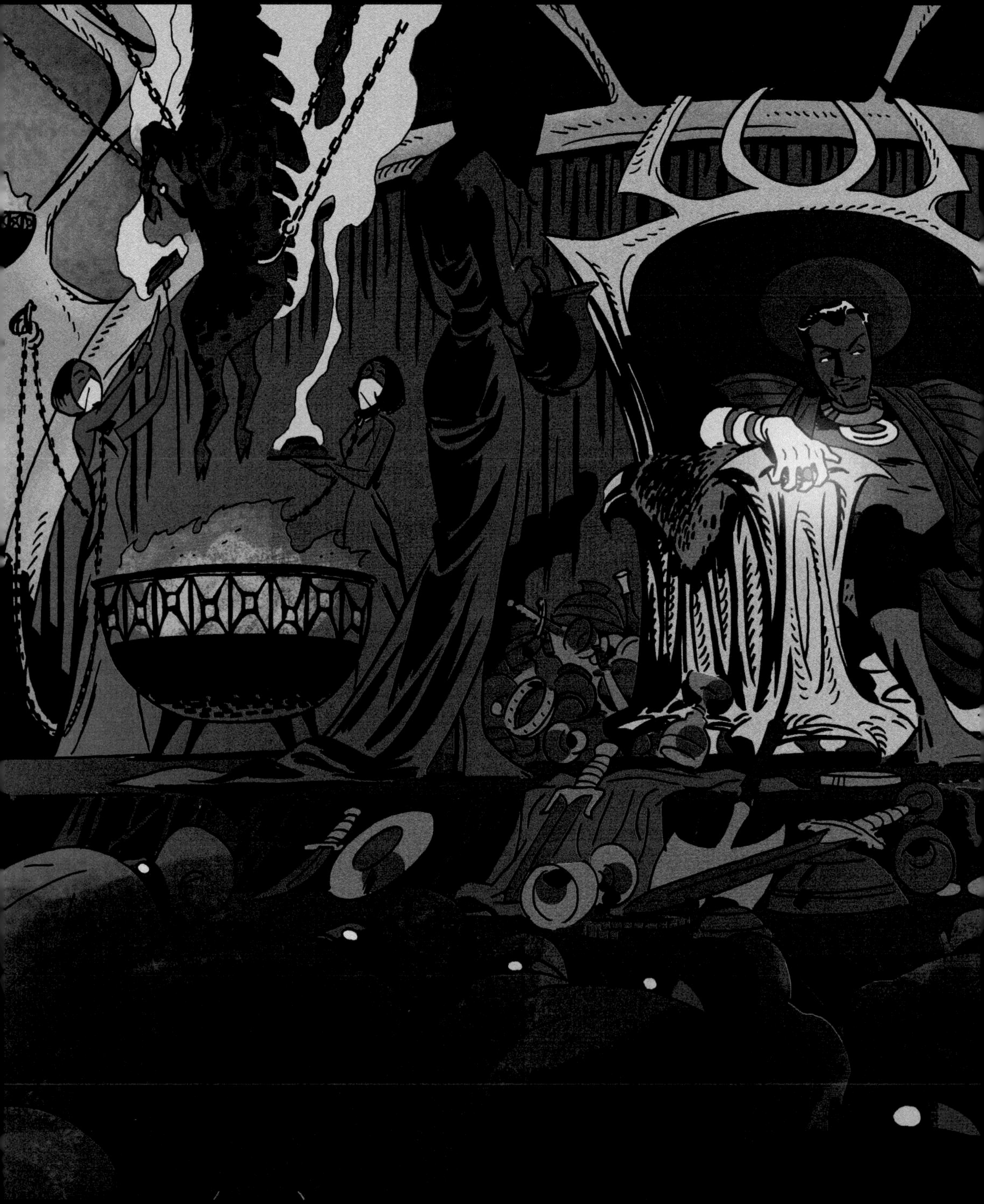

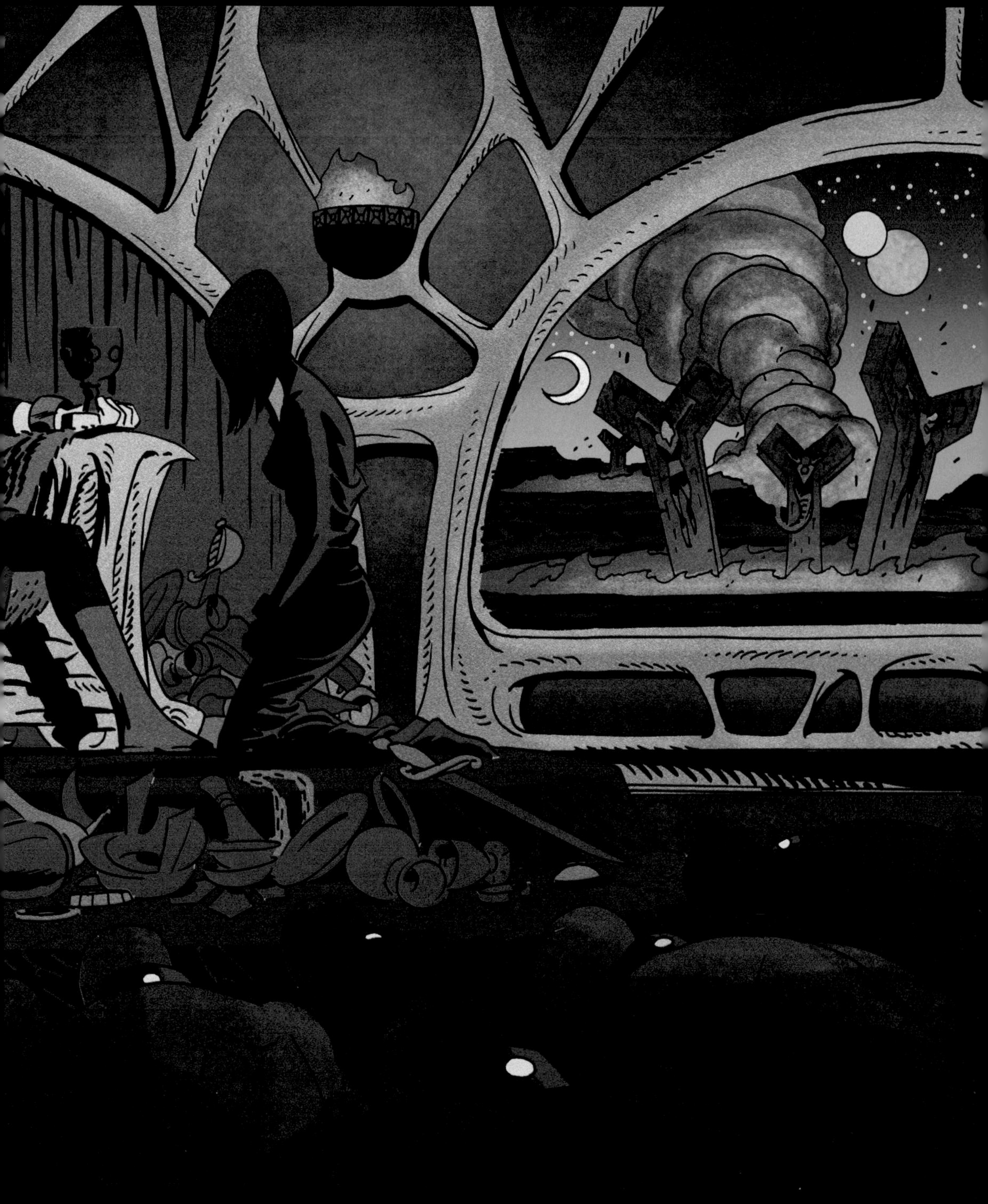

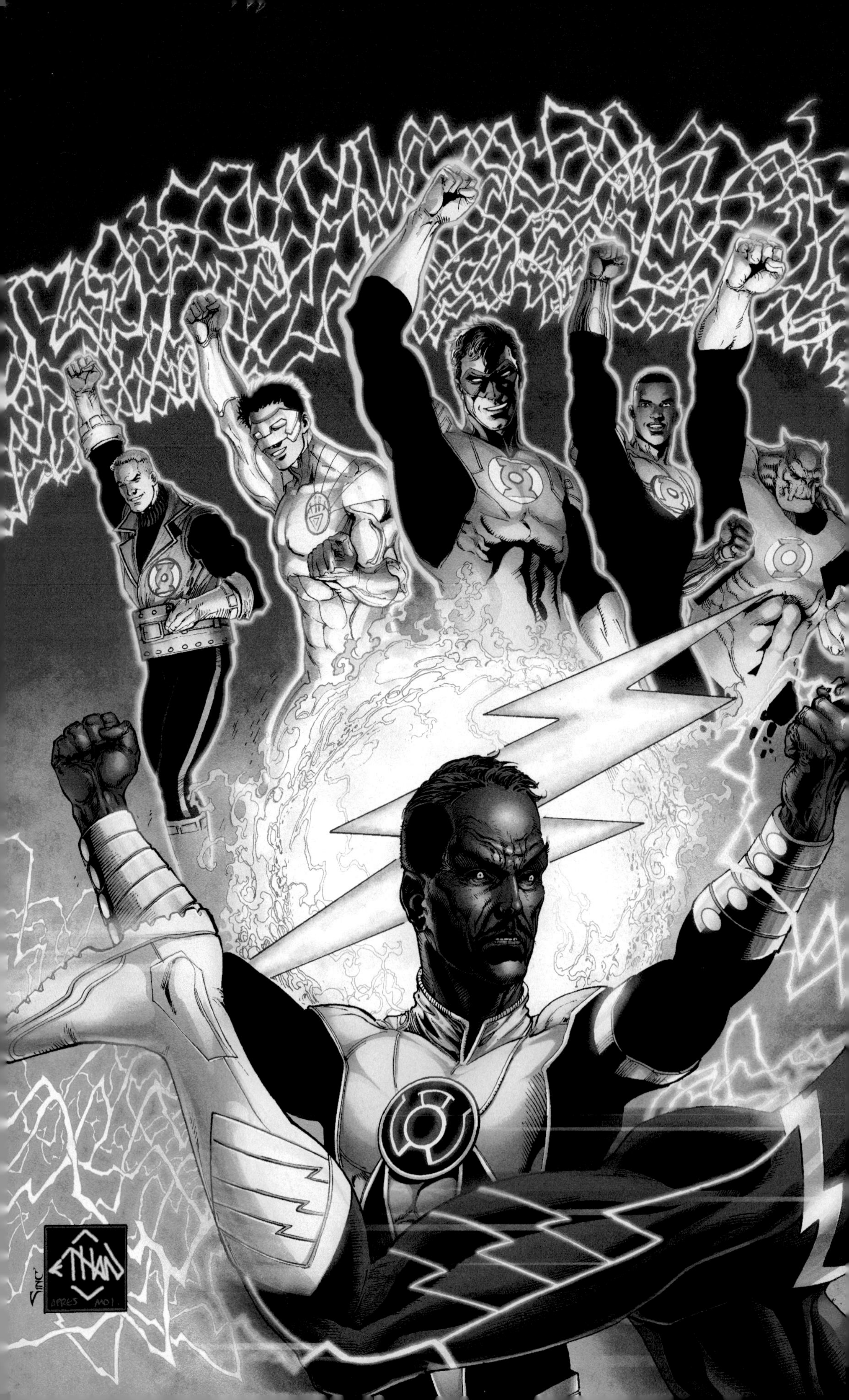

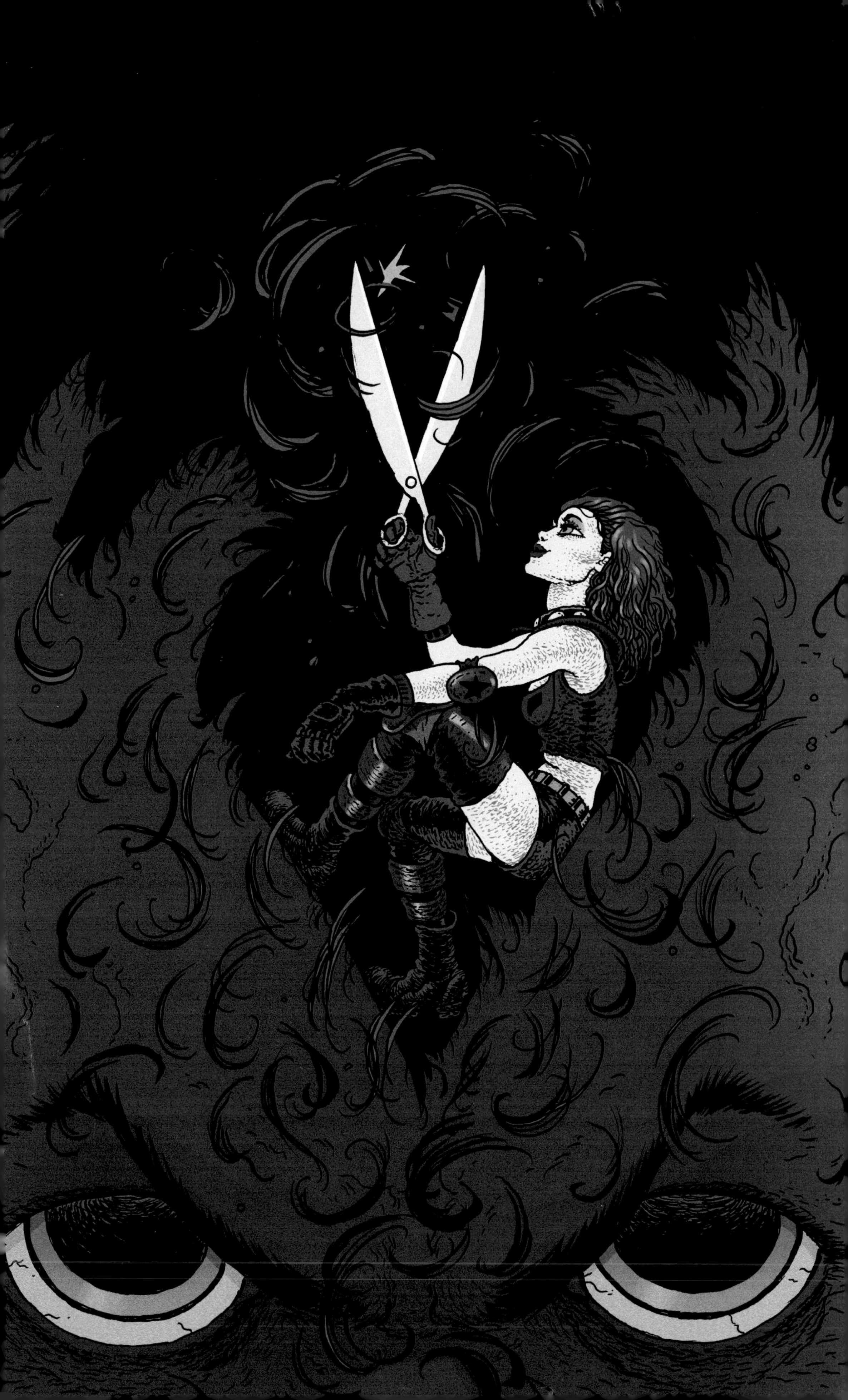

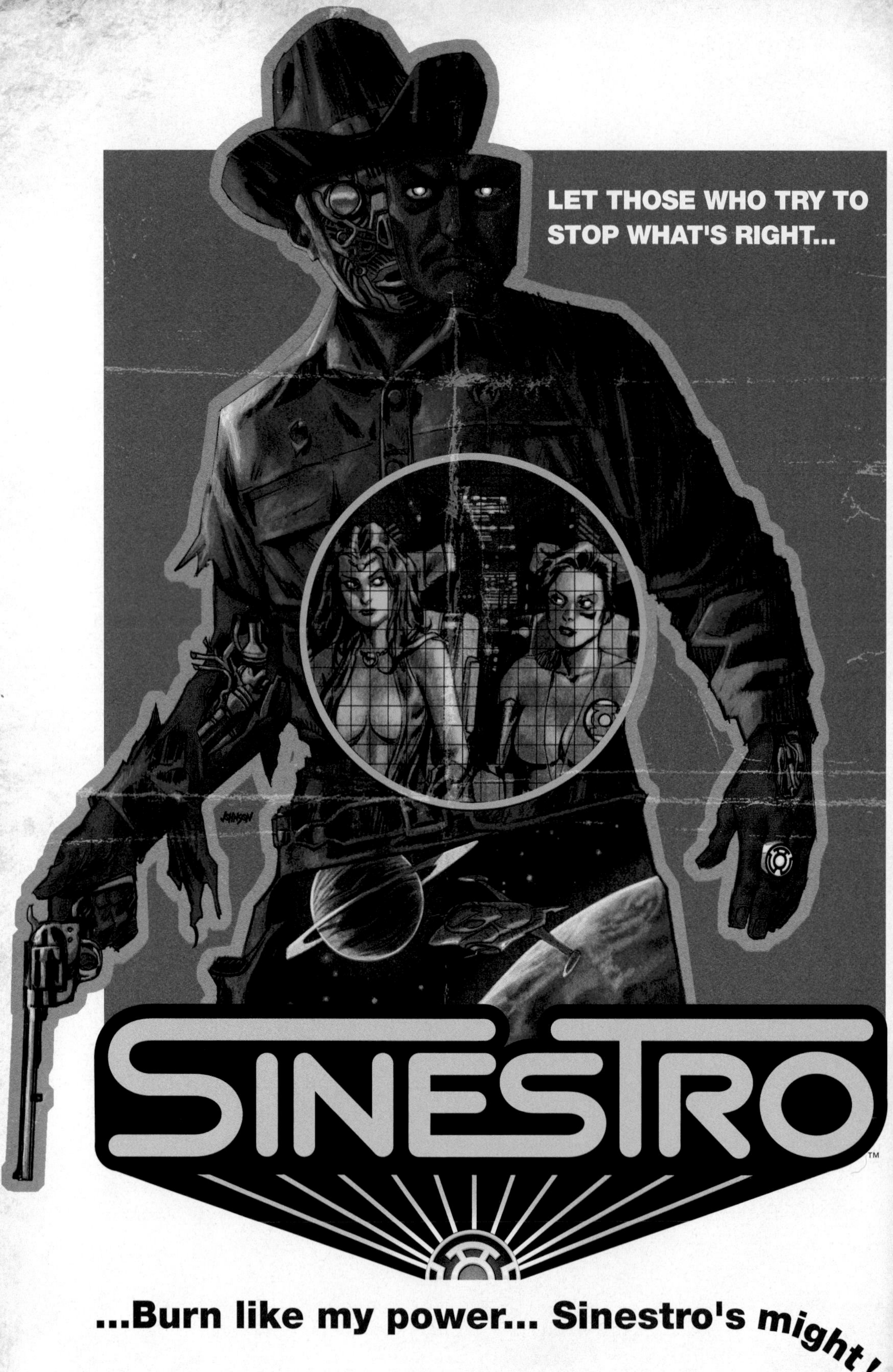
LET THOSE WHO TRY TO
STOP WHAT'S RIGHT...
SINESTRO™
...Burn like my power... Sinestro's might!

DC Comics Presents

DIANE NELSON President DAN DIDIO and JIM LEE Co-Publishers

GEOFF JOHNS Chief Creative Officer · BOB HARRAS Senior VP – Editor-in-Chief

RATED T TEEN

MAY 2015

START AT THE BEGINNING!
GREEN LANTERN
VOLUME 1: SINESTRO

GREEN LANTERN CORPS VOLUME 1: FEARSOME

RED LANTERNS VOLUME 1: BLOOD AND RAGE

GREEN LANTERN: NEW GUARDIANS VOLUME 1: THE RING BEARER

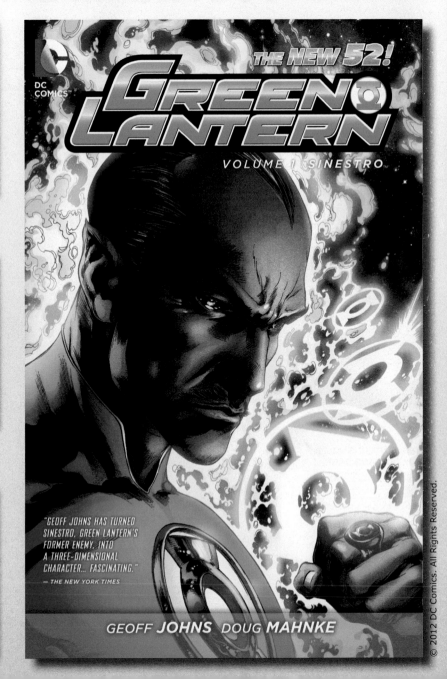

GEOFF **JOHNS** • DOUG **MAHNKE**

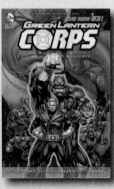

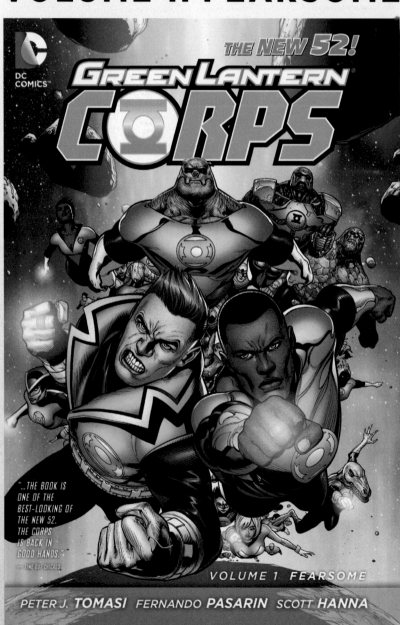